DEVILS ON
HORSES

Also by Terry Kinloch:

Echoes of Gallipoli: In the words of New Zealand's Mounted Riflemen (Exisle 2005)

DEVILS ON
HORSES

IN THE WORDS OF THE ANZACS IN THE MIDDLE EAST 1916–19

TERRY KINLOCH

Foreword by Dr Christopher Pugsley

To my parents
Jack and Shirley Kinloch

First published 2007; reprinted 2008
This paperback edition published 2016
Exisle Publishing Limited,
P.O. Box 60-490, Titirangi, Auckland 0642, New Zealand.
'Moonrising', Narone Creek Road, Wollombi, NSW 2325, Australia.
www.exislepublishing.com

National Library of New Zealand Cataloguing-in-Publication Data
Kinloch, Terry, 1958-
Devils on horses : In the words of the Anzacs in the Middle East
1916-19 / by Terry Kinloch ; foreword by Chris Pugsley. 1st ed.
Includes bibliographical references and index.
ISBN 978-1-77550-263-1
1. New Zealand. Army. New Zealand Mounted Rifles Brigade.
2. World War, 1914-1918—Campaigns—Egypt—Sinai.
3. World War, 1914-1918—Campaigns—Palestine.
I. Title.
940.41293—dc 22

This book is published with the assistance of a grant from the History Group
of the Ministry for Culture and Heritage.

Text design and production by *BookNZ*
Cover design by Dexter Fry
Maps drawn by Jonette Surridge
Printed in China

Contents

Maps and figures

Maps

Figures

Abbreviations

AIF	Australian Imperial Force
ALH	Australian Light Horse
AMR	Auckland Mounted Rifles
CMR	Canterbury Mounted Rifles
CWGC	Commonwealth War Graves Commission
CYC	Canterbury Yeomanry Cavalry
DMC	Desert Mounted Corps
EEF	Egyptian Expeditionary Force
ICC	Imperial Camel Corps
LH	Light Horse
MEF	Mediterranean Expeditionary Force
NCO	Non-commissioned officer
NZEF	New Zealand Expeditionary Force
NZMFA	New Zealand Mounted Field Ambulance
NZMGS	New Zealand Machine Gun Squadron
RHA	Royal Horse Artillery
WMR	Wellington Mounted Rifles
YMCA	Young Men's Christian Association
Z-Day	The day that an operation was scheduled to begin

Key for all maps

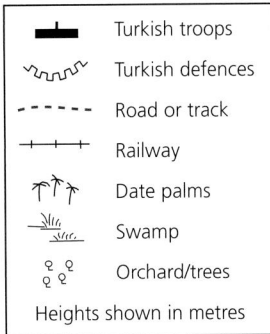

	Turkish troops
	Turkish defences
	Road or track
	Railway
	Date palms
	Swamp
	Orchard/trees
Heights shown in metres	

Glossary

13-, 18-pounder   The two types of field gun used by RHA batteries.

Advance guard   The force that moves ahead of a larger body of troops to detect, and deal with, light opposition.

Aucklands   Colloquial term for the AMR Regiment.

Battalion   In the British and Imperial forces, an infantry unit of about 1000 men, or a camel unit of 800 men.

Battery   In the British horse artillery, a unit of four 13- or 18-pounder guns.

Bivouac   A field camp without huts or tents.

Bridgehead   An area on the enemy side of a river or other obstacle.

Brigade   A grouping of several regiments or battalions and supporting units.

Cacolet   A bed or chair fitted to a camel to carry wounded or sick men.

Camelier   A soldier who rode a camel.

Canterburys   Colloquial term for the CMR Regiment.

Cordon   A ring of troops placed around an objective to prevent people from entering or leaving.

Corps   A grouping of several divisions, and supporting units.

Desert Column   The strike force of the EEF from December 1916.

Desert Mounted Corps   The successor to the Desert Column, formed in August 1917.

Division   A self-contained formation consisting of several brigades, and supporting units.

Eastern Force   From August 1916 to August 1917, that part of the EEF east of the Suez Canal.

Establishment   The authorised strength of a military organisation, in men, animals, weapons and equipment.

Field ambulance   A military medical unit.

First line   Ammunition and other combat supplies held by a unit for its immediate replenishment.

Flank guard   A small force deployed to protect the flanks of a larger body of troops.

Garrison   A force defending or guarding a position.

Heads   Colloquial term for senior commanders.

Hejaz   The coastal region of modern Saudi Arabia extending south from the Gulf of Aqaba.

Horsemastership   The science of the care of horses under all conditions.

Hotchkiss gun   Automatic rifle issued to EEF mounted troops in April 1917.

Lewis gun   Light machine gun issued to EEF mounted troops in July 1916.

Listening post   One or two men positioned forward to listen for enemy activity.

Main Body   The first NZEF contingent of men and horses that sailed from New Zealand in October 1914 (with the First Reinforcements).

Martial law   Military-controlled justice system.

Maxim machine gun   First machine gun used by regimental MG sections and by the NZMGS. A similar weapon was used by the Turks and the Germans throughout the war.

Mesopotamia   Turkish province encompassing the area of modern Iraq and Kuwait.

Mountain gun   A small artillery piece that could be disassembled and carried on camels or mules.

Mounteds   Colloquial term for mounted riflemen.

Outpost   A small protective element between the enemy and a stationary main force.

Palestine   The southern district of Turkish Syria, approximately equivalent in area to modern Israel, southern Lebanon, the Gaza Strip and the West Bank.

Pasha   Senior Turkish honorific title, and the name of two German military forces.

Railhead   The furthest point of a railway under construction.

Range card   A sketch of the ground in front of a defensive position, showing the distances to key features.

Redoubt   A self-contained defensive position.

Regiment   A mounted force of about 550 men.

Reinforcement   A replacement soldier.

Remount   A replacement horse.

Screen   Light forces placed to provide early warning of an approaching enemy.

Section   Four horsemen in a mounted rifles troop.

Squadron   A mounted force of about 160 men.

Staff   The operations, personnel and logistic officers who helped commanders plan and execute operations.

'Stand to'   The periods before dawn and after dusk were the most likely times for an enemy attack, and troops stood to in these periods, ready to repel such an attack.

Stunt   Colloquial term for an operation.

Syria   Turkish province encompassing the area of modern Syria, Lebanon, northern Israel and western Jordan.

Troop   A mounted force of about 32 men.

Vickers machine gun   Later type of machine gun used by the NZMGS.

Wellingtons   Colloquial term for the WMR Regiment.

Yeomanry   British Territorial Army cavalry.

Yildirim   Thunderbolt.

Arabic/Hebrew

Abu   Father

Ain   Spring

Bedouin   Nomadic Arab desert dwellers

Beit   House

Bir   Well

Birket   Pool

Deir   Monastery

Fanatis   A metal water container

Hod   A sandy depression containing date palms and (usually) a well

Jebel   Mountain

Jihad   Struggle

Jisr   Bridge

Khamsin   A hot desert wind that was believed to blow for 50 days in a year

Khan   Inn

Khurbet   Ruin

Nahr, wadi   River

Neby   Prophet

Ras   Head, top

Sabkhet   Salt lake, marsh

Sheikh   Chief, elder

Tel   Mound or hill, often on the site of an ancient settlement

Author's note

THERE IS A surprisingly large amount of written and photographic material available relating to the Middle East campaign fought by the New Zealand Mounted Rifles Brigade. Archives New Zealand holds most of the relevant regimental, brigade, and divisional war diaries, along with hundreds of original orders, reports, maps, signals, personnel files and copies of official and personal letters.[1]

The other vital primary reference sources are the photographs, diaries and letters left by the men who fought in the campaign. For this book I have drawn from the letters, diaries, published memoirs, and interview records of nearly 60 New Zealanders, plus a number of Australians and Britons. Letters and diaries are most reliable for those events that the writers witnessed, and often omit discussion of the more unpleasant aspects of the war.[2] The reminiscences of First World War veterans recorded by the Oral History Centre of the Alexander Turnbull Library are useful sources, although the effects of failing memories and post-war influences mean that caution is required in their use. The other key personal records in this book are the photographs. In New Zealand, Australia and elsewhere, there are hundreds of photographs taken by soldiers and official photographers during the Middle East war. Although those from small personal cameras often suffer in comparison with those taken by professional photographers, I have deliberately used many for this book, as most have never been published before. Taken collectively and used with care, they add vital colour and detail to the often dry and sometimes sparse official records.

There are two categories of published accounts dealing with the Middle East campaign: those written immediately after the war by veterans or war correspondents, and those written by historians years or decades later. Three New Zealand regimental histories and a 'popular' campaign history of the New Zealand Expeditionary Force (NZEF) in the Middle East appeared soon after the war, along with official British and Australian accounts. These books are valuable sources of information, but they are becoming scarce and inaccessible to the general reader, and they do not always tell the whole story. Unpalatable facts were often left out and criticism of senior Allied commanders was seldom permitted. There is an ever-increasing number of new books that deal with the Middle Eastern campaign of the First World War, but few of them pay much attention to New Zealand's contribution. Some modern authors who should know better commit the inexcusable sins of assuming that New Zealand's mounted riflemen are interchangeable with Australia's light horsemen, or of simply ignoring the two middle consonants in the word 'Anzac'.[3]

It is impossible to write credible military history unless you are familiar with the ground. I had access to a number of good maps relating to the Middle East campaign. More importantly, I was able to walk over most of the actual battlefields in Egypt, Israel and Jordan and visit nearly all the cemeteries in which New Zealanders lie buried.[4]

I do not discuss the operations of other Allied forces in detail, or dwell on strategic or policy matters, except to provide context for the activities of the New Zealanders. The narrative focuses almost entirely on the fighting regiments and squadrons of the NZMR. This is partly out of choice, and partly out of necessity. I had access to very few records from Turkish or German soldiers, and to none from the Egyptian, Arab, Jewish and other inhabitants of the lands across which the combatants fought, so their stories are not told here.[5]

In keeping with contemporary usage, I refer to the mounted riflemen's enemy as Turkey, despite the fact that the Ottoman Empire (to use its correct title) included many other ethnic groups.[6] In order to make the quotations more readable, I have corrected obvious spelling and grammatical errors, standardised the spelling of place names and occasionally changed the case of the initial letter of a quotation to make it fit the structure of the associated sentence.

Devils on Horses was written with the help of many people. For their assistance in the 'field phase' of the project, I thank Lloyd Mendes, who accompanied me on several visits to Sinai battlefields, and Israeli Colonel (Retired) Itzhak Brenner, who showed me the Ayun Kara battlefield. Closer to home, my former wife Jenny taught me the basics of riding and horse management.

In addition to the archives listed in the bibliography, I conducted research at the Library of Congress, the National Defense University and the Pentagon Library in Washington DC, and with the staff of the Commonwealth War Graves Commission in England. In New Zealand, the staffs of the Defence Library, the New Zealand Society of Genealogists, the Royal New Zealand Returned and Services' Association, the Trentham Camp Library and the University of Otago Library all provided valuable help.

The following individuals made special contributions. Noel Taylor tirelessly tracked down diaries, letters and photographs on my behalf. Mark Rhodes generously permitted me to publish photographs from his grandfather's magnificent album. Mike Smith allowed me to refer to the manuscript of his forthcoming biography of Major General Sir Edward Chaytor, as did Lieutenant Colonel Peter Wood with his thesis on the tactics of the NZMR Brigade. Dr Christopher Pugsley, Mike Smith and Lieutenant Colonel Paul van den Broek reviewed the manuscript. Gal Shaine's photographs and descriptions of Ayun Kara and other battlefields in Israel were a great help, as was his review of my account of the Ayun Kara battle. Barry O'Sullivan's knowledge of NZMR uniforms and equipment was very helpful. Thanks also to Graeme Barber, Greg Bradley, Rob Burrowes, Tony Edwards, Joe Evans, Patricia Forsyth, Captain Ian Hunter, RNZIR (Retired), Windsor Jones, Matthew O'Sullivan, Jeff Pickerd, Matt Pomeroy, Richard Shenley, Captain Simon Strombom, Bill Wilson and Michelle Winn, for their assistance with photographs. Professor Noel Dunbar and Phil Deed generously granted me access to their rare and extensive collections of First World War maps, and Bill Woerlee sent me copies of several contemporary map sheets. Steve Becker, Geof Mansfield, John Ruf, Geoff Smith and the other knowledgeable contributors to the Internet discussion forums listed in the bibliography were useful sounding-boards and valuable sources of information. Lastly, thanks to Steve Butler, Peter Curtis, Egidia DesRoches, David Lackey, Lynne Mackie, John McDonald, Susanna Norris, Brigadier Kevin Riordan and Simon Wilson.

I must acknowledge the splendid work of the Commonwealth War Graves Commission, which maintains the graves and memorials of 1,700,000 British and Commonwealth soldiers who died in the First and Second World Wars. The CWGC's new on-line Debt of Honour Register was invaluable for finding the last resting places of many of New Zealand's mounted riflemen, and I gained a sobering insight into the human cost of the war by visiting their immaculately maintained graves and memorials.

I thank New Zealand military historian Glyn Harper for introducing me to Exisle Publishing Ltd. The high technical quality and the excellent design of both of my books is a credit to Gareth St John Thomas, Ian Watt and the rest of the Exisle team. The publication of the book was aided by New Zealand's Chief of Defence Force, Lieutenant General Jerry Mateparae, ONZM, who, as Chief of Army, funded the production of the maps and the purchase of the publishing rights for many of the photographs. Dr Christopher Pugsley, New Zealand's leading military historian, kindly wrote the foreword. Jonette Surridge produced the superb maps, which are based, in the main, on maps from the British official history of the campaign. The maps took nearly 18 months to produce: Jonette's patience and professionalism during this protracted period are greatly appreciated.

I would like to thank everyone who granted me permission to publish photographs and excerpts from diaries, letters and interviews. In the case of those copyright holders I was unable to locate, I hope that the material quoted meets with your approval. My publisher and I would be grateful for any information that might help to trace those copyright holders whose identities or addresses are not currently known.

My dear wife Carol has shared my life with New Zealand's mounted riflemen for many years. She generously accepted the long hours when I was shackled to a computer keyboard, or delving into dusty archives around the world. Carol also reviewed the manuscript, assembled the casualty database and accompanied me to many of the CWGC cemeteries in Egypt, Israel and Turkey. Thank you above all, sweetheart.

For anyone whose assistance I have inadvertently omitted to acknowledge, please accept my apologies and my thanks. Without all of this help, I could not have produced this book, but the final responsibility for the result remains mine alone.

Foreword

DEVILS ON HORSES is a very important book for New Zealanders, and for those who read military history. We now have an account of the New Zealand Mounted Rifles Brigade in Sinai and Palestine that at last does justice to their story. This was perhaps the finest body of New Zealanders ever to serve overseas, and now we can see why.

Kinloch tells the story across the spectrum of command, at troop, squadron, regimental, and brigade levels, allowing us to see what bound this body of horsemen together and made it such an effective fighting force. He also places it in the context of the Middle East campaign, which evolved from the defence of Egypt and the Suez Canal into the clearance of the Sinai Peninsula in 1916 and the driving of the Ottoman Turkish forces from Palestine and Syria by the end of 1918. He brings out the importance of the mounted element of the Egyptian Expeditionary Force, consisting of British Yeomanry, Australian Light Horse, New Zealand Mounted Rifles and, for most of the campaign, cameliers of the Imperial Camel Corps, which included both New Zealanders and Australians within its ranks. This mounted arm, and the light horsemen and mounted riflemen in particular, was critical to the defence of the Suez Canal. We see that in the author's vivid account and dissection of the Battle of Romani. He tells how the Turkish breakthrough was stopped by the quick intervention and gritty defence of the Australian and New Zealand (or Anzac) Mounted Division, which included the New Zealand Mounted Rifles Brigade.

This book is more than a good read for New Zealanders looking to explore who we were and what we did in the Great War. Kinloch's professional understanding of the campaign makes it essential reading also for students of warfare and of the Sinai and Palestine campaign in particular. He brings out the critical importance of logistics, which is the bedrock of tactical success. Progress in this campaign was measured by the inching of the railway track and water pipeline across the Sinai desert. We see that the availability of water was the knife edge on which success or failure in each battle was balanced. Taking ground had no value if there was no water there for the horses. Kinloch shows the risks that commanders at all levels took in fighting for this lifeblood that made campaigning in Sinai and Palestine possible.

Kinloch also makes us appreciate a clever enemy who realised that he could cripple the Egyptian Expeditionary Force's strike capability if he could deny them water by defending or blowing up the wells. In *Devils on Horses,* the Turkish forces are more than a backdrop to the New Zealand story. They are fully present in all their strengths and weaknesses. We see the skills of Turkish and German artillery, and the dogged courage and endurance of their machine gunners and infantrymen. They in turn understood the Anzacs' strengths and weaknesses and, for example, at Bir el Abd, at Gaza, and in the two raids across the Jordan, bested them and showed their skill as soldiers and commanders.

This book is also an important study in command. One appreciates again the strengths of Harry Chauvel, the commander of the Anzac Mounted Division, first articulated in A. J. Hill's *Chauvel of the Light Horse*. New Zealanders will also be able to appreciate for the first time in detail the skill and judgement of Ted Chaytor as a brigadier general commanding the New Zealand Mounted Rifles Brigade. He could sense how the battle was going and how his mounted riflemen should be used, not as mounted infantry but as horsemen who could close with the enemy quickly, then use their skills of fire and manoeuvre to drive the Turk from his defensive position or block his advance. Kinloch brings this out better than has ever been done before, giving the reader a real understanding of Chaytor's brilliance.

Chaytor was matched by the quality of his regimental commanders within the brigade: 'Fix-Bayonets' Bill Meldrum (who succeeded him in command), Findlay, McCarroll, Mackesy and the equally impressive collection of commanders at squadron level, some with Boer War experience, who underpinned the New Zealand success. It took experienced men to compensate for the real weakness of mounted horsemen who, always short of critically important artillery, had to employ speed of manoeuvre, careful use of ground and then infantry skills with rifles and machine guns to attack positions in which the enemy often outnumbered them. It is this tactical skill that emerges again and again in Kinloch's study.

At the trooper level, we see what it was like to endure the conditions in this campaign – the long hours where the horse had to be cared for first before the rider could look to his own welfare, the heat, the flies, the monotony of tinned rations, the shortage of water and the inevitable impact of all of this on the health of the men. They endured these conditions because there was a job to be done and because their mates in the tightly knit four-man sections could not function without them. Fierce loyalty and a consciousness of who they were as New Zealanders marked them out. They took harsh revenge on those who slighted them and the reader will appreciate their hatred for the Bedouin, some of whom killed the isolated wounded and stripped the dead. The massacre at Surafend is the terrible finale that casts a shadow over the exploits of an outstanding body of men. It cannot be excused but Kinloch shows the speed and skilful planning that went into its dreadful execution; it, too, tells us much about these men.

With this book, Terry Kinloch has written a new page of New Zealand history that most New Zealanders have never before read. It is a seminal study that will stand the test of time, and it is a fitting tribute to the New Zealand Mounted Rifles Brigade.

Christopher Pugsley
Department of War Studies
Royal Military Academy Sandhurst

Introduction

There is nothing glorious in death on the field for the soldier who dies.... For the broken, bruised body covered with blood and dust, there is a hasty, shallow grave and a hurried prayer, and sometimes neither.[1]

ALEC McNEUR

In September 1918, the First World War was finally drawing to a close. Germany, Austria-Hungary and Turkey were on the verge of defeat at the hands of the British Empire, France and the United States. More than nine million soldiers, sailors and airmen were dead and thousands more would be killed before the guns finally fell silent. In France and Belgium, the German Army's last great Western Front offensive had failed, and it was now retreating in disarray in the face of a massive, co-ordinated Allied counter-attack. The hard-fighting infantrymen of the New Zealand Division were nearing the end of a long and gruelling Western Front campaign, punctuated by very heavy losses on the Somme, at Messines and in the mud of Passchendaele.

Far away from the Western Front, in the Middle East, another force of New Zealanders was approaching the end of a quite different campaign. Since April 1916, approximately 2000 horsemen of the New Zealand Mounted Rifles (NZMR) Brigade had continued the fight against the Turkish Army that began on Gallipoli in 1915, on battlefields stretching from the Suez Canal to the Dead Sea and beyond.

The NZMR Brigade was part of General Sir Edmund Allenby's Egyptian Expeditionary Force (EEF), which broke through the Turkish front line near Jaffa on 19 September 1918, opening the way for thousands of British, Indian and Australian cavalrymen to gallop up the coastal plain of Palestine (modern Israel) towards Haifa and Nazareth. One hundred kilometres to the east, across the Jordan River, a small force that included the NZMR Brigade was poised to attack the enemy-held village of Amman. On the afternoon of Wednesday 25 September, 104 horsemen from the Auckland Mounted Rifles Regiment were selected for a risky mission. They were ordered to sabotage a section of the Hejaz Railway, which lay some 20 kilometres behind enemy lines. The track was the only viable escape route for the Turkish 4th Army, which was fighting around Amman (see Map 2, p.27). The men were heavily armed and they rode the fittest horses available. The

The Hejaz Railway at Amman.

demolition party was equipped with two picks, two shovels and a few spanners. The New Zealanders quickly stripped their saddles of all but essential gear, received their orders, gulped down a hurried cup of tea and rode out. All they knew about the route was that an easterly course from the village of Suweile would eventually bring them to the railway.

Scouts led the way, navigating by the stars and with a luminous compass, and searching for signs of the enemy. The route was difficult and the horses' hooves often struck sparks as they stumbled over unseen rocks. After the scouts discovered a rough track leading more or less in the right direction, this was followed until a party of Turkish soldiers was heard digging a defensive post in the darkness ahead. Silence was imperative, so the New Zealanders had to avoid this small enemy post. After retracing their steps for a few hundred metres, they found and followed an even smaller goat track. The men often had to lead their horses on foot in single file. As the night wore on, the party silently detoured around several Bedouin encampments. Finally, the mounted riflemen reached the railway line between Amman and Zerka. While the horsemen dismounted under cover, two officers climbed a small knoll overlooking the railway to reconnoitre. On reaching the top of the hill, they were astonished to see a large column of Turkish soldiers marching northwards on a road alongside the track.

Fascinated, the two officers watched the scene in the indistinct haze of moonlight, while a confused medley of sound floated up to them on the night air – the cracking of whips, creaking of wheels, and the shouting of the Turkish drivers. Had these unsuspecting Turks known that two enemy officers were watching them, and a hundred of the dreaded 'death riders' were within easy rifle range of them, they would hardly have cracked their whips and shouted to each other with such abandon.

Once this unsuspecting enemy column had passed out of sight, eight New Zealanders crept down to the railway to begin work, under the protection of covering forces on high ground to the north and south. There was little cover at the railway and a very good chance that more Turks would turn up at any time. Indeed, the demolition party had barely loosened the nuts on the selected section of track when a Turkish troop train steamed around a bend in the railway to the south.

There was no time to get back from the line to cover, and the only cover near the line was composed of two small rocks, about eighteen inches high, not fifteen yards from the rails, behind which the party crawled – four behind each. If they were discovered the game was up, so be sure they lay very, very still in the moonlight, and it was a tense few moments as the big Turkish armoured truck, pushed by an armoured engine, approached. Both truck and engine were crammed full of Turks, singing and talking. Just as they passed the spot, travelling quite slowly, where the eight figures were lying so still, one of them gave a shout. Then the party on the ground thought they were 'for it', but the train moved on, and presently went out of sight round another bend. How they passed without seeing the khaki figures on the ground and opening fire on them remains a mystery to this day.

The relieved demolition party continued its work, swearing at the inadequate tools. A few minutes later, sentries spied a lone enemy soldier who seemed to be watching the demolition party from the far side of the track. 'As he lay there throughout operations it was assumed that he was either sick or wounded, or else mistook the party on the line for Turkish railway men.' Next, a mounted railway patrol appeared. One rider stopped and looked in the direction of the demolition party for a full minute before riding on, apparently unconcerned. The sweating troopers finally loosened the bolts holding the rails to the wooden sleepers and removed an entire section of track. After carefully disguising the resulting gap, the New Zealanders mounted their horses at 3 a.m. and retraced their tracks. On reaching safety at dawn 'everyone indulged in a much longed for smoke'. The 'poor old neddies' were 'dead beat'. Later that morning, a Turkish supply train heading south towards Amman was derailed on the sabotaged section of track. The cutting of the Hejaz Railway by the New Zealanders contributed to the capture of 10,000 prisoners and a large quantity of weapons, ammunition, trains, rolling stock and other booty around Amman in the following days.[2]

This adventurous action typifies the type of 'stunt' at which New Zealand's mounted riflemen excelled. The plan was daring and the risks were high, yet the raid was a complete success, with no casualties suffered by the New Zealanders. Although the story reads almost as a *Boy's Own* yarn, it is entirely true. The operation was carried out by men of the Auckland Mounted Rifles Regiment, one of the three combat regiments in the New Zealand Mounted Rifles Brigade. Who were these 'death riders', and what were they doing dodging Turks in the hills around Amman, Jordan, in 1918?

Eleven weeks after the outbreak of the First World War on 4 August 1914, 8500 men and 4000 horses sailed from New Zealand, bound for England. A quarter of the men and half of the horses belonged to the NZMR Brigade.[3] The New Zealand Expeditionary Force (NZEF) was supposed to complete its training in England, before crossing the English Channel to fight the Imperial German Army alongside the British in France and Belgium. That plan came to nought when Turkey joined the war on Germany's side while the convoy transporting the NZEF and the larger Australian Imperial Force (AIF) was still at sea. The men were diverted to Egypt in December to train, and to help defend the vital Suez Canal against Turkish attack from southern Palestine (modern Israel).

In April 1915, the NZEF and the AIF, now known formally as the Australian and New Zealand Army Corps (ANZAC) and colloquially as the Anzacs, took part in the invasion of Turkey at Gallipoli. The men of the NZMR Brigade landed in May, without their horses. In the eight months of the Gallipoli campaign, 2721 New Zealanders (including 599 mounted riflemen) lost their lives and 7473 others (970 mounted riflemen) were wounded. Many hundreds of others were sick. The original NZMR Brigade was effectively destroyed on Gallipoli; the exhausted survivors were evacuated to Egypt in December 1915.[4]

In 1916 one New Zealand and four Australian infantry divisions sailed from Egypt to the Western Front. There was no need for more horsemen there and someone had to defend Egypt against the Turks, so the NZMR Brigade and four Australian Light Horse (ALH) brigades stayed in the Middle East.

On Easter Sunday 1916, 1850 New Zealand mounted riflemen crossed the Suez Canal and rode into the Sinai desert to take on the Turkish Army. Many of the riders had already tasted defeat at the hands of the Turks at Gallipoli so they felt they had a score to settle. The mounted riflemen and light horsemen (who were by now grouped into the Australian and New Zealand Mounted Division) led the Egyptian Expeditionary Force across the arid Sinai peninsula in 1916, almost single-handedly defeating the Turks at Romani, Magdhaba and Rafah. In 1917, the EEF invaded the Palestine district of Turkish Syria. After a shaky start and some hard fighting, Gaza, Beersheba, Jerusalem and Jaffa were all in the hands of the EEF by the end of the year. In early 1918, the Anzac horsemen crossed the rocky Judean Hills and descended through the barren Wilderness to the Jordan Valley, capturing Jericho from the Turks. After enduring a hellish summer in the valley and suffering two more galling defeats at the hands of the Turks, the New Zealand and Australian riders captured Amman and an entire Turkish corps in September 1918. With its armies in Syria and elsewhere beaten or on the verge of defeat, Turkey was forced out of the war at the end of October.

Malaria and influenza ravaged the ranks of the New Zealand brigade just as victory was achieved. The brigade's return to New Zealand was delayed, first because of a lack of shipping and then because the men were needed to quell Egyptian riots in 1919. New Zealand's mounted riflemen finally returned home in the winter of that year. Only one of their horses ever tasted New Zealand grass again. A few hundred sick or old horses were sold to local Egyptians or Arabs, or were shot; the rest were handed over to British garrison units in Egypt.

Excluding Gallipoli, the New Zealanders fought 14 significant battles against the Turks. The mounted riflemen defeated the Turks on seven occasions, and they were beaten seven times. Regardless of the outcome, each encounter cost New Zealand lives and disease took a low but steady toll throughout the war. Five hundred and twenty-two New Zealanders were killed or died of wounds or sickness during the Middle East campaign, and thousands more suffered from non-fatal injuries or illnesses.

On the western slopes of Jerusalem's Mount Scopus stands a cemetery maintained by the Commonwealth War Graves Commission (CWGC). Among the serried rows of headstones filling this peaceful graveyard are 34 that bear the names of New Zealand mounted riflemen. The names of another 46 New Zealand horsemen 'whose graves are known only to God' appear on the nearby memorial wall. The Jerusalem War Cemetery is one of 16 CWGC cemeteries between the Egyptian port city of Alexandria and the Lebanese and Syrian cities of Beirut and Damascus, which contain the remains of New Zealand mounted riflemen. If the scarcity of signatures in the visitors' books is anything to go by, very few

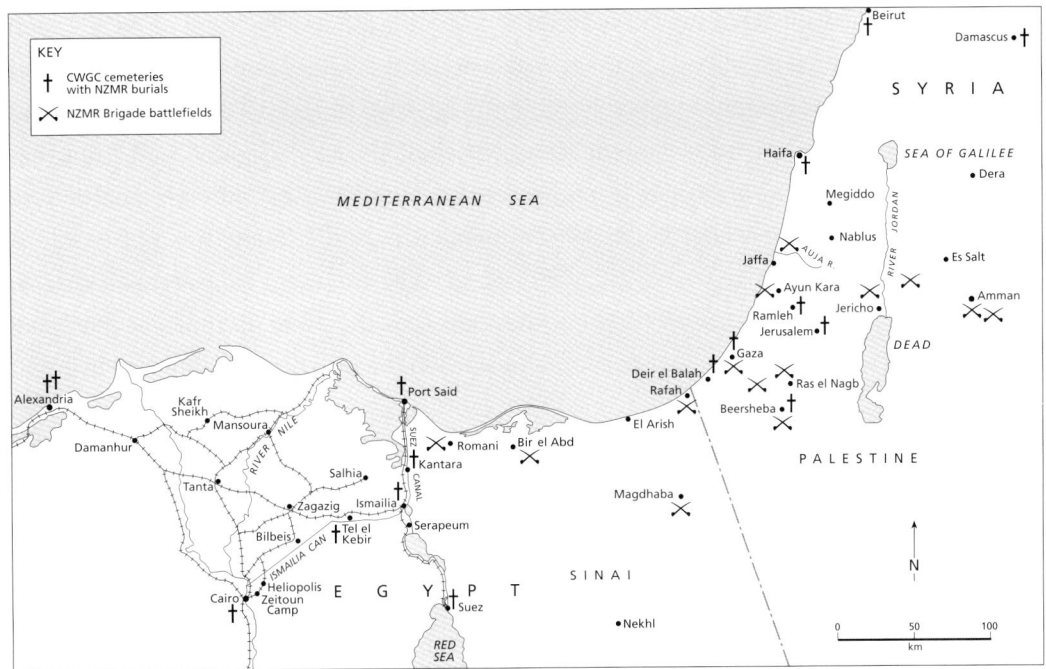

Map 1: NZMR Battlefields and Cemeteries.

The Jerusalem War Cemetery.

New Zealanders are aware of the existence of any of these graves. The rows of well-tended plots and the columns of names on memorials contradict the commonly held belief that the New Zealand Expeditionary Force fought only at Gallipoli and on the Western Front.[5]

The post-Gallipoli experience of the mounted riflemen was very different from that of the rest of the NZEF, and their losses were a fraction of those suffered by the New Zealand Division in France and Belgium. The mercifully short casualty lists of the NZMR Brigade led some people in New Zealand to accuse the mounted riflemen of being so busy sunbathing and frequenting Egyptian brothels that they had no time for any 'real' fighting. Such criticism was unjustified, and it incensed the mounteds when they heard it.

The Turk was a tough and courageous fighter who could never be taken for granted. Besides this human foe, New Zealand's mounted riflemen also had to contend with venomous snakes, scorpions, giant poisonous centipedes and tarantula spiders in their beds and in their boots. They endured hardships that are almost unimaginable today. They lived for months on a few litres of heavily treated water per day. A wash in more than a few teaspoons of fresh water was a rare luxury, and a bath was an impossible dream for months on end. As a result, their bodies were usually crawling with lice. Their menu usually consisted of hard army biscuits and greasy corned beef. The poor diet and the harsh environment meant that the men sickened easily and took months to recover from minor wounds or illnesses. They usually slept on the cold sand, wrapped in a smelly, sweat-soaked horse blanket and using their saddle for a pillow. As the years passed, they endured intense heat and numbing cold, sometimes made worse by suffocating sandstorms or freezing rain. They lived among an indifferent, or outright hostile, local population. When they were wounded, they often suffered unnecessary agony because of inadequate evacuation systems. They enjoyed few of the compensations available to the rest of the NZEF in France and Belgium. Leave was available, but rarely beyond Egypt. Rest periods in friendly French villages or in England were an impossible dream for the horsemen.

The campaign fought by the New Zealand horsemen in the Middle East has received little attention from historians and few New Zealanders know anything about it. There are, I believe, several reasons for this. First, the small size of the NZMR Brigade and the open nature of the fighting in the Middle East meant that New Zealand's casualties were very low compared with those suffered on the Western Front and at Gallipoli. As a result there is no great sense of national loss associated with the Middle Eastern campaign. Second, the mounted riflemen had no official war correspondent or historian with them to record their exploits, and they received little recognition from British or Australian correspondents.

Finally, I believe that there still exists an element of what one veteran described in 1920 as the 'fairly common fallacy' that the horsemen were 'merely tourists'.[6]

Many of the places that were familiar to New Zealand horsemen 90 years ago are front-page news today, for all the wrong reasons. Cairo, Tel Aviv, Jerusalem, Beersheba and Amman have all been the targets of terrorist attacks in recent years, and it is a foolhardy Westerner who ventures into the Gaza Strip or the West Bank these days. New Zealand military personnel continue to work in the Middle East. The Sinai headquarters of the Multinational Force and Observers (MFO), in which a small contingent of New Zealand defence personnel serves (as I did in 2000 and 2001), is just a short drive from the battlefields fought over by some of their grandfathers and great-grandfathers. Other New Zealanders serve with the United Nations in Israel, Syria, Lebanon and Iraq. All these New Zealanders are dealing with the unforeseen consequences of political decisions that were made during, and immediately after, the First World War.[7]

The title of this book comes from a discussion that took place at Gallipoli between New Zealander Clifton Bellis and Turkish veterans of the Middle East campaign in 1965. The Turks told Bellis that the Anzacs were known as 'devils on horses' because 'they never knew where they would strike next. The Turks' reconnaissance planes would report no movement in the enemy camps at sundown, yet by daybreak the Anzacs would be attacking a position 20 miles away from their base, which the Turks had never thought possible.'[8]

Every year thousands of New Zealanders make the journey to Gallipoli and smaller numbers visit the Western Front cemeteries, but very few travellers visit the graves of the New Zealanders who died in the Middle East campaign. Until now, New Zealand's 'devils on horses' have been the forgotten men of a forgotten campaign in a dimly remembered war. The purpose of this book is to ensure that they are forgotten no longer.

Terry Kinloch
Washington DC
31 January 2007

Prologue

AT THE HEIGHT of its power in the 16th century, the Turkish Empire stretched from the border of Persia (modern Iran) to the gates of Vienna. By 1914, the empire was tottering on the edge of dissolution, but it still held sway over an enormous area of the Middle East. Turkey controlled two vital strategic waterways: the Suez Canal, which linked Europe to the riches of the East, and England to East Africa, India, Australia and New Zealand; and the Dardanelles, which dominated Russia's only year-round sea route to Europe.[1] Turkey also possessed the newly discovered oilfields at the head of the Persian Gulf, and its Sultan was recognised as *caliph* (the successor to the Prophet Muhammad) by the majority Sunni sect of Islam.

In the decade before the First World War, Turkey lost much of its European territory, mainly in two Balkan wars in 1912 and 1913. Thousands of experienced Turkish officers and a quarter of a million soldiers were also lost, along with most of the army's artillery. Its ammunition stocks were almost exhausted and its medical and transport services were in a state of near collapse. The army was exhausted and demoralised and the Turkish economy was nearly bankrupted by the wars.[2]

H12323, AUSTRALIAN WAR MEMORIAL

The German Kaiser, Wilhelm II, in Istanbul before the war, with Enver Pasha to his left.

Germany had invested time and money in Turkey for many years. One significant result of this association was the building of a railway from southern Anatolia, through Syria, and deep into the Hejaz region of Arabia towards Mecca. In 1913 the German Army established a military mission in Istanbul (led by General Otto Liman von Sanders) to help the Turks rebuild their broken army. This, however, was no alliance and Turkey's rulers realised that they needed the protection of some major European powers to help fend off others as they greedily eyed the sprawling and unstable empire.[3]

Turkey's overtures to Paris, London, Berlin and even to its old enemy in St

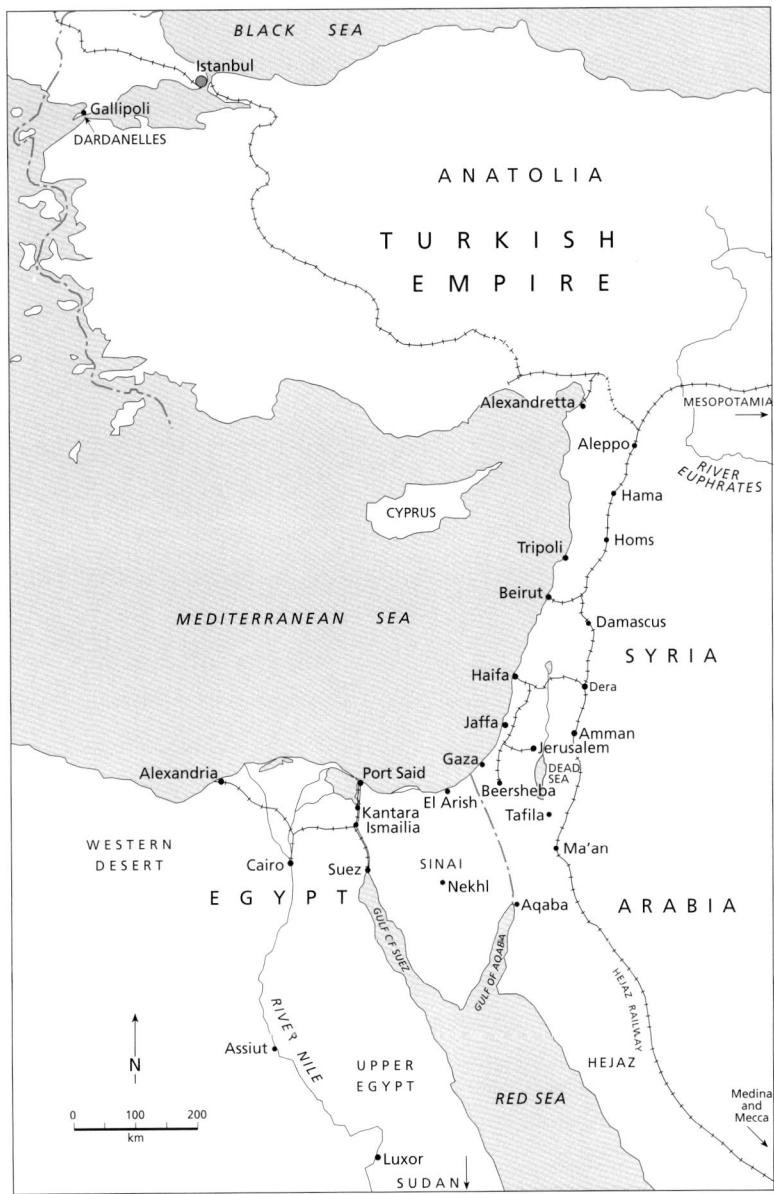

Map 2: Middle East, 1916.

Petersburg were all rebuffed, but as war loomed, Germany reconsidered her position and when Istanbul proposed formal talks in late July 1914 the Kaiser ordered his reluctant ministers and generals to respond positively. The ink on a secret Treaty of Alliance signed on 2 August was barely dry when Germany began urging its new ally to attack the Russians and the British. Turkey would not be rushed, however, and declared herself to be neutral. This pause was necessary while the army mobilised, and while its leaders argued about whether another war was really in Turkey's best interests. Allied offers to guarantee Turkey's security if she remained neutral were insufficient to sway the pro-German Minister of War, Enver Pasha, who wanted an immediate declaration of war against the Allies.[5] Even after the Germans handed over two warships and several million Turkish pounds in gold, Enver could not persuade his colleagues to declare war on the Allies, so he decided to provoke Russia into declaring war on Turkey. The Turkish Navy bombarded Russian warships and ports in the Black Sea on 29 October. Russia duly declared war on the Turkish Empire on 2 November, followed, three days later, by France and the British Empire.

The die was cast. On 14 November, Istanbul's senior Islamic cleric called upon the 270 million Muslims around the world to launch a *jihad* (struggle) against the infidel Allies. In response, the British replaced Egypt's pro-Turkish *khedive* (viceroy) with his more co-operative uncle, declared Egypt to be a British protectorate, placed it under martial law and began to reinforce the small pre-war garrison.

As 'an agricultural state which had thrown itself into an industrial war', Turkey was woefully ill-prepared for what was to come. When its traditional sea-lanes of communication were closed by Allied fleets, its primitive road and railway network could not take up the slack. Turkey lacked modern motor vehicles, railway engines and rolling stock: it took up to a month for a soldier to travel from Istanbul to southern Syria, 2000 kilometres away, via the single railway line. Turkey had few reserves of ammunition and weapons and it lacked modern communications, aircraft and other technical systems. The massive mobilisation meant that there were not enough men left in the provinces to harvest crops and this led to famines. Even horses, mules and cattle were in short supply.[5]

Apart from a small professional cadre, the large Turkish Army was composed entirely of conscripts. All Muslim males over the age of 20 were liable for two to three years of active service in the army, followed by up to 20 years in the reserve. Since Christians and Jews mainly served in labour battalions, the fighting troops were Anatolian Turks, Kurds or Arabs. Thanks to the efforts of the German military mission, the army's doctrine and organisation closely resembled that of the German Army, but it lacked the equipment and training to make this much more than a superficial similarity. The Turks were desperately short of weapons and those riflemen lucky enough to have their own Mauser rifle sometimes had only 150 rounds of ammunition. The standard of training varied enormously: 1500 general staff officers had trained abroad or under German instructors in Turkey, and many of them were capable commanders and planners, but lower-ranking

Turkish infantry in the desert.

officers were less well trained, and many were illiterate and lacking in leadership ability. Corruption and laziness were widespread faults.[6]

The greatest strength of the army lay in its soldiers, affectionately referred to by the Turks as *Mehmetçik* (Little Mehmet). Turkish infantrymen, especially the ethnic Turks from Anatolia, were tough and tenacious fighters able to endure extreme hardship. Their lack of mobility and poor tactical leadership meant they usually fought best from static defensive positions. 'Once settled down', the Turkish soldier 'is a dangerous man, and the best method of dealing with him is to rush him and keep him moving.'[7]

A Turkish infantry division was about half the size of its European equivalents. Around 10,000 soldiers were organised into three infantry regiments, each consisting of three battalions and a machine gun company, supported by a regiment of mountain or field artillery. Turkish cavalry regiments typically fielded five squadrons, each of about 100 men. The cavalrymen were usually ethnic Turks but some less effective 'tribal' Arab and Kurdish irregulars also served. Their horses were small but tough.[8]

Medical support for the soldiers was extremely poor. The medical service comprised volunteer Red Crescent staff, equipped with whatever medical and surgical equipment and supplies they could requisition from local hospitals and pharmacies.[9]

Turkish soldiers usually wore German-style grey or khaki uniforms, but their headgear was unique. The *tarbalak* or *Enveriye*, which consisted of a long strip of cloth wound around a wickerwork frame, offered no protection against shrapnel or rifle fire. Arab troops usually wore traditional *keffiyeh* head-cloths. Personal equipment and weapons were German in origin. Because clothing often could not be replaced on operations, many Turkish soldiers fought in little more than rags, held together by string, dirt and sweat. Barefoot soldiers were often captured, especially in the final years of the war.

Turkey's first land campaign, against the Russians in December 1914, was a disaster. At the same time, and with German encouragement, planners in Istanbul decided to attack the British forces in Egypt. Berlin hoped that a Turkish advance on the Suez Canal would force the Allies to keep troops in Egypt, away from the Western Front. Turkish aims were more grandiose: it was hoped that the Muslim Egyptians would rise in jihad against the British and help the Turks throw them out of Egypt. Allied naval supremacy in the Mediterranean Sea meant that the Turks could approach the Suez Canal only by crossing the Sinai peninsula from Palestine. To defend the canal, the British built a defensive line along its western bank. The low-lying plains to the north-east of the waterway between Kantara and Port Said were flooded and warships were anchored in the waterway to lend the weight of their heavy guns to its defence. Egypt's small pre-war British garrison was quickly replaced by Indian troops, and the Australian and New Zealand expeditionary forces were diverted to Egypt in December 1914 to help defend the canal.[10]

On 15 January 1915, 20,000 Turkish and Arab soldiers marched from Beersheba into Sinai. Awaiting them on the banks of the Suez Canal were 30,000 Indian and British troops, supported by artillery and naval guns. The Turks attacked the canal defences on 3 February, but they were beaten back. Turkish hopes for an uprising were unfulfilled: the Egyptians had no love for the British, but they did not want the Turks back, so they did nothing. The Turks broke off the attack and withdrew across the desert to Palestine.[11]

Two months later, most of the British and Anzac (as the Australian and New Zealand troops were known) troops in Egypt were committed to the invasion of Turkey's Gallipoli Peninsula. Many planners in London believed that the Turks would give up as soon as the Allies landed but, far from collapsing, the Turks forced the Allies to withdraw eight months later. The Gallipoli campaign had shown that the Turkish Army was not to be underestimated, Many Anzac veterans developed a grudging respect for the enemy they knew as 'Abdul' or 'Johnny Turk', appreciating his toughness and 'sense of fair play'.

In 1915, with the attention of both sides firmly focused on the fight for Gallipoli, Egypt reverted to the quiet backwater it had been in 1914. However, as the Gallipoli campaign wound down in late 1915, war planners in London aired their concerns about another Turkish attack on the Suez Canal.[12]

Brigadier General Edward Chaytor commanded the New Zealand Mounted Rifles Brigade from December 1915 until April 1917, when he took command of the Australian and New Zealand Mounted Division. The professionalism and ability of this largely unknown New Zealand commander contributed significantly to the success of the NZMR Brigade.

Chaytor was born in Motueka in 1868. He became a trumpeter in the Marlborough Hussars at the age of 18 and by 1892 had reached the rank of captain. In October 1899, Chaytor left the family farm to fight the Boers in the South African War. He completed two tours there, finishing the war in command of the South Island Battalion of the Eighth Contingent. The experience he gained commanding mounted troops in the harsh conditions of the South African veldt was to prove invaluable in his later military career. Chaytor returned to New Zealand in July 1902 to receive a commission in the army's Permanent Force. On the outbreak of war in 1914, Colonel Chaytor became the senior personnel and logistics planner for the commander of the New Zealand Expeditionary Force, Major General Alexander Godley. His efforts were instrumental in preparing the NZEF contingents that deployed at short notice to German Samoa and Europe.[13]

Chaytor played an important role in stabilising the chaotic situation at Anzac Cove on 25 April 1915. On 19 May he received a serious wound to his right arm and shoulder and was evacuated to England. By the time Chaytor returned to Gallipoli in August, the campaign was almost over. He left the peninsula on 23 November to take up the command of the New Zealand Rifle Brigade, which was being assembled in Egypt, but he was summoned back to Gallipoli two weeks later to take command of the NZMR Brigade.[14]

A well-built man of medium height, with receding red hair, Chaytor had 'a

Edward Chaytor.

thinnish face with a prominent Roman nose, sharp blue eyes, a slightly jutting jaw, a resolute mouth, and a moustached upper lip'. He was known as 'a wise and a just commander, of great personal bravery and strong moral courage. Simple and direct in all he did and said, he at once gave those who came in close contact with him a feeling of trust.... He ... [combined] a wide knowledge of the intricate detail of feeding, clothing and moving of large bodies of mounted men, with a quick grasp of tactical situations and a sure decision as to his own course.' Chaytor's nickname of 'Fiery Ted' was not entirely due to the colour of his hair, and he was respected, rather than worshipped, by his men.[15]

Chaytor was one of a very few career officers in the NZMR Brigade. Although many of his officers had fought in South Africa, few had been in uniform permanently since 1902. Most of his officers were enrolled in the Territorial Force (TF) and the more senior ones had commanded TF regiments or brigades in New Zealand before the First World War. All three of Chaytor's regimental commanders fought on Gallipoli.

Lieutenant Colonel Charles Mackesy, a 55-year-old land agent and accountant from Whangarei, commanded the Auckland Mounted Rifles Regiment (AMR). The Irish-born Mackesy had lived in the United States before emigrating to New Zealand in the 1890s. Well educated and fluent in French and German, he was also a practical soldier and a firm disciplinarian. His men referred to him as 'German Joe' or 'Old Joe'. Three of his sons also served in the war, and one was killed on Gallipoli.[17]

Lieutenant Colonel William Meldrum, a 50-year-old farmer and retired solicitor from Hunterville, commanded the Wellington Mounted Rifles Regiment (WMR). Known as 'Corn Cob Bill' or 'Fix Bayonets Bill', Meldrum was a modest man who took great interest in the welfare of his men, but he was another strict disciplinarian who expected his orders to be obeyed without question. Meldrum's heroic efforts on Chunuk Bair in August 1915 after its capture by William Malone's Wellington Infantry Battalion deserve far greater recognition than they have received to date. He was the best of the NZMR Brigade's regimental commanders.[17]

Forty-seven-year-old Lieutenant Colonel John Findlay, another farmer, commanded the Canterbury Mounted Rifles Regiment (CMR), the only regiment in the brigade from New Zealand's South Island. The only one of the three original regimental commanding officers who had fought in the South African War, Findlay was brought out of semi-retirement in the Army Reserve to command the CMR. He was seriously wounded on Gallipoli during the August offensive and he had not returned to the regiment when it was evacuated from the peninsula in December 1915.

At this stage of the war, all New Zealand's mounted riflemen were volunteers.

Charles Mackesy.   *William Meldrum.*   *John Findlay.*

Throughout the war, the majority of the horsemen came from the rural areas of New Zealand. Many had ridden since childhood and were used to fending for themselves in harsh conditions. The men joined up for many reasons, including a desire to see the world, adventure and (for a lesser number) a patriotic desire to fight for the British Empire.[18]

A regular flow of trained reinforcements was necessary to keep the NZMR Brigade up to strength. According to pre-war British plans, 70 per cent of a force of mounted troops would have to be replaced in the first year of a war. The unexpectedly heavy losses of mounted riflemen on Gallipoli, where they fought as infantry, upset these calculations and the scale of reinforcements had to be increased temporarily. New Zealand's Defence Department increased the maximum age from 40 to 45, reduced the minimum height and chest measurements and abolished the upper weight limit of 76 kilograms in order to provide this short-notice surge of reinforcements. Even so, the required number of extra volunteers was difficult to meet and many in New Zealand considered conscription for the first time. The shortage of volunteers was particularly serious in the rural districts, which were the main recruiting areas for mounted riflemen. Conscription began in New Zealand in November 1916 and by August 1917 all NZEF reinforcements, including mounted riflemen, were conscripts.[19]

During the First World War 16 million horses were used as cavalry mounts, and to pull guns, ambulances and supply wagons.[20] Every fighting soldier in the NZMR Brigade had a horse, and senior officers often had several each. Packhorses carried machine guns, ammunition and other essential equipment and supplies; draught horses pulled supply and ambulance wagons and artillery guns. Military regulations were quite specific about what was acceptable in a military horse. Remounts, as they were known, were expected

PEF/P/RHODES/128. PALESTINE EXPLORATION FUND, LONDON.

A well-conditioned New Zealand horse.

to be between four and seven years of age, and between 14 and 15.2 hands in height. Stallions were not permitted and geldings were preferred to mares. Any colour was allowed, as long as it was not too light. All experts agreed that a remount needed to have some thoroughbred breeding, although a pure thoroughbred was not suitable. The horses had to be sound, well muscled, without vices and safe to ride. They needed to be able to carry heavy weights over long distances without losing condition. Remounts also had to be obedient, steady in and out of the ranks, used to weapons firing near them, good jumpers, unafraid of deep water and swimming, willing to stand still when being mounted and happy to be led.[21]

New Zealand was responsible for providing the NZEF's horses for the first few years of the war. Horses were purchased by Department of Agriculture inspectors and delivered by rail to the main Remount Depot in Upper Hutt, where they were fed and exercised until ships arrived to transport them overseas. When the vessels reached their destination, the horses were transferred by rail to field remount depots. After a period of acclimatisation and rest, the remounts were available for issue to units.

Remount shipments from New Zealand ceased towards the end of 1916 because of a

The Remount Depot in Upper Hutt, New Zealand.

lack of shipping: the last 455 New Zealand horses arrived in Egypt in November of that year. Once these horses were used, remounts had to be drawn from imperial depots, which held horses from Britain, France, the United States, Argentina and elsewhere. Remounts were carefully examined in the regiments before they were accepted, as unsuitable mounts were often sent up to the units. Some Argentinian horses, 'although apparently in the pink of condition when they arrived, were soft, of poor heart, and could not stand up to the hardships as the original New Zealand-bred horses had done, with the result that they were evacuated from the active list as fast as they appeared'.[22]

In addition to the normal range of equine diseases and injuries encountered at home, New Zealand horses in the Middle East were exposed to tropical diseases and infestations, war wounds, exhaustion and poisoning. They endured extreme heat and bitter cold, and were, on occasion, soaking wet and covered in mud.[23]

The mounted riflemen had a large and efficient veterinary organisation to help them care for their precious horses. The brigade had a Mobile Veterinary Section (NZMVS), every regiment had a professional veterinary officer and a farrier quartermaster sergeant, and each squadron had one farrier sergeant and one shoeing smith per troop. The regimental veterinary officers and their assistants treated minor equine illnesses and injuries and the NZMVS collected and evacuated horse casualties from the battle zone. Seriously ill or injured animals were evacuated to veterinary hospitals, usually by rail. Recovering horses, as well as tired and worn-out animals, passed through convalescent depots. Once they were fit, the horses were sent to remount depots. Animals that were too ill or badly injured were humanely destroyed, usually by shooting.

Horses evacuated to veterinary hospitals or convalescent depots were struck off the unit strength and replaced. If no New Zealand horse was available, the rider would receive a remount from somewhere else. Clearly, it was in the best interests of every mounted rifleman to keep his original horse fit and healthy, to avoid the risk of losing it and receiving an inferior replacement.[24]

Well-trained horsemen could spot a sick or injured animal from its general appearance or behaviour. A horse that was standing oddly, constantly changing its position or hanging its head was probably not well, and one that was inattentive, listless or uneasy was also worth watching closely. Dull eyes, flattened ears, a dull coat and a runny nose were danger signs, as was an irregular or uncertain gait. A loose shoe or a small lump under the saddle, if detected in time, was easily remedied; if it was not fixed in the unit, the horse might have to be evacuated to a veterinary hospital – and the riders knew what that meant.[25]

The horsemen devoted hours each day to the care of their mounts. It was impossible, and against regulations, to wash the animals in the desert, so regular daily grooming was essential to keep the pores open, to remove dead skin and hair and to remove disease-

G-8687-1/1, PAColl-3031, The Press (Christchurch) Collection, Alexander Turnbull Library.

The Canterbury Mounted Rifles Regiment at full strength, paraded in New Zealand before embarkation.

causing organisms. Regimental farriers inspected the feet of all horses daily and horseshoes were replaced regularly.[26]

Horses in hard and sustained work require a mix of hard feed (in the Middle East this consisted of oats, maize, bran, dhoura or barley) and roughage (grass, hay, berseem, chaff, tibbin or straw). Little and often was the guiding principle for feeding horses and they were not supposed to be worked hard immediately after eating. 'Often … the horses were so tired that they refused to eat, and weary troops would knead dry grain into little balls moistened with a few last drops of water and feed the animals by hand.' Whenever extra fodder was lying around, men would gather it up in sacks and tie it to their saddles for later use.[27]

The New Zealand Mounted Rifles Brigade was organised into a small headquarters, three fighting regiments and several small support units. A brigadier general commanded the brigade with the assistance of several dozen officers, clerks, military policemen, signallers and orderlies. Each of the mounted rifles regiments had 549 men and 608 horses under the command of a lieutenant colonel, arranged in three squadrons and a machine gun section. Each of the latter contained a pair of Maxim machine guns, which were carried on packhorses. A mounted rifles squadron of 158 men and 169 horses was subdivided into a headquarters and four troops; each troop consisted of eight four-man sections.[28]

The section was the basic building block of the regiment. In combat, one man in each section was responsible for holding the horses while the other three fought on foot. These four men lived, worked and fought together and usually became close friends. Camp duties were shared: one man was responsible for cooking, another for looking after the horses, the third for keeping the campsite clean and tidy, while the fourth took care of the section's share of guards and fatigues.[29]

In addition to its mounted riflemen, each regiment had a veterinary officer, a doctor and three medical orderlies, a chaplain, an armourer (to look after the weapons) and a number of signallers, cooks, farriers, saddlers, trumpeters, clerks, batmen, grooms, drivers, stretcher-bearers and sanitary staff. The regiments left New Zealand with bicycles, packhorses and horse-drawn wagons, but only the packhorses could operate in the Sinai desert, so all supplies were moved by rail or by huge camel convoys from the Egyptian Camel Transport Corps (CTC).[30]

The New Zealand Mounted Brigade Field Ambulance (NZMFA) provided immediate medical support to the brigade. Up to 50 badly injured or seriously ill men could be stabilised at the ambulance at any one time. Serious cases were evacuated from the ambulance to

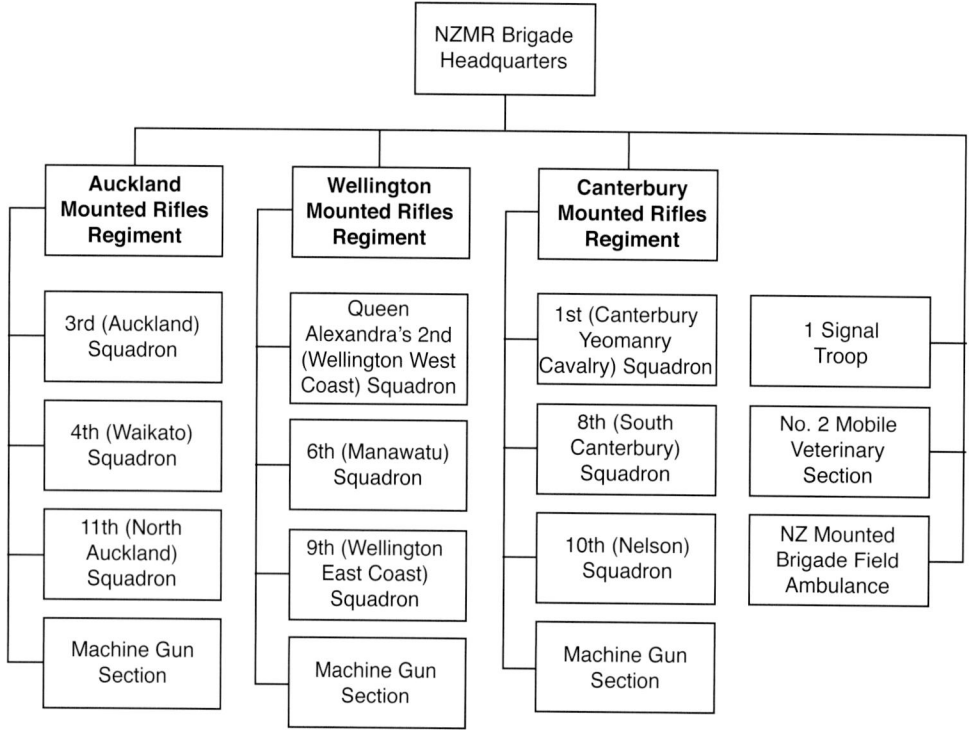

Figure 1: The NZMR Brigade in April 1916.[31]

military hospitals, while minor cases were treated and returned to their units. At first, the field ambulance was poorly equipped for desert warfare. Its ambulance wagons were converted delivery vans that needed six horses to drag them through the deep sand, even when empty. The situation improved in May 1916, when sand carts and camels were issued to the unit.[32]

The New Zealand Engineers provided a Field Troop and a Signal Troop. The original Field Troop was removed from the NZMR Brigade and sent to France with the new infantry division; a replacement troop of 77 men was raised in 1917. Its role was to construct and repair wells, reservoirs, troughs and water points, carry out minor demolitions, improve camp sites and other minor engineering tasks. They also carved and painted crosses for battlefield graves.[33]

The Signal Troop was manned by 33 men from New Zealand's Post and Telegraph and Railways Departments whose job was to provide communications between brigade HQ and the regiments. This they did using field telephones, semaphore flags, pigeons, heliographs and (eventually) radios. They exchanged their bicycles and most of their motorcycles for horses and camels before the Sinai campaign began.[34]

A Royal Horse Artillery (RHA) battery from the British Territorial Army supported the New Zealanders. The battery was equipped with four 18-pounder field guns. These well-designed and reliable weapons fired an anti-personnel shrapnel shell to a range of about six kilometres. Each 1-tonne gun and its ammunition limber was towed by a team of six or eight horses, and operated by 10 gunners. According to Guy Powles, the historian of the NZMR Brigade and the Canterbury Mounted Rifles, these batteries were 'as keen and efficient as any regular batteries, and were magnificently horsed'. The British gunners quickly became favourites of the New Zealanders.[35]

Had the brigade reached the Western Front in early 1915, as it would have done had Turkey not entered the war, it would probably have been incorporated into a British or Australian mounted or cavalry division. Although its men rode horses, the NZMR Brigade was not a cavalry force. Mounted riflemen (and light horsemen, the Australian equivalent) were doctrinally different from traditional British cavalrymen. Mounted riflemen rode their horses to a battle, where they dismounted under cover and fought on foot as infantry, using rifles and bayonets, and supported by horse artillery and machine guns. Their horses were led to nearby cover by the No. 3 man in each section. Cavalry, on the other hand, were trained and equipped primarily to fight on horseback, charging in massed formations into enemy cavalry and defeating them with swords and lances. Shock action, as this was called, could be employed by mounted riflemen, but only in special emergencies. Cavalry and mounted rifles units did share some roles, such as scouting and providing security for the infantry. Because the NZMR Brigade could put only as many riflemen in a firing line

A typical mounted rifles troop in the Middle East.

PEF/P/RHODES/166, PALESTINE EXPLORATION FUND, LONDON

A section of four mounted riflemen.

as a single infantry battalion (900–1000 men), it could not fight protracted actions on its own against large or entrenched groups of enemy infantry. Its role was to use its mobility to seek out and find the enemy, to deal with small or isolated outposts and patrols and to delay larger enemy forces until infantry brigades caught up and took over the fight. A single detached brigade could operate independently for only a few days at best. After that, it needed the support of the division to which it belonged for supplies, medical and veterinary care, reinforcements and remounts.[36]

The men in the mounted rifles regiments were known informally as 'the Aucklands', 'the Wellingtons' and 'the Canterburys'. Mounted riflemen as a whole were colloquially known as 'mounteds'. These terms will appear throughout this book, as will the abbreviations AMR, WMR and CMR for the Auckland, Wellington and Canterbury mounted rifles regiments. Each squadron in the brigade was maintained throughout the war by its parent Territorial Force mounted rifles regiment. The service squadrons were named after these regiments, and the men wore their badges throughout the war (see endpapers). For example, in the Canterbury Mounted Rifles Regiment, the squadron provided by the 1st (Canterbury Yeomanry Cavalry) Regiment was known as the 1st (CYC) Squadron, and those from the 8th (South Canterbury) and the 10th (Nelson) regiments were known as the 8th (South Canterbury) and 10th (Nelson) squadrons. The mounted riflemen were equipped with the reliable and efficient Short Magazine Lee Enfield (SMLE), a bolt-action rifle with a 10-round magazine of .303-inch bullets. A well-trained rifleman could supposedly fire 15 aimed shots per minute, and even a mediocre shot could hardly miss his target at ranges out to 200 metres. The rifle was short enough to be handily carried on horseback. A long bayonet was attached to the weapon for close fighting on foot. In mounted rifle regiments, the rifle was usually carried on a sling over the right shoulder, not in a rifle bucket. Officers, machine gunners and some other specialists carried a pistol (usually a heavy Webley .455-inch revolver) instead of a rifle. Cavalry swords were not issued to the New Zealanders during the war, although at least one NZMR officer carried, and used, a sword at Rafah.[37]

At first, each regiment possessed two water-cooled Maxim machine guns. Although a single Maxim had the equivalent fire effect of several dozen rifles, it was extremely heavy: the weapon, its tripod and one box of belted .303-inch ammunition weighed nearly 60 kilograms. The Maxims were gradually replaced by slightly lighter and more reliable Vickers guns.[38]

Uniforms were supposed to be worn in accordance with Dress Regulations but these rules were seldom enforced in the field. Headgear was common to all ranks, although officers often had better-quality hats than the men. Many men retained the cork Wolseley helmets they had worn on Gallipoli to protect themselves from the desert sun. Otherwise, a felt hat was worn, with a khaki-green-khaki puggaree wrapped around the base of the crown. A regimental badge was usually worn on the front of the crown and later in the war cloth regimental patches were worn on each side of the puggaree. Steel helmets were trialled, unsuccessfully, in the Desert Mounted Corps in 1918.[39]

Officers wore an open-collared 'drab' service dress jacket over a shirt and tie. Embroidered rank was worn on the cuffs at first, but by the end of the war many officers wore metal rank badges on their shoulders instead. Metal 'NZMR' shoulder titles and regimental badges (often blackened or unpolished for field service), medal ribbons and New Zealand Forces buttons were worn on the jackets. Mounted officers wore well-cut riding breeches made of cavalry twill or Bedford cord material. Their footwear consisted of high brown leather riding boots or brown ankle boots with spurs; if they wore the latter, their lower legs were protected by woollen puttees or brown leather gaiters. Officers wore a leather Sam Browne belt, fitted with a pistol holster and a 12-round ammunition pouch. They usually also carried binoculars, a whistle, a clasp knife, a prismatic compass, a water bottle, a map case and a haversack.

The uniforms of the soldiers were simpler in design. Jackets and trousers were made of a heavy woollen serge material. Puttees enclosed the lower legs above ankle boots and steel spurs. A brown leather bandolier, holding ninety rounds of .303-inch ammunition in five-round clips, was worn over the left shoulder, and extra ammunition pouches were attached to the leather waist-belt alongside the bayonet. In addition to the rifle, a water bottle and haversack were carried. Embroidered rank was worn on the upper arms of the jacket; wound stripes, trade and proficiency badges and service chevrons were worn on the forearms. A lightweight khaki drill (KD) uniform was available for officers and men to wear in the summer months; mounted-pattern woollen greatcoats were issued for use in cold weather.[40]

Jim McMillan thought the New Zealand uniform compared poorly with that worn by the Australian light horsemen.

[On parade] the Mounted Rifleman looked positively dowdy beside his smartly-dressed companion of the Light Horse, who wore a tunic of fine, soft material, well-cut, and of similar style to that worn by the officers – his mate from across the Tasman wore one of coarse, rough serge, with no pretensions whatever for either cut or style. The Australian's hat was of good quality felt, with a bound edged brim that prevented it from falling, and with one side tilted up against the crown. Depending on what regiment he belonged to, he might also have a feather adorning the side – emu he claimed, but we maintained that they were kangaroo

Uniforms of officers and men in the NZMR Brigade. The soldier on the right wears a khaki drill uniform. The officer on the left is Second Lieutenant William Johns, killed at Beersheba on 31 October 1917.

feathers. His opposite number across the way also wore a felt hat, but that is as far as the resemblance went, for it was made in such a way and of so poor material, that the brim was probably flopping down over his ears. The only thing that gave it any sort of status at all was the green band in the centre of the puggaree.

The next item in the sartorial elegance of the Australian trooper was his shapely riding breeches, well cut and roomy around the thighs, and cutting in sharply to be tight at the knees. Compare them with those on his poor relation who is getting round in a pair of pants that could be described as something between plus-fours and jodhpurs, but not actually resembling either, and still less looking like a pair of riding breeches – tight where they should have been baggy, and vice versa.

What capped everything in the comparison between the two uniforms was the fact that the Light Horseman wore leather leggings to complete his outfit. From both the appearance and utility aspect, they were far superior to those abominations that the New Zealanders were required to wear – puttees.[41]

The horsemen used the excellent British Universal Pattern (UP) 1902 saddle, which was designed to spread the weight of the rider and his equipment evenly over the horse's back. A folded brown saddle blanket was placed on the horse's back beneath the saddle, which was secured with a girth strap (sometimes supplemented by a surcingle, a thin strap over the top of the saddle). The total weight carried by a troop horse was about 110 kilograms: 70 kilograms for the rider, 20 kilograms for saddlery and the balance for clothing and personal effects, rations, weapons and ammunition. Strapped to the saddles were two leather wallets (usually containing spare clothes, toiletries, and emergency rations), a greatcoat, a rubberised groundsheet, a canvas water bucket, one or two shoe cases, a sand muzzle, a second saddle blanket, a picketing peg and rope, mess tins and a nose-bag or sack holding grain for the horse. With all this kit around him, it was virtually impossible for a rider to fall off a horse except sideways. Later in the war, a second ammunition bandolier was placed around the horse's neck.[42]

The leather Universal Pattern 1902 bridle consisted of two parts: a head-collar, which was never removed unless the horse was in a fenced enclosure, and a separate bridle-head. The bridle-head was issued with a reversible Portmouth bit but a simpler and less harsh snaffle or Pelham bit was almost invariably used in the field. Whenever time permitted, bridle-heads were removed to allow the horses to drink and eat more comfortably. A head-rope, used to secure the horses in camp, was attached to the head-collar and looped around the horse's neck.[43]

1

Return from Gallipoli

How I wish J. Turk would come, it would break the monotony some.

BERT HARRIS

ON 26 DECEMBER 1915, a motley flotilla of troopships steamed into the Egyptian port of Alexandria. On board were thousands of tired and dispirited evacuees from Gallipoli, including nearly 1400 men belonging to the New Zealand Mounted Rifles Brigade. The mounted riflemen caught trains to Zeitoun Camp, near Cairo, where their horses and several thousand reinforcements awaited them.[1]

Although a large number of reinforcements had joined the brigade during the closing months of the Gallipoli campaign, the regiments were still sadly under strength. The Wellington Mounted Rifles Regiment (WMR), for example, could muster only 360 officers and men out of its establishment of 549. Many sick or wounded mounted riflemen who had been evacuated from Gallipoli during the campaign were in hospital or convalescent homes in Egypt, Malta or Britain. Others were already on their way home, judged unfit for further service. Even the unwounded evacuees were generally weak and malnourished. Reinforcement Harry Mitchell described the Gallipoli veterans as 'silent men, very silent'. He did not ask them about Gallipoli. 'We minded our own business, because we were new chums.'[2]

The few hundred fit Main Body and First Reinforcement men were reunited with their original horses. They happily handed in their infantry equipment, receiving in its place spurs, bandoliers, saddles and bridles. Their worn-out weapons were overhauled or replaced and the number of Maxim machine guns in each regiment was increased to four.

During the three and a half weeks that the brigade spent at Zeitoun, training focused on hardening of the horses and horsemanship tests for the reinforcements. After seven or eight months out of the saddle, and with little fat left to soften the seat, many Gallipoli veterans had an uncomfortable first few weeks on horseback. Many of the professional warrant officers and non-commissioned officers (NCOs) in the brigade had died on Gallipoli and this

A hod in the Sinai desert near Romani.

slowed progress until their replacements were trained. On Gallipoli, some of the mounteds had worried that the horses would be gone, or so neglected that they would be useless, by the time they got back to Zeitoun. Their fears were groundless: the animals were healthy, fit – in Edwin McKay's words, 'full of beans'[3] – and thoroughly acclimatised.

It was mid-winter in Egypt, but the days were fine and warm, with temperatures of 20° to 30°C, and the nights were mild. The invigorating climate, plentiful rest and good food quickly refreshed the weary Gallipoli veterans. Walter Carruthers wrote home on 10 January 1916 that 'we will be fit for killing and curing in a week or two. You wouldn't know us for the same crowd that landed back here about three weeks ago.' Hundreds of reinforcements were posted to the regiments and, according to Guy Powles, the NZMR Brigade was 'fully armed, magnificently horsed, properly equipped and at full strength' in 12 days.[4]

As the NZMR Brigade reconstituted itself at Zeitoun, war planners in London and Istanbul considered their next moves in the Middle East. The Allied evacuation of Gallipoli had released a large, confident and aggressive Turkish Army for operations elsewhere and Allied planners expected another Turkish invasion of Egypt in 1916. This threat was taken seriously in London. The loss of the Suez Canal would be a significant blow to the Allied cause: it would sever the shortest sea link between Britain and its empire, and it would provide another demonstration – after Gallipoli and another British failure in Mesopotamia – of Allied inferiority to Islamic Turkey. If this resulted in a worldwide Muslim uprising, the consequences for the Allies would be extremely grave.

The War Office believed that the Turks would advance across the top of the Sinai peninsula and seize the Katia oasis area, 40 kilometres east of the Suez Canal, and attack the canal from there. The generals in London decided to pre-empt the enemy by occupying the Katia district first. However, the British commander in Egypt, Lieutenant General Sir John Maxwell, deferred the occupation of the oases until the close-in defences along the entire length of the Suez Canal were completed to his satisfaction.[5]

Despite the need to guard the Suez Canal, there was a much more important use for most of the nearly 400,000 Allied soldiers in Egypt. The inconclusive fighting on the Western Front in 1914 and 1915 had resulted in more than one million French and British casualties. Allied planners decided in late 1915 that the war could only be won by defeating the main German and Austro-Hungarian armies in Russia, Italy and on the Western Front, and major Allied attacks on all three fronts were planned for the following summer. The War Office in London needed to collect enormous numbers of reinforcements over the winter to replace losses and to create the new divisions needed for the planned Anglo-French offensive on the Somme. One important source of men was the now-unemployed Mediterranean Expeditionary Force (MEF) in Egypt.

However, as the MEF's temporary commander noted, 'we shall have a lot of reorganizing to do in Egypt before we are fit to take the field again'. Many of the men in Egypt, or arriving

Cemal Pasha (second from right), the commander of the Turkish 4th Army.

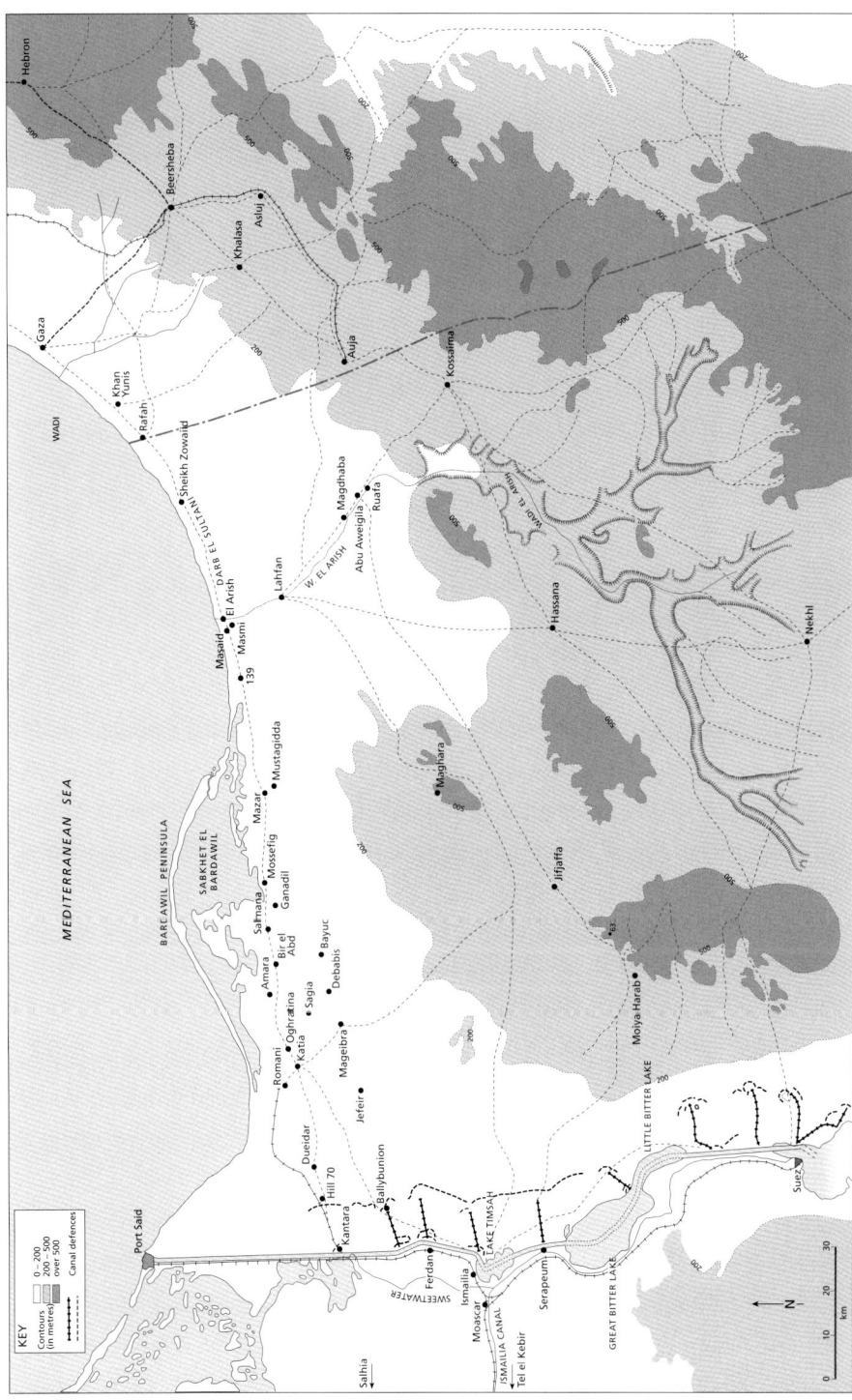

Map 3: Northern Sinai Peninsula, August 1916.

A group of New Zealanders at Serapeum, on the bank of the Suez Canal.

from Gallipoli, were recovering from wounds or sickness, or were simply exhausted, and the force needed re-equipping for European warfare. Commanders were urged to reinforce and outfit their units, and to get some training done quickly, so that the divisions could be shipped to France in time for the Somme offensive, scheduled to begin in August 1916.[6]

There were around 65,000 Turkish soldiers of the 4th Army in the Syrian district of Palestine, under the rather inept command of Cemal Pasha, Turkey's Minister of Marine, who, luckily for him, was assisted by a capable German officer, Colonel Friedrich Kress von Kressenstein. As the War Office had predicted, the Turks decided to send part of the 4th Army back into Egypt in the spring of 1916. It was to block the Suez Canal by sinking ships with artillery fire from a defensive position near Romani. The Turkish infantry were to be supported by German and Austro-Hungarian aircraft, machine guns and artillery.[7]

Apart from the Nile River valley and delta, Egypt is a desert nation. In 1916 the barren desert regions were occupied by a few thousand Bedouin (nomadic Arabs) scratching a meagre living by harvesting dates and raising livestock. Metalled roads were rare outside of the cities and non-existent in Sinai. There was a good railway network in the Nile Delta and fresh water from the River Nile was carried to the canal towns of Port Said, Ismailia and Suez via the Ismailia and Sweetwater canals.

The Sinai peninsula extends nearly 400 kilometres from the Mediterranean Sea to its southern tip, and 180 kilometres from the Suez Canal at Port Said to the border post at Rafah. Beyond Rafah was Turkish Syria. The northern third consists of large sand dunes and flat stony plains dotted with small prickly shrubs. A large water-bearing area exists between Mazar and Romani, marked on the surface by ancient wells, called *hods*, in the midst of small patches of date palms and shrubs. The many large *wadis* (river valleys) throughout the peninsula are dry for most of the year. The sub-surface water is always slightly salty and quite bitter wherever palm tree roots touch the water.[8]

The Sabkhet el Bardawil is a large, swampy salt-water lagoon between the Mediterranean coast and the desert. Although slightly below sea level, parts of it are dry in summer. With a salt crust on its surface that might, or might not, be hard enough for horses and men to ride on, it was a treacherous place for the unwary.

Today it is possible to drive across Sinai in air-conditioned comfort in a couple of hours. Ninety years ago, the peninsula was a far more formidable barrier. There were three main approach routes from Turkish Syria to the Suez Canal, but only the first is relevant here. The impressive-sounding Darb el Sultani, or 'King's Highway', reputed to be the oldest road in the world, was nothing more than an unpaved track alongside a single strand of telegraph wire. The track followed the coastline from Rafah through El Arish, Bir el Abd

Horses being watered at Serapeum.

and Katia, reaching the Suez Canal at Kantara. There was little or no fresh water between El Arish and Mazar, and the soft sand along the track made for slow and exhausting marching.[9]

In January 1916, Lieutenant General Sir Archibald Murray arrived from England to assume command of what soon became the Egyptian Expeditionary Force (EEF). In addition to keeping the Suez Canal safe from Turkish attacks out of Palestine, General Murray also had to keep an eye on pro-Turkish Senussi tribesmen in the Western Desert and maintain control in Upper Egypt and the Sudan. He was also expected to 'interfere with' Turkish bases and lines of communication in southern Palestine. Murray had to achieve these tasks with a steadily reducing number of troops as, one after the other, his best divisions were sent to France.[10]

Murray decided that the long-term security of the Suez Canal could best be achieved from the far side of Sinai. He estimated that five infantry divisions and four mounted brigades, operating on a line between El Arish and Kossaima, would be sufficient to block a Turkish advance along the coast and to attack the flank of any enemy movement along the central route. Murray initially thought that he faced up to 250,000 Turks in Syria, but the planners in London disagreed and continued to take forces from him. Murray's mind was eased in February, when he decided that no large-scale Turkish offensive into Egypt

P02132.001, AUSTRALIAN WAR MEMORIAL

Men and horses in the Suez Canal in March 1916.

J05877, AUSTRALIAN WAR MEMORIAL

The pontoon bridge over the Suez Canal at Ferry Post.

was likely before the winter months at the end of 1916; by then, he wanted to be in El Arish. The War Office authorised Murray to advance as far as Katia but deferred a final decision on El Arish.[11]

An enormous amount of preparatory work was required before the EEF could venture into the desert wastes of Sinai. The canal defences, and an extensive network of supply depots, training camps, railways and roads behind them needed to be finished, or built from scratch. Railway swing bridges across the canal had to be built, along with pipelines, pumps and filtration and chlorination stations for the Nile water in the Sweetwater Canal. Because the Bardawil Lagoon would prevent the force from being resupplied from the sea as it crossed the western half of the peninsula, Murray also had to build a railway and a water pipeline across the peninsula.[12]

Construction of the desert railway began at Kantara in March 1916 and 25 kilometres of line were laid in the first month. At this rate, Murray expected that the railhead would reach Katia by the end of April. This would allow him to station an infantry division and a mounted division there, supported by other infantry divisions along the canal. Mounted patrols would be able to operate from this base as far eastward as Bir el Abd.

Murray's Anzac and British mounted brigades also needed to reorganise and re-equip. The horse artillery guns and limbers were fitted with wide wooden blocks on their wheels

51

H01793, AUSTRALIAN WAR MEMORIAL

New Zealanders leading their horses along the bank of the Suez Canal.

and hitched to eight-horse teams to give them reasonable mobility across the sand. Horse-drawn wagons were useless in the deep sand of Sinai, so away from the railway all stores and supplies had to be carried on the backs of camels. Seventy-five thousand riding and transport camels were needed, but few had yet been collected.[13]

Cemal's plans to invade Egypt were delayed when Russian attacks near the Black Sea diverted some of the Turkish reinforcements earmarked for his Sinai offensive. The German and Austrian forces were also slow in arriving in Syria. While he waited, Cemal authorised Colonel Kress von Kressenstein to launch a spoiling raid against the advancing British railway in April 1916.[14]

On the warm, sunny morning of Sunday, 23 January 1916, the New Zealand Mounted Rifles Brigade rode out of Zeitoun Camp on a seven-day, 140-kilometre trek to the banks of the Suez Canal. As the horsemen followed the causeway alongside the Ismailia Canal into the mixed desert and farmland to the north-east of Cairo, the pyramids and the minarets sank slowly into the west behind them. After the fine start, heavy rain fell on most days. At Bilbeis, the troops endured what locals said was the wettest and coldest night in many years. The wagons carrying the rations and tents became bogged in the soft, wet sand, so the horsemen just lay on the sand and covered themselves with two blankets and a waterproof sheet. Everyone was miserable until scouts 'liberated' a pile of creosote-soaked railway sleepers from the Bilbeis railway yards. According to William Peed, 'they made good firewood and we made ourselves fairly comfortable for the night'. Indignant Egyptian State Railway authorities later forwarded 'a most exorbitant bill to NZEF Headquarters'.[15]

When the brigade rode out from Bilbeis the next day, 'the mission school children were out cheering us, and we made the children very pleased by answering them back. It was a very windy day and everyone was miserable. The sand was very bad on the eyes, and we were pleased when the wind ceased.' The brigade passed through Tel el Kebir, Moascar and Ismailia, before arriving at Serapeum, close to the banks of the Suez Canal, on 29 January (see Map 1, p.23). Lieutenant General Godley watched them arrive, commenting later that 'they looked very well, and were very fit, and are, of course, delighted to have their horses again'. The strength of the brigade at the time was 2429 men, 2336 riding horses, 352 draught and packhorses and 100 mules.[16]

Training began immediately. After a few days of rifle and machine gun shooting, the men were reacquainted with patrolling and outpost duties. They practised dismounting and handing their horses to section No. 3s and attacking on foot. They rehearsed the tactical formations used to move across the desert and relearned the principles of attacking, defending, pursuing and withdrawing under fire. One squadron at a time was sent across

A camp at Serapeum, with a camel convoy on the skyline.

the canal to patrol in front of the trenches, which were manned by Australian infantrymen. The patrols returned to the trenches each day to water the horses.

As Peed recorded, the work was not very demanding: 'we are not doing much in the way of training'. The AMR historian, Charles Nicol, described life at Serapeum as 'exceedingly pleasant'. Wednesday and Saturday afternoons, and all day on Sundays, were devoted to boxing, rugby and swimming in the Suez Canal. The canal was still in use by Allied shipping, and lookouts were posted to warn the naked swimmers when merchant ships with women passengers approached.[17] On 19 February, Lieutenant Colonel 'Old John' Findlay, the popular Commanding Officer of the Canterbury regiment, rejoined the brigade after a lengthy period of treatment and convalescence in Britain.

It was common knowledge that most of the men in Egypt would soon be heading for Europe. 'Deep down, there was no doubt whatsoever that France was the country most desired.... Every little arrangement with regard to clothing, equipment or training which gave any indication of probable climatic conditions was eagerly discussed.'[18] Although they did not yet know it, very few Anzac horsemen would ever get to France, where the Western Front had long since solidified into an unbroken series of trenches extending from the North Sea to Switzerland. Until the Allies figured out how to break through the formidable German defences and into the open, there was no mounted work for the tens of thousands of British and Indian cavalrymen already there, let alone for the light horsemen and mounted riflemen in Egypt.

Before anyone could sail for Europe, the recuperating Gallipoli divisions and the 40,000 Anzac reinforcements had to be reorganised. On 10 February the old Anzac Corps became 1 Anzac Corps. It retained the veteran 1st and 2nd Australian infantry divisions and the New Zealand and Australian Division, all under Godley's command. Three new Australian infantry divisions were combined into 2 Anzac Corps. Godley's more experienced men were put in charge of the defence of the central part of the Suez Canal, while 2 Anzac Corps was assembled and equipped nearby at Tel el Kebir. As soon as they were ready, both corps were to be transferred to Europe.[19]

General Godley wanted to create a New Zealand infantry division. Although this marked a major escalation in New Zealand's commitment to the war effort, he managed to gain the approval of the New Zealand government on 17 February. Finding the smaller new units for the New Zealand Division was relatively simple, and one squadron of the Otago Mounted Rifles (OMR) Regiment became Divisional Mounted Troops. (The OMR was then disbanded, and the remaining men were transferred to other units). Raising four

1000-man infantry battalions and 10 artillery batteries was another matter. Godley found many of the officers and soldiers he needed from the 7500 New Zealand reinforcements already in Egypt, but he also needed experienced officers and NCOs, and men who were familiar with horses. Some were transferred from the NZMR Brigade at Serapeum, and the final shortfall was made up by raiding the training squadrons of the regiments, where many Gallipoli veterans were convalescing. A total of 50 officers and 2000 men was compulsorily transferred to the New Zealand Division from the NZMR Brigade and its reinforcement drafts.[20]

This did not go down well with many mounted riflemen. Gordon Harper wrote that 'the poor old mounted brigade has been turned aside by the very man whose reputation we made on Gallipoli [Godley] … if anyone goes away to hospital, he never comes back, but finds himself in a new branch, amongst strangers, when he gets out.' Leslie Smith was indignant. 'We decided to break camp and go ten miles down the canal to Serapeum to see our … officers…. Colonel [Mackesy] was very indignant about … Main Body men being transferred. He is going to see the General.' When Major General Andrew Russell, formerly the commander of the NZMR Brigade and now the commander of the infantry division, spoke to the disgruntled transferees on 6 March, he gave them the choice of remaining with the mounted rifles brigade and staying in Egypt 'indefinitely', or going with their new units to 'a new country'. Smith changed his tune after Russell's intervention. 'We were all delighted at the prospect of leaving hot, old Egypt. We thought it over and decided to stay in the artillery'.[21]

Reinforcements who were not needed for the mounted regiments were fair game as far as the Gallipoli veterans were concerned. However, to take many of the veterans themselves and, worse, to reduce some of them in rank, without giving them or their commanders the opportunity to object, was insensitive to say the least. As if this were not bad enough, officers and NCOs taken from the brigade were replaced in command appointments, not by promoted veterans, but by inexperienced reinforcements. As Gordon Harper noted, 'there is much feeling here against these latecomers who are [now] nearly all senior to those who are here. I am afraid we badly need another battle to straighten things out again.' Benjamin Colbran agreed: 'There is a lot of discontent amongst us and it would not take much to start a row. As is generally the way, men were picked out by favouritism. A man wants to drink and crawl with his NCOs to get on. This I will not do, so have been cut out and an 8th Reinforcement man put in my place. It is an insult, and I have not felt so annoyed since joining the army.' Word of the complaints got back to New Zealand, but

Godley reassured the Minister of Defence, James Allen, that 'the non-promotion of non-commissioned officers has been very much exaggerated, and as usual the loudest cry has been made by those who were the least deserving'. At the end of this needlessly painful process, the NZMR Brigade was a little smaller than it had been in 1914. Although various references quote slightly different numbers, the new establishment of the brigade was about 1760 men and 2100 horses.[22]

On 5 March, the NZMR Brigade crossed the Suez Canal via a pontoon bridge at Ferry Post near Ismailia and took over responsibility for a 16-kilometre stretch of the central defence zone from an Australian infantry brigade. The Auckland and Canterbury regiments were split up into squadron camps along the front line about 15 kilometres out from the canal, and the Wellingtons were held in reserve back at the canal. The riders patrolled the desert to the east by night and day. Above them, flimsy British aircraft scouted beyond the horizon. Egyptians required passes to move anywhere near the canal and a strip of sand adjacent to the waterway was swept smooth each day so that any footprints appearing in it overnight would be detected at dawn.[23]

According to Guy Powles 'there was no doubt about being in the desert now. As far as the eye could see not a tree was to be seen, nothing but miles of sand extending in broken ridges to the horizon.' The desert was unlike anything the New Zealanders had experienced before; for those old enough to remember, even the parched South African veldt was more hospitable.

Nearly every day dawned clear, with cloudless blue skies. The men completed their morning routine – washing, feeding the horses, cleaning their weapons and eating breakfast – and then the work started. Some lucky men rode off into the desert on patrol but most faced a day of backbreaking labour in the trenches under the hot sun. Jim McMillan found 'shovelling the sand from the bottom of the trenches … a never-ending and thankless task, for almost as fast as it was thrown out, it ran in again. A diversion from this seemingly futile way of expending one's energy was provided by the job of erecting barbed wire entanglements, which, to the men who had enlisted as horsemen, was only slightly less unpleasant than coping with the sand.'[24]

Guy Powles described this time:

There were rumours of the enemy being about, and patrols daily scoured the desert in front of the Brigade's position…. Patrolling by day far out into the desert, and providing standing patrols by night, were only varied by cleaning out and improving the trenches of our main line. The weather was hot, and work in the trenches during the day was very trying … Each squadron had its own allotted task and camp, and the rivalry between them to gain the approval of the CO [Commanding Officer] tended to keep everyone in a high state of efficiency. Horses were in the hardest condition, well-groomed and well-fed. It was here that men began to realise the necessity of keeping the horses perfectly fit, and although regular stable hours were kept and horses groomed for 2½ to 3 hours daily, yet many men were to be seen at odd times giving their mounts an extra polish. And here it was that the Regiment learned how to load and how not to load the 'Ship of the Desert'. For the desert to the east of the Canal is so soft that all wheels [wagons] were left at Serapeum, and everything that everybody owned had either to be piled somehow on a camel or be left behind. Rations were plentiful but monotonous, consisting of tinned beef and hard biscuits. Water was very scarce, and all that was required for drinking and washing and for the horses came to the camps on camels, each carrying two fantasies [fanatis], as the large tin vessels were called, holding fourteen gallons [64 litres] apiece.[25]

On 15 March the New Zealand and Australian mounted brigades were transferred to the new Australian and New Zealand Mounted Division. The idea of combining the mounted riflemen and light horsemen into a mounted division was first suggested in December 1914 but it had been rejected out of hand by the War Office.[26] Now, with four Anzac mounted brigades available and unwanted on the Western Front, there was no argument from London. The new division was placed under the command of Major General 'Harry' Chauvel, an Australian who had commanded the 1st Light Horse (LH) Brigade and later

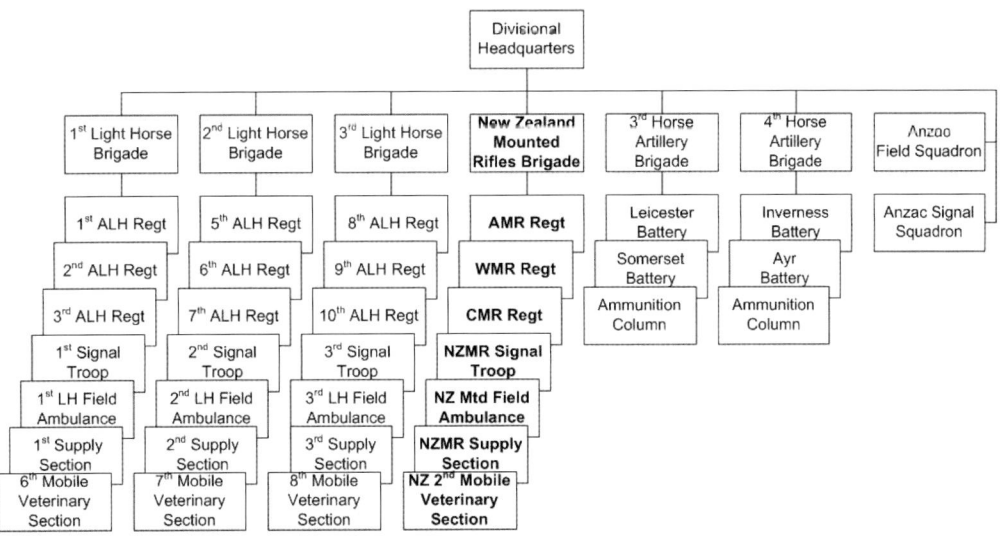

Figure 2: The Anzac Mounted Division in April 1916.[27]

New Zealand horses ready for desert operations.

the 1st Australian Division on Gallipoli. Chauvel, a 51-year-old professional soldier with South African War experience, was described by one historian as 'perhaps the least dashing of the truly distinguished leaders of mounted soldiers in history. Shy, gentle of speech, and quiet of bearing, he was a zealous disciplinarian but a very just one, deeply respected, but in no way a soldier's idol.'[28]

General Chauvel's division was immediately, and forever afterwards, known as the Anzac Mounted Division. It consisted of the NZMR Brigade, the 1st, 2nd and 3rd Light Horse (LH) brigades, four Royal Horse Artillery (RHA) batteries equipped with 18-pounder field guns, and various divisional troops. NZMR and ALH volunteers supplemented specialists in the new Anzac Field Squadron and Anzac Signal Squadron, and experienced officers were transferred from the brigades to help form the Divisional Headquarters.[29]

As soon as his brigades were released from their canal defence duties, Chauvel intended to assemble them at nearby Salhia to train and re-equip for desert operations. Before this could happen, the young Prince of Wales visited the NZMR Brigade in the desert. Godley wrote that the men were 'thrilled at seeing the heir to the throne, and gave him a wonderful reception', but not everyone was quite so thrilled, as Percy Doherty noted. 'HRH The Prince of Wales inspected the brigade's line of trenches today … He appeared to be … bored to death and didn't seem to be over-interested in us or anything else … these inspections bore a poor soldier more than any one else, they always mean a deuce of a lot of extra work and messing about, and to us are anything but pleasant.' Jim McMillan, who was part of the Guard of Honour for the royal visitor, had cause to remember that particular parade for years afterwards: he dropped his rifle in front of the prince.[30]

The New Zealand brigade, 'shorn of some of its best officers and men' and topped up with partly-trained reinforcements, was far from ready to face the Turks, so it was fortunate that no enemy action occurred along the canal during March. Although this made life 'dreary and monotonous for all concerned', it did give Chaytor a chance to train his brigade. 'How I wish J. Turk would come,' wrote Bert Harris, 'it would break the monotony some.… There is really nothing very exciting about this life at present.' One thing did not change, according to William Peed: 'Fatigues the same as per usual, and plenty of them'.[31]

The NZMR Brigade and the 2nd LH Brigade were relieved of their canal-guarding duties by an Australian infantry division on 30 March. The New Zealanders returned to Serapeum to pack up, before riding to Moascar to farewell the men of the New Zealand Division, who were about to leave for France. The celebrations were boisterous. Five Greek canteens were burnt down during the night and Egyptian merchants also suffered. 'When the troops knew they were going away, of course that night they tore every one [of the Egyptian food stalls] apart. Every poor Egyptian lost all his gear and all his stuff. … All the ones that were left behind paid for the damage. We were fined so much; it was stopped in your pay book.' When the mounteds were stood down for the invasion of Gallipoli in April 1915, many of them had been bitterly disappointed. A year later, their diaries and letters record no comparable reaction to being left behind in Egypt. Perhaps the terrible experiences on Gallipoli had dampened their enthusiasm for fighting, or maybe they believed that the Turks would give them plenty of work in the desert.[32]

On 5 April a Training Regiment was established at Moascar to support the NZMR Brigade. Major Albert Samuel was transferred from the WMR and promoted to command the regiment. Newly arrived reinforcements received their last training here before being certified ready to join the brigade. Training focused on the use of gas masks, shooting and field work. Enough horses were available to mount a squadron at a time. The staff of the training regiment were experienced officers and non-commissioned officers (NCOs) sent down from the brigade on three-month secondments.[33]

Training at Salhia consisted of shooting, bayonet fighting practice and revision of reconnaissance and reporting procedures. According to Charles Nicol, 'the horses had the benefit of plenty of water and green feed, and they put on condition.' Australian Ion

Idriess described the village as 'a little Eden in the desert. The ground all green under intense cultivation, a splendid grove of date palms, the big clean village, the minaret tower gleaming under the sun, and a picturesque population of Arabs, Egyptians, and Greeks.' Kingston Hull wrote home: 'We have been here some days and are having the easiest time struck so far, [we] are in the tent most of the time.' On one occasion training was 'rudely interrupted … in a most unpleasant manner by a … sand storm of full desert fury, which smothered everyone and everything while it lasted'. As Guy Powles recorded, the storm subsided towards evening 'but it seemed like days before one felt clean again. The sand seemed to penetrate the very pores of the skin.'[34]

When the Sinai railway was extended past the canal defences in mid-April, the British 5th (Yeomanry) Mounted Brigade was sent out into the desert to protect the line from Turkish attack and to search for water. General Chauvel ordered the 5th Australian Light Horse (ALH) Regiment forward to Katia on 22 April to reinforce the cavalrymen, to be followed a day later by the rest of the 2nd LH Brigade. Brigadier General Chaytor was under orders to send two of his New Zealand regiments to Kantara on 25 April.[35] On the afternoon of Easter Sunday, the Wellingtons were preparing to play the Aucklands at rugby when bad news arrived. That morning the British cavalry brigade had been surprised and routed by a Turkish attack out in the desert and the survivors were retreating in disorder towards the canal. Johnny Turk was back.

2

The cold-footed mounteds

This was no country for horses, or for men, or for any live thing for that matter.

C.G. LYTTELTON

_____

ONE BRITISH CAVALRY squadron was at Katia; two others and an engineer water survey party were six kilometres further east at Oghratina. A strong detachment of Scottish infantrymen and Indian cameliers was at Dueidar and there were several reserve cavalry troops at Romani. A sizeable Turkish force was known to be at Bir el Abd: small detachments had already attacked some of the Yeomanry positions. The cavalrymen were novices in the desert; their posts were lightly-manned, few trenches had yet been dug, and little barbed wire was used. They had no artillery with them because the guns could barely be moved in the soft sand and there was no water for the extra horses. The posts were too far apart to support each other with rifle or machine gun fire and little effective patrolling took place. German scout aircraft often flew over the camps and local Bedouin, some of whom were believed to be receiving Turkish pay, had free run of the Yeomanry positions.

The 5th ALH Regiment reached Kantara by dusk on 22 April, but it was too late to save the British cavalry. At dawn on the foggy morning on 23 April, 3500 Turks and Arabs, under the command of Colonel Kress von Kressenstein, attacked. They pinned down the troops at Dueidar and overwhelmed the cavalrymen and engineers at Oghratina and Katia. Many of the cavalrymen chose not to escape on their horses, since that would have meant abandoning the engineers, and fought until they were either killed or were so badly wounded that they were unable to move. Losses were heavy: about 130 men were killed and as many surrendered. The leading squadron of the 5th ALH Regiment arrived on the battlefield at noon and pursued the withdrawing Turks, but it could only round up a few stragglers.[1]

The remainder of the 2nd LH Brigade left Salhia at midday. That afternoon, after news of the attack arrived, the NZMR Brigade was also ordered into the desert. The New Zealanders could carry only what would fit on their saddles, so precious gift parcels from

Horse and man at rest in the desert.

home, which had been distributed that day, had to be unceremoniously dumped. The brigade was in the saddle by 8 p.m. and riding towards Kantara. The brigade's brass band played a rousing tune as 1516 men and 1690 animals rode away into the darkness.[2] It was almost exactly 12 months since the landings at Anzac Cove.

After riding all night, the New Zealanders crossed the Sweetwater Canal on a narrow railway bridge with planks laid between the tracks and no guard rails. As Guy Powles recorded, 'The majority of the horses took it quietly, but some, whose owners had evidently been visiting the feed bin in unauthorised hours, were feeling above themselves.' Two horses fell off the bridge into the water. According to Joseph Laws, one survived but the other was so badly injured that it had to be destroyed. The mounteds crossed to 'the business side' of the Suez Canal via a pontoon bridge at Kantara at 7 a.m. After a hurried breakfast they carried on into the desert for another ten kilometres, passing demoralised cavalrymen on foot, going in the opposite direction. The NZMR Brigade arrived at Hill 70 soon after 9 a.m., completing a forced march of 35 kilometres.[3]

Not long after the tired riders got their heads down, the Royal Flying Corps (RFC) reported that another large enemy force was heading towards Romani. The 2nd LH Brigade rode forward, eager for battle, but the 'enemy column' turned out to be 400 Egyptian railway workers coming in to complain about not being fed during the recent excitement. According to Percy Doherty, 'it was wonderful how keen and alive we all were in a few minutes, although just before the alarm we all felt half-dead after the long night march and the want of sleep'. Chaytor sent the Canterbury regiment up to Romani to support the Australian brigade.[4]

With the Turks gone, little happened for the next fortnight. NZMR patrols rode out from Hill 70 to Dueidar and Romani every day, linking up with the Australians and the Canterburys. In early May the CMR tried to cut a canal from the sea to the western end of the nearly dry Sabkhet el Bardawil in an attempt to flood it, but the waves defeated their efforts and the task was abandoned.[5] On 12 May the entire brigade moved up to Romani and Bir Etmaler to take over the outpost line from the 2nd LH Brigade.

When the Anzacs occupied the ground lost by the Yeomanry in April, they were disturbed and scandalised by what they found. A few days after the Easter raid, 25 dead and 14 wounded cavalrymen were found at Katia, alongside the carcasses of 60 horses and 30 camels. Machine gunner Gordon Harper deployed his Maxims 'in the moonlight amongst gruesome objects of all kinds. The ground was covered with helmets, boots, swords, and dead men.' Kingston Hull also saw grim evidence of the raid. 'Out where the Yeomanry were smacked up the poor chaps are half buried and frizzling in the sun.... By the heaps of empty cartridges, they fought while they had any left. Their bandoliers are all empty.' Percy Doherty, too, recorded his impressions. 'Horses lay dead in rows … where they had been mowed down by machine guns, they still had their halters and heel-ropes … Some corpses were hardly buried at all and the stench was anything but pleasant.' Arthur Rhodes was struck by other things. 'One cannot realise the amount of stuff the officers had, consisting of golf clubs … and all sorts of pictures, carpets, cut-glass candlesticks … under their beds. I have never seen such a camp in my life. I found a list of silver they had with them and alongside each item was the price.'[6]

The Katia raid highlighted the danger of complacency when dealing with the Turkish Army. Commenting upon the disaster, Lieutenant General Murray compared the British horsemen with the Anzacs. 'The bulk of the yeomanry officers are ignorant of the rudiments of mounted work…. In any serious mounted work, I rely entirely on my Anzac Mounted Division, who are excellent under hard conditions.'[7]

Murray's earlier assessment that the Turks would not attack before the winter was obviously incorrect. The enemy was clearly in an aggressive mood, but no one yet knew if the raid was the precursor of a larger Turkish offensive or a one-off effort before they settled down for the summer. The Anzacs used the following months to learn how to live and fight in the unforgiving Sinai desert. 'By trial and error we gained the needed experience…. We found out what we really needed, and what could be dispensed with. The redundant horse covers were scrapped: hung around the animal's neck they took more strength from him during the day than their doubtful protection at night warranted. Much of our own clothing was more suited for the Arctic than the desert – that was slowly remedied.'[8] As far as Gordon Harper was concerned, the environment was a more challenging adversary than the Turks.

> *It was the desert which is our chief enemy. There is nothing so inscrutable as its changeless face; there is so little indication of the hidden enemy, and there is no warning of the scorching blast which rises from its red hot sands and envelopes the unfortunate troops who are struggling in its grip…. One sinister warning it will always give. Unlike the sea, it always insists on giving up its dead. Nothing will it cover with its sands and the whitened bones of years ago are added to by the fair haired Tommies who are quite preserved when the white sand has drifted from them. Yet when the sun goes down everything seems to breathe again and life seems easy again.*[9]

The 35,000 Bedouin who lived in oases and wadis scattered across the Sinai peninsula had no interest in the war, other than for the opportunities that it presented to them.

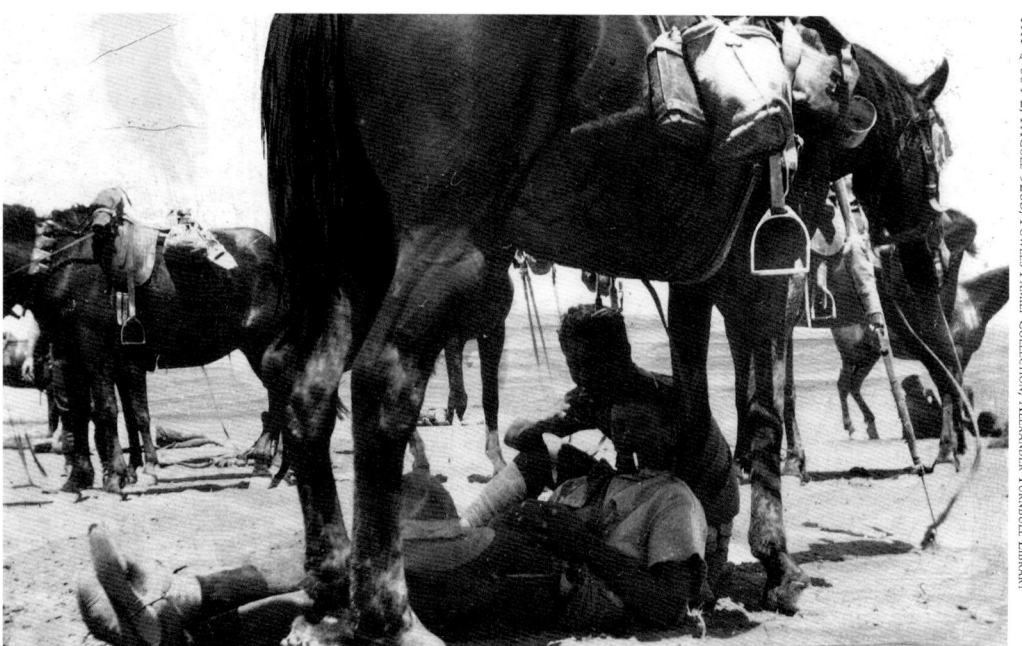

Two troopers resting in the shade.

Before long they were despised by the Anzacs. 'They are of no use to their fellow men,' wrote Lieutenant Arthur Moore, 'producing nothing beyond that barely essential to their own needs, and on many occasions were suspected of carrying information to the Turks of British movements.' Percy Doherty recorded a report about how the Bedouin treated the British wounded after the Katia raid. 'News has been received that the Turks treated the wounded Tommies well in the last smack-up of a few days ago, they left them with food and water and bandaged their wounds, but the Bedouin afterwards stripped them of all their clothing, and one body was found with wire round the neck, showing that the wounded man had been strangled by the inhuman brutes.'[10]

The Sinai Bedouin were considered to be pro-Turkish. Orders were issued to round them up and send them to the canal but this was easier said than done. The wily tribesmen quickly spotted search parties and hid among the sand dunes or, on one occasion, down a well. They could move so quickly across the soft sand that they could easily outpace a mounted column. Usually it was only old men, women and children who were caught, along with what Australian light horseman Ion Idriess described as 'their flocks of scraggy goats and mangy camels'.[11]

The Bedouin did not entirely deserve such animosity. Desert nomads who lived by their own rules and customs, they scratched a living from one of the most inhospitable habitats in the world. According to Harry Mitchell, 'you never see a fat one'. Bedouin saw nothing wrong in taking what was left behind on the battlefields – including stripping clothes and equipment from the bodies of dead or wounded men – or in selling information to the highest bidder. Britons, Anzacs, Germans and Turks were all foreigners to the Bedouin, and they all had resources that the Bedouin could exploit.[12]

The daytime temperatures in the desert soared with the approach of the summer of 1916, which would be one of the hottest on record. Percy Doherty thought that the heat in May 'was just like passing along a road with gorse fires burning on the side, it just seemed to practically scorch the skin'. According to John Masterman, 'if one placed an egg on the sand, it would cook in about two minutes, but we had no eggs to cook'. To make matters worse, the *khamsin* season was under way. 'Day after day blew this dreaded hot wind from the south. The summer sun burned with fiendish ferocity.... Packets of candles melted until the wicks alone remained.'[13]

The water in the desert oases varied in quality from unpleasant to undrinkable. Chlorinated Nile River water was brought forward on camels for the men but the horses, forced to drink the oasis water, lost condition until they became used to it. As Edwin McKay wrote, 'until we reached Palestine ... [the horses] never knew the taste of one drop of fresh water'. In the early days, water had to be exposed by digging wells. Because sand flows back into a hole almost as quickly as it is removed, these wells had to be large and carefully constructed, and it could take a troop of 30 men a day or more to gain access to water a few metres below ground. Fortunately, Australian engineers introduced the spear-point pump, with which water could be obtained without any digging at all. Each troop had a medical orderly, whose job it was to test the water and classify it as 'drinking water', 'fit for horses' or 'not fit for horses'. Sometimes even the men had to drink local water, which needed to be boiled or treated with chlorine tablets to make it safe. When dissolved in a bottle of water, a chlorine tablet was, in Ion Idriess's words, 'guaranteed to kill all germs. It does. It will also burn leather and eat the rust off stirrup irons – which is what we use them [the tablets] for.' According to Edwin McKay, 'the toughest of germs would not live long in such a nauseating fluid'.[14]

The daily water allowance in camp was about four litres per man. About half of that went to the cookhouse for cooking and making tea and a little over a litre went into each man's water bottle, leaving about half a litre for washing. On patrol, each man had a single bottle of warm, treated water to last him through the heat of the day. Camels carrying water would usually, but not always, rendezvous with patrols at dusk. 'The water was … often almost too hot to drink, after travelling for hours in . . . metal tanks exposed to the sun – not the best kind of thirst quenchers for parched throats, but eagerly drunk by the thirsty horsemen for all that.'[15]

The men saw little wildlife during the day, as sensible animals stayed underground to avoid the heat. 'As the sand cooled in the evening, all sorts of life appeared – spiders, many kinds of lizards, kangaroo rats, and tortoises and chameleons. The men often carried a chameleon on the hat, and in the evening, it would catch the flies that rested on us.… There was a black spider that, as we rode past, would turn and face us and raise its fore-legs in an angry and defensive attitude, a nasty and dangerous-looking beast.' Apart from one white pup which was kept as a pet, the men shot wild dogs 'because they … eat the dead'.[16]

Men and horses alike were tormented by insects. 'Eating became one long fight between hungry men and hungry flies,' wrote Guy Powles. 'One ate with one hand while the other was continually brushing away the pests.' The eyes of the horses were often shielded from flies, and the sun, by string fringes fitted to the brow bands of their bridles, and some men carried fly whisks to swat the flies. Lice, or 'chats', were another trial. Ion Idriess described them as 'damned wretched things. A man's daily tally is about thirty, except when he's right off duty and gets a chance to take his pants down, and

A water-carrying camel in Sinai.

then God knows how many he gets.' Under such unhygienic conditions, small scratches inevitably became infected, forming weeping sores that attracted more flies and took weeks or months to heal. There was also the ever-present threat of dysentery, spread by flies which flew from the toilets and rubbish heaps straight to the food in the men's mouths. Fortunately, typhoid and cholera were kept at bay by regular inoculations and smallpox vaccinations were administered whenever there was an outbreak of the disease in the area.[17] The horses also had to endure the attention of ticks and fleas. Ticks made their way to the horses from the camel convoys, crawling up their legs and attaching themselves to the animals' bellies. The only way to remove the blood-sucking parasites was to burn them off with a lighted cigarette.

Theoretically, the in-camp menu included meat, bread or biscuits, bacon, jam, milk, vegetables, potatoes, sugar, tea, cheese and lime juice. But Ted Andrews wrote that 'our rations … were hopelessly monotonous. Porridge and dirty rice, a shaving each of greasy, fat bacon ... bully [beef], biscuits, jam and the life-saving tea! Why the hell the army chiefs could not have got us dried fruits and vegetables, produced in Egypt, or occasional issues of fresh vegetables and fruit from the Delta, we never knew.' Tins of condensed milk arrived 'in a state of putrefaction. The daily ration of marmalade which every man had received *ad nauseam* since he crossed the Canal had acquired a blended flavour between kerosene and castor oil.' The 'Mobile Ration' consisted of bully beef, biscuits, jam, tea, cheese, milk and sugar. Each man carried an 'Iron Ration' of biscuits, bully beef, tea, and sugar, to be consumed only when ordered. Edwin McKay wrote that 'the army biscuit was … perforated here and there, presumably to give breathing space to the weevils that boarded and lodged in so many of them…. When speaking of war atrocities, don't fail to include the army biscuit ration.' Army rations were supplemented from home and, occasionally, by the enemy. Charitable societies and individuals in New Zealand and England sent the men parcels of biscuits, cakes, soup tablets, chewing gum, sweets, cigarettes or tobacco, and cans of tinned salmon, fruit and milk. These were gratefully received, and, if one man got a cake from home, he would typically share his good fortune by splitting the food among his section. When Turkish rations were captured, their rolled sheets of pressed dates or apricots were very popular.[18]

Night starts for patrols were usual in the desert, but they were not without risk to the horses. Feeding and watering could not be conducted properly, and saddles were difficult to adjust in the dark. Fifteen minutes after starting a march, riders stopped and checked the horses' saddles and bridles for rubbing or chafing and to ensure that no equipment was about to fall off. Whenever possible, bits and saddles were removed during brief halts. The horses were given a small feed and their backs were rubbed to restore circulation. To cool the horses down, the last few minutes of a march were conducted at a walk with the riders dismounted. Despite this careful management, the horses were so tired at times that they would lie down fully saddled during brief halts.[19] The walk was by far the most common gait used, as anything quicker could not be sustained for long without injuring the overloaded horse. A steady, calm walker was worth its weight in gold, but a jogger was a trial for its rider.

Wherever possible, horse picket lines were sited near water, on firm ground, out of the wind and near the men's bivouacs. To help conceal them from aerial observation, horse lines were arranged in irregular patterns, and, if possible, placed under cover in hods. The horses required constant supervision to prevent them getting themselves into trouble. Horse-line sentries were posted to watch the horses, especially when feeding, to stop their head- and heel-ropes from tangling, to report horses that were off their food and to clean up the animals' droppings.[20]

Apart from small-scale scouting in Sinai, the Turks concentrated on building up their forces in southern Syria. The experienced and combat-hardened 3rd Division arrived from Gallipoli in April, as did the first German reinforcements.

When the railway reached Romani on 19 May, the British 52nd (Lowland) Division was sent forward from the Suez Canal. Romani was an ideal place from which to protect the railway (see Map 4, p.90): a raised tableland dominated the flat ground towards Katia and it had plentiful water in wells at Romani and Etmaler. Romani's northern approaches were partly blocked by the Bardawil Lagoon while to the south there was an area of deep, relatively waterless sand. Wellington Ridge, named after the WMR, formed the southern edge of the plateau upon which the camps and the railway rested. This ridge, which rose steeply from the flatter land to the south, was pierced by many narrow gullies. Whoever held Wellington Ridge dominated the camps and the railway. South of Wellington Ridge were two sandhills, Mount Meredith and Mount Royston, which would become key terrain in the coming battle.[21]

The Scottish infantry began work on a chain of redoubts extending south from the Mediterranean coast near Mahemdiya to a high sandhill called Katib Gannit, and then westward for a short distance along Wellington Ridge. Major General Chauvel, placed in command of all the mounted troops east of Hill 70, brought his Anzac brigades forward and put them to work patrolling the desert to the east and south-east. Determined to avoid a repeat of the Yeomanry disaster, Chauvel sent his mounted troops out on daily patrols from the strong infantry base at Romani.[22]

New Zealanders watering their horses behind a sandhill at Romani.

General Murray's desert pipeline. 'KILO 86' is the distance in kilometres to Kantara.

British infantry could march only about 10 kilometres a day in the soft sand, so they were no use for patrolling. Unlike the 'beetle-crushers', 'the mounted men … could reach the enemy at a walking gait in five hours, including the regulation halt of ten minutes in every hour. They could then dismount, fresh to fight, feel the pressure, and locate the position of the enemy, and return to camp the same day.' Over the succeeding weeks, the mounted riflemen and light horsemen hunted for Turks, searched for water and rounded up 'spying' Bedouin.[23] Guy Powles wrote the following description of troop-level patrolling in the desert.

Small parties of men left camp in the darkness of the early morning bound for Katia, Oghratina, or Mageibra. Once clear of the camp, they spread out in one line, riding three or four yards apart, with a section of four men in diamond formation in front, and two men far out on each flank. As daylight increased, the men in front and on the flanks spread out and kept further away from the main body, but never so far that they could not communicate by signals.... Out in the desert where the different landmarks constantly changed, the compass and map carried by the troop leader were the only guide. Riding on, halting only to spell their horses for a few short minutes, they would probably reach the particular spot they were bound for about 11 a.m. Posting a lookout with a pair of field glasses on the most prominent ridge, the rest of the party would make a thorough search through the palms for any trace of the enemy, such as camel tracks, footmarks, or signs of fires. Nothing being discovered, sections would then go out a couple of miles south and east on further reconnaissance. Stray Bedouin … were brought in to be interrogated, and then sent to concentration camps in Egypt. About 2 o'clock the troop would start to return to camp. … Riding on, the deep silence of the desert broken only by the swish of the horses' feet in the sand, or the howl of a desert dog, the patrol would listen with anxious ears for the challenge from the night post in front of the camp. Half an hour's ride brings it to its own lines, where a welcome and hot tea awaits the tired men. The troop leader goes to make his report, and the day is ended. Very few of these patrols covered less than thirty miles [50 kilometres] a day, and sometimes considerably more.[24]

The northern faces of the largest sand dunes were often very steep and dangerous. On moonless nights, the horses could not detect the edge of the drop until it suddenly appeared beneath their hooves. Some adventurous men developed a novel approach to these precipices: horses 'were tobogganed down the steep sides, sitting back on their haunches in the soft sand. All that was required was for the rider to start his horse quite straight down the slope, leave his horse's head free, and keep his own head. Then the glissade was great fun and quite impressive to watch.... And it really was not difficult, though a fool of a horse would sometimes try to turn in the middle of the slide, with the inevitable result in a roll to the bottom, man and horse jumbled up together, very unpleasant.' The deep sand slowed the horses to a walk, at an average speed of no more than four kilometres per hour; the camels were even slower. General Murray admitted that 'it is not easy to … round up Bedouin and Turks at that rate'.[25]

Desert navigation was very difficult. Magnetic compasses and basic maps were available, but recognisable landmarks were scarce. Usually all that could be seen were seemingly endless, identical waves of sand dunes stretching into the shimmering distance. A sighting of the telegraph line along the Darb el Sultani was often a great relief to anxious troop leaders. Patrols frequently covered long distances entirely on compass bearings, looking for a tiny clump of date palms hidden in a depression. These hods were often invisible until the riders were within a few metres of them. Fog and mirages made navigation even harder. 'During the night,' Moore noted, 'heavy fogs would often complicate the already difficult travelling in the dark without landmarks, and daylight, on one occasion at least, found the advance guard on the tail of their own rear guard.' Some officers were better navigators than others. One CMR raid apparently failed because 'Col. Findlay … was, in more senses than one, completely fogged, and the result was that we got completely lost

... and we had to halt and wait for daybreak to find out where we were, and even then the mist was still too heavy, and I think it was between 6 and 7 a.m. before we started on again. ... Goodness only knows how we would have fared had the Turks got wind of it and surrounded us, which they could easily do as they are much more at home on this wretched desert than we are ... I am afraid it would be "finish" for [the] CMR.' In these circumstances, it is amazing that very few patrols ever got lost. Most objectives were reached on time, and without the riders being detected by the Turks.[26]

'Stunts', as operations were usually known, of one to four days' duration were often ordered with as little as 30 minutes' notice. In that time, 'a man had to draw his own rations, fill his water bottle, and draw his horse's rations. This last had to be done up in nosebags and secured properly to the saddle, this being no mean art in itself. Horses had to be saddled, picket and head ropes done up, and all necessary gear strapped to saddles.'[27]

MATT POMEROY COLLECTION

The original caption for this photograph, 'Tired', says it all.

A 'Special Reconnaissance' of the wells at Jefeir, Mageibra and Bayud was conducted on 15–16 May 1916. On the first day the Canterbury regiment rode forward to Oghratina. Before dawn the following day, the regiment was to ride forward to Debabis, providing support to an Australian regiment that was going to Bayud. At the same time, the CMR's 1st (CYC) Squadron and a light horse squadron would scout Mageibra and Jefeir. Each man was to carry one water bottle and a camel convoy would bring extra water up to Oghratina and Sagia.[28]

The 16th of May was a cruelly hot day, with a scorching khamsin raising the temperature to 50°C in the shade at Etmaler. What it reached in the sunshine was not recorded, but Arthur Rhodes recalled that the reins on his horse were so hot that 'I could hardly hold them, and as for the stirrups, well, they nearly burnt my boots'. A yawning rider was cautioned by a companion, 'Don't open your mouth so wide, Bill, when you yawn – you'll be getting your stummick sunburnt, an' it hurts somethin' awful!'[29]

The reconnaissance itself was uneventful. A CMR patrol spotted two enemy camel riders in the distance, but they 'refused to stay to be interviewed', so the riders withdrew to Oghratina – to find no camels and no fresh water.[30] By now, Gordon Harper wrote, 'the wind was like a blast furnace, and men began to double up…. I fell off my horse, and for some hours, men kept pouring well water over me and the others who were down, and ultimately pulled us round.'[31]

Lieutenant Colonel Findlay signalled Brigade HQ to 'send water and ambulances to Oghratina at once'. Shortly afterwards, he sent another, more urgent, message: '40 down with sun, must have ambulance'. According to Arthur Rhodes, 'every man ran around and worked like blazes to get water and food to the Canterburys. Special [camel] trains were sent off [as] matters by this time were very serious. They had got into a heat wave which knocked them all out, and if it had not been for a few who doused the remainder with water, I fail to see how they would have got on. After many wires, one came through saying they were recovering and would start for camp at 6.30 p.m. This they did and managed to crawl into camp at 11.30 p.m.'[32]

Other Anzac patrols also suffered from the fierce heat and 31 New Zealanders suffering from sunstroke were evacuated to hospital. Others were so thirsty when they reached camp that they 'flung themselves from their horses and on all fours struggling between the heads of excited, thirsty, whinnying animals, and devoured the brackish water from the troughs together'. Rhodes noted that 350 horses in the New Zealand brigade were temporarily unfit for work after that terrible Tuesday. Many men were demoralised by the shocking heat. Harry Judge wrote that 'old Anzacs say they never suffered so much on Gallipoli from the frost and snow as they did here yesterday from heat and thirst'.[33] Despite the awful conditions, the tasks were completed to General Murray's satisfaction: 'The Commander-in-Chief wishes to convey ... his appreciation of the splendid work done in the very arduous reconnaissance yesterday. [He] does not think that any other troops could have undertaken this operation successfully in the present weather.'[34]

After this salutary experience, the men were issued a second water bottle and long-distance moves began to be conducted at night as a matter of course. The men learned to drink as much as they could before departing on patrol and tried not to open their water bottles until they were on their way back towards camp after the stunt.

The first operation involving the entire New Zealand brigade took place at the end of May 1916. Its purpose was to surprise the Turks at Salmana, 40 kilometres from Romani. The regiments were accompanied by one 18-pounder gun from the Ayrshire Battery and by 850 camels carrying water, food and ammunition. The brigade rode out from Etmaler at 10 p.m. on Monday 29 May, reaching Debabis eight hours later. 'Wells were sunk and a supply of very salty water obtained, but the horses were so thirsty that they drank it with relish.' According to Arthur Rhodes, the men 'had a huge feed, as we took plenty of tinned stuff and also beer, which was ... a huge success'.[35]

After resting for the day at Debabis, the men resumed the march after dark. Everyone was 'very excited'. At midnight, the 3rd (Auckland) Squadron of the AMR was sent ahead to Bir el Abd, where there was a small enemy post. The Aucklands were to cut the telephone wires, then put a block in place behind the enemy position. The rest of the brigade would then advance and push the Turks into the arms of the Aucklands. It did not work out that way. 'Through some delay, the advance was not made for two hours after the wires were cut by the 3rd squadron ... and by that time the Turks had got away.'[36] Harry Judge's horse got tangled in the telephone wires.

He is a bad brute ... and now he went clean mad and bucked and twisted and turned until he got both himself and me completely tumbled up and it was not many seconds before he sent me flying clean out of the saddle ... I held on to the reins and this of course pulled him right on top of me, and he placed one of his hind feet on my back and his fore-feet on my head. Fortunately I had my [Wolseley] helmet on, and this saved my head, and, of course, the sand was soft underneath. This knocked me out for a few minutes, and when I recovered my senses and looked up, I saw my hack had succeeded in throwing himself, and that one man was sitting on his head while one or two more were cutting the wire clear.[37]

A02435, Australian War Memorial

Camp at Hill 70, protected by low barbed wire entanglements in front. The canvas covers behind the tents provided shade for the horses.

Although it was likely that the element of surprise had been lost, the column pressed on to Salmana, reaching it at 3 a.m. The CMR and AMR were sent north and south to encircle the position. The Aucklands attacked a small enemy post near Salmana.

> *The three squadrons galloped across the intervening flat ground towards the sand-hill, upon which 200 to 300 Turks were in position. The astonished Turks hardly fired a shot, even when the regiment dismounted near the base of the hill. Fixing bayonets, the troopers rushed the hill, but before they got to the top, the Turks were in fast retreat. A brisk fire was opened on the Turkish rearguard, five of whom stood their ground until shot.*[38]

The Aucklands came under 'friendly fire' from the Canterbury regiment to the north-west, but no casualties were inflicted. An enemy force of camel riders attempted a counter-attack from the east, but it withdrew when the rising sun revealed the strength of the attackers. Chaytor called off the operation and the brigade withdrew at 8 a.m. Fifteen enemy soldiers were killed and two prisoners and a box of telegraph pole insulators captured. Four Bedouin women and a baby were also brought back. The only EEF casualties were two men who were slightly wounded. With Chaytor, Arthur Rhodes 'rode up to see the position at 6.15 [a.m. and] saw the dead Turks – all told 15 – quite nice to see dead Turks again'. The force returned to Etmaler the following night, having covered 100 kilometres in 36 hours. 'Dog-tired, the men were sound asleep the moment the horses had been cared for.'[39]

British aircraft had bombed the Turks as they retreated from Salmana. The Turks returned the favour at dawn the next day, by bombing and machine-gunning the 1st LH Brigade's horse-lines at Romani. Eight Australians and 36 of their horses were killed, and many other terrified animals stampeded, some never to be seen again.

Being bombed from the air is probably the worst experience that men undergo in modern warfare. One sees a plane flying at anything from three to eight thousand feet [900 to 2500 metres] up; then comes the sound, a whirr, gradually rising to a shrill shriek of the descending bomb, then the explosion and a cloud of thick blackish-grey smoke slowly rising from the ground. If the bomb falls into horse lines, the sight is not a pleasant one. Men and animals are gashed and torn in an indescribable manner.[40]

Knowing the total reliance of the mounted brigades on their horses, enemy pilots hunted

The twelve Vickers guns of the New Zealand Machine Gun Squadron, photographed later in the war.

for the led animals during battles, and for the horse lines in camps. To counter this menace, the camps were spread out and air sentries were posted on surrounding sandhills with orders to blow whistles if enemy aircraft appeared. On hearing a whistle blast, Ion Idriess wrote, 'the oasis springs to life. Every man rushes to his horse, leaps on and gallops straight out into the desert in a thundering scatter of six hundred horses'. According to Clifton Bellis, 'after a few air alarms ... the horses could hear a plane long before we could, and get restless'.[41]

Aerial dog-fights were watched avidly by those on the ground, even though the enemy aircraft easily outmatched the 'odd-looking [British] contraptions'. British pilots sometimes also suffered from the attention of trigger-happy troops on the ground. According to Robert Wilson, some pilots said 'they'd sooner fly over Turks than Colonials'.[42]

The men soon grew weary of the never-ending patrolling. 'Nothing much doing here,' noted Percy Doherty, '... things are getting very stale here now.' Kingston Hull wrote that 'the best part of war is the time when the band is playing and the people cheering the departing soldiers. The rest is so silly and useless, when all is said and done.' Hull heard that 'we are going to England next month.... I do not know what good it would do us going there – unless we went as infantry and they seem to have plenty of them. I would

PEF/P/RHODES/29, PALESTINE EXPLORATION FUND, LONDON

A Lewis gun on an improvised anti-aircraft mount.

not come again as Mtd. – there is too much fooling around looking for water, getting feed etc. Where an infantryman would be resting, we are working.'[43]

When they were not out on patrol, the horsemen lived in camps at the Romani or Etmaler wells. A typical in-camp day began with reveille at 5.30 a.m. Sick parade was held at 6 a.m., after which the horses were watered and fed. The men had their own breakfast at 7.15, before cleaning up the tent lines and the horse lines in preparation for an inspection at 9. The horses were fed and watered again at 11 a.m., 4 p.m. and 8 p.m.; the men ate at noon and 5.30 p.m. The bugle call for lights out was sounded at 10 p.m. During the day, those men who were not sleeping after a long night out on guard were kept busy doing fatigues, escorting camel convoys, digging wells or guarding water troughs and supply dumps. With a few troops always out on outpost duty keeping an eye on nearby hods, it was an exhausting routine.[44]

'The [Mediterranean] sea is about five miles from here,' William Peed noted. 'It was delightful and we gave our horses a good swim in the sea.' According to John Masterman, 'our Postal Service was working well. They received the mail at Suez, took it to Ismailia, sorted it out there, then sent it on by train to Kantara, then transported it across the Canal to another train. That train would bring it up to the railhead, there camels would be loaded with it and taken to our camps.' Not all of the mail was welcome, though, according to Edwin McKay. 'It appeared that some unspeakable swine [in New Zealand] … had enclosed a note in one soldier's parcel expressing the hope that it would not reach any of the "Cold-Footed Mounteds" …'. The story went the rounds of the division, and the sulphurous air could almost be felt for a while.[45]

After eight months of being spoiled rotten while the NZMR Brigade was away at

Gallipoli, the horses now endured real hardship for the first time. Strenuous efforts were made to keep them fit and healthy in the inhospitable desert. 'We rode very slowly all night, resting for half-an-hour … at a time [so as] not to give the horses too much before we may have to go into action with them.' A lot of extra equipment was needed on the long patrols, and it had to be carefully arranged on the horses to avoid giving them sore backs and other injuries. Each man carried '240 rounds of ammunition in two bandoliers – one on the man himself and one around the horse's neck. The wallets in front of the saddle were filled with a change of clothes, and a blanket and overcoat covered the wallets.' So much was carried that, according to Alexander Wilkie, 'little could be seen of the saddle except the seat, and an acrobatic feat was necessary to get into it'. The heavily laden horses often sank to their bellies in the deep sand. The doctrinal sequence of riding for 20 minutes, walking for 10 minutes, riding for 20 minutes and resting for 10 minutes in every hour was abandoned; it was too tiring for the men, and the constant mounting and dismounting of the horses exhausted the animals. With no grass in the desert, all horse fodder had to be brought forward from the Suez Canal. Usually, it was barley and tibbin, often supplemented by berseem, millet, hay, maize or oats. Molasses was sometimes issued as a supplement to tibbin.[46]

The health of the horses was 'a matter of constant anxiety; in spite of all possible care they began to fall away in condition. This was no country for horses, or for men, or for any live thing for that matter.' Edwin McKay recalled that 'our splendid, over-wrought horses just broke their great hearts and spirits in silence. What grand, gallant animals they were!' John Masterman was 'quite sure they would love to get back to their native land, poor creatures, where they could have a good feed of green grass and a scamper round the paddock and away from the broiling hot sand. They are never loose from one year and to the next.' William Peed wrote in June that 'the DVS [Director of Veterinary Services] … came and had a look at our horses and was overheard to say that we would have to give our horses a rest'. This did not happen.[47]

On 24 June the NZMR Brigade handed over its duties to the 2nd LH Brigade. Leaving the Wellington regiment with the Australians and taking the 5th ALH Regiment in its place, the New Zealanders rode back to Hill 70 for a rest. As Charles Nicol recorded, 'Plenty of fresh water was … available, and the horses had the advantage of shelters from the sun.' While the brigade was at Hill 70, some magnificent chargers belonging to British artillery officers were stolen by New Zealanders and quickly disguised. When the owners arrived in the horse lines and demanded their mounts back, everyone present protested their innocence. Unfortunately, the British officers were able to identify their animals by the number and parent unit tattooed on the inside of the horses' lips, which the New Zealanders did not know about. The horses departed with their rightful owners, apparently with no ill feelings on either side.[48]

In July 1916, two significant organisational changes occurred in the NZEF. The first of two New Zealand camel companies, each comprising 183 officers and men, was created in the Imperial Camel Corps (ICC). The company was manned by mounted rifles reinforcements, and key appointments were filled by officers transferred from the NZMR Brigade.[49]

Also in July, the regimental machine gun sections were amalgamated into the New Zealand Machine Gun Squadron (NZMGS), under the command of Captain Robin Harper. This squadron of 230 men and 321 horses was as mobile as the regiments it supported, with its 12 heavy Maxim and Vickers machine guns carried into action on the backs of packhorses. As dismounted attacks developed, the machine guns would be galloped forward on the flanks in order to provide effective covering fire throughout the assault. The machine gunners became so expert that the guns could be firing within 60 seconds of being ordered to halt from the gallop. N.W.H. Beaven was proud of his job as a machine gunner, but he still found plenty to complain about. 'A tall pack horse is an abomination, as the extra few inches require a great deal more brute strength to hoist the gun and ammunition on to the pack.' Grooming the horses every morning resulted in the animals quickly becoming bored, 'their faces bearing an expression of great resignation as they are wondering if they would ever get breakfast'. Pack saddles were difficult to secure, and the girth straps sometimes came loose, resulting in the pack saddle and its contents slipping underneath the horse. 'An amiable horse … generally stops while you adjust the whole turn out, and looks at you as if to convey the one word, "Idiot".' In place of the Maxim machine guns, each mounted rifles regiment received three Lewis machine guns, on a scale of one per squadron. As a result of these changes, the firepower of the NZMR Brigade was increased significantly, making up to some extent for its limited artillery support.[50]

A third, more distant, event that would affect the New Zealanders took place in June 1916, when the Arabs in the Hejaz district of Arabia rose in revolt against the Turks. The ill-disciplined and poorly equipped tribesmen achieved little against the Turkish troops for some time, but their actions convinced planners in London that the EEF should be given more ambitious tasks in support of the Arabs.[51]

By mid-July, Anzac mounted patrols had thoroughly scouted the northern Sinai Desert to a distance of 80 kilometres from the Suez Canal. The Turks withdrew many of their advanced posts and gave up trying to intercept the Anzac patrols. The Anzac mounted brigades were already developing an enviable reputation. 'The Light Horse and Mounted Riflemen are desert-wise, know the area like the back of their horses' heads, and are physically hardened to an incredible degree. ... It's hard to imagine a group of men better fitted for battle in this tract of land.' In May, General Murray cabled the War Office: 'I am assuming that you are leaving the three Australian light horse brigades and the New Zealand brigade with me. Otherwise I shall be deprived of the only really reliable mounted troops I have.' Murray also stated that the men under his command were adapting to the hot weather, 'especially the Anzac mounted troops, who have a genius for this desert life'. In June he wrote that 'the Anzac Mounted Division proved itself a unit on which I could absolutely depend to display energy, resource and endurance'. A month later, as Guy Powles recorded, Murray sent the following message to General Chauvel: 'Whatever I ask your people to do is done without the slightest hesitation and with promptness and efficiency. I have the greatest admiration for all your Command.'[52]

In July 1916, Chauvel's brigades were at Hill 70 (NZMR Brigade less the WMR), Romani (1st LH Brigade), and Etmaler (2nd LH Brigade and the WMR). The 52nd Division was busy digging in at Romani and the 42nd (East Lancashire) Division was preparing to move up from Kantara. The 3rd LH Brigade was still back on the canal, along with two other British infantry divisions.

Up to 2000 Turks were known to be at Bir el Mazar, 70 kilometres east of Romani, but they appeared to be inactive. 'It seemed as if the great heat would stop even the Turks from moving troops on a large scale, and that, apart from aeroplane bombs, the Anzac Mounted Division and 52nd [Division] were to have a quiet summer. Some authorities regarded a desert campaign by either side in the months of July and August as virtually impossible.[53]

Then, on 17 July, German aircraft suddenly became very active over Romani. Two days later, Brigadier General Chaytor flew on an aerial reconnaissance mission as an observer. The 2nd LH Brigade was about to begin a sweep to round up Bedouin between Oghratina and Bir el Abd and Chauvel told Chaytor to fly the mission to ensure that the ground ahead of the light horsemen was clear of Turks. It was a good thing that he did, for it certainly was not clear. Chaytor spotted camps containing about 8000 Turks and 3000 camels between Bayud and Bir el Abd, just 30 kilometres from Romani. In the words of Martin Eccles, Chaytor's report 'made us sit up sudden'. Johnny Turk had once again done the unexpected.[54]

3

The Battle of Romani

When one is going through a hail of bullets, the sensation is like walking through a
rain storm. You put your head down and you go on.[1]

KINGSTON HULL

MAJOR GENERAL CHAUVEL ordered the 2nd LH Brigade to halt at Katia and to send out patrols
at first light on 20 July 1916 to locate the approaching enemy force. The Turkish advance
guards were waiting for them near Oghratina. According to William Peed, 'We almost got
into a trap, but horsemanship got us out.' Martin Eccles, whose Wellington regiment was
attached to the Australian brigade, wrote, 'We retired like hell, and it was a marvellous
thing that no-one was hit.' Prisoners captured by another WMR patrol revealed the
strength and intentions of the Turkish force.[2]

In February 1915 the Turks had tried and failed to seize a bridgehead across the Suez
Canal. This time they intended to capture the water-bearing Romani area, from where they
would use artillery to sink Allied shipping on the canal. Colonel Kress von Kressenstein
commanded around 18,000 men, two-thirds of whom were good Anatolian infantrymen,
many with Gallipoli experience. Kress also had 30 artillery pieces, 38 machine guns, 12
aircraft and two mobile field hospitals, all commanded and partly manned by Germans or
Austrians. Kress planned to tie down the strong British infantry defences on the eastern

The low sandhills of Romani, as seen from Katia.

flank of the Romani position, using artillery fire and small-scale attacks by one of his three regiments. At the same time, the other two regiments would approach Romani from the south at night. At dawn, they would attack north over Wellington Ridge, overrunning the camps, capturing the wells and cutting the railway. Finally, the Turks would destroy the isolated British infantry before reinforcements could arrive from the Suez Canal.[3] Delays in the arrival of some German units meant that the Turkish advance did not begin until high summer. The stakes were high: in the extreme heat, whoever controlled the water supply would win the battle. The Turkish force left Gaza and Beersheba on 4 July, arriving at El Arish 10 days later. It took as long again for the bulk of the force to reach Bir el Abd. As his force advanced towards the enemy, Kress prudently safeguarded his withdrawal route by preparing a series of fall-back defensive positions. Within a few days of their detection by Chaytor, the Turks reached Mageibra and Oghratina. Then, on 24 July, they stopped.

Major General the Honourable Hubert Lawrence, the tactical commander responsible for the defence of Romani, wanted the Turks to attack him there and he had a plan to defeat them if they did.[4] To protect the railway and to provide a firm base around which the mounted brigades could manoeuvre, 7000 Scots of the 52nd Division had laboured for weeks under the hot sun to build a string of defensive positions from near Mahemdiya to Katib Gannit. Although the infantry defences seemed to end at Katib Gannit, they actually continued in a well-concealed westward loop, to protect the wells and the railway station at Romani.[5] Each redoubt accommodated up to 150 riflemen and several machine guns. They were well entrenched and protected by barbed wire. An infantry brigade of about 5000 men from the 53rd Division was in reserve at Romani Station and the 42nd Division was moving forward to the banks of the Suez Canal (see Map 4, p.90).

The area south of Wellington Ridge was not entrenched, to create the impression that it was undefended. General Lawrence wanted the Turks to attack there, in the hope that they would exhaust themselves marching through the heavy, waterless sand in the heat. The British infantry and Chauvel's Anzac Mounted Division were ordered to interfere with this Turkish advance and to force them to commit their reserves.

General Chauvel could call upon 1600 men in the 1st and 2nd LH brigades and two horse artillery batteries, based at the Romani and Etmaler wells. He prepared a secret defensive line extending five kilometres from Katib Gannit, past Mount Meredith, to Hod el Enna, to be occupied as soon as the Turks began their final approach to Romani. These light horsemen were expected to halt the enemy, force them to deploy into attack formation and then to conduct a slow fighting withdrawal back to Wellington Ridge.

Once the enemy was blocked and exhausted, the EEF was to counter-attack and destroy him. In the original plan, two groups of mounted troops were to play the central role in this part of the battle. Chaytor's Section Mounted Troops were a half-day's march away, at Hill 70 and Dueidar. This force included the NZMR Brigade (the AMR, the CMR and the new machine gun squadron), the 5th ALH Regiment, a Composite Regiment of several British cavalry squadrons, and two artillery batteries. The recently arrived 3rd LH Brigade was twice as far away, at Ballybunion. These forces were to sweep around behind the Turks from the vicinity of Mount Royston, a large sandhill at the western end of Wellington Ridge.[6]

When the advancing Turks were spotted by Chaytor on 19 July, Romani's defences were not yet complete. Most of the infantry redoubts were ready, but there were not yet enough machine guns, artillery pieces or soldiers in place to make it secure. Had the Turks attacked immediately, instead of stopping at Oghratina for 10 days, they might have stood a better chance of capturing Romani. The unexpected pause gave Lieutenant General Murray time to send up more machine guns, to assemble another counter-attack force (the Mobile Column, consisting of camel, light horse and Yeomanry units) and to provide the infantry of the 42nd Division with enough camels to allow them to operate in the desert away from the pipeline. When the battle finally began, Kress's 18,000 Turks were heavily outnumbered by 30,000 EEF men, supported by 50 artillery pieces.[7]

The Turks had halted at Oghratina to await their heavy guns, which were held up in the soft sand near El Arish. In an amazing feat of strength and perseverance, these massive weapons, including six guns weighing 2 tonnes apiece and two 6.5-tonne behemoths, were dragged all the way across the Sinai Desert by men and cattle. The soft sand was dealt with by the simple but backbreaking method of placing planks of wood or brush beneath the wheels of the guns.[8]

General Lawrence ordered Chauvel to maintain contact with the Turks, but to avoid being decisively engaged and to keep his men and horses as fresh as possible. Each night, one of the Australian light horse brigades rode out at midnight and halted near Katia until dawn. When the sun came up, the brigade spread out and advanced eastwards until it met the Turkish screen. Weak enemy posts were attacked but the horsemen were under orders to withdraw if the enemy counter-attacked in strength. At dusk the tired riders withdrew back to the camps, leaving several small officers' patrols behind to maintain contact with the Turks until the relieving brigade arrived. The New Zealand brigade was equally active to the south along the telegraph line, where mounted riflemen patrolled and manned observation posts to watch Mageibra and Bir Nagid.[9]

View from near Romani south towards Bir Etmaler, with Wellington Ridge in the distance.

This was highly dangerous work. The Turks had an uncanny ability to move noiselessly through the sand, and the location of the mounted patrols could inadvertently be given away by a nervous neigh or by the jingling of a bit or stirrup. The result could be disastrous, with sudden Turkish bayonet attacks being launched from very close range. If the men could not escape in time, they were killed or captured. Riders returning from these stressful patrols managed a few hours' sleep before being roused for stand to before dawn. The heat and flies of the daylight hours, and the need to look after the horses, gave little further opportunity for rest and, before they knew it, they were away out again. Under this ceaseless pressure, men and horses quickly lost condition.

On 28 July, 50 Turks occupied Hod Umm Ugba, just nine kilometres from the Romani defences. Lieutenant Colonel Meldrum immediately attacked them with two WMR squadrons, supported by two 18-pounders and several machine guns. Sixteen Turks were killed and eight were captured, while Meldrum lost one man killed and two wounded. Robert Tuke recalled that 'Jeff Fitzherbert's horse was hit half-way between the eyes and the tip of the nose. The bullet is still in his head, but the horse is just as fit as he was before he was hit.' Tuke was honest enough to write in the same letter that, 'if a chap gets a bullet, it may mean a trip to New Zealand, which would be just the thing'.[10]

On 3 August a Turkish prisoner captured by an Auckland patrol at Nagid revealed that the main attack was to be launched that night. The Aucklands also found out that a strong Turkish force was moving towards Nagid. Chaytor immediately ordered the AMR to send a patrol to Bir Abu Raml and to relieve the 5th ALH Regiment at Dueidar, so that the Australians could scout past Nagid at dawn the next day.[11]

By the morning of 3 August, the Turks had occupied Katia in strength, with their left flank at Bir el Hamisah. When the sun set that day, the Turks were on a line extending from Hill 110 in the north, through Katia, and south to Nagid. As the 2nd LH Brigade retired to the camps at Etmaler and Romani at dusk, they realised that the Turks were following them. Chauvel already expected the Turks to attack that night (the last day of the Muslim festival of Bairam) and this report was all that he needed to send 500 light horsemen of the 1st LH Brigade into their secret defensive line south-west of Katib Gannit.[12]

The night of Thursday 3 August was clear but hazy, calm and illuminated by a low crescent moon. At 10 p.m., a flashing light was seen at Katia and 30 minutes later a single shot echoed through the darkness near Hod el Enna. Just before midnight, the tense light horsemen in the line between Mount Meredith and Hod el Enna detected hundreds of Turks advancing silently out of the gloom towards them.[13]

The light horsemen levelled their rifles, checked the belts in their Maxim guns and waited with their hearts in their mouths. The first shots were fired at midnight and the surprised Turks halted. Then, at one o'clock in the morning of 4 August, 8000 Turks advanced towards the light horsemen, shouting 'Allah!' and 'Finish Australia! Finish Australia!' By 2.30 a.m. the Turks were near enough to begin launching bayonet charges. Turks toiling up the steep slopes of Mount Meredith were plainly visible in the moonlight and many of them were shot by Australians lining the crest. However, the hill was being outflanked to the south and at 3 a.m., as the moon set and complete darkness descended, the Australians abandoned Mount Meredith. The Turks immediately emplaced machine guns along the crest of the hill, which caused some casualties among the withdrawing light horsemen. Some Turks were so close that one rider, lifting what he thought was another Australian onto the back of his horse, discovered that the man was actually a Turk.[14]

Around the same time, the AMR patrol at Bir Abu Raml spotted several columns of Turkish troops. Lieutenant Frank Alsopp sent Sergeant Ernest Cheetham and a few men out to investigate. They confirmed the sighting and Cheetham left his men there to keep an eye on the enemy while he rode back to make his report. He could not find Alsopp so decided to ride to Pelusium Station to report what he had seen. He soon found himself in the midst of two large enemy columns, between Bir Abu Raml and Bir el Dhaba. Cheetham coolly rode alongside one column until he found a gap and made good his escape. The other eight members of the patrol were captured. 'What a hell of a time they'll have, trudging back across the desert to a Turkish prison camp hundreds of miles away! Poor chaps! I'm glad it wasn't us.'[15]

In accordance with Chaytor's earlier instructions, the 5th ALH Regiment rode out from Dueidar just after midnight to establish the strength of this enemy force and where it was going; part of the Auckland regiment moved up to Dueidar to replace it. The light horsemen reached Nagid before dawn, from where they saw two enemy battalions, 1500 men, trudging north-westwards towards Hod el Enna. They were on their way to reinforce the Turkish attack on Wellington Ridge but they stopped and engaged the light horsemen, losing two precious hours in the process. The presence of this large enemy force confirmed that the Turks intended to attack Romani, not bypass it. They seemed to be falling into Lawrence's trap.[16]

As dawn approached, the Australians between Mount Meredith and Wellington Ridge could finally see what they were facing – but so could the Turks. When the thinness of the opposing line became apparent to the attackers, they intensified their efforts. The Australians continued their measured withdrawal. Men in the firing line kept up a heavy fire until another line of riflemen and machine gunners was ready to take over behind them. The men in the forward line then ceased firing and ran back to their led horses, which were waiting close behind them in low ground. They mounted up and rode back to their next position. In this manner, troop by troop and squadron by squadron, the light

Mount Meredith, viewed from the direction of the Turkish advance.

Canvas water troughs below a sand hill at Romani.

horsemen withdrew to Wellington Ridge. The Turks hunted for the end of the light horse line; once found, they could work around it to get behind the Australians.

As soon as there was enough light for them to see, the gunners on both sides added their weight of fire to the battle. At 6 a.m. British horse artillery fire drove the Turkish machine gunners from the crest of Mount Meredith. The heavier Turkish guns bombarded the infantry redoubts and the camps along the railway. Air-bursting shrapnel from the smaller calibre guns was deadly but the high explosive shells from the heavy German howitzers were smothered in the deep sand. German aircraft bombed whatever they could see but most of their bombs also exploded harmlessly in the soft sand. To the north, the 31st Regiment reached Bir Abu Hamra but, in accordance with its orders, it did not press its attack against the Scottish redoubts in front of it.[17]

Chauvel could see that he was being outflanked so at 4.30 a.m. he ordered the 2nd LH Brigade to extend the 1st Brigade's line west along Wellington Ridge. Two regiments went into the line immediately and the WMR remained in reserve. The New Zealanders waited with the horses of the two Australian regiments in a depression behind the ridge. The massed horses offered a splendid target for the marauding enemy aircraft but their luck held and they were not seen.

By 7 a.m. the light horsemen had abandoned the eastern end of Wellington Ridge. The 2nd LH Brigade retained its hold on the central part of the ridge for a little longer but Turkish pressure soon forced this brigade back too. An hour later, the Turks occupied

Wellington Ridge and began to fire into the camps along the railway. For a short period, only the WMR stood between the Turks and the Etmaler camp. Meldrum was told by his Australian brigade commander that he could give up no more ground or the camps would be lost. '"If they get through my line here", replied the New Zealander grimly, "they can have the damned camps".'[18] Max Aldred was wounded on Wellington Ridge.

> A Turk about twenty yards in front of me seemed to take up my whole attention. He had a horrible grin on his yellowish face and he looked straight at me – I can see that grin yet – and he was in the act of putting his rifle to his shoulder. I took a snap shot at him with my revolver, and he doubled up. Immediately afterwards I felt a blow on the side of my head – then there is a blank.[19]

Nervous clerks in the camps began to burn regimental records to prevent them falling into enemy hands. When the WMR quartermaster arrived from the firing line to find his cooks preparing for a hurried departure, he ordered them to unpack their kettles and make some tea for the men in the firing line. 'The cooks responded readily,' wrote Wilkie, 'and in the face of heavy artillery and rifle fire they carried the tea to their comrades, who, having had no time for breakfast, fully appreciated it.' The immediate threat to the camps passed when shrapnel fire from the horse artillery batteries of the Anzac Division drove the Turks back off the crest of Wellington Ridge. They did not reappear until mid-afternoon.[20]

While the Turks paused along Wellington Ridge, other enemy columns pressed on towards Mount Royston. Chauvel had already sidestepped some of his light horse regiments across to meet them, but he could do no more and 2000 Turks occupied Mount Royston soon after dawn. As Lieutenant Colonel R.R. Thompson later recorded, to the Scottish infantrymen of the 52nd Division, 'who could see the Turkish shrapnel bursting on the hills far behind us, it looked almost as if the Turk had succeeded in his object and that we were being caught like rats in a trap. It looked as if our only escape would be northwards by the sea.' In fact, the crisis of the battle had nearly passed. The Turks had drunk their water, and none was to be found in the sand dunes south of Romani and Etmaler. Under the burning sun the Turkish infantrymen struggled against the deep, heavy sand. All the time, the light horsemen and the Wellingtons shot at them and shrapnel thinned their ranks. About 7 a.m. a squadron of British cavalrymen from Pelusium Station attacked the Turks near Mount Royston. This slender force, along with a few light horse squadrons on Wellington Ridge, held up the threatening Turkish outflanking movement for two more vital hours.[21]

Back at Hill 70, General Chaytor was woken at 2 a.m. with news of the Turkish attack at Romani. At 5.35 a.m. his Composite Regiment was ordered forward; two hours later, the NZMR Brigade followed. Its orders were to pick up the Aucklands at Dueidar and then to 'operate vigorously [towards Hod el Enna] so as to cut off the enemy, who appears to have got round the right of the A. & N.Z. Mounted Division'. However, the Turks' capture of Mount Royston forced General Lawrence to amend these orders. According to Arthur Rhodes, the New Zealanders 'marched on Dueidar but after going three miles [they] received an urgent wire to alter direction and attack Canterbury Hill and Mount Royston'.[22]

At 10 a.m., with no sign of Chaytor's force, General Chauvel asked the commander of the reserve infantry brigade to help him out by taking over part of the defensive line north of Wellington Ridge. This would allow Chauvel's mounted regiments to water their horses before joining Chaytor's Section Mounted Troops in their envelopment of the Turkish left flank. The officer refused and Chauvel could not compel him to obey.[23] Chaytor's force finally came into view in the late morning and exchanged heliograph messages with the Australians north of Mount Royston.

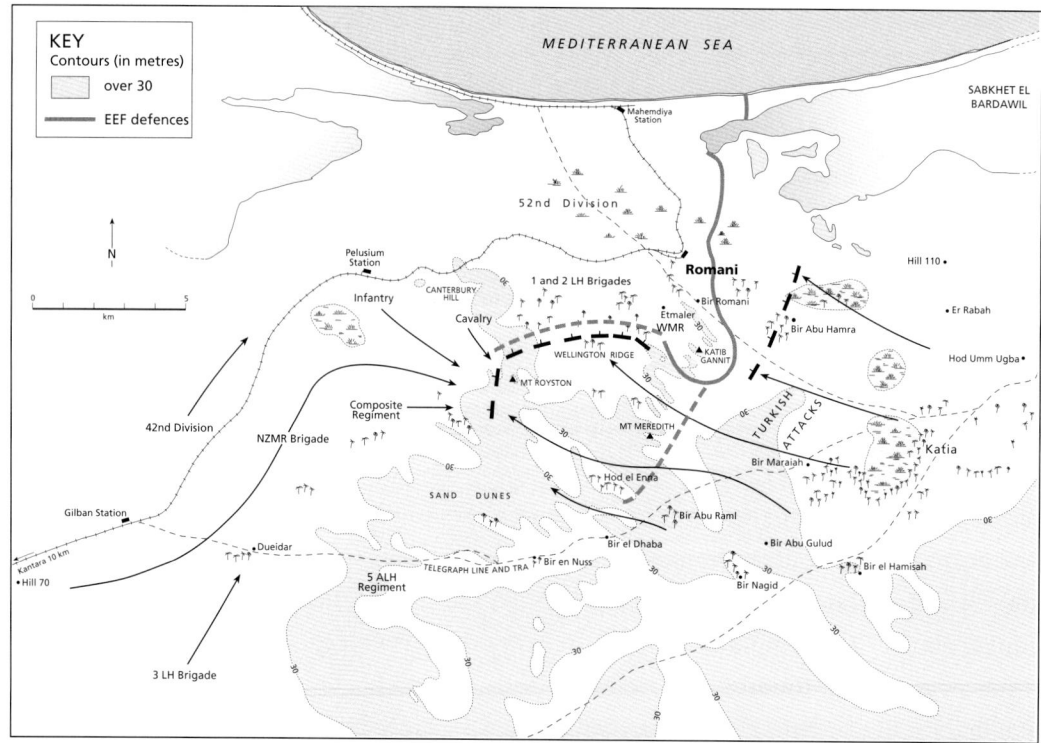

Map 4: The Battle of Romani.

90

'Who are you?'

'Chaytor.'

'Will you attack Mount Royston?'

'Advancing to attack Mount Royston.'

At 11.30 a.m. the NZMR Brigade rode into the line south of Canterbury Hill, between the light horsemen and the Composite Regiment, which had arrived earlier. According to a British doctor, Captain Oskar Teichman, 'it was a great relief to everyone to hear that the New Zealand Mounted Brigade … was just coming into action on our extreme left.… As soon as the New Zealanders joined in, the pressure on our left flank was considerably reduced.' By noon, two infantry battalions from the 42nd Division had detrained at Pelusium Station and were making their way towards Mount Royston, but Chaytor decided not to wait for them. He launched the Canterbury regiment, a squadron and a half of Aucklands and the Composite Regiment against 2000 Turks on Mount Royston. They were supported by the Somerset Battery and by the New Zealand Machine Gun Squadron.[24]

After quickly driving in the advanced enemy posts, the pace of the attackers slowed. The sand dragged at their feet, there was no cover, the midday sun was scorching hot and the fire of the Turkish riflemen and machine gunners was heavy and increasingly effective as the attackers came closer. By mid-afternoon, the Turks abandoned a trench line at the base of Mount Royston and a few crest-line trenches at the southern end of the hill, but their main position held firm. At 2.30 p.m. Chaytor issued orders for a general assault, to begin at 4.45 p.m.[25]

Covered by the artillery battery and the machine gunners, the assault regiments retrieved their horses, mounted and galloped forward through the deep sand to the base of the hill. British cavalrymen charged the southern flank of Mount Royston at the gallop with swords drawn. The Turks declined to stay and meet the charge, and the cavalrymen captured the crest, from where they were able to shoot down onto an enemy mountain gun battery, killing the pack camels. The gunners and large numbers of Turkish infantrymen surrendered. Englishman Robert Wilson, who took part in this charge, described the New Zealanders as 'marvellous fellows, but very slow – we left them standing once when we had orders to take a hill where a battery of guns were; we had collared guns and all by the time they got there'.[26]

After several of the machine gun squadron's packhorses were shot earlier in the day, the gunners dismounted and went forward on foot, lugging their heavy weapons with them through the soft sand. As the charge started, they mounted their guns and at ranges of 500 to 1000 metres 'quickly got on the target.... A few of the enemy on the forward slopes endeavoured to get back, but were quickly cut down by the gunners; the remainder surrendered.'[27]

General Chaytor and Captain Arthur Rhodes watched 600 New Zealanders and 200 British cavalrymen take on the Turks on Mount Royston.

It was a chance and a big gamble.... The brigade mounted and galloped for Mt. Royston – such a sight I have never seen, it was too wonderful for words.... The Turks gave very heavy rifle fire but [caused] little damage. The top was gained – huge excitement – and hundreds of white flags went up. The Turks saw they were cut off [and] we stopped firing. The General and I rode out, Turks everywhere. They had dropped their rifles and put up their hands. The sight was wonderful.... A wonderful day for the mounteds – we had waited for two years for this to come off.[28]

Twelve hundred Turks surrendered at Mount Royston. Jim McMillan described it as 'a wonderful sight to the ... very weary troopers, who were only too ready to call it a day if the opposition felt that way'. According to Guy Powles, 'competition was very keen for the Zeiss glasses [binoculars] of the prisoners'. The machine gunners came forward and placed their guns on the high ground, engaging retreating Turks until they were out of range. Mount Royston was firmly in the hands of the EEF by 6 p.m. The battalions of the 42nd Division took over the hundreds of prisoners and marched them towards Pelusium Station, followed by the tired horsemen.[29]

Just before dark, the Turks to the east made a final attempt to push northwards over Wellington Ridge but British artillery fire broke up their attack. A general advance by the four EEF mounted brigades at sunset came to nothing. Two Scottish infantry battalions and the 1st and 2nd LH brigades tried to retake Wellington Ridge at 7 p.m. but the Turks showed no inclination to give it up. Not long afterwards, Colonel Kress ordered his forces to withdraw under the cover of darkness to Katia.

The reaction of the New Zealanders to their first mounted action was generally positive. 'We captured several hundred Turks,' wrote Robert Tuke, 'and I think altogether 4 or 5,000 were captured. Not bad, was it?' As Charles Nicol noted, 'Perhaps the proudest man of all [in the Auckland regiment] was the padre, who had the distinction of getting a piece of metal through his hat without receiving any injury.'[30] Before the fighting Max Aldred 'had always been "afraid of being afraid". At Romani I found that, once the thing started, there was so much to do that you simply had not time to think of being afraid. Also, I learnt that when a man is killed – even if he is a close friend – it does not upset you as it would at an ordinary time. You expect people to be killed, and it might be your turn next.'[31]

The fighting on 4 August cost the lives of four New Zealanders and 35 others were wounded. The light horse brigades lost many more men: 71 killed, 344 wounded and 28 missing. The desert was dotted with the still forms of men who had been killed by the Turks. Men who died on the battlefield were

British horse artillery in action at Bir Etmaler.

left where they fell, with the location of their bodies marked by their rifle and bayonet stuck upright in the sand. After the battle the bodies were buried in shallow graves, the locations of which were carefully recorded on maps. If they were lucky, a damp saddle blanket kept the sand from their faces. The dead were then left to the mercy of the local inhabitants, human and otherwise, until they could be reinterred in centralised cemeteries.[32]

The NZMR Brigade and the Yeomanry cavalry rode back to Pelusium Station for the night. 'Firing continued long after dark along the line, the enemy also using his artillery, and the firing did not die down till midnight. The enemy also expended a number of star shells, from time to time, presumably in anticipation of an advance.' As the horsemen rode through the darkness, they were machine-gunned by a British aircraft. Luckily the pilot was a poor shot and no casualties resulted.[33]

The parched horses became excited as they approached the camps and smelled the water. Oskar Teichman described Pelusium as a scene of 'indescribable confusion – mounted troops coming in to water, infantry detraining and marching out, busy ASC [Army Service Corps] depots, camel convoys loading up, ammunition columns on the move, wounded arriving in sand carts, and large columns of prisoners being marched in'.

There seemed to be representatives of many races amongst them, from the desert Arab and negro soldier to the fair-haired and blue-eyed European Turk. Infantry wearing the enverene hats, brown fezzes or skullcaps, dressed in dark brown khaki and corduroy breeches (most unsuitable for this climate), gunners in Astrakhan caps and blue uniforms. Arab irregulars

The west side of Mount Royston, attacked by the New Zealanders on 4 August 1916.

in flowing garments, transport drivers with red facings to their uniforms and yellow sashes,
and German machine gunners in khaki drill and wearing yachting caps.[34]

All the prisoners were exhausted and thirsty, and their packs contained little more than handfuls of unripe dates. To compound their misery, many were suffering from dysentery.[35]

The EEF's infantry divisions and mounted brigades had suffered few casualties on 4 August and it looked as if they had a golden opportunity to finish off the Turks on the following day. They were about to relearn a lesson that many of the Gallipoli veterans already knew: never take Johnny Turk for granted.[36]

4

A terrible day

The big oasis was the hub of streams of machine gun bullets; all our troops seemed to be fighting now in isolated squadrons; we needed far more men than we had.

ION IDRIESS

THE PURSUIT OF the Turkish forces began long before dawn on 5 August. Major General Chauvel's Anzac Mounted Division was ordered to advance south-east between Mount Meredith and Hod el Enna. To its left, an infantry brigade was to march on Mount Meredith, while, to the right, the 3rd LH Brigade was to advance from Dueidar through Bir el Nuss to attack Hod el Hamisah from the south. The rest of the infantry and the 5th Mounted Brigade were to support the advance.

The Turks and Germans left behind at Wellington Ridge stood little chance when Chauvel's advance began at 4 a.m. The men of Meldrum's Wellington regiment and the 7th ALH Regiment crested the ridge with fixed bayonets and charged down into the valleys to the south, shouting as they went. To the demoralised and exhausted Turks and Germans, the Anzacs must have presented a terrifying sight, as Lieutenant Colonel J.D. Richardson conveyed: 'Gaunt from prolonged sleeplessness, their eyes bloodshot from glare and strain, their faces begrimed with dust and sweat, and bristly with a few days growth of beard, the Australians and Wellingtons might have unnerved troops in better condition than the unfortunate Turks opposed to them.' A number of machine guns and their crews were captured without resistance; many of them were Germans. Fifteen hundred prisoners were quickly rounded up.[1]

Meldrum immediately called up the horses and remounted his regiment. Without waiting for orders, and taking an Australian machine gun section with them, the WMR, in the words of their historian, Major Alexander Wilkie, 'relentlessly pursued the enemy, capturing hundreds of prisoners, till it approached Katia, where it came under heavy fire'. The Wellingtons stopped in a position overlooking Bir Maraiah and waited for the mounted brigades to catch up. Most of the men sat in the shadow of their horses to gain some respite

Date palms at Katia. The shade provided by these trees, and the ample water, greatly assisted the Turkish defenders on 5 August.

from the growing heat. Outposts backed by machine guns kept a wary eye on the Turks and patrols captured 93 prisoners, 80 camels, a field ambulance and an ammunition dump. At 9 a.m. Meldrum sent two of his squadrons to assist two British artillery batteries that were being attacked east of Katib Gannit. An hour later, he was placed in command of the 2nd LH Brigade as a temporary replacement for its wounded Australian commander. Major Charles Spragg took over the WMR, while Meldrum contacted the approaching 6th and 7th ALH regiments and began to assemble his new command. Around this time, all the mounted troops except the Mobile Column were placed under General Chauvel's command. Chauvel sent his mounted brigades forward over the ground that had been partially cleared by Meldrum, with orders to concentrate in the low ground in front of Katia.[2]

After spending three hours watering its horses, the New Zealand brigade was in the saddle by 6 a.m. and riding towards Bir en Nuss, where it found the 3rd LH Brigade, the 5th ALH Regiment and a squadron and a half of Aucklands. By noon, all Chauvel's horsemen were assembled in the low ground three kilometres west of Katia. The infantrymen were lagging far behind, so Chauvel decided to launch a mounted charge into Katia. The plan was for the brigades to 'rush the Katia position, it being believed that a resolute advance would cause the Turks to surrender'.[3] The NZMR Brigade was to attack from the south, the 1st and 2nd LH brigades and the 5th Mounted Brigade from the west and north-west respectively. The 3rd LH Brigade was to move through Hamisah, on the New Zealanders' right, then wheel northwards behind Katia to cut the enemy's withdrawal route. The 52nd Division was ordered to do its best to advance on Bir Abu Hamra.[4]

The charge could succeed only if the Turks were weak, demoralised and caught in the open, if the intervening ground was passable and if there were no enemy machine guns to worry about. Chauvel must have believed that all these conditions existed at Katia on 5 August but in fact none did. The Turks still outnumbered the mounted troops and they still had all their heavy guns and most of their machine guns. In front of them lay a 2000-metre-wide salt swamp, which was covered by machine gunners and artillerymen in well-concealed, shaded positions under the date palms. The defenders, some of whom were fresh reserves, had good cover and plenty of water. According to the WMR war diary, the enemy 'was well supported by artillery, at least ten guns being used, ten shells often bursting simultaneously'.[5]

The mounted attack began at 2.15 p.m. The 1st and 2nd LH brigades surged towards the apparently dry salt swamp between them and the enemy. After a kilometre of exhilarating galloping, their ride ended abruptly when some of the leading horses broke through the thin salt crust into the soft swamp below, in full view of the amazed Turks. The horses were hastily led into cover, where they were shelled heavily. Some animals were killed or badly wounded but casualties among the riders were surprisingly few. Jim McMillan was unimpressed. 'Whoever conceived the idea must have had visions of Waterloo or Balaclava in his mind ... but, if so, the vision soon faded.'[6]

Chaytor ordered the 5th ALH Regiment and the AMR to capture a battery of Austrian guns that was believed to be deployed in a hod at Bir Maraiah. The light horse commander decided that his men should carry their rifles with fixed bayonets. According to Charles Nicol, 'the gallop was a thrilling spectacle. The horses simply raced towards the palms, leaving a high cloud of dust behind them. The troopers, expecting the guns to open on them any second, leaned forward in their saddles.' The hod was deserted, apart from a dozen Turks who were quickly rounded up.[7] Kingston Hull described the capture of three Turkish snipers: 'We [dismounted and] advanced [on foot] with fixed bayonets – like hunting out a rat. It would have been better to have shot them while their rifles were in their hands, but they gave themselves up, and no-one could bring themselves to bayonet them in cold blood.'[8]

The Yeomanry attack to the north was held up by enemy artillery and machine gun fire. This failure exposed the left flank of the WMR and Major Spragg had to adjust his line quickly to prevent Turkish machine guns being placed there. The expected envelopment by the 3rd LH Brigade on the right of the Aucklands did not eventuate. Spotting this gap, the Turks sent troops towards it and Chaytor had to put the reserve CMR regiment into the line to restore the situation.[9]

With their flanks now secure, the Turkish defenders at Katia could concentrate on the frontal attack. The attackers managed to capture the western and south-western edge of the oasis area but all efforts to advance further failed. Without significant artillery and infantry support, the mounted regiments were far too weak to capture Katia. For the rest of the day, the Anzac and British mounted regiments struggled to come to grips with the Turks in the tree lines of the oasis. Conditions were extreme. 'This Saturday was desperately hot, about the hottest day in an exceptionally-warm Egyptian summer.'[10] There was no water, except in Katia. The fighting was desperate and unrelenting, as Ion Idriess recalled.

> *A few New Zealanders panted up near us – they kept in a scattered group, running and firing, running to farther sand mounds to drop to their knees and blaze away again – the sweat streaming from their red faces and bared chests.... So we pressed slowly, but surely forward, ever nearer the huge Katia oasis and the firing flamed to a roar, then to a point-blank crackling that rebounded among the trees. The mystery was that a man could live through it.... The sun was setting. The big oasis was the hub of streams of machine gun bullets; all our troops seemed to be fighting now in isolated squadrons; we needed far more men than we had.* [11]

The Katia oasis, viewed from the west. The dark area in the middle distance is the salt swamp, into which some horsemen galloped on 5 August.

General Chauvel ordered the tired regiments to hold on until dark to allow the wounded men to be evacuated and then to withdraw. Thirteen Aucklands remained on the battlefield overnight as a listening post.[12]

The attack on Katia had stood little chance of success and EEF casualties were relatively heavy: five New Zealanders were killed that day and 58 wounded. The regimental medical officer of the WMR, Captain George Wood, and his medical orderly, Sergeant William Moseley, were mortally wounded when they galloped forward under fire to rescue a badly wounded Lewis gunner near the enemy line. After the jubilation of the first day's fighting, many of the men were disappointed. The Turks were not behaving like a beaten force. 'Their fire was hot and well-directed, while their artillery out-gunned the … Ayr and Somerset Batteries.'[13] Arthur Rhodes was critical of the Australians in the 3rd LH Brigade.

> *Turk guns got into Canterbury and gave the 8th [squadron] hell. The Turks were reinforced on the flat by 600 men who attacked the Canterbury men, who held on. At this critical moment, the 3rd Australian Brigade pulled out at 4.15 p.m. - they left without a word to anyone. At this time the Turks – about 3,000 – were getting the worst and had started to retire, but, as soon as the 3rd Brigade left, they reinforced and attacked again. We held them until dark and retired at dark … It was very sad having to retire, but the NZMR could not hold as there was about six to one. Canterbury has done wonderfully well.*[14]

The men and animals on both sides were exhausted. 'A reaction had now set in, and the men and animals were feeling the strain. During the short halts that night, it was no uncommon thing to see the horses, as soon as their riders dismounted, lie down on the sand, thoroughly tired out.' The NZMR Brigade got lost, finally reaching its bivouac at half-past-midnight. Many of the men missed out on fresh water and food when their camel convoy got lost.[15]

The 1st and 2nd LH brigades, temporarily incapable of further effort, were sent back to the railway for a rest. The New Zealand and British brigades, and the 3rd LH Brigade, continued the fight as best they could on 6 and 7 August. When scouts rode cautiously into Katia, they found that the oasis, which 'had been alive with the sound of death yesterday was now silent as the grave. Here and there we rode past a dead horse, sometimes a forlorn group of Turkish dead, and here two New Zealanders.' Mounted patrols re-established contact with the Turks at Oghratina, but no serious fighting eventuated. The enemy was still too strong to be dislodged by a few weak mounted brigades. Nine New Zealanders were wounded by artillery fire on 6 August.[16]

The two British infantry divisions were unable to advance beyond Katia. The deep sand, the extreme heat and their lack of acclimatisation resulted in widespread heat stroke and exhaustion. The New Zealand Mounted Field Ambulance rescued many of these men who, in A.M. Davidson's words, 'were suffering from extreme thirst and heat exhaustion from marching on the scorching sand. The timely assistance saved many of the poor fellows, who were far spent.'[17]

On 7 August three mounted brigades tried again at Oghratina but the Turks held them off easily with artillery fire, as Arthur Rhodes recorded. 'They shelled us very heavily – 400 shells fell within a radius of 70 yards around Brigade Headquarters in one hour. I don't know if you can imagine what this means, but I can tell you it is perfect hell.' During the day, a New Zealand patrol stumbled across an intact telephone line that had been abandoned by the enemy. Listening in, Lieutenant Colonel Mackesy, who understood German, and an interpreter heard that the Turkish retreat was to continue. The horsemen also found a notice above a grave, warning that the occupant had died of cholera. The riders withdrew at dusk, leaving patrols out overnight to keep an eye on the enemy.[18]

The Turks withdrew to Bir el Abd that night. The next day, it took the pursuing horsemen some time to get through Oghratina: 'They had entrenched the whole place, so [we] had to go carefully in case men were hiding in the trenches. The Turks had made dummy men in the trenches that looked very real, also dummy guns.' New Zealanders found a note that read, 'Here was a German Artillerie Observation Poste and had seen all the movements of the English cavaliere. Lieutenant Alsopp, A.M. Rifles, now prisoner of war – a gentleman – had eaten in our Batterie. Dated 5/6. VIII.16.' The New Zealanders ran into heavy resistance when they approached Bir el Abd. They maintained contact with the Turks all day, but obeyed orders to avoid becoming seriously engaged. That night, the mounteds withdrew to a bivouac site at Debabis.[19]

That day Lieutenant General Murray received a congratulatory message from King George V: 'Please convey to all ranks engaged in the Battle of Romani my appreciation of their efforts, which have brought about the brilliant success they have won at the height of the hot season in the desert country.'[20] But the royal congratulations were slightly premature, as the Anzac horsemen were about to discover.

Chauvel obtained Major General Lawrence's permission to attack Bir el Abd on 9 August. The British infantry divisions could not take part but Chauvel had all the mounted brigades under his command for the operation. His plan was to pin the Turks with a frontal attack and to encircle both flanks to cut off their retreat. The NZMR Brigade was to make the frontal attack along the axis of the telegraph line into Bir el Abd. The slightly rested and

Machine gunners in action near Katia.

understrength 1st and 2nd LH brigades were combined into one force named Royston's Column. (Meldrum still commanded the 2nd LH Brigade.) This column was to march from Katia to Hod Hamada, then attack around the northern flank of the enemy position at Bir el Abd as the New Zealanders launched their frontal attack. The 3rd LH Brigade was to attempt to get around the enemy's southern flank and capture Salmana, cutting off his retreat. The small Mobile Column was ordered to make a wide sweep through Bir Bayud; the 5th Mounted Brigade was held in reserve.[21]

General Chauvel's plan to take on the Turks with a single understrength brigade, and to launch two other equally weak brigades behind them, was daring, to say the least. 'If the enemy were demoralized, it had a chance of success. If not, very little.' As it turned out, Chauvel underestimated the recuperative powers and the determination of the 6000 Turks at Bir el Abd, who were now rested, watered and fed and 'full of fight'. The main enemy line consisted of 'a series of entrenched redoubts with rifle pits in front ... all these redoubts were connected by telephone to their artillery – three batteries of 77 mm and one 4.2 [inch] battery [105 mm] and several 5.9 inch [150 mm] howitzers.' The Turkish line was anchored to the north on the Bardawil lagoon, making any attempt to outflank it there impossible. Against this formidable defensive layout, Chauvel's mounted brigades could put about 3000 men into the firing line; some regiments could contribute only 180 men. Chauvel had just four horse artillery batteries, and he was entirely without infantry support. The supply lines of the Turks were shortening, while the mounted brigades of the EEF were getting further away from their own supply bases, 30 kilometres distant at Romani. Not surprisingly, the battle at Bir el Abd was to be one of the hardest fought by the New Zealanders after Gallipoli.[22]

By 2 a.m. on 9 August, the men of the New Zealand brigade were awake and feeding their horses. At 5.30 a.m. they were in the saddle and riding towards the enemy waiting at Bir el Abd. Forty-five minutes later, the New Zealanders chased off the enemy outposts in front of them and reached the high ground overlooking Bir el Abd. They dismounted, sent the horses back under cover and advanced on foot against the main Turkish trenches. The mounteds attacked with two squadrons of Aucklands on the right, and the Canterburys on the left, both reinforced with machine guns. The 5th ALH Regiment and the rest of the Aucklands were kept in reserve. To the left and right of the New Zealanders were Royston's Column and the 3rd LH Brigade. The three brigades covered a front of eight kilometres, giving a density of one rifleman to every three metres of frontage.[23]

In Royston's Column, a troop of 20 Wellington men pushed forward 'with characteristic Anzac impudence' and captured a ridge 2000 metres north-west of Bir el Abd. One hundred and fifty Turks 'lost their heads, refused the steel, and bolted'. Later that morning, as the Wellingtons pushed forward another 400 metres, they 'drew fire of every description, high explosive shells, shrapnel, and bullets tearing up the ground ... most of the casualties in the WMR during the day were inflicted there'. Fortunately, the soft sand again deadened the effect of the high explosive shells; otherwise the casualties would have been much heavier. Royston's Column was held up 1000 metres from the Turkish line and a gap 800 metres wide opened between it and the New Zealanders. Chaytor had to send several of his reserve squadrons forward to close the gap.[24]

To the south, the 3rd LH Brigade was unable to maintain contact with the Aucklands and at 6.45 a.m. the reserve AMR squadron was ordered up to extend the New Zealand line to the right. A couple of hours later, Chaytor had to send a squadron from the 5th ALH Regiment into the line there as well. Despite these reinforcements, a 1500-metre gap opened between the NZMR brigade and the Australians, who had been brought to a halt by fierce Turkish resistance from a strong redoubt at Hod el Bada. At 8.30 a.m., General Chauvel reluctantly ordered the 3rd LH Brigade to abandon its attempt to outflank the Turkish line and to close up on the right of the NZMR Brigade. Not long afterwards he ordered Royston's Column to do the same to the left of the NZMR Brigade. This effectively meant the abandonment of the plan to encircle the Turks. From now on, it was to be a simple frontal attack to push the Turks out of Bir el Abd.[25]

As the sun rose higher over Bir el Abd, keen-eyed observers spotted lines of transport camels assembling behind the Turkish defences. British artillery fire killed many of these animals, forcing the Turks to set fire to their stores. The columns of smoke seemed to indicate that the Turks were about to withdraw and Chaytor's New Zealanders pushed forward down the eastern slopes of the ridge towards them. However, they 'only succeeded in advancing sufficiently to expose their line to flanking attacks, as the Australian brigades were unable to conform to the movement. By 10.30, all progress was over.'[26]

According to a German staff officer present at the battle, Colonel Kress did not initially feel strong enough to face another hard fight. He had decided to retreat from Bir el Abd, but when it became clear that the attacking horsemen were not supported by infantry

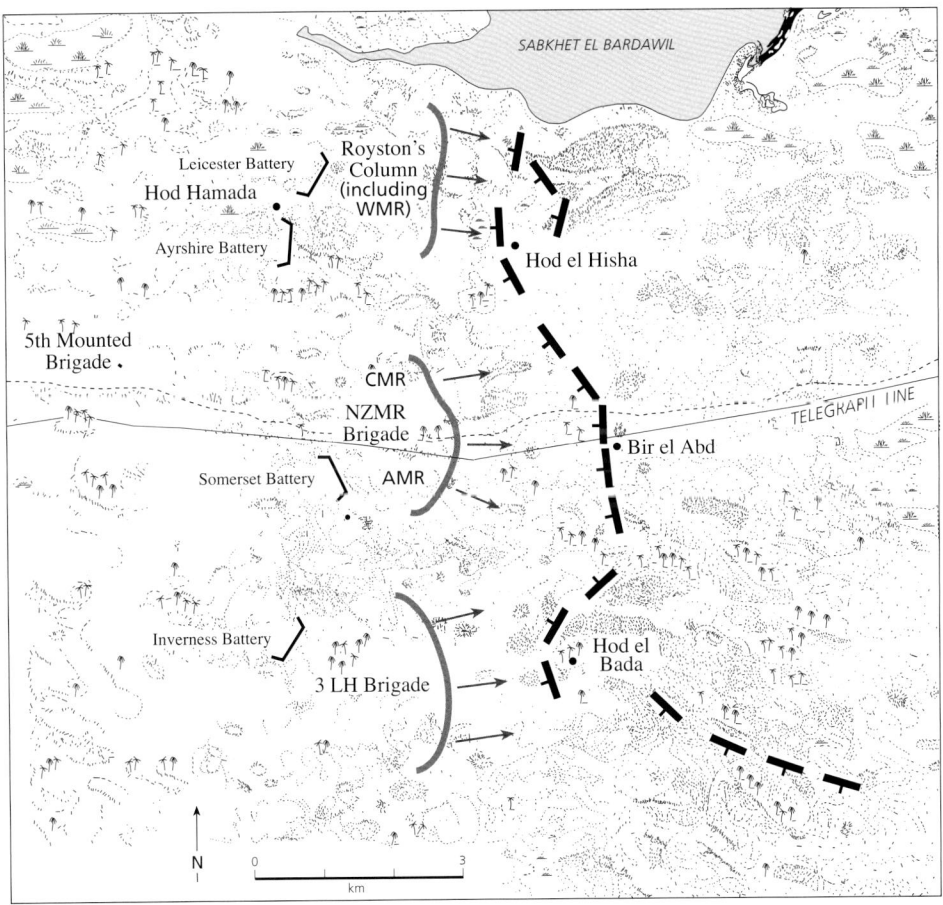

Map 5: Bir el Abd.

H03788. AUSTRALIAN WAR MEMORIAL

An 18-pounder gun from a British horse artillery battery. The wheels were fitted with wide wooden blocks in the desert.

or heavy artillery, Kress decided to stay and fight. The Turks pushed back both flanks of Chauvel's force but the New Zealanders stood 'firm as a rock' in the centre until the late afternoon. There is some evidence that fresh Turkish reserves, brought up from El Arish, were used in the fight at this stage. In the heaviest attack, three enemy battalions were launched at the centre of the New Zealand line, which was still out in front of the flanking brigades. The Turks were barely beaten off by the Canterburys and Aucklands, who were forced back for nearly a kilometre, until reserve cavalrymen and an artillery battery arrived to help.[27]

The Turks were winning the artillery battle easily. The sharp crack of the horse artillery guns sounded pathetic compared with the deep boom of the heavy German cannon. According to Arthur Rhodes, 'the shelling was very heavy. We were shelled from 6.15 [a.m.] to 1.45 [p.m.] with not five minutes rest. Thanks to the misjudgement of their gunners ... not a single [NZMR] man or horse was killed.'[28] However, when a heavy shell did land on top of other horses or men, the result was disastrous. The horses of the dismounted riflemen and gun batteries were a prime artillery target: if the Turkish gunners could kill the animals, the guns would be immobilised and the Anzacs would be at the mercy of the fleet-footed Turkish infantry. That morning, 37 artillery horses and four gunners in the Ayrshire Battery were killed by artillery fire in minutes, temporarily stranding the guns. The enemy artillery fire gradually increased in intensity during the day, reaching a higher level than that experienced at Romani or on Gallipoli.

Turkish small arms fire also took a toll of the horses that day.

We'd hear a heavy smack! and know a horse had been hit. The poor brutes mostly got it through the stomach. Some of them, apart from the shivering grunt, hardly moved, others shook themselves a little – it depended on where they were hit. One reared wildly and pawed the air. Another plunged yards forward on its knees, blood pouring from its nostrils as its head lay over on the sand. But mostly they were hit through the stomach and would just shake themselves a little. The owner would take the saddle off immediately, for it was always a case [a mortal wound]. The horse would nose around among his mates, shake himself, and five minutes later roll on the sand. It was the beginning of the end.[29]

By mid-afternoon the NZMR Brigade was in 'a very difficult position … well down the forward slopes with both flanks exposed, and had it not been for the accurate shooting of each individual man, backed up by the machine guns and the Somerset Battery, the entire Brigade would have been overwhelmed'. At 3 p.m. a final attempt was made to gain some ground, but it was a waste of time and men. The Turks were simply too strong to be budged by such a weak attacking line. At 5.30 p.m. Chauvel decided to withdraw but even this manoeuvre was fraught with danger. It was especially risky for the New Zealanders, who were under very close and intense fire from large numbers of Turks. The dangers of a daylight withdrawal were too great so the New Zealanders were told to hang on until nightfall.[30]

As soon as the sun set and the New Zealanders began to pull out, the Turks attacked ferociously. The AMR, the 5th ALH Regiment and the cavalry withdrew troop by troop, squadron by squadron, leaving the Canterbury regiment as rearguard. The CMR's withdrawal was then covered by fire from the New Zealand Machine Gun Squadron, under Chaytor's personal direction. The machine gunners fought what Major John Luxford described as a 'textbook rearguard action. The led horses were brought up to the gun teams, and gradually the guns dropped back by sections to successive covering positions, until the retirement was complete. In this rearguard action the gunners inflicted terrible casualties upon the Turks.' All 12 of the New Zealand machine guns were blazing away at the Turks, some of whom were only 100 metres away. As the darkness deepened, British cavalrymen placed their Wolseley pith helmets over the muzzles of the New Zealand machine guns to help hide the flash from Turkish observers. This concentrated, point-blank machine gun fire was too much for the Turks, who lay down in the sand and returned a desultory rifle fire. The machine gunners then withdrew, a pair of guns at a time. A Canterbury squadron covered them as they mounted their guns on their packhorses and made their escape.[31]

Everyone was clear by 7.30 p.m. and back at Oghratina before midnight. Fred Dill's horse Bob was shot during the withdrawal: 'I felt him falter, I knew he got hit somewhere'. The bullet broke Bob's jaw and he had to be destroyed. When Old Ginger also stopped a bullet during the withdrawal, his rider Harry Porter led him on foot to Etmaler, where he received an enormous 18-hand horse as a replacement.[32]

Arthur Rhodes described 9 August as 'a terrible day – may I never see another like it'.

The fire was hell and casualties very heavy.... The heat was awful and Turks very strong all day.... How our men held Lord knows.... I never want to fight with Australians again, they left us again. At 3.30 the 3rd [LH] Brigade retired without telling us. and at 4.15 the 1st and 2nd [LH brigades] also retired, leaving the NZMR to fight ... by itself.[33]

At one point during the day, with the Turks within 50 metres and 'the air ... thick with machine gun bullets and shells knocking us over with the concussion', Kingston Hull

British artillery horses killed at Bir el Abd.

'gave up all hope of ever getting out'. He shot three Turks at 100 metres range, writing afterwards that 'it is perhaps an awful thing to kill men, but I never felt more satisfied as when I saw them drop'. Hull thought that the fighting went well for the first few hours. 'We were driving them back and killing a good many.... But all at once their artillery opened up from away back somewhere.'

> *The shells began to land behind us and all the time shortening up, the last salvo landing about 40 yards to the rear. We decided to move to the left and were not there a minute when we saw hundreds of Abduls not more than a hundred yards off. A machine gun opened on us also, and they fire awfully fast. Things were now desperate for our little party. Our way of retreat lay across about 200 yards of open [ground] and up a hill on the other side. None of us expected to win back again. [Captain Maxwell] Aldred got a bullet graze on the head which made him silly for a while. He got one [Turk] with his revolver only a few yards off. It was here that I dropped three of the enemy for sure. They did not seem particular about getting under cover, they were coming on upright. We were all so done up and exhausted with the heat that none of us could go at more than a walk out of it. The feeling comes to you that it cannot be helped, if you are hit, it doesn't matter.... Chaps who had been on Gallipoli had not seen anything hotter. I do not want to go through it again, anyway. For the rest of the day it was a case of hang on with six to one against us. I suppose someone must come out of it, but while it is on, each one thinks that the bullets are all for him.*[34]

Not once during those long, hot hours did the Turks close to bayonet fighting range. The battle was fought in extreme heat – 38°C according to one report – in heavy, deep sand. The men had one or two water bottles to sustain them through the day and the summer sun heated the water to near boiling point. 'We fired until the rifle barrels grew so hot they burnt our hands. I rinsed my throat with hot water – no man had a cool drink that day.' As an indication of the intensity of the fight, the four artillery batteries fired 2500 rounds of 18-pounder shrapnel during the day. General Chauvel's casualties at Bir el Abd were heavy: 73 men were killed, including 30 New Zealanders, and 243 were wounded, 77 of them New Zealanders.[35]

The 3rd LH Brigade was left near the battlefield as a rearguard, while the other brigades rode back to Oghratina. As the battered horsemen withdrew to lick their wounds, the Turks continued their orderly withdrawal. On 12 August Bir el Abd was found to be abandoned and men sent up to bury the dead New Zealanders found that some of the bodies had been stripped by Bedouin. According to Kingston Hull, 'it was hard to tell who they were after being two days in the sun. One satisfaction, judging from the amount of enemies about, we must have finished three or four times as many of them.[36]

That same day, a German aircraft dropped six bombs on the New Zealand camp, killing three men and 10 horses. Arthur Rhodes witnessed the attack.

> *The General [Chaytor] and I lay down on the ground, and we heard this bomb coming, [making] an awful row. I could have sworn that it was going to get us. 15 yards [away is] quite close enough. A second one came and landed nine yards from us but did not burst; if it had, there would have been no more Arthur.*[37]

For the next few days, weary Anzac and British horsemen maintained contact with the Turks. An enemy rearguard at Salmana was driven off by horse artillery fire while the CMR 'sat and watched … neither side seemed very keen on forcing a fight'. The Turks finally withdrew all the way back to El Arish, leaving an outpost at Mazar (see Map 3, p.47). 'The Turk has gone for good,' wrote Arthur Rhodes, 'and I hope never to see him again.' That was too much to hope for, but the fighting was over for now.[38]

The EEF casualties in August 1916 totalled 1130; 200 were killed. Most of the losses were sustained in the Anzac mounted brigades: according to Anzac Mounted Division records, between 28 July and 13 August 167 men were killed, 616 were wounded and 36 were listed as missing. According to the War Diary, the NZMR Brigade lost 46 men killed, 181 wounded and 10 missing. The Anzac division also lost 826 horses.[39]

Lieutenant Gordon Harper was badly wounded by a Turkish shell at Bir el Abd. His brother Robin, who commanded the machine gun squadron, carried him from the field, but Gordon died in a Cairo hospital. Lieutenant Colonel Findlay, the CMR commander, was hit in the hand by shrapnel from the same shell that wounded Harper. Major Herbert Hammond, commander of the 8th (South Canterbury) Squadron of the CMR, 'was very ill on the morning of the battle … but [he] insisted on remaining and leading his squadron'. He was killed at Bir el Abd.[40]

Many of the wounded casualties suffered needlessly during their evacuation. In theory, a man wounded in the firing line was carried back to a collecting post near the led horses. From there, he was moved to the regimental aid post (RAP), 500 metres or so further back, by stretcher-bearers. Once the regimental medical officers (RMOs) had assessed the casualties, their further evacuation was the responsibility of the New Zealand Mounted Field Ambulance. This unit was also responsible for the immediate medical and surgical

Two New Zealand casualties in camel cacolets. The ride was far less comfortable than it looks.

treatment of wounded men, usually at a brigade advanced dressing station (ADS) a few kilometres behind the firing line. From the ADS, those casualties requiring further medical attention were supposed to be evacuated to hospital via motorised or horse-drawn ambulances, or trains.[41]

The reality was very different. The means of moving casualties along the evacuation chain were completely inadequate. Wounded men were dragged out of the front line on corrugated-iron sleds or carried out on blankets stretched across rifles. Horse-drawn sand carts could not travel far in the deep, trackless sand, so many badly wounded men had to be dragged back to the railhead at Romani on horse-drawn sleds or carried on the backs of camels in cacolets (flimsy frames that could carry two sitting or lying casualties). 'When the beast moves off, the patient is thrown and bumped about to a degree sufficient, in many cases, to produce nausea and vomiting. To a man with a painful wound, such as a fractured thigh, the torture of a long trip in one of these contrivances was extreme.' As Powles wrote, 'Happy indeed was the man whose wound permitted him to be lashed instead to his horse.' Under these conditions, seriously injured men stood little chance of surviving unless they received their wounds close to the railhead at Romani. According to Alexander Wilkie, 'one instance at least is recorded for a NCO with a broken thigh having to ride a horse for some miles. Needless to state, he died later.'[42]

For the wounded men who survived to reach the railway at Romani, their torments were not over. There were no proper hospital trains; the one train that was provided consisted of a line of open trucks, containing nothing, not even straw. Stretcher cases were placed on the floor and walking wounded sat around the sides of the trucks. Captain Oskar Teichman, a British doctor working on this train on 4 August, was appalled.

> *On reaching Pelusium, our engine broke down and the train waited for a considerable time; then the shrieks and groans of the wounded broke the stillness of the quiet night. But worse was to come: we had to be shunted in order to let a supply train pass through. ...Casualties were taken to Kantara in open [railway] trucks, the journey occupying from six to fifteen hours, during which time the men were without lights or attendance. Not a few of them died en route from neglect and exhaustion.*

Teichman told of several wounded New Zealanders, including 'a trooper ... [who] had been shot through the spine, [who] kept up a pitiful wail ... but could not have survived long.... Opposite me was a Captain of the New Zealand Medical Corps, who ... was in such a critical state that he could not be moved. Machine gun fire had removed a large part of his femur and the greater part of his thigh.'[43]

The Turkish attack at Romani never threatened Allied shipping on the Suez Canal and it did not prevent any Allied divisions from leaving Egypt for the Western Front. Between 3 and 9 August the Turks lost half of their force: 1250 men killed, 3750 wounded and nearly 4000 prisoners, including many Germans and Austrians. Most of the dead Turks were never buried but the Kantara War Memorial Cemetery contains the graves of four German soldiers who died in August 1916. That the Turks were not annihilated is a tribute to their fighting and marching qualities and to Kress's masterful withdrawal. In the words of Lieutenant General Sir A.P. Wavell, 'the Turk showed his finest qualities as a soldier at Romani. He attacked with resolution, struggled gamely when checked in his assault, outmarched the British infantry when he withdrew, and held off the pursuing horsemen in his retreat.' And, at the end of the fighting, he dragged his enormous artillery pieces all the way back to El Arish.[44]

The British infantrymen played their part in the initial battle by blocking the direct approach from Katia to the railhead at Romani; after that, they were ineffective. The inexperienced and poorly acclimatised riflemen could not march, let alone fight, in the soft sand under the terrible summer heat. In comparison, the better trained and well-acclimatised mounted troops fought well. The New Zealanders, competently led at regimental and brigade level, fought aggressively and with determination. The months they had spent living in the desert before the battle paid off handsomely and they withstood the extreme climatic conditions of August 1916 as well as any non-native could.

The machine gun squadrons were a particular success, especially at Bir el Abd. The firepower of massed machine guns was a significant force multiplier and the 'moral effect' of such machine gun fire on the Turk was 'very great'. Even taking this new capability into account, however, the combat power of unsupported mounted troops was still relatively low. They needed considerable artillery and infantry support if they were to prevail against enemy forces of any size. A fully manned regiment could put only about 300 rifles into a firing line. That number reduced further when sickness and 'absenteeism' were taken into account.[45] According to Kingston Hull,

> *It is very strange where a squadron's strength goes to when a fight is on. Chaps seem to disappear in a marvellous manner. It is a fact [that] our squadron did not have more than 40 men for the last day's go [at Bir el Abd]. Take horse holders out of that, and there are few left. Pay day or ration time is the time to see a full muster.*[46]

The endurance of the horsemen in the severe summer conditions was still quite limited. The lack of water, the deep sand and the extreme heat meant that they could only fight continuously for about a week before they were too exhausted and weak to continue. The soft sand prevented the horses from travelling much faster than a walk, and it became apparent after the August fighting that Turkish infantrymen were nearly as mobile as the Anzac horsemen. The critical difference was the condition of the soldiers at the end of a long march: Turkish foot soldiers would be exhausted, whereas mounted troops would be fresh when they dismounted to begin the fight.

General Murray was full of praise for the Anzacs. 'I cannot speak too highly of the gallantry, steadfastness, and untiring energy shown by this fine division throughout the operations.' Apart from this comment, there was little else in Murray's dispatches to please the Anzacs. Their part in the battle was downplayed while the British infantry received undeserved praise. Very few Anzacs received awards after the battle. According to Ted Andrews, 'a very small honours list appeared for the Anzac Mounted Division, the only recipient being Sgt H.A. [Harold] Martin, who received a Russian decoration.' It was widely believed that twenty-six staff officers in Murray's HQ in Cairo received decorations, and that two others resigned because they missed out.[47]

Despite his failure to reward their efforts with 'gongs', Murray was well aware of the importance of his Anzac mounted brigades. At the conclusion of the Romani fighting, he told the War Office that 'these Anzac troops are the keystone of the defence of Egypt'. In a congratulatory letter to Brigadier General Chaytor, Godley wrote:

> *I am so glad that you have been well rewarded for having to stay in Egypt by having had such a good fight. The cavalry here [in France] are very miserable, and all that possibly can are [transferring] to the infantry. There does not seem to be the slightest chance for them, and you may tell your fellows that they really are very lucky to be in Egypt, where they can do some mounted work, instead of being here where they would have no chance at all.*[48]

The Australians nicknamed the Wellington regiment, which had fought as part of the 2nd LH Brigade throughout August, the 'Well and Trulies'. For light horseman Ion Idriess the 'En-Zeds are first-class fighting men, and I don't think they grumble as much as we do. They shave oftener, anyway.' The New Zealanders knew that they had come through a trying initiation with credit and they were well satisfied with their performance. Robert Tuke wrote: 'I expect NZ people are beginning to realise that the old Mounted Brigade is not having such a nice big picnic after all.'[49]

5

El Arish by Christmas

It was quite evident that the enemy were not expecting visitors,
at least not for breakfast anyway.

JIM McMILLAN

LIFE IN SINAI was relatively quiet for the next three months, as the railway and the pipeline inched eastward towards El Arish. This was fortunate. The Anzacs and their horses were exhausted by their exertions in August and the British infantry divisions needed more time to acclimatise before they would be fit to fight in the desert. Although the main role of the horsemen and cameliers was to protect the railway and pipeline, they also scouted widely, hunting for Turks, Bedouin and water. Behind them, the infantrymen slowly marched forward on a special wire-netting road.

Soon after the fighting ended at Bir el Abd, the NZMR Brigade moved forward to Hod el Amara. Two cholera-infected Turks were found at Amara. A message 'extended compliments to the British ambulance, and expressed regret for having to leave behind two cholera suspects. The German medical officers had considerately marked all infected wells. Fortunately, precautions had been taken by the Anzac medical officers; for all troops had been regularly inoculated against cholera and typhus. These measures bore good fruit, for there were only a few mild cases of cholera, and only one New Zealander died.'[1]

The Anzac horsemen also visited the treacherous Sabkhet el Bardawil, its surface a mixture of thick salt crystals overlaying thick mud, and open water. 'The temptation to seek an easier route led horse and rider on to places where the weak surface was not able to support the weight. Then man and beast found themselves floundering hopelessly in the black oozy mud.'[2] The men were surprised to find large patches of figs and watermelons at the edges of the salty lagoon. 'Those [melons] that were considered to be not quite mature enough by the troops were soon demolished by the horses.'[3]

On 17 August, General Murray moved his headquarters from Ismailia back to Cairo.

F-66830-1/2, BARBARA EVANS COLLECTION, ALEXANDER TURNBULL LIBRARY

Three AMR men shaving in the shade at Etmaler.

Lieutenant General Sir Charles Dobell arrived to take command of the troops east of the Suez Canal, which became the Eastern Force. Meldrum relinquished command of the 2nd LH Brigade on 27 August and returned to the WMR.

At the end of August, the Wellington regiment went back to Swing Bridge Camp near Kantara for a rest. One of the first items on the agenda for William Peed was a swim in the Suez Canal. A consignment of letters and parcels arrived from home and Peed received several letters plus 'one tin of biscuits and two pair of socks, six tins of tobacco, and one large tin of assorted lollies'. A few days later, he wrote, 'We are hoping to be here till the end of the war. No such luck I don't think [*sic*].'[4]

On 11 September, the rest of the brigade (apart from the field ambulance and the machine gun squadron) left Amara for a month's rest at Etmaler. Leave for up to seven days was granted to Cairo, Port Said and a new rest camp at Sidi Bishr on the coast near Alexandria. On his way to Cairo on leave, William Peed 'dined on the train amongst the officers. How they stared, but damn it, I was hungry, and I had a good feed.' As George Berrie recorded, Alexandria was a popular destination, as it was inhabited by 'more Europeans and fewer Arabs, and one decent pub was actually left in bounds'. Not everyone could take advantage of these opportunities. As Harry Judge wrote, many men were 'too hard up to go, including myself, as we have been spending all our money on extra stores without which we would be nearly starving'. Many of these men, in Martin Eccles's words, gave the 'wet canteens' (bars) in Kantara 'a real good hearing' instead.[5]

On 11 September, Kingston Hull offered his brother Burton some free advice. 'Don't … be in any hurry to come to this old war. It is no good, and a man or two cannot make any difference. I am quite sure if ever I get out of it, I will have nothing more to do with the Army.' In another letter, Hull expressed his disappointment about his first combat experience.

> I hope if it comes to a fight again soon, I get in a few more good shots. Many chaps come all the way here and get knocked out and have not the satisfaction of getting one back, as it were. It is not too nice to have your rifle refuse to fire, [as] happened to me … and I was a couple of hours lying behind a small lump trying to fix it. Bullets were whacking about, and now and then, one would hit the top of the mound and shower sand in my face.

Despite his disillusionment, he believed the desert to be 'the healthiest place in the world. I know we could not have lasted out so long where it is wet and muddy. The horses now are far fitter than for many months, and should stand a bit of work.'[6]

An interesting view of life in the NZEF in Egypt at this time was provided by pioneering safe sex campaigner Ettie Rout. The first contingent of her Volunteer Sisterhood arrived in Egypt on 30 November 1915; Rout and a second group sailed from New Zealand at the end of December, reaching Port Said on 9 February 1916. The first 10 sisters had been working in Cairo. When the NZEF deployed to the banks of the Suez Canal, Ettie and five of her volunteers followed. On 23 May 1916, they opened the Tel el Kebir Soldiers' Club, which consisted of a few mud brick houses and some large marquee tents. The club quickly became popular with the Anzac soldiers training nearby. Fresh fruit, home-cooked food and drinks were available to supplement the men's uninspiring army rations. 'On a big day, the soldiers got through six to eight barrelfuls of fruit salad, a tankful of lemon squash, three bathfuls of pudding, two of plain trifle, 200 loaves of bread, thousands of buns and small cakes, and three to four hundredweight of cut cake.'[7]

Rout's club at Tel el Kebir closed in September 1916, as most of the troops were well beyond the Suez Canal. Before opening a new club at Kantara early in December, Rout continued to look after the men in the desert as best she could. She distributed fresh fruit, cakes and bread to the camps near the Suez Canal and provided sandwiches and hot cocoa to men departing on desert patrols. 'She made sure the men right out at the front, and in the outposts, got their share by sending boxes of cocoa, milk and sugar with men who were on their way out there'. Later in December, Rout handed over the Kantara club to two Australian women, Alice Chisholm and Verania McPhilamy, and left Egypt for England.[8]

Rout loved living among the New Zealanders and Australians, whom she regarded as 'a bunch of scruffy lads who needed attention'. In her words they had 'a deadly job – seemingly quite worthless and yet important to keep being done, but boring and brain-saddening to the last degree'. As far as she could see, most of the time the men 'had nothing to do, and unbearable heat to do it in'.[9]

General Murray's next objective was the Turkish garrison of El Arish, but the slow pace of the railway and pipeline construction prevented him from doing anything about it until the closing months of 1916. In the meantime, two mounted raids were conducted. The first, which involved the New Zealand machine gunners, was launched against the Turkish rearguard at Mazar on 16–17 September. The New Zealanders saw no action, however, and rejoined the brigade at Etmaler on 20 September. The Turks took this breathing space as an opportunity to withdraw from Mazar. The second raid cleared an enemy post at the inland settlement of Maghara. By not seriously attempting to interfere with these raids or to conduct offensive operations themselves, the Turks effectively handed over control of the Sinai desert west of El Arish to the Anzac horsemen and the cameliers.[10]

An NZMR camp at Bir el Abd.

In early October the New Zealand brigade was warned to prepare to move back up to the front. A few last courses in elementary signalling and Lewis gunnery were conducted, saddles were overhauled and equipment issues were completed. The WMR rejoined the brigade at Etmaler on 10 October. Two weeks later, the New Zealanders rode to Bir el Abd and took over the forward outpost line at Bir el Ganadil from an Australian light horse brigade (see Map 3, p.47). It was more of the same for the New Zealand horsemen, but the almost complete lack of water beyond Bir el Abd seriously hampered their activities. Mounted patrols scouted ahead of the railway, protected the Egyptian workers from surprise attack, rounded up Bedouin and surveyed the country. The regiments established bivouacs successively at Mossefig, Mazar and Mustagidda and patrolled from these bases. When the Aucklands returned from one patrol with some Bedouin women and infants, 'The cooks that evening prepared condensed milk for the babies, to the delight of the troopers, who had remarks to make about the start of the regimental nursery, and the appointment of a sergeant nurse'.[11]

While the regiments were forward, 'football became the rage, and regular matches were played between squadrons and regiments. It was really wonderful how the NCOs managed to have footballers available about a camp, though men for fatigues were always scarce.'[12] The tarantula spiders and scorpions of the Sinai desert also provided good entertainment. It was considered good sport to place one of each together in a box, where they would immediately begin fighting. As Corporal Jim McMillan recalled, 'From the beginning of the battle to the end, it was very evident that this was a duel to the death, with no quarter expected on either side, consequently the two fairly evenly matched foes usually both ended up dead on the battlefield. If by chance one of them survived, it was not for long, however well he had fought. There was no sympathy to be found among the onlookers for either victor or vanquished.'[13]

On 27 November, a patrol of 10 New Zealanders reconnoitred an enemy outpost at Masmi, five kilometres south-west of El Arish. The riders took a wide detour into the desert south of the telegraph line, marching entirely on compass bearings. They reached their objective after daybreak and withdrew without being spotted by the enemy. The total distance travelled was almost 75 kilometres.[14]

The stillness of the desert and the vivid colours of the morning and evening skies impressed many men. 'Perfect silence reigned,' Dr Teichman wrote, 'and there appeared to be no sign of life except an occasional vulture hovering over the old Turkish battlefield, or a jackal slinking homewards to his lair.'[15] Guy Powles described the sunsets and dawns as among 'the few glories of the desert':

Night after night on outpost, one watched and marvelled at the wondrous tints. As the sun sinks below the rim of the horizon, the whole sky glows with coloured bands of light, then these gradually fade out, leaving a clear blue sky studded with innumerable stars.... At dawn, streaks of colour spread over the sky, and begin to brighten the darkness, then quickly comes a full blaze of light across the sky, the colouring is gone, and it is broad daylight.[16]

Pretty colours were not enough for George Ranstead, however, who was bored by the lack of action. 'Things go on just as usual, and we always hope that there is something going on [on] the other fronts. I think it would be an everlasting war if everyone carried on as we do.' There was little that could be done to speed up the war: General Murray's railway and pipeline were 'a typically British piece of work – slow, very expensive, immensely solid'.[17]

On 7 December a British cavalryman, Lieutenant General Sir Philip Chetwode, arrived from France to take command of the leading elements of Eastern Force, which he christened the Desert Column. This consisted of the Anzac Mounted Division, the new Imperial Camel Corps (ICC) Brigade, several Yeomanry cavalry regiments and the 42nd and 52nd infantry divisions.

By now the mounted troops had thoroughly studied the land right up to the outskirts of El Arish. On 11 November, Chauvel received preliminary orders for the move towards El Arish. 'Never was an order more welcome to troops.'[18] Detailed plans were drawn up for the attack. When the railway was 20 kilometres from the objective, two infantry divisions were to capture the village, once the mounted forces had encircled it and cut the Turkish withdrawal route. After that, the small Turkish garrisons at Magdhaba, Abu Aweigila and Kossaima were to be destroyed by the mounted brigades while the infantry divisions pushed up towards Rafah as quickly as the railway could get them there. Once he was reinforced, General Murray planned to march on Beersheba.

El Arish was 'a little Eastern town with the usual flat-roofed houses, Sheikh's tomb, and a minaret, and to the east of it is a plain on which are the welcome shade and greenery of tamarisks and fig trees, a relief to eyes strained and weary of constant sand. Water is plentiful from several groups of wells, and the beach is a fine one, with groves of date palms close to it.' RFC reconnaissance aircraft revealed that the Turkish position at El Arish was defended by some 1600 men. Aircraft also spotted enemy positions up Wadi el Arish at Magdhaba and Abu Aweigila, covering the Turkish railhead, which had reached Kossaima. Preparations were not complete until 20 December – too late. The RFC on that day reported that the enemy apparently had abandoned El Arish. General Murray decided

AUTHOR'S COLLECTION

The desert railway under construction.

to push his mounted troops forward immediately, leaving the infantry and artillery behind.[19]

When the New Zealanders left their desert bivouac on the evening of 20 December, they were expecting another short ride to a new camp site.

The Christmas mail from home had just been received, and, as the column moved out, many men resembled travelling Christmas trees, with parcels ... tied all over themselves and [the] horses. Many also carried long 'bivvy' sticks for rigging up their next temporary blanket shelter, and these sticking up in the air enhanced the general comic effect. When it became known that the column was bound for El Arish, where fighting was expected, parcels, sticks, and all other unnecessary gear were shed right and left into the desert, until everyone was in fighting trim. This necessitated later the telling of many 'white lies' in letters home as to the enjoyment of cakes and other good things that were never eaten.[20]

The night of 20–21 December 1916 was very cold and many men regretted leaving their overcoats on the baggage camels. For once, they 'were glad of the opportunity to walk and lead the horses occasionally, so as to get some warmth through exercise'.[21] As they rode on in the darkness, 'to their delight' they 'felt their horses pass from the sand which they had known for so long to firm soil. And with morning light, though sand dunes mile on mile lay to the south and east of them, their eyes were gladdened by green patches of cultivation, with wheat and barley just sprouting, and many palms.'[22]

The NZMR column was guided by Captain Alexander Finlayson. 'So excellent was his judgement and skill in finding his way that, when daylight appeared, the column was found to be within 200 yards of the small sand-hill to which he had been asked to guide it.' The New Zealanders arriving at Masmi at dawn on 21 December. Ahead of them, the defences of El Arish looked suspiciously quiet.[23]

A ring of outposts was quickly thrown around the village. At 9.30 a.m., a New Zealand patrol reported that El Arish was empty of Turks. The village was found to consist of 'closely packed mud houses … accommodating, during the day, the family, the poultry, and the domestic animals, and in which the domestic refuse of ages had gradually gathered. There are few things on earth more repelling to every sense than the yard of an Eastern house, and El Arish was no exception. Unless on duty, you did not linger long in its narrow, winding streets.' Only the orchards of apricot, peach, and orange trees, and the new crops of barley and wheat, were appreciated by the Anzacs – and the fact that there was plenty of good water in the village. A few prisoners revealed that the Turkish garrison had gone inland along Wadi el Arish to Magdhaba, 37 kilometres away.[24]

On the morning of 22 December, the 3rd (Auckland) Squadron escorted some engineers up Wadi el Arish to Lahfan to see if there was water there. For the rest of the horsemen, the day passed quietly until General Chetwode arrived and ordered a pursuit to be launched up the wadi that night. His haste arose from an intercepted Turkish message dated 21 or 22 December that apparently ordered the Turks at Magdhaba to withdraw immediately to Auja (see Map 3, p.47).[25]

Major General Chauvel was placed in command of the force, which consisted of the Anzac Mounted Division (minus the 2nd LH Brigade) and the Imperial Camel Corps (ICC) Brigade, supported by two batteries of horse artillery and a mountain gun battery. If Chauvel failed to capture the wells at Magdhaba, the horses would face a long, thirsty trek back to El Arish before they could have a drink, unless water was found at Lahfan. The Anzac Mounted Division concentrated near the wadi south of El Arish after dark. Chauvel's water convoy became mixed up with the incoming 52nd Division, delaying the beginning of his march to Magdhaba until after midnight.[26]

The men were loaded with three days' rations for the horses and themselves and with as much water as they could carry. The horses and camels walked on either side of the stony wadi bed, which was reserved for the artillery. Even though the wheels of the 18-pounder guns made a tremendous racket on the stones, the men were ordered to maintain strict silence and smoking was forbidden. The only other sounds were 'the pounding of hooves, the clank of stirrup against stirrup, and the occasional neighing and snorting of the horses'. The flat plains on either side of the wadi were covered in fine white limestone clay, from which choking clouds of chalky dust rose as the riders passed.[27]

At 4.50 a.m. the column halted and dismounted about six kilometres from the village of Magdhaba, within sight of the Turks' camp fires. To Jim McMillan, 'it was quite evident that the enemy were not expecting visitors, at least not for breakfast anyway'. Martin Eccles remembered arriving at Magdhaba 'just on daylight, very cold and sleepy'.[28]

As dawn broke, the men and their horses and camels breakfasted while General Chauvel took his brigade commanders forward to survey the enemy position. The heavy pall of smoke that covered the position once the Turks extinguished their fires made this very difficult. After several hours of peering into the murk and listening to reports from scout aircraft, Chauvel was able to determine the rough layout of the Turkish defences, but the assault troops attacked with 'only a very general idea of the ground'. Australian aircraft that flew over the enemy position took heavy fire from the ground. A message dropped on Chauvel's headquarters confirmed that 'the [bastards] are there all right!'

Anzacs inspecting a beached German mine at El Arish. When another of these weapons exploded, two Australians were blown apart.

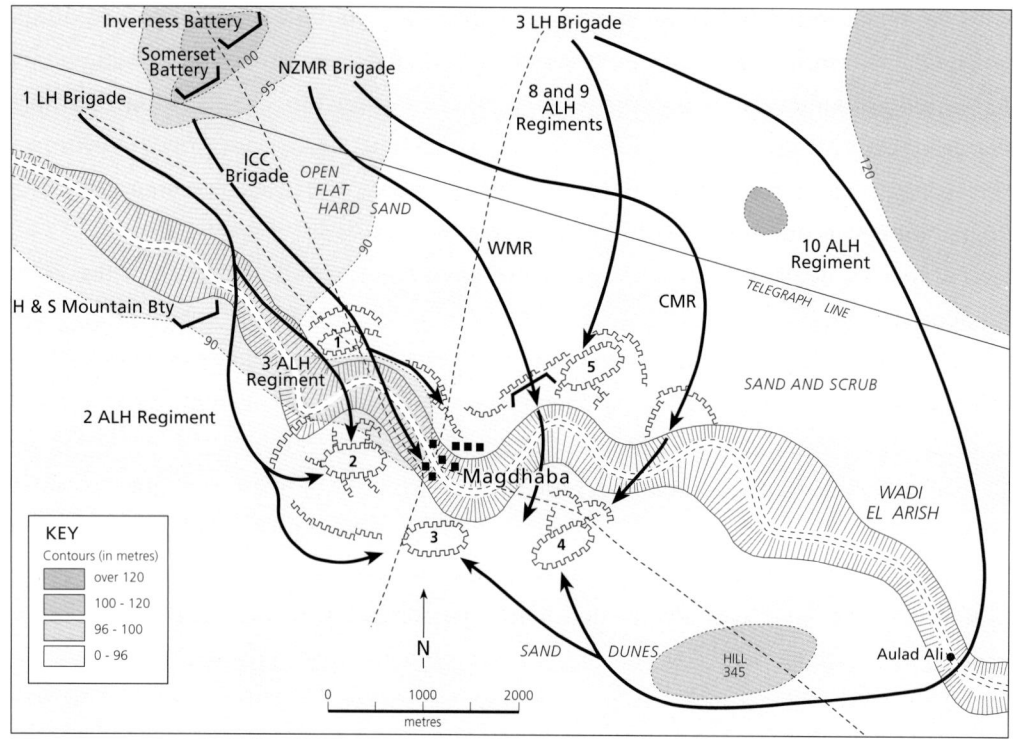

Map 6: Magdhaba.

Aircraft observers also reported that there was no sign of enemy reinforcements as far out as Ruafa, 13 kilometres south-east of Magdhaba.[29]

The enemy position was centred on the tiny village of Magdhaba, straddling the dry bed of Wadi el Arish. Two battalions (about 1600 men) from the 80th Regiment, 27th Arab Division, and a few cameliers manned five redoubts and a few connecting trenches. Four old mountain guns were emplaced on high ground, protected by the forward infantry positions. To the west, the sand dunes bordered the wadi, but to the east a flat, hard plain stretched for more than two kilometres from the village to the edge of the sand dunes. This plain was dotted with scrubby bushes and desert flowers and there was a large enemy redoubt (No. 5) sited on it. Another defensive position was sited on the wadi bank (No. 1) and three others (Nos 2, 3 and 4) were located on the far side of the wadi. The latter, up to eight metres deep, with many side gullies, afforded excellent cover for the garrison.[30]

Chauvel issued his orders at 8.22 a.m. He had decided to concentrate his strength on the hard ground east of the wadi, where the mobility of his mounted troops could be used to best advantage. He intended to seize the eastern redoubts (Nos 1 and 5) and the village with its wells, thereby cutting off the western redoubts from water. The attack was to begin as soon as the assault forces and the guns were in position and it was to be pressed home relentlessly. Brigadier General Chaytor was ordered to attack Magdhaba from the north and the north-east and to cut the enemy's line of retreat along the wadi bed, using the 3rd LH Brigade and his own New Zealand brigade. The ICC Brigade, Chauvel's strongest striking force, was ordered to advance directly on Magdhaba from the north-west. The 1st LH Brigade, Chauvel's reserve, had orders to be prepared to move up on the right of the cameliers.[31]

At 9.25 a.m. Chaytor was in position five kilometres to the north of Magdhaba. Almost immediately, he was told that small groups of mounted enemy troops were escaping along the wadi bed. He sent the 10th ALH Regiment right around the enemy position towards Aulad Ali to cut them off. Brigadier General 'Galloping Jack' Royston led this slender force personally, arriving at the wadi in time to capture 300 Arab soldiers.[32]

Chaytor then saw that the enemy appeared to be retiring from Hill 345, on the far side of the wadi. If the ICC Brigade would push forward in support, Chaytor said, he would seize Hill 345. Fifteen minutes later, he gave up waiting for the cameliers and sent the Canterbury and Wellington regiments towards No. 5 Redoubt. The 3rd LH Brigade was brought forward to support the New Zealanders and to get around the enemy's right flank in the village.

At first, the CMR and WMR advanced on horseback, with the AMR in reserve. The horsemen rode to within 1500 metres of No. 5 Redoubt, before mountain gun and rifle fire forced them to dismount and send the horses back to cover. The WMR screen, commanded by Lieutenant Edward Levien, actually galloped right up to the enemy trenches under fire from the entire enemy garrison. It then retired 400 metres to cover, where it was quickly reinforced with Vickers and Lewis guns. The enemy positions were well concealed and the ground across which the New Zealanders had to advance was flat and open, with only occasional stunted bushes here and there to provide illusory cover. As a result, progress soon slowed to a crawl.

At 10 a.m. a pilot landed near General Chauvel's HQ and told him that the enemy 'were off'. Chauvel immediately ordered his reserve, the 1st LH Brigade, to advance straight into Magdhaba. Brigadier General Charles Cox led his brigade into the open at the trot. Coming under enemy shrapnel fire as he passed the cameliers on his left, he changed direction slightly and increased the pace to a gallop. 'For a minute or more, the light horsemen enjoyed the excitement of a cavalry charge, as the horses fought for their heads, and the quart pots and other gear clattered against the saddles.' The Australian horsemen came under increasingly-heavy and accurate fire from two enemy redoubts, and it became obvious that the Turks were not 'off'. To continue the advance on horseback, in the face of such heavy fire, would lead to heavy casualties for men and horses, so Cox abandoned his spectacular charge and led his brigade into cover in the wadi. Once there, he sent two regiments on foot towards the enemy in the nearest redoubt. His third regiment was sent out to the south-west around the enemy flank.[33]

As noon approached, the New Zealanders were still slowly advancing towards the village and the nearest redoubt. To their right, the cameliers and Cox's light horsemen were also moving slowly forward. The 10th ALH Regiment was at Aulad Ali and the rest of the 3rd LH Brigade was still held in reserve by Chaytor. The British and Indian gunners were finding it very difficult to silence the enemy artillery, as only one redoubt was visible. Heat mirages and dust clouds reduced visibility and made communications difficult.

As the two New Zealand regiments advanced, an 800-metre gap opened between them. Just after noon, Chaytor sent the 8th and 9th ALH regiments of the 3rd LH Brigade into this gap, in an effort to force a result. The two Australian regiments galloped up, dismounted under heavy fire and advanced on foot.

At 1.05 p.m. Chauvel heard that the engineers had been unable to find any water at Lahfan. This was bad news. Since the horses had not had a drink since before leaving El

The village of Magdhaba, viewed from the west.

Arish the previous evening, Chauvel would soon have to withdraw his force back to El Arish to water them. The slow progress of the attack suggested that the prospects of capturing Magdhaba quickly were poor so Chauvel told Chetwode by telephone at 1.50 p.m. that he intended to break off the action and return to El Arish. General Chetwode urged Chauvel to fight on, even if it cost him some of his horses. He also told Chauvel that he was collecting every camel he could find in order to send 3000 litres of water to Lahfan. Chetwode suggested that the fire of the artillery should be concentrated on one redoubt, which could then be taken by a bayonet charge after dark. Chauvel agreed to try one more time.[34]

Even as Chauvel was talking to Chetwode, the enemy redoubts began to fall in quick succession. After pausing to draw breath and to bring up more ammunition, the Wellington regiment and the 8th and 9th ALH regiments captured No. 5 Redoubt and the mountain gun battery.

> With the Wellingtons on their right, the two Australian regiments fixed bayonets about eighty yards from the enemy trenches, and then charged right home. For a few minutes the Turks engaged fiercely in a hand-to-hand encounter, and several of their men were killed with the bayonet before the general surrender. The Australians then covered … the advance of the Wellingtons, and, as the New Zealanders advanced to close quarters, the Turks in front of them raised the white flag.[35]

As Powles recorded, 'By 3.30 p.m. the New Zealanders with fixed bayonets were swarming over the trenches to the east of the houses and the Turks were surrendering in all directions.' Wilkie wrote, 'Some of our men, unfortunately, exposed themselves too quickly, under the impression that the whole line of Turks had surrendered, but they were fired on from the right, and the attack was immediately resumed. Lieutenant [Maurice] Harding … was mortally wounded by this burst of fire. Machine gun, Lewis gun, and rifle fire was then directed for some minutes at the wavering Turks, who again hoisted white flags and, coming out of their trenches unarmed, surrendered.'[36] As Nelson Hughes recalled,

> Harding … had just borrowed my rifle and fired a few shots 'to join in the sport' as he said. He then crawled a few yards over to join Dick Bowen on my left when he got hit between the eyes. We dragged him back under cover but he died soon after…. My section mate, Mollie Morgan was killed this day as well as Trooper [Reginald] Gamlin … His friends at home had sent him over a Waimate football jersey, amber and black…. He insisted on wearing it into action despite his … cobber [James] Bashford pleading with him not to, on account of snipers.[37]

Meanwhile Cox's light horsemen and the cameliers attacked the redoubts in front of them. Covered by machine gun and rifle fire, the troops charged across the open, flat ground and captured No. 1 Redoubt at the point of the bayonet, taking 95 prisoners. Machine guns were brought forward into the redoubt, from where they could fire into the next one, No. 2. The cameliers clambered out of the first redoubt and continued their advance towards the village, while the light horsemen attacked the next redoubts on the western side of the wadi (Nos 2 and 3), which finally fell at 4.20 p.m. Among the prisoners captured in No. 3 Redoubt was the Turkish regimental commander.

To the south, the 10th ALH Regiment crossed the wadi and advanced back up towards Nos 3 and 4 redoubts. Because there was better cover on this side of the wadi, the Australians were able to get very close to the enemy on horseback. One half-squadron of light horsemen, carrying rifles with fixed bayonets in their hands, galloped straight through No. 4 Redoubt, which was defended by 300 Turks. They survived by sheer boldness, helped by the enemy's poor marksmanship. A little more cautiously, the light horsemen turned and attacked the redoubt on foot, aided by squadrons from the 2nd ALH Regiment and the WMR, which had crossed the wadi from the village. The 8th and 9th ALH regiments and the CMR also crossed the wadi. Together these regiments captured the last redoubts by 4.30 p.m. and organised resistance ended. Light horse regiments chased down a few escaping Turks and scattered shots were fired from sand dunes south of Magdhaba until dark.[38]

The mounted men assembled in the village as the sun set. The regiments were mixed up so it took some time to sort them out, bring up the horses, water some of them and collect the prisoners. As it got dark, dozens of small fires were lit to mark the positions of the wounded men for the stretcher-bearers.[39]

Ninety-seven dead enemy soldiers were buried on the battlefield. Nearly 1300 prisoners were rounded up, along with four mountain guns, one machine gun, 1200 rifles, 100,000 rounds of ammunition, 50 camels and 40 horses. The commander of the 80th Regiment and both of his battalion commanders were among the prisoners. The attackers lost 22 men killed and 134 wounded, mostly in the camel battalions. In the NZMR Brigade, nine men and three horses were killed; 56 men and seven horses were wounded.[40]

Magdhaba had fallen after a long, hard day's fighting. The defensive position had been well designed and the redoubts and rifle pits were very difficult to see. A critical weakness seems to have been its lack of machine guns and artillery. The enemy resistance had been determined until the attackers closed to within bayonet range: few defenders had the stomach to fight on from that stage. Perhaps they had also realised by then

The NZMR Brigade advancing on Magdhaba. The soldier in the foreground is wounded.

that no reinforcements were coming. General Chauvel appreciated that, had Turkish marksmanship been better, his assault forces would have suffered heavy casualties.[41]

Chauvel left part of the AMR, which had seen no fighting, the 1st ALH Regiment and a squadron from the 3rd ALH Regiment to clear the battlefield and destroy the buildings. These men bivouacked on the battlefield overnight and continued their work at dawn. The other horsemen and cameliers set off for El Arish, taking the fit prisoners and a few trophies with them. According to Chauvel, 'it was a devil of a business getting brigades assembled, prisoners counted and started off with escorts, convoys of men's water distributed and water issued, all at one signal lamp in the desert which marked my Headquarters'.[42]

The returning riders met Chetwode's resupply column of 400 camels at Lahfan. Some regiments stopped to water their mounts while others continued on towards El Arish. The night was very cold, the men and horses exhausted. Many men, who had not slept for three days and nights, were so tired that they experienced hallucinations during the long ride. 'Men saw, or fancied they saw, plantations, towns with large buildings lighted up, precipices, or a gradually-closing wall. A man would halt, thinking he was on the edge of a cliff, then seeing others riding on he knew it to be imagination only.' Other men reported seeing silent armies of strange-looking soldiers on weird beasts. At one point, General Chauvel and another officer suddenly spurred their horses and galloped off into the darkness. After a few minutes, they quietly rode back and rejoined the column. They had imagined they had seen a fox and taken off in pursuit.[43] As Powles recorded,

> *Men and horses were dropping off at the oddest times and in the oddest of positions, and many men and horses came down in the dust; and this long night ride may safely be regarded as one of the most trying of the many wearisome marches experienced by the brigade. Apart from the intense cold which penetrated to the bone the lightly clad horsemen, the men were fatigued to such a degree that words fail to adequately describe.... Dense clouds of dust almost blinded the tired horses, which collided with one another in the dark.*[44]

A New Zealand machine gunner wrote that 'the dust seemed to glue the eyelids together and make it impossible to keep awake'. Jim McMillan recalled that 'Immediately a halt was made, the weary men just dropped to the ground and in most cases, fell asleep at once, right there among the horses' hooves. There was little danger of being trodden on – the tired animals being just as disinclined to move as were their riders. Nevertheless, they always responded as soon as they were remounted and carried on steadily until the next halt was made.' As riders fell asleep, the pressure on the reins eased and the horses would step out towards home. Many a trooper suddenly awoke to find himself passing regimental or brigade headquarters.[45]

The horsemen eventually reached their bivouac area on the beach near Masmi at 6 a.m. on Christmas Eve. Breakfast was interrupted by the appearance of a German aircraft which bombed the camps but no one was particularly concerned. The prisoners were handed over to the infantry to guard and feed them. 'In order to ration them, our friends of 52nd Division had to go short for a day or two. The "Scotties" were amusingly indignant, and repeatedly told our fellows they had taken too ****** many prisoners, and should have used the ****** bayonet more.'[46] The New Zealanders were 'very tired but very pleased with themselves'. After watering and feeding the horses and themselves, the exhausted men slept the day through.[47]

Back at Magdhaba, Magnus Johnson and a few other Aucklanders 'slept in a Turkish tent [to keep warm] and got covered with lice'. They left Magdhaba at 2 p.m. on Christmas Eve but got lost after dark and had to wait until Christmas Day dawned before they could find the route again. It was a far from joyous Christmas and the trooper who suggested that carol-singing might be a good idea quickly realised his mistake.[48]

The first casualties were evacuated to El Arish on the night of the battle, on camel cacolets, sledges and sand carts. Others were taken to a Turkish hospital in the village. At dusk on Christmas Eve, these men were evacuated to the coast. 'A hideous night followed, as the long column of 150 camels, each bearing its burden of two jolted, groaning men, moved slowly through the intense darkness.'[49] At El Arish, the men were already strapped into comfortable sand carts for land evacuation, when it was decided that they would be evacuated by sea. They waited for four days before heavy seas forced the cancellation of the sea evacuation. They were sent back by sand cart, as originally planned. It took some of these wounded men up to nine days to reach hospital. On 29 December an enormous ambulance convoy carrying 150 wounded men left for the point on the railway known as the 139 Kilometre peg, where a hospital train awaited them.[50]

That same day, Lieutenant General Chetwode addressed the troops at El Arish: 'The mounted men at Magdhaba had done what he had never known cavalry in the history of war to have done before, i.e., they had not only located and surrounded the enemy's position but they had got down to it as infantry and had carried fortified positions at the point of the bayonet.' Soon after their defeat at Magdhaba, the Turks withdrew their remaining posts from Sinai, with the exception of a position near Rafah.[51]

By now, the New Zealanders had been living and fighting in the desert for nearly a year. They were fully acclimatised, as were their horses. They knew how to survive, move and fight in one of the most inhospitable environments that New Zealanders have ever

Arab prisoners captured at Magdhaba, not looking too upset about the fact.

fought in. Although they had the measure of the Turks in open warfare, they had relearnt the Gallipoli lesson of not underestimating 'Abdul' as a defensive fighter. And they had yet to come up against the main Turkish army in Syria.

6

A damned good scrap

Over the swelling sand-hills they come, line upon line … no song, no laughter, no talking, not a light to be seen; no sound but the snort of a horse as he blows the dust from his nostrils; or the click of two stirrup irons touching as two riders close in together; or the jingle of the links on the packhorses; or perhaps a neck chain rattling on the pommel.

GUY POWLES

CHRISTMAS 1916 WAS not a particularly festive period for the Anzac horsemen, although they were pleased with their success at Magdhaba. With winter now upon them, the men began to suffer from the rain and cold. No tents had been available since Romani so they had to fashion shelters from whatever they could. Captured Turkish bivouac sheets and odd scraps of leaky sacking, canvas or Bedouin cloth were draped over holes scraped in the sand. Two days after Christmas, as a new camp was set up in a date-palm grove on the beach at Masaid, a storm began that lasted 12 days. It became even colder; the heavy rain and strong winds made everyone miserable. As the AMR's historian recorded, 'During the gale a supply of fresh meat . . . was buried by the wind-shifted sand, and it had to be dug out. The stew on that occasion was more gritty than usual.' After grimly sitting it out on the beach for a few days, the brigade was moved back to the railhead on New Year's Day 1917. This new camp was more easily supplied but it was exposed to the wind, and the water for the horses was poor. After four uncomfortable days, the brigade moved back up to Masaid, on a wet day that resulted in another thorough soaking for everyone.[1]

On 27 December the RFC reported an enemy defensive position on a small knoll called Magruntein, near the police and customs border post at Rafah. At least two Turkish battalions and four mountain guns were observed, but no other enemy forces were visible within 15 kilometres. It seemed too good to be true: another small Turkish garrison was sitting on its own, seemingly far from support, but well within reach of General Murray's mounted troops. Murray wanted to attack the position with his infantry and

The NZMR Brigade riding from El Arish towards Rafah on 8 January 1917.

mounted troops but that strike force would take some time to prepare. General Chetwode convinced Murray to allow him to launch a quick surprise 'cutting-out raid', using the Anzac Mounted Division (still without the 2nd LH Brigade), three battalions of the ICC Brigade, the 5th Mounted Brigade and four light cars armed with machine guns.[2]

Kress, seeing that the Turkish 31st Regiment at Magruntein was exposed and vulnerable, wanted to pull it back into Palestine immediately after the defeat at Magdhaba. He was overruled by Cemal Pasha, his incompetent commander, who insisted that it stay where it was for political reasons. By the time the German managed to reverse Cemal's decision, it was too late.[3]

On 28 December the 1st LH Brigade scouted part-way along the El Arish–Rafah track, discovering that the route was hard enough to support guns and light vehicles. Two days later they undertook a second reconnaissance to Sheikh Zowaiid (see Map 3, p.47), where they found the villagers to be friendly, and plenty of good water available in a fresh-water lagoon. A scout section pushed a little further forward and observed the Turks busily improving their defensive position at Magruntein. The light horsemen also brought back 'tidings of … rolling stretches of pasture and young crops, brightly starred with poppies and other wild flowers'.[4]

General Chetwode issued his orders on 7 January 1917. The first step was for the assault force to concentrate at Sheikh Zowaiid, 30 kilometres from El Arish. From there the three horse brigades of the Anzac Mounted Division were to cover the last 14 kilometres to Magruntein. Riding east, then north, they were to attack the enemy at dawn on 9 January. The ICC Brigade would attack the enemy frontally, in concert with the Anzacs. The 5th Mounted Brigade was to wait in reserve. If the enemy withdrew before he was surrounded, he was to be pursued, but only as far as Khan Yunis. Chetwode had no intention of remaining at Rafah, even if the attack was successful, so only one day's food and forage was to be carried from El Arish. Regimental medical officers were warned to collect all their wounded patients before dark, in order to save them from the attentions of a Bedouin tribe in the neighbourhood which was 'known to have the reputation of mutilating their enemies'.[5]

At noon on 8 January 1917, 1605 men and 1851 horses and mules in the NZMR Brigade rode out from their camp site near El Arish to join the assault force assembling on the eastern bank of Wadi el Arish. The river was in flood, with the water lapping up to the horses' girth straps: this delighted the men, reminding them of New Zealand rivers. At 4 p.m. the entire force moved out, following the telegraph line to the east.[6]

The first part of the way lay over very heavy sand dunes, which tried the double gun teams and ammunition wagon teams to the utmost; and it was some miles before the Old Road in its defined form … appeared, and then the column took to that great shallow trough worked down by the feet of countless generations. The guns and ammunition teams were given the hardened centre, and the horsemen rode on each side. Let us stop and watch them go by in the moonlight.... Over the swelling sand-hills they come, line upon line – noiseless they go – no song, no laughter, no talking, not a light to be seen; no sound but the snort of a horse as he blows the dust from his nostrils; or the click of two stirrup irons touching as two riders close in together; or the jingle of the links on the packhorses; or perhaps a neck chain rattling on the pommel. No other sound is heard unless one be very close, then there is a low swish swish as the sand spurts out in front of a horse's foot slithering on from step to step.[7]

The advance guard encircled Sheikh Zowaiid soon after sunset and the main body of the force bivouacked there at 10 p.m. The village was 'a delightful spot of greenness that showed up in the moonlight'. The troops rested in silence; smoking and camp fires were prohibited. As Powles wrote, everyone felt 'unbounded surprise [when] the good steeds, instead of standing as usual as quiet and steady as statues and dozing also, immediately got their heads down and began cropping … many a man gave up entirely any thought of sleep and helped his horse to a "real green feed".' Others were kept awake by the intense cold, and, in one case, by heavy snoring.[8]

The march resumed three hours later. Against the wishes of his subordinate commanders, Chetwode inexplicably ordered the wagons carrying the reserve artillery and machine gun ammunition to be left behind in Sheikh Zowaiid. The Anzac Mounted Division led the column towards Karm Ibn Musleh (see Map 7, p.137). At 3.30 a.m. the troops halted seven kilometres south-west of Rafah for an hour. A few stray Turks were rounded up, but not before they fired a warning flare.

At 5.15 a.m. the New Zealand brigade was sent ahead to round up the Bedouin that 'infested' the area around Rafah. Cordons were thrown around the camps at Karm Ibn Musleh and Shokh es Sufi and the New Zealanders collected 30 old men, women and children armed with ancient swords and a few pistols. 'They gave a warning … before the New Zealanders could reach them – the long drawn Arab "lu lu lu!" which travels a great distance – and as dawn appeared smoke signals went up from one Bedouin camp after another.' Trooper William Harris was shot dead by an Arab at Shokh es Sufi. The killer stole the New Zealander's rifle and bandolier before escaping on his horse. While Trooper Albert Watson was searching the same camp, his horse broke away and ran to another camp site, chased by Watson.[9]

The Reduit, photographed after the battle.

One of the Arabs there caught the horse and was about to hand it over to Trooper Watson when he suddenly struck him over the head with a heavy sword in a scabbard. Watson fell to the ground, when three or four other natives rushed in, kicked and punched him and took his bandolier and rifle away. Corporal [Ernest] Sweetman, seeing that Trooper Watson was in trouble, galloped to his assistance. The Arabs fired four shots at Sweetman, but as this failed to stop him, the natives, of whom about 20 had assembled by this time, scattered, taking with them Watson's horse, saddle, bandolier, rifle, and bayonet.[10]

Chaytor reported that the ground near Shokh es Sufi was suitable as an assembly area so Chauvel brought up the rest of the Anzac Mounted Division. The ICC Brigade, the 5th Mounted Brigade and Chetwode's headquarters remained further to the west.

When the AMR reached the frontier of Palestine, Lieutenant Colonel Mackesy halted the regiment and rode forward alone. Passing a stone pillar marking the border, he took off his hat and 'thanked Almighty God that he had at last been permitted to enter the Holy Land … and came back smiling'. The rising sun revealed 'rolling turf-covered downs, all green from the winter rains, and already sprinkled with early spring flowers. Here and there, patches of young barley showed darker green against the fresh dew-spangled grass, while in sharp contrast a belt of sand dunes some two miles wide lay to the north along the sea coast.' An Australian doctor later recalled that 'the matting tents of the Bedouin, with their camels, sheep, and donkeys grazing peacefully, and the smoke of their fires mingling with the wreaths of mist from the wet green slopes, made a picture which brought to mind the stories of the Old Testament'.[11]

As General Chauvel studied the enemy position, the Turks suddenly awoke to their peril: 'The confusion which followed confessed their surprise. There was an immediate and disorderly rush of troops to their numerous earthworks.'[12]

The enemy position at Magruntein was skilfully sited and well constructed. The key to the position was the Reduit on Point 255, an 80-metre-high, smooth, grassy knoll that dominated all approaches. The Reduit was linked by communications trenches to an irregular and nearly invisible outer complex of trenches arranged in three 'systems', referred to as the A, B and C works. A gently sloping grass-covered plain extended for at least 1000 metres in front of this ring of defences. Scattered across this 'glacis' were hidden rifle pits 'crowded with picked sharp-shooters'. Several small-calibre mountain guns were concealed within the defences.[13] General Chetwode wrote afterwards: 'I confess I thought the task was almost beyond the capacity of dismounted cavalry to carry through'. The enemy position did have weaknesses and Chetwode and Chauvel quickly identified them with the help of ground and aerial reconnaissance. In particular, no barbed wire had been used and the defences were weaker on the north-eastern side.[14]

At 8.30 a.m. Chauvel was told that the roads to the east and south-east of Rafah were clear of enemy troops. Reassured, he immediately issued his orders for the attack. The NZMR Brigade was to attack the Reduit and the C4 and C5 trench systems. The 1st LH Brigade was to assault C1, C2 and C3. Both attacks were to be launched from the east and north-east. Chaytor was also told to be prepared to stop the garrison from escaping via the coastal sand dunes. The ICC Brigade was to attack the B works. The 3rd LH Brigade was held back as Chauvel's divisional reserve and Chetwode retained the British 5th Mounted Brigade as his own reserve.

Chetwode intended to 'soften up' the formidable defences with an artillery barrage. The 30-minute bombardment was to end at 10 a.m. This was to be the signal for the attack to start. At 9.35 a.m. the New Zealanders rode out from the divisional assembly area, led by Chaytor and followed by 'a horde of Bedouin chattering like monkeys'. As Powles explained, 'The 8th Squadron ... formed the advanced guard to the Canterbury regiment. As it rode to the north of Rafah to cut the Turks' communications it came into full view of the enemy, who opened on the squadrons with shrapnel and rifle fire, but, riding in open order, the regiment escaped with only two or three casualties.' The CMR chased down an escaping camel column, cut the telegraph line and captured the customs and police post at Rafah, rounding up nearly 200 prisoners (including six Germans).[15]

Major James McCarroll led the 3rd and 4th squadrons of the AMR around the back of the Turkish position.

We went off at a trot. As we neared the position, the shelling and machine gun fire increased. Our pace increased to a steady gallop. The horses seemed to enter into the spirit of the job, and ... we galloped on over green crops. It was a beautiful sight, the lines regular just like on parade. We raced over an outer trench and a number of Turks surrendered. An officer and three or four men [ran] back [towards] their units. I ... galloped after them, drawing my sword. I induced them to halt and return to us. One of them caught my horse by the bridle but I hit him on the back of the neck with the sword back. The Aucklands cleared another line of incomplete trenches, capturing more prisoners and a machine gun post.[16]

Chaytor ordered Meldrum to send small patrols to the east to watch for approaching enemy reinforcements. A reinforced section of WMR men scouted to the east towards

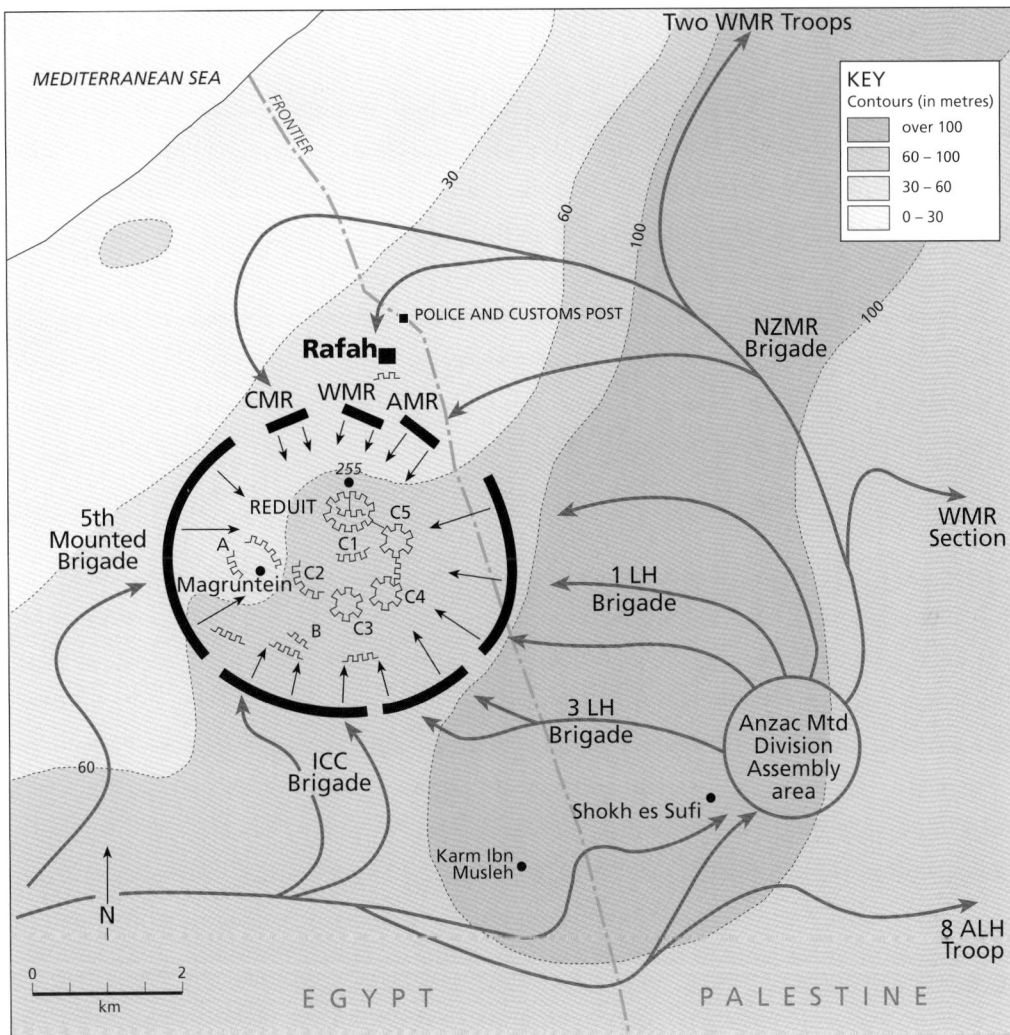

Map 7: Rafah.

Shellal while two Wellington troops patrolled north-east towards Khan Yunis. By 9.45 a.m. the New Zealand mounted regiments, with Brigade Headquarters in the lead, had galloped to within 2000 metres of the closest Turkish trenches. It reminded Guy Powles of another war: 'How like South Africa was that ride … the little red man [Chaytor] and Brigade Headquarters leading with the whole brigade at a gallop.'[17] As the regiments moved into position, the artillery batteries began their bombardment of the enemy defences. Aircraft fitted with primitive radios were employed to spot targets and to correct the fire of the guns. Some of the gunners 'had the rare experience of seeing their targets, but they themselves were even more visible to the enemy, who shelled them severely with his mountain guns'.[18]

This was the mounteds' first fight on ground that was still occupied by its original inhabitants, many of whom watched the fight 'with interest … from their tents, or while tending their flocks between the two firing lines'. Grazing donkeys 'galloped as fast as their legs would carry them alongside the excited horses'.[19]

So confident were the natives that they would be unharmed that they sent their womenfolk to graze flocks and herds behind our lines, and at one period there was actually a girl with some sheep between the [enemy] trenches and our firing line. The whistling shells overhead neither interfered with the feeding sheep, nor disturbed the girl's equanimity. And when the Light Horse made their rush to the trenches, a cow and her calf accompanied them.[20]

As soon as the artillery bombardment ended, the New Zealanders dismounted and began their attack. The Canterbury and Auckland regiments led the assault, with the Wellingtons in reserve. Two machine guns were allocated to support the Aucklands and four to the Canterbury regiment. The remaining six were held in reserve. The regimental Lewis guns were also in action, 'doing excellent work, and the machine guns, from a low ridge in our rear, supported the firing line. The advance was slow but steady, the men advancing on foot as though they were carrying out manoeuvres. Everything worked like clockwork. A troop would rise from the ground and, covered by the fire of their comrades on either flank, dash forward a few yards, the men throwing themselves down, and bringing fire to bear on the trench in front of them till the remaining troops had come into line.'[21]

Many men who took part in that frightening advance recorded their experiences in writing. For some, the waiting was the worst. 'Ahead were those sandbag covered trenches behind which grim-faced German machine-gunners and experienced Turkish regulars were waiting, finger on trigger, for us to rush forward. The more we stared at those trenches and the open ground that lay between, the more impregnable they seemed to be.'[22]

Others chose to emphasise the comic aspects. One man who was lightly wounded in the thigh 'was picked up by the stretcher-bearers, who started to carry him to a place of safety, in order to dress his wound. On the way to cover, a shell landed a few yards in front of them and exploded. For a moment they were lost to view in a cloud of smoke and dust; gradually the smoke cleared away, and revealed the stretcher-bearers gazing with a puzzled look into the empty stretcher, while the "case" was seen disappearing over the sky line, bidding fair to break the record for the 100 yards sprint.'[23]

The [CMR] Padre also caused some amusement. He was with the Colonel, whose headquarters were about 2,000 yards behind the firing line…. Suddenly the enemy's shells began bursting around, and the order was passed around for everyone to dig for cover, and the Padre was observed furiously attempting to dig himself in with a spoon.[24]

This was a serious business, however: men were shot down all over the battlefield. Casualties in the front line had to be carried out on stretchers to the waiting sand carts and sledges. As some machine guns were being galloped forward, the gunners came under enemy machine gun fire.

Trooper [Robert] Reid was leading a gun pack[horse] when he was shot through the spine. In spite of this, he continued in the saddle and led his packhorse another 250 yards, to where the gun teams halted under cover; he then fell from his horse, and was at once examined by the doctor. His officer, thinking he would comfort him, said: 'You'll be alright, Reid. You're hit in the muscles of the back.' Reid replied: 'Ye'r lying, sir, I'm shot through the back, but I hung on to my horse, though.' He died two days later. For a packhorse leader to let his charge get loose was an unpardonable sin in a Mounted Machine Gun Section; this stolid Scotchman, in spite of his terrible wound, determined that his record should not be broken at the last, and succeeded.[25]

PA1-q-605-05-3, POWLES FAMILY COLLECTION, ALEXANDER TURNBULL LIBRARY

The New Zealanders beginning the assault on the Reduit. Note the complete absence of cover.

New Zealand machine gunners firing from a captured enemy trench.

To the left of the New Zealanders, the 1st LH Brigade advanced against the C system of enemy trenches. Further south, the cameliers began their attack on the B system. At Chauvel's request, General Chetwode ordered his reserve cavalry brigade to divert Turkish attention by attacking the A trench system. As soon as Chetwode was assured that all exits were sealed, he ordered all reserves to be thrown into the battle and for the attacks to be pressed home. The 3rd LH Brigade came into the assault line between the ICC Brigade and the 1st LH Brigade, and the Wellington regiment joined the fight between the other two New Zealand regiments. By 11 a.m. all the available troops were committed.

> *The circle was yet far too wide for contact; each brigade was more or less isolated, with its flanks exposed; and the admirable placing of the enemy posts left most of the British troops open to enfilade [flanking] fire. For a time the Turks shrewdly withheld their fire, and all the regiments made rapid progress until they came within about half a mile of the earthworks. Then the Turks opened [fire] vigorously with all arms, and Chauvel's men, still beyond charging distance, were held by a hail of lead which each moment increased in intensity and deadliness.[26]*

By 12.15 p.m. the New Zealanders had closed to within 500 metres of the Reduit but they could make no further progress. Four of their machine guns were out of ammunition by 1.30 p.m. Disaster was averted when Major Alexander Wilkie, the Quartermaster of the WMR, commandeered a cable wagon from the signallers, filled it with 24,000 rounds of small arms ammunition at Sheikh Zowaiid and brought it up to the firing line at the gallop.[27]

At 2 p.m. the Canterburys on the New Zealand right flank joined up with the left of the 5th Mounted Brigade, finally completing the encirclement of the enemy garrison. Apart from this lateral movement, the New Zealanders had made little progress since noon. The attack was grinding to a halt. 'The very slight undulations of the ground gave hardly any cover, and every yard seemed to be beaten by machine gun fire.' The Turkish mountain guns were ineffective but enemy aircraft were bombing whatever they could see and the rifle and machine gun fire from the redoubts and trenches was heavy and sustained. At 3.15 p.m. the Inverness Battery, which had been supporting the New Zealanders, fired its last round and was sent away from the battlefield. 'There was no weight in our attack anywhere, and lack of coordination resulted in wasted efforts by individual units.' The attackers and defenders settled down to a short range fire fight, in which the former were at a distinct disadvantage. The ground was so open and the enemy positions were so dominant that the attackers, lying flat on the ground, were plainly visible to the Turks, as were the supporting horse artillery batteries and machine guns.[28]

Lieutenant General Chetwode was worried. Prisoners revealed that he was facing 2000 ethnic Turks of the 31st Regiment in Magruntein, supported by four mountain guns and German machine guns, and that another regiment had left Shellal to reinforce the garrison at Magruntein as soon as the Allied attack had begun. This last piece of news was confirmed by Chetwode's air and ground patrols. At 2.30 p.m. Chetwode called for a last concentrated effort against the Reduit. His remaining horse artillery batteries shelled the trenches until they too began to run out of ammunition. The attack gained no ground and by 4 p.m. the situation was critical. The Turks were fighting stubbornly, reinforcements were closing in and the 1st LH Brigade reported that it could not advance – in fact it was forced to withdraw slightly to find better cover. The New Zealanders were coming under occasional 'friendly' artillery fire from the British batteries on the far side of the hill.[29]

At 4.30 p.m. Chetwode decided to cut his losses and break off the attack. Orders for the withdrawal were issued and some assault units immediately pulled back. Chetwode mounted his horse and began to ride back to El Arish. Chaytor, however. had already issued orders for a brigade advance at 4 p.m. Squadrons of the Wellington and Auckland regiments got up and advanced in a series of rushes, with other squadrons and the machine gunners providing close-range covering fire. The Reduit 'stood out clearly nearly a mile away from the New Zealand line, on the crest of an absolutely naked, grassy slope.... It was a wild, impetuous rush rather than a precise and steady advance.... despite the hail of lead the Turks, resisting with fine courage, could be seen standing up to take aim with their rifles.' Captain Arthur Herrick and Corporal Ben Draper fired a Lewis gun as they ran. 'While one held the gun under his arm and directed it, the other worked it, spraying the Turks along the trenches with a stream of bullets.'[30] Aucklander James McCarroll, who took part in this assault, described the experience.

> *The three regiments moved as one, covered by a portion of each regiment. The glistening steel, the dark forms on the green slopes with not a bit of cover. Steady as a rock. Here and there a man dropped.... Then the whole line [got] up as one man for the final rush, firing had ceased. It was here we got a number of casualties. Oh, that picture will never fade from my memory. Men fell quickly, the others pressed on, and with a cheer they reached the top of the hill where they had a business interview with the Turk.... The appearance of our brigade on top of the hill altered the whole position, and in ten minutes the Turk was beaten.*[31]

MILDRED FUNNELL COLLECTION

Turkish prisoners, probably captured at Rafah. The officer on foot, with his back to the camera, is believed to be Meldrum.

Chaytor wrote afterwards that 'the covering fire from machine guns and rifles was excellent, [it] made the Reduit appear a smoking furnace, and kept the Turks' fire down. The men covered the last 600 to 800 yards in two grand rushes, everyone having made up his mind to get home, and the result was that the position was taken with very little loss to ourselves.'[32]

It was not entirely one-sided. The Turks facing the NZMR charge surrendered but machine gunners on the right fired into the New Zealanders, causing several casualties. Kingston Hull got into the enemy trenches and was about to bayonet a Turk when 'he put his hands up, so I let him off'. Chaytor wrote that 'there were few places in the trenches free from [Turkish] dead or wounded, and in several places I saw they were three deep'. After a short pause, the New Zealanders brought up several machine guns and, covered by their fire, climbed out of the captured redoubt and attacked the next one, known as the Sandy Redoubt or C5. Before they reached it 'the garrison stood up and surrendered.... The Turks had had enough, and everywhere they threw down their arms.'[33]

With the loss of the vital high ground at the Reduit, the lower enemy positions were immediately rendered indefensible. The Australian light horsemen and the cameliers quickly secured them. The lead battalions of the ICC Brigade 'went on with gathering speed against heavy fire, although, as the Camels closed, the enemy shooting became erratic and ineffective. When 200 yards away [the] men could plainly see the Turks fixing their bayonets; accepting the challenge with a great roar, they rushed at the stronghold. But as they reached the trenches, the Turks raised a number of white flags, and a moment later the panting assailants ... were shaking hands with the enemy all along the line.' According to William Owers, some Turkish prisoners 'didn't seem too distressed at being caught'. Afterwards, New Zealanders told a story that 'old Brig. Royston, of the ALH, "Galloping Jack" we called him, seeing us storm [Point] 255, yelled to his men to attack at once – "or those NZ b...s will take the lot!"'[34] By 5.15 p.m. it was all over. John Masterman remembered that the enemy commander hid under a tent to avoid capture. 'However our boys, always after loot, were poking about and looking round for stuff, thought they found something and found it to be the Turk commander.'[35]

With the position captured, the force had to quickly gather its wounded and its prisoners and withdraw. The wounded New Zealanders were collected 'in heaps' for the sand carts to pick up. Firing continued for a little longer to the east, as the enemy reinforcements approaching from Shellal and Khan Yunis exchanged rifle and machine gun fire with the New Zealand outposts. At 6.30 p.m. the Desert Column withdrew to Sheikh Zowaiid, where it spent the night. 'Never did prisoners find themselves on the march quicker than did the Turks and Germans taken at Rafah.' As Robert Wilson recalled, 'among the prisoners was a German Major who was in charge of their machine guns, a magnificent, well-dressed figure. I said, "Good morning," to him and he replied in perfect English "Good morning to you – wasn't that a damned good scrap?" He had been at Oxford for three years just before war broke out.'[36]

The CMR reached Sheikh Zowaiid soon after 10 p.m. but, as Guy Powles explained,

the day's work was not yet finished. Horses had to be watered … it takes a long time to water two thousand animals at three small troughs. Horses once watered, the allotted camp sites were found, where rations and fodder had been dumped. After a few hours very welcome sleep, the Regiment saddled up and rode quietly back to camp at Masaid, watering the horses en-route at the 52nd Division troughs in … Wadi el Arish. The infantry gave the Division a splendid reception, each camp turning out and cheering as it rode past. Also, what was appreciated very much, they volunteered to man the pumps till all horses had been watered. The column arrived in camp about 2.30 p.m., tired but proud. In just forty eight hours it had covered over seventy miles, taken 1,450 prisoners, a battery of mountain guns and much other booty.[37]

The Anzac Mounted Division's field ambulances remained on the battlefield overnight to collect the last of the wounded, protected by two regiments of light horsemen. However, the New Zealand dressing station had been withdrawn at 5.20 p.m. so the stretcher-bearers and the regimental medical staffs had to evacuate the wounded without it. One hundred wounded men lay in an Australian dressing station 'with few blankets, no food, and no lights, all these conveniences having, in the confusion, gone back to Sheikh Zowaiid on the equipment camels…. All telephonic communication had accidentally been cut off, the enemy was close at hand, the night was a bitter one. Cold, hungry and hourly expecting capture, the wounded suffered severely.' With insufficient sand carts and sledges left behind for the wounded, and only a light screen between them and the advancing Turkish reinforcements, it seemed that capture was the most likely outcome for anyone still on the battlefield. Some of the casualties were worried that they would be abandoned but the medical staff assured them that they would stay with them, come what may. When a staff officer rode up in the early evening and ordered everyone to leave the battlefield within 10 minutes, abandoning any wounded who could not be moved immediately, the medics refused to go. Fortunately, the approaching enemy reinforcements stopped and then returned to Khan Yunis and Shellal. Extra sand carts were sent forward from Sheikh Zowaiid and the battlefield was finally cleared by 1.30 a.m. on 10 January. Later that day the Turkish wounded were also brought in.[38]

'Hun' prisoners captured at Rafah.

Most of the wounded men faced a four-hour journey in sand carts over a rough track to the casualty clearing station at Sheikh Zowaiid. At 11 a.m. the next day the casualties continued their journey to El Arish in camel cacolets. Those men who survived the evacuation were put on hospital trains at El Arish and moved back to hospitals in canal towns, or in Cairo.

Fred Dill was shot in the shoulder 10 minutes before the Turks surrendered. Dill recalled that he was placed on a stretcher and left out on the ground. At midnight, he was seen by a doctor, then put in a tent with others who were going to die. The next morning, when an orderly came around covering the faces of those who had died during the night, Dill asked him for water. 'He jumped a bit and said, "Oh, you're not dead yet?"' Dill's dressing was changed and he stayed in the tent for three more days before being evacuated by camel cacolet to El Arish: 'that was agony'.[39]

Kingston Hull was probably referring to this battle when he wrote:

It is wonderful sometimes how one can come through when bullets are coming thick, and yet at other times they may be not so bad and yet some poor chap gets one. The best way is to take your time when lying down, to keep well down. In the case of a shell it is – she will, she won't, she will, she won't – until it bursts and the suspense is over.[40]

145

Turkish cavalry and cameliers made a half-hearted attack on the rearguard early the next day but they were easily beaten off. The dead were buried on the battlefield, although some bodies stayed underground for only a short period. At dawn the local Bedouin searched the battlefield for anything of value. According to Australian historian Henry Gullett, the dead of both sides, and those wounded Turks still on the ground, were stripped of clothing and boots. Graves were opened and the contents rifled by the 'wretched natives'. This was the first time that most of the Anzacs had seen the Bedouin tribesmen at work on a battlefield: they were appalled and angered.[41]

At Magdhaba and Rafah, the Turks had left weak and immobile infantry garrisons with inadequate artillery support too far forward. On each occasion they lost an entire regiment. The Turkish 31st Regiment was destroyed at Rafah: 200 Turks were killed, and 162 wounded and 1473 unwounded prisoners (including 10 Germans) were captured. Most of the prisoners were Anatolian Turks, considered by the Anzacs to be better fighters than the mainly Arab defenders of Magdhaba. As Wilkie noted, 'In face of the terrific fire which was directed against them, they could frequently be observed exposing themselves to get a more deliberate aim.' According to Powles, 'The Turks were confident almost to the last that they could hold their position; and one captured officer admitted that he thought it was impossible for the attackers to succeed in the time available, and before the arrival of the Turkish reinforcements.' A captured German officer told New Zealand camelier Beethoven Algar that 'if he'd been in charge, we'd never have taken the place because they were really impregnable he reckoned, but the Turks forced them into surrendering'.[42]

Seventy-one Turks were killed and 415 wounded – three times their casualties at Magdhaba. In the Anzac Mounted Division, 42 men were killed in action and 242 were wounded. Chaytor wrote afterwards that the NZMR Brigade's casualties – 17 killed and 93 wounded – had been 'phenomenally light'. As Ted Andrews recalled, 'One … trooper killed that day was Gordon Abercrombie, right at the last trench we captured.... Also, Tpr. Ewen Elmslie was hit in a leg. We put a tourniquet on it, but he had to ride his horse out. By the time he got to hospital (El Arish) it had been left on too long, gangrene set in, and he died. It was so sad to see him go as well as Major Jim on Gallipoli, another sacrifice by this fine … family.'[43]

Twenty-three horses were killed in the Anzac division. In the New Zealand brigade nine horses were killed or subsequently destroyed, three went missing and four were wounded. Robert Tuke described the death of one horse in his section: 'We were all resting in a small dip in the ground holding our horses, when a bullet hit a horse's head and killed him. We were lying at the horse's feet, so when he was shot he rolled over three of us, and woke us up, as we were nearly asleep.'[44]

The New Zealanders received the lion's share of the credit for this last-minute victory in what some men called 'The Parade-ground Battle'. Chetwode stated that 'excellent as was the work of all the troops engaged, the part played by the New Zealand Brigade was outstanding. That the action terminated favourably was largely due to its dashing assault upon the Reduit, for from that moment Turkish resistance began to crack.'

> *It was New Zealand's day. The Brigade had advanced across grassy slopes, with no cover but an occasional clump of the Iris Lily, planted to show the boundary of a field. The covering fire from the machine guns, Lewis guns, and rifles was perfect, and was the great feature of the attack.... Another feature of the final charge was the spectacle of many of our men firing as they ran.*[45]

Chaytor was critical of the light horsemen, who, he thought, 'mostly dismounted too far from their objective and lost their drive long before they got close up – many men lay down and fired at long range instead of pressing on.... The Camel Corps had the same fault, but I understand that camels must be left a long way off.'[46] Some more junior participants criticised the method of attack.

> *Many of us held the opinion that the position could have been galloped in the dark before the Turks were aware of our presence; and probably with far fewer casualties than we suffered. The enemy had been taken too cheaply. It was thought that the appearance of horsemen right round him would bluff him into surrendering.... The result was we had no strength to press an attack anywhere in daylight. In the dark a bayonet advance against Magruntein would have settled the matter in 15 minutes.*[47]

Horsemen inspecting the captured trenches at Rafah.

The Sinai campaign had been fought and won by Australian, New Zealand and British horse- and camel-mounted troops. The British infantry divisions were unable to march far enough or fast enough to take a useful part in any of the desert battles. This was about to change: once the EEF entered Palestine and encountered better marching conditions for its infantry, and stiffer enemy resistance (divisions instead of regiments), the Anzac horsemen would become a smaller and smaller part of the strike force. The conditions under which the horsemen fought were also about to change, seemingly for the better. After El Arish, 'conditions for the horses were much better, with harder ground and some green fodder. Water was also much better. The stunts from here were longer, but easier on the horses.'[48]

7

Someone has blundered

Attack in Gaza seems to have failed. Awful mess. Somebody wants hanging.

FRED STERLING

_____

AFTER THE RAFAH battle, the New Zealanders rode back to the beach near El Arish. Tents were brought up by train and the men settled in for a well-earned rest period, interspersed with regular sporting fixtures. 'Whenever opportunity offered, the officers of the CMR and WMR were sure to play a football match. The rival teams tried conclusions on the beach at El Arish, when, after a most strenuous game, the Wellingtonians won.'[1]

East of El Arish 'the country was undulating; it was green, and horses tugged impatiently at their bits in their eagerness to taste grass once more. Around the patches of young crops, poppies showed in splashes of scarlet, and the horsemen passed a mud hut with melon vines and tomato plants thriving inside the sod wall enclosure. There were orchards of apricot trees laden with young fruit. Skylarks rose from beside the road and fluttered upwards, singing.… There was more life in the stunted scrub, and rough grasses grew in the hollows; there were even occasional fig trees and flocks of goats shepherded by ancient Bedouin.' The barley crops were out of bounds, but 'this did not seem to be understood by many of the horses'.[2]

After months of sinking into soft sand, the horses could now step out on the hard ground and the riders detected a new spring and energy in their mounts. At last, the mounted regiments could make the most of their mobility, the horse artillery could travel at the gallop for the first time and supply wagons and light cars could be used. The sleds and sand carts used to evacuate wounded men were supplemented, then replaced by motorised and horse-drawn ambulances, although the hated cacolets were retained for use in the hills of Palestine.[3]

At Gaza, the coastal plain is about 35 kilometres wide. Inland of a narrow coastal belt of sand dunes, the land between Khan Yunis and Gaza is flat or gently rolling, cut by numerous dry wadis. The largest is Wadi Ghazze, which reaches the sea about eight

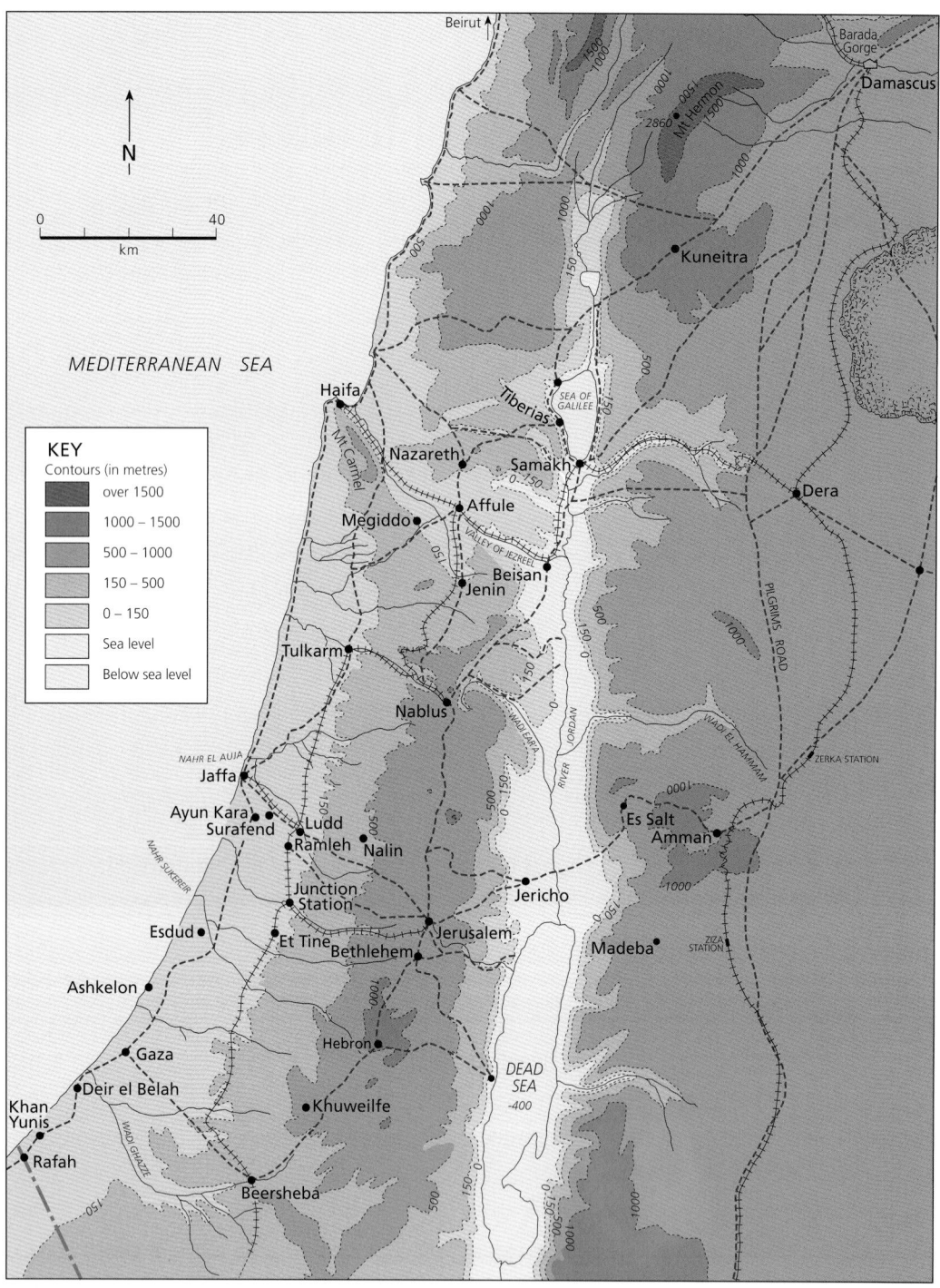

Map 8: Palestine, 1916.

kilometres south of Gaza. Its banks are steep and dangerous to come across unexpectedly. In early 1917 there were major crossing points on the coast, at Shellal and Esani (see Map 11, p.176). The inland crossing points were dominated by large earthen mounds on the banks of the wadi, marking the sites of ancient towns. On the far side of Wadi Ghazze, the land rose gently towards a long, low ridge, along which ran the Gaza–Beersheba road.

Gaza had sat astride the coastal invasion route between Egypt and Palestine for thousands of years. It was sited on rising ground at the edge of the coastal sand dunes, about three kilometres inland from the sea. Adjacent to Gaza was a long rise, known as the Es Sire Ridge to the south and (later) as Anzac Ridge to the north. Whoever held Ali Muntar, the highest point on the ridge, controlled Gaza. The village was surrounded on most sides by a band of fields, olive groves and gardens, separated by cactus hedges. Up to three metres high and five metres wide, these hedges were formidable barriers to men and horses. The village consisted of a chaotic maze of flat-topped mud-brick buildings around the tall minaret of the ancient mosque. By 1917 the pre-war population was much reduced, with a few hundred inhabitants rubbing shoulders with the Turkish garrison.[4]

The New Zealanders spent the first three weeks of February camped near El Arish, before moving up to Sheikh Zowaiid. On 23 February, Brigadier General Chaytor led the NZMR and 2nd LH brigades to the village of Khan Yunis, which had reportedly been abandoned by the Turks. The stunt also aimed to capture Sheikh Ali el Hirsch, a resident who was alleged to be a Turkish spy. After a shaky start at dawn, when the horses of the advance guard got loose and galloped wildly through Brigade Headquarters, the village was surrounded. The suspect was not there, but strong Turkish forces were, so the operation was broken off at 7.30 a.m. Ten Turks and five armed Arabs were killed, along with one New Zealander. A few days later, the Turks did evacuate Khan Yunis, withdrawing to a new line along Wadi Ghazze anchored at Shellal. The Desert Column occupied Khan Yunis on 28 February.

On 5 March, as the EEF was about to attack them at Shellal, the Turks withdrew again, this time across Wadi Ghazze to a new defensive line between Gaza and Hareira. When horsemen rode up to the abandoned enemy defences, they discovered several rows of horse traps. These cone-shaped pits, about 1.5 metres in diameter at ground level, each had a sharpened wooden stake set in the bottom. After two weeks at Sheikh Zowaiid, the Anzacs moved up to a new camp site on the Rafah battlefield. When Harry Judge visited the graves of New Zealanders, he was angered to find that 'the Bedouin had dug up their bodies and stripped them, and had not even re-interred them'.[5]

While the troops waited for 'the heads' to come up with the next plan, they relaxed on the beach at Rafah. Life was almost pleasant for a while, as Walter Macfarlane recorded.

Friday 9 March 1917: On camel escort after breakfast ... went to YMCA, bought biscuits and chocolate. Two Taubes over, anti-aircraft [guns] shelled them but did not get a hit.... Played the CYC this afternoon after stables, with four of our men away they only beat us 6-0. Had a bathe in sea in afternoon, one before stables and another later after football. Warmest day we have had for months.[6]

The Desert Column's First Spring Meeting (also known as the Rafah Races) was held on 21 March 1917 at the site of the Rafah battle. The course encircled the old Turkish Reduit, which served as the grandstand.

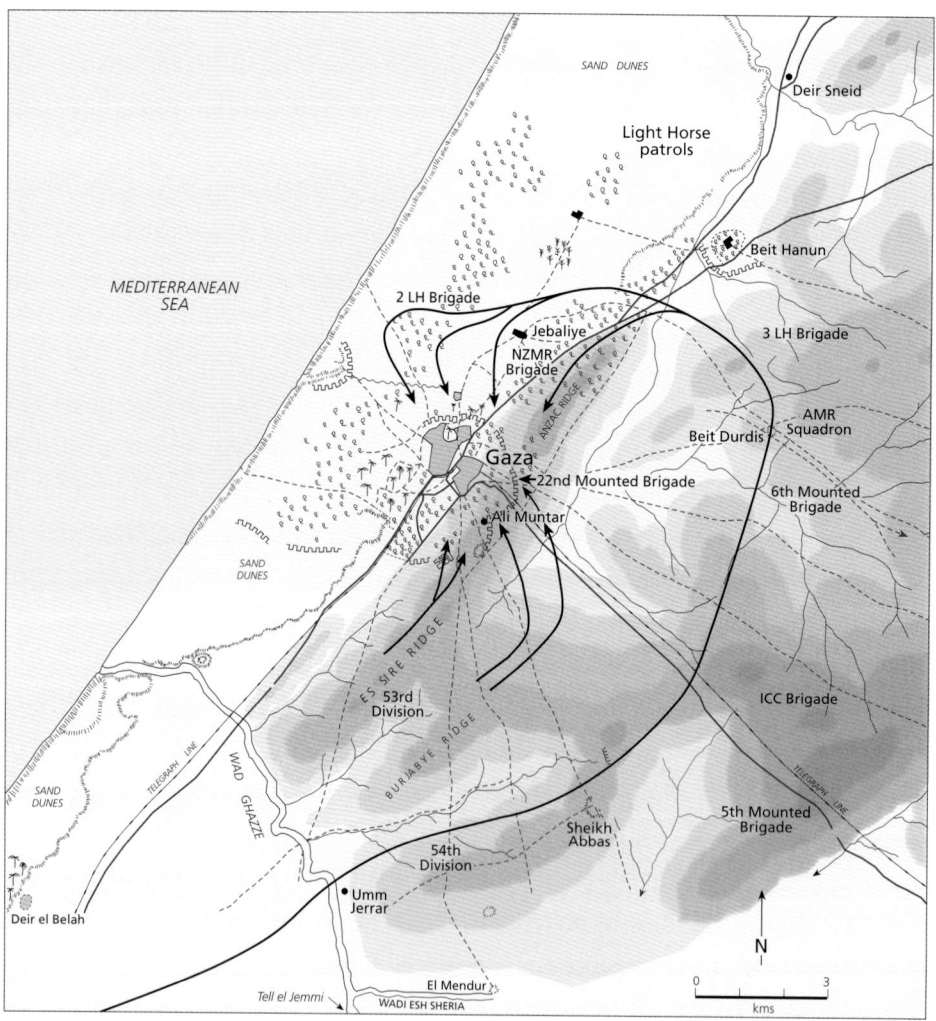

Map 9: First Battle of Gaza.

As much of the usual paraphernalia of a racecourse as resources allowed was recreated in the desert – an enclosed paddock, totalizator enclosure, jumps, a marked course – trophies were ordered from Cairo, and a programme printed. General Chauvel gave a cup for the Anzac Champion Steeplechase open to all ranks of the Desert Column; the Sinai Grand National was won by a horse wounded earlier on that very battlefield, and the Jerusalem Scurry, the ninth and last event of the day (for mules), was won over five furlongs by No Name for the 2nd Battalion Sikh Pioneers! There was no charge for admission, but over £200 was made for charities.[7]

The senior New Zealand medical officer earned 'undying fame and a win for New Zealand, by pulling off the 'Promised Land Stakes' with a little horse called 'Maori King' (alias 'The Rat') from Canterbury.'[8]

Political changes in Great Britain at the end of 1916 had a dramatic effect on the campaign in the Middle East. A new prime minister, David Lloyd George, came into 10 Downing Street keen to gain a quick military success that would bolster flagging morale at home. Seeing little likelihood of that occurring on the Western Front, Lloyd George looked eastwards. Encouraged by the EEF's success in 1916, he thought the Turks in Palestine and Mesopotamia were ripe for the plucking. He encouraged the War Office to come up with plans to defeat them, but the generals convinced him that the major theatres of war had to take priority. In December 1916 Lieutenant General Murray was told to expect no reinforcements – he had asked for two more infantry divisions and some extra mounted troops – and not to begin large-scale offensive operations into Palestine before the autumn of 1917. Murray decided to capture Gaza immediately, to secure a good start line on the far side of Wadi Ghazze for these later operations.[9]

In order to obtain some of the additional fighting men that he wanted, Murray reorganised Dobell's Eastern Force. He brought the 52nd (Lowland) and 53rd (Welsh) infantry divisions across Sinai to join the 54th (East Anglian) Division at El Arish, and created the 74th (Yeomanry) Division from dismounted British cavalry brigades. Murray also expanded his mounted force to two divisions. Major General Henry Hodgson, a British cavalryman, took command of the new Imperial Mounted Division, which consisted of the 3rd and 4th Light Horse brigades and the 5th and 6th (Yeomanry) Mounted brigades. The 1st and 2nd LH brigades and the NZMR Brigade remained under General Chauvel's command in the Anzac Mounted Division, where they were joined by the 22nd (Yeomanry) Mounted Brigade. Lieutenant General Chetwode's Desert Column now comprised the two mounted divisions and the 53rd Division.[10]

General Dobell allocated the Gaza operation to the 22,000-strong Desert Column (reinforced with the 54th Division), promising Chetwode other Eastern Force troops if he needed them. General Chauvel's Anzac Mounted Division (without the 1st LH Brigade) was ordered to encircle Gaza to prevent the escape of the garrison. The responsibility for holding off the enemy reserves further inland was given to the Imperial Mounted Division (without the 4th LH Brigade). Once the Gaza garrison was isolated by the mounted troops, the 53rd Division, and one brigade from the 54th Division, would launch 12,000 men against Ali Muntar. H-Hour for this part of the attack was 8 a.m. Chauvel was warned that his troops might be needed to assist the British infantry by attacking Gaza from the north. The assault divisions lacked sufficient transport – horse-drawn wagons, camels and light trucks – to operate away from the railway for more than 24 hours, so Gaza had to be captured within one day.[11] Z-Day for the attack was 26 March 1917.

British intelligence was wrong in its assessment that the Turks would withdraw from Gaza if they were attacked. In fact, they had decided to stand and fight on the Gaza–Beersheba line. Gaza was initially defended by two infantry battalions, totalling about 2000 men, and the nearest reinforcements were about 20 kilometres away at Sheria and Jemmame (see Map 11, p.176). After German air reconnaissance convinced Kress that the British were about to attack Gaza, he reinforced the garrison, increasing its strength to about 3500 rifles, 42 machine guns and 20 field guns. The Turkish 53rd Division, stationed near Jaffa in case of a British amphibious landing there, was warned to be prepared to march towards Gaza if it was attacked. The Gaza garrison commander was ordered to hold out in any attack until reinforcements arrived.[12]

At 2.30 a.m. on 25 March, the NZMR Brigade and the 22nd Mounted Brigade rode from their camping grounds on the beach to Wadi Ghazze. Their task was to provide security while the assault force commanders selected their crossing points. As Fred Sterling recorded in his diary, 'It was as dark as Hades and very still, except for the roar of the breakers on the shore. Occasionally, a horse would neigh or a man cuss as his horse floundered into soft sand.' After a number of crossing points were identified and secretly marked, the New Zealanders rode back to Deir el Belah. As the sun rose, Sterling saw a 'splendid sight'.

Plains that we had left [the night before] with hardly anything upon them except a few cattle, sheep, and Bedouin, were now massed with troops almost as far as the dust would let one look. Huge trains of transport camels, limbers, wagons, guns, and thousands of moving, perspiring men. Drums were beating and Tommies singing, while the screech of bagpipes added tone to the whole picture.[13]

Gaza, photographed after its eventual capture.

The men spent the rest of the day resting and preparing for the night's work that lay ahead.

The night of 25–26 March was cold, still and very dark when the 53rd Division began its approach march from Deir el Belah at 1 a.m. on 26 March. Ninety minutes later, General Chauvel led the Anzac Mounted Division, the Imperial Mounted Division and the ICC Brigade towards their crossing points on Wadi Ghazze. The strength of the NZMR Brigade that day was 1773 men and 2064 horses.[14]

A heavy fog descended before the regiments reached the wadi, limiting visibility to less than 20 metres. According to Fred Sterling, 'the cold of it seemed to bite right into my bones'. After detouring around an infantry unit that had inadvertently camped across the track, the Anzac division reached the Umm Jerrar crossing point. The leading light horse regiment crossed quickly and safely at around 5 a.m., despite the darkness and the murk. 'Men could see those next to them, and the rumps of the horses immediately in front. They moved slowly across the wide and broken approaches to the wadi, and halted many times until the column was safely on the other side. Silence was broken only by the click of horseshoes on the metal lying loosely on the scaly hillsides.'[15] Ion Idriess described the atmosphere.

The ride was a constant stopping and starting, with our horse's muzzle rammed up against the horse's rump in front. No talking, no smoking, just darkness and fog and muffled hooves – the smell of horses – the expectancy of a volley, the feeling of unseen life all dense around us everywhere. We wondered where the hell we were; wondered if we might ride into the great fortress of Ali Muntar itself.... Occasionally our horses slithered down ravines so precipitous that they could never have faced them in daylight. All a man could do was lean back in the saddle and hold his breath as his horse's ears disappeared down into the fog.[16]

After pausing for 30 minutes while the guides oriented their compasses, the mounted regiments rode on into the damp gloom. At 6 a.m. the 2nd LH Brigade was approaching Sheikh Abbas, where the Australian scouts surprised two German aircraft on the ground. They galloped towards them but were too late to prevent them from taking off. The ground crews were captured, but the aircraft returned to machine-gun the leading squadrons.[17]

The widely dispersed regiments rode on quickly, galloping when necessary to capture enemy patrols. They were machine-gunned from the air several more times, with little effect other than a slight delay each time men dismounted to shoot back. At 9 a.m., 10 wagons and 30 Germans were captured on the Gaza–Beersheba road. Soon afterwards, the Anzac Division reached Beit Durdis, which was still shrouded in fog. Communications via telegraph and radio were established with Chetwode's HQ, although the radio transmitter was jammed throughout the day by a more powerful Turkish device in Gaza. After a short halt, the 2nd LH Brigade pushed on towards the coast, and at 11 a.m. the 7th ALH Regiment reached Jebaliye and the nearby seashore, closing the ring around Gaza.

Light horse patrols and an armoured car patrol were sent to the north towards Beit Hanun and Deir Sneid to watch for enemy reinforcements. Almost immediately, the 6th ALH Regiment captured the commander of the Turkish 53rd Division, as he drove in a carriage towards Gaza. The 'disgusted general' was abandoned by his escort and quickly surrounded 'by a body of grinning, unkempt Australians on their great steaming horses'.

His ... Kaiser moustache was continually a-twitch, as vainly he turned his back on the unkempt troopers who threatened him at every angle with all breed of cameras. When he was taken to the Old Brig. he complained bitterly of our disgusting coarseness. He demanded some of us at least should be shot.[18]

According to Guy Powles, the Turkish officer was disappointed that his servant had not been captured with him.[19]

While the NZMR Brigade waited at Beit Durdis, Chaytor dispatched two AMR squadrons eastwards towards Huj to keep watch for enemy reinforcements. Pools of water were found in several nearby wadis so many of the horses were watered while they waited. The 22nd Mounted Brigade and Chauvel's headquarters also stopped at Beit Durdis for a few hours.

The Imperial Mounted Division crossed Wadi Ghazze behind the Anzac division and took up outpost positions between the Gaza–Beersheba road and Beit Durdis. The ICC Brigade extended this line south to the banks of Wadi Ghazze. Behind them, the 54th Division crossed the wadi and dug in along the Sheikh Abbas Ridge.

All was now ready for the 53rd Division to begin its attack on Ali Muntar and Gaza. Unfortunately, the division had trouble crossing the wadi in the fog and the leading brigades were not across until well after dawn. By 9 a.m. they were ready to begin the assault along the Es Sire Ridge but the artillery preparation was slow and there was some confusion about the exact locations of the assault forces. Chetwode and Dobell became concerned at these delays and at 11.45 a.m. General Chetwode ordered the commander of the 53rd Division to attack at once. He complied, but precious hours had already been lost.

The mounted troops at Beit Durdis watched the infantry attack begin in the early afternoon. They marvelled at the courage and discipline of the English and Welsh

AUTHOR'S COLLECTION

This photograph is believed to show the two guns captured by the WMR in Gaza.

New Zealanders resting in the shade. The newspaper is the Feilding Star.

infantrymen as they advanced uphill in broad daylight, with no cover and inadequate artillery support, against well-sited Turkish machine guns and under heavy shrapnel fire from artillery batteries in Gaza. Hundreds of men were shot down and it seemed to the watchers that the infantry attack was failing.

Colonel Kress had correctly assessed the scale of the enemy attack by 8 a.m. He immediately ordered the reserve 3rd and 16th Divisions to march to the relief of the Gaza garrison and the 3rd Cavalry Division in Beersheba was put on the march towards Khan Yunis. The leading regiment of the Turkish 53rd Division, whose commander the Australians had captured that morning, could not reach Gaza from Jaffa for 24 hours. The Gaza commander was once again ordered to hold out to the last man.[20]

A Turkish prisoner told interrogators that the Gaza garrison was much larger than the two battalions that Chetwode believed to be there and that reinforcements had been requested by the Turkish commander at 10 a.m. Chetwode decided to give the 53rd Division some help. At 1 p.m., he placed the Imperial Mounted Division under General Chauvel's orders, and told him to use his own division to attack Gaza. At 2.30 p.m. the New Zealand brigade was warned to prepare to move into Gaza. Chauvel issued his final orders for the assault 45 minutes later. At 4 p.m. the 2nd LH Brigade was to attack southwards between the sea and Jebaliye. The New Zealanders were to advance between the road and Anzac

Ridge; the Yeomanry regiments of the 22nd Mounted Brigade would move into Gaza along the Beit Durdis track.[21]

The horsemen began their advance into Gaza on time. The Turks in the town were concentrated to the south and south-east against the British infantry: initially this allowed the mounted regiments to make good progress. The New Zealanders galloped from Jebaliye across an open valley and seized the undefended northern spur of Anzac Ridge, before dismounting and advancing on foot along the ridge and towards the village. 'We had to gallop some distance across a flat intersected with ditches and low mud walls,' Harry Judge recorded in his diary, 'and we jumped these in great style, and, as far as I know, no one came to grief.' The WMR was on the right, the CMR on the left, with the AMR in support. Brigade HQ established itself on a knoll (later known as Chaytor's Hill) on the northern part of the ridge. As they advanced up an open valley, the New Zealanders came under fire from Turks concealed behind rows of cactus hedges in the valley, and from Anzac Ridge. One Canterbury squadron advanced quickly along the lightly defended crest of the ridge, reaching the abandoned enemy redoubt at Ali Muntar at 6.40 p.m., just as British infantry arrived from the south.[22]

At 4.25 p.m., the WMR captured a fully equipped Turkish field hospital. The Wellingtons worked their way through a thick belt of olive groves and cactus hedges to reach the outer streets of Gaza. Having hacked their way through the cactus hedges with their bayonets they fought the enemy at close quarters. On the left of the Wellington line, Lieutenants Cecil Allison and William Foley led two Wellington troops across a shallow lagoon to clear a Turkish trench near a cemetery. Sixteen defenders who put up their hands were captured but an equal number who continued fighting were bayoneted by the New Zealanders.[23]

The centre of the Wellington line was forced to halt briefly on the outskirts of the cemetery. To their right, near a small lake, two enemy field guns could be seen firing from behind the cover of thick cactus hedges. Major John Sommerville's squadron captured the guns, bayoneting or shooting 48 defenders in the process. A determined Turkish counter-attack launched to recapture the guns was defeated by the New Zealanders and by the 7th ALH Regiment, which fired machine guns into the flank of the Turks as they charged the New Zealanders. The Wellingtons used the captured guns to help fight off this attack, then consolidated their line along the edge of the cemetery.[24]

A Turkish strongpoint in a group of houses about 70 metres away held up further progress.

[Corporal Claude] Rouse got [a captured] gun pointing towards the red house, put the trail

159

against a telegraph post, opened the breech, twiddled away with the controls until he could see the building through the barrel, then in with a round and let go. The shell ploughed up the ground in front, the trail jerked off the pole and the gun ran back over the crew, scattering them.[25]

After three or four rounds were fired into the building, 20 terrified Turks emerged from the dust and rubble with their hands in the air. One projectile knocked down so many buildings that Rouse said that the New Zealanders had created a new street in Gaza.[26]

To the west of the New Zealanders, the 2nd LH Brigade was making slower progress through the sandhills and cactus hedges. This delay exposed the right flank of the WMR and the regiment prepared to meet a counter-attack there. The officers armed themselves with captured Mauser rifles to assist in the defence of the captured ground and the guns. The Turkish assault never came and spare horses from the machine gun squadron were sent forward to bring out the captured guns. As the Wellingtons fought on in the gathering gloom, a few men of the 2nd LH Brigade came up behind them. Assuming that anyone in front of them must be Turkish, the Australians mistakenly opened fire on the New Zealanders, forcing them to take cover.[27]

The British cavalrymen of the 22nd Mounted Brigade reached the outskirts of Gaza

New Zealanders watering their horses in Wadi Ghazze during the Second Battle of Gaza. The horses are watered from troughs to prevent the wadi water becoming muddied.

along the Beit Durdis track, encountering little opposition. Meanwhile, the infantrymen of the 53rd Division had made slow but steady progress up the Es Sire Ridge towards Ali Muntar. Their casualties were heavy but, with New Zealand assistance, Ali Muntar was in British hands by nightfall. As darkness descended, the horsemen in and around Gaza were in high spirits. They believed that the enemy was beaten and that the town was theirs for the taking. The Anzacs confidently expected to complete the capture of the town and its garrison at dawn the next day.

At dusk, Turkish reinforcements finally began to make their presence felt. Some leading elements came within range of Aucklander Fred Sterling's outpost squadron at 4 p.m.

We could see them through our glasses being unloaded from a train. They formed up amid the green barley, and then spread out and made for our thin outpost line. We got our machine guns to work upon them at long range ... They seemed to have hosts of machine guns, which they kept up a ceaseless cackle with. We hung on and rattled away at them. The affair was fast assuming a serious aspect, when suddenly they called a halt. I guess if only they had known how few were opposed to them, all finished would have been our lot. We could not afford to blaze away recklessly, for our ammunition would not stand the strain.[28]

News of these reinforcements alarmed Chetwode and Dobell. They also believed that Chauvel's horses had not been watered since crossing Wadi Ghazze before dawn and that the only water was inside Gaza. They also thought that Ali Muntar, the key to Gaza, was beyond their grasp.

The generals were wrong on all counts: the Gaza garrison was on the point of collapse, the enemy relief forces were about to be ordered to halt, many of Chauvel's horses had had a drink during the day (the Anzacs were in possession of several good wells) and EEF actually held Ali Muntar. Nonetheless, Chetwode acted on his fears and at 5 p.m. ordered the slow-moving support elements of the mounted brigades back to Wadi Ghazze. An hour later, he began to withdraw all the mounted troops. The infantry divisions were ordered to pull back to a defensive position on the enemy side of the wadi.[29]

Two Australian sources claim that Chaytor would not withdraw his men until he received a written order. Ted Andrews wrote that Meldrum 'flatly refused to move until he had accounted for everyone . . . . One of our boys was badly wounded, his thigh bone broken by a bullet. We had to use his rifle as a splint and his puttees as bandages, but he died before we got him far.'[30]

The extraction of the mounted regiments was a difficult and protracted affair. The 7th

ALH Regiment was six kilometres away from its horses, and all the regiments were badly mixed up in the streets and gardens of Gaza. The horse artillery, the captured guns, the prisoners and the wounded men were sent back first, under escort. Once they were clear at around 7.45 p.m., the mounted riflemen and light horsemen began to trudge back to their horses. The exhausted Turks apparently did not notice them go.[31]

The Anzacs were despondent and angry but not too upset to prevent hundreds of them from falling asleep on their horses as the animals plodded back to Wadi Ghazze. A khamsin wind blew up during the night, increasing the trials of the riders and their mounts. Fred Sterling 'marched all night, cold as charity, dark as Hades'. Packs of howling jackals added to the unpleasantness of the night. On the way out, the Wellingtons halted for a brief rest and quickly lit fires to boil the billies for a cup of tea. It was then discovered that they had halted right next to Ali Muntar; fortunately, it was unoccupied. The fires were hastily extinguished and the withdrawal continued. By 2 a.m. on 27 March, the Anzac Mounted Division had passed through Beit Durdis and General Hodgson put the Imperial Mounted Division on the march behind them towards Wadi Ghazze. By dawn, all of the mounted troops were on the home bank of the wadi.[32]

During the night, the true situation in Gaza gradually became clear to the British commanders. Lieutenant General Dobell sent orders for the 53rd Division to hold fast and ordered reinforcements forward. The division's commander apparently did not receive these orders and, not knowing that the 54th Division was covering his right flank, believed that his men were exposed to Turkish counter-attack. At 10.30 p.m. he ordered his brigades to pull back across Wadi Ghazze. By 4 a.m. on 27 March, the evacuation of the enemy side of the wadi was complete.

An hour later, as the sun rose on a new day, Chetwode realised that the Turkish reinforcements had stopped and that all of his own forces were behind Wadi Ghazze. He made an attempt to reoccupy Ali Muntar and other key positions before the Turks could. Small forces re-entered some enemy trenches but were quickly driven out again by Turkish counter-attacks.

Fred Sterling noted, 'Attack in Gaza seems to have failed. Awful mess. Somebody wants hanging.' James McCarroll agreed: 'I can't understand what has happened. Someone has blundered.' According to Gullett, the withdrawal from Gaza was 'one of the sorriest movements undertaken by Australians and New Zealanders during the war'. In Nicol's words, the New Zealanders 'were very tired, but even fatigue was forgotten in their disgust at being pulled out of a great victory. Their spirits went down to zero, and a period of dark depression was ushered in.'[33]

His Majesty's Land Ship Kia Ora, *one of the tanks used in the Second Battle of Gaza.*

Defeat had been snatched from the jaws of victory and the first Battle of Gaza was over. The Turks lost about 300 men killed, 1000 wounded and 1000 prisoners. The Anzac Mounted Division captured half of these prisoners, including a divisional commander, and the two field guns. In the EEF 523 men were killed, nearly 3000 were wounded and 250 became prisoners of the Turks. Six men in the Anzac division died and 64 were wounded. Twenty-five horses in the division were killed.[34]

The War Diary states that the NZMR Brigade lost two men killed and 29 wounded. One of the fatalities was Arthur Fitzherbert, a 64-year-old trooper from the Rangitikei province. Unable to enlist locally because of his advanced years, Fitzherbert went south to try his luck and managed to convince recruiters in Canterbury that he was 40 years old. After reaching Egypt late in 1915, he wangled a transfer to the Wellington regiment, where he ended up in the same section as his son, also named Arthur. During the dismounted advance into Gaza, 'Dad' Fitzherbert, as he was known in the regiment, was shot in the neck. He carried on until blood loss forced him to seek medical attention. On his way back to the dressing station, he stopped to help another wounded man and was struck by shrapnel. Because he could not be moved, he was bandaged and left where he fell. He insisted on keeping his rifle with him. He died later that day.[35]

General Chetwode wrote to Chauvel to thank him 'for the very fine work accomplished by the Division under your command ... and especially for the skilful way in which you withdrew the cavalry in the dark after their long day's work against the enemy'. After asking Chauvel to pass on to his men his admiration of their 'splendid behaviour before the enemy', Chetwode praised their delaying of 'greatly superior' enemy reinforcements. 'Two hours more daylight would have enabled the cavalry to finish the job, and it must have been most disheartening to your men, after such a fine effort, to have the prize snatched from their grasp by darkness. The harder the task I give the mounted troops of the Desert Column, the better they carry it out, and no man could ask to command finer troops.'[36]

In his next dispatches to London, General Murray misleadingly claimed that a great success had been achieved, and that the Turks in Gaza had barely escaped annihilation. After greatly exaggerating the number of enemy casualties, Murray told the War Office that his troops were delighted with themselves and that none of them had been hard-pressed during the battle. 'It is proved conclusively that in the open the enemy have no chance of success against our troops, but they are very tenacious in prepared positions. In the open our mounted troops simply do what they like with them.' Newspaper reports of 'A Brilliant Victory' and '20,000 Turks Defeated' hit the streets in Great Britain within days. When these headlines eventually reached the despondent EEF troops, they were amazed and annoyed. Had they missed something?[37]

When read alongside the good news from Baghdad, which had been captured from the Turks in March 1917, General Murray's dispatch suggested that the Turkish Army was on its last legs and that an immediate advance by the EEF into Palestine stood a good chance of success. The War Office estimated that fewer than 30,000 enemy troops stood between Murray and Jerusalem. He was told to finish the job at Gaza, then to go for the Holy City. Murray had backed himself into a corner: he actually had little hope of success if he attacked Gaza again but he had no choice but to obey.[38]

After the Gaza battle, the men and horses of the NZMR Brigade spent several periods resting on the beach at Deir el Belah. At around this time, each squadron handed in its single Lewis gun and received four new Hotchkiss automatic rifles.[39] While Murray grappled with the problem of how to capture Gaza, the horsemen patrolled towards Sheria and Beersheba and dug strongpoints on important features. Each night, a regiment from each brigade rode out to form an outpost line on high ground. Guy Powles described this as 'a most difficult and tedious operation'.

Colonel Findlay watching helplessly as his regiment's horses are bombed during the Second Battle of Gaza.

The Regiment would leave camp after dark with instructions to hold a line detailed on a map. Knowing nothing of the general formation of the country, on reaching the appointed place it was very hard to place the posts in the best positions, or where they could do most good in the event of being attacked. Usually two squadrons held the line in a series of detached posts, while the remaining squadron was held in readiness to support. Mounted patrols, each consisting of five or six men, were sent out at intervals during the night, patrolling, in open country, for two or three miles to our front.[40]

General Murray decided to renew the attack directly against Gaza. Beersheba was known to be lightly held but he believed that the lack of water ruled out an assault by the EEF at that end of the enemy's line. His own railway ran along the Mediterranean coast, so that was where he had to attack again. Unfortunately, he faced a very different situation from that encountered in March. A dense network of Turkish trenches now laced the ground in front of Gaza, transforming it into a fortress. A series of strong redoubts was built along the high ground in front of the Gaza–Beersheba road. Although not linked with continuous trenches, they were well sited to dominate the long, gently rising slopes in front of, and between, them. Apart from scattered crops of barley, there was no cover on any approach to the enemy positions. For the first time, belts of barbed wire and overhead cover protected many of the Turkish redoubts.

The Turkish reinforcements that had started moving towards Gaza during the first battle did not return to their reserve locations. The 3rd Division now defended Gaza, the

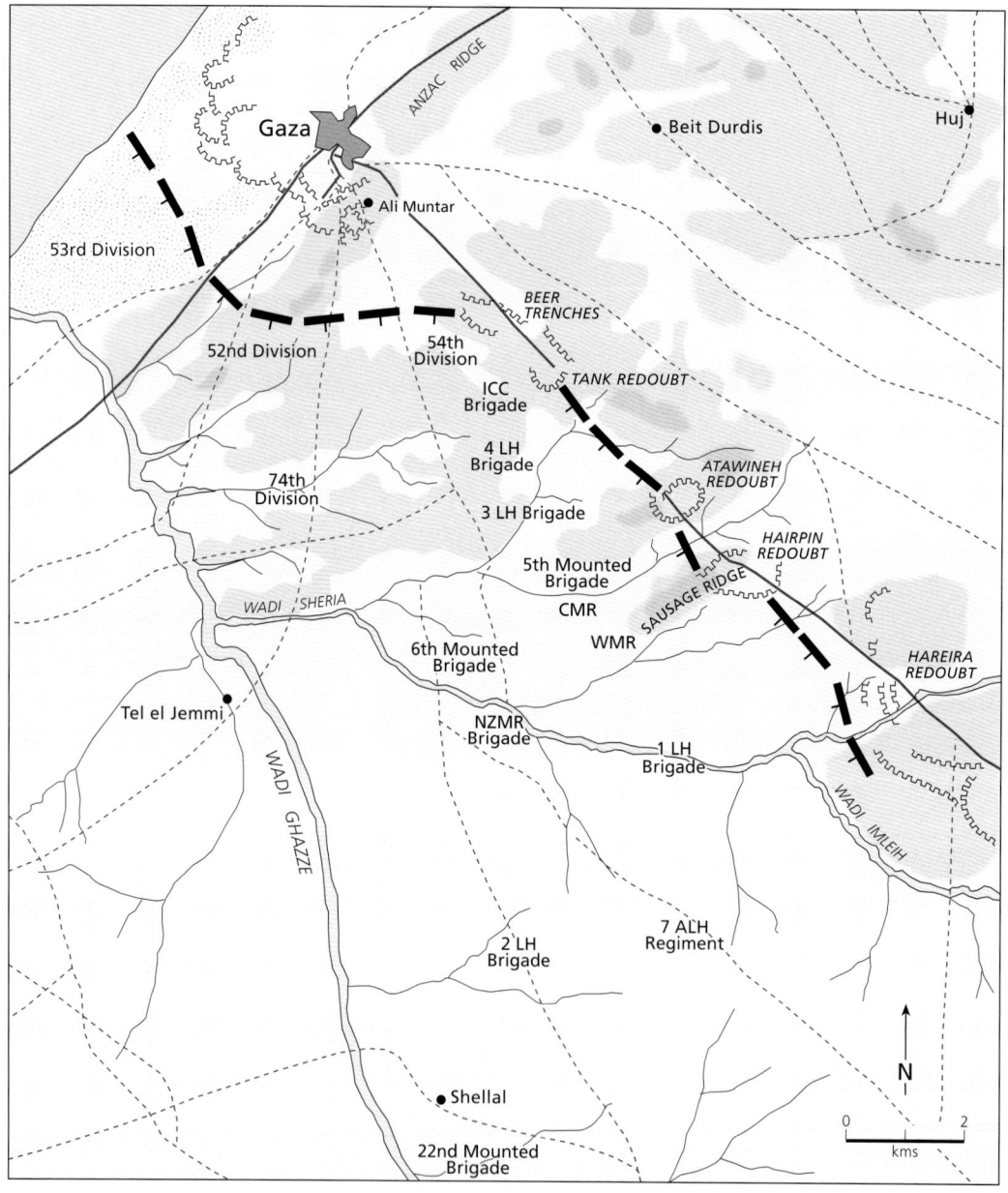

Map 10: Second Battle of Gaza.

reinforced 53rd Division covered the centre of the line and the 16th Division was centred on the Atawineh and Hareira redoubts. The 3rd Cavalry Division was held in reserve near Huj. This time, no undefended gaps were left for the EEF's mounted troops to ride through. The line from Sheria to Beersheba was thinly held and a single infantry regiment and a few guns defended Beersheba. In all, about 18,000 Turks occupied the defensive line between Gaza and Tel el Sheria;100 guns and 86 machine guns covered all approaches. As the Turks perfected their defences, German scouting aircraft flew overhead, informing their commanders about EEF activity.[41]

These enemy preparations ruled out a repeat of the tactics adopted for the first Gaza battle. What was needed now was a deliberate, massed infantry assault in the Western Front style, supported by heavy artillery, eight tanks and 4000 gas shells. Murray decided to use all four of his infantry divisions, with the mounted troops protecting their right flank. After a heavy artillery and naval bombardment, the infantry would attack Gaza, Ali Muntar and the western redoubts. The Desert Column, now consisting entirely of mounted troops – the Anzac and Imperial Mounted divisions and the ICC Brigade – was to protect the right of the infantry divisions by holding the Turkish defenders of the Atawineh and Hareira redoubts in place. Part of the mounted force was to be held in reserve, ready to pursue the enemy if he withdrew, or to envelop Gaza from the north.[42]

The Anzac Mounted Division was to 'demonstrate against … Hareira, in such a manner as to prevent the enemy there from detaching troops towards Gaza'. The demonstration was to be conducted on horseback; Chauvel was told not to launch a dismounted attack. The NZMR Brigade was ordered to protect the right flank of the division against any Turkish attack from the direction of Beersheba. If the enemy broke and ran, the Anzac Mounted Division was to pursue him. As it was thought likely that the Turks would retaliate to the use of poison gas by using it themselves, gas masks were issued to the horsemen in March.[43]

The attack was scheduled to begin on 17 April. In the first phase of the battle, the infantry divisions were to secure an advanced position close enough to the enemy defences for the EEF's artillery to reach them. After a day's interval, the main attack on the Turkish defensive line was to begin. With around 35,000 troops, including 11,000 mounted men, and 170 guns, Dobell and Chetwode were very confident of success. As Chetwode told Murray, 'If one division plus a brigade could do what they did on the 26th [of March] with only the amount of reconnaissance possible in what was almost a battle of encounter, our deliberate preparations and extra gun power should make the matter very safe.'[44]

The infantry divisions crossed Wadi Ghazze in the pre-dawn darkness on 17 April and moved up to their start lines, while the mounted forces rode out to their assembly areas to the south-east. The NZMR Brigade led the Anzac Mounted Division from Deir el Belah to Wadi Ghazze near Shellal. 'We marched all night,' Sterling wrote, 'and the dew fell like rain.' As they crossed the wadi, the horsemen were machine-gunned from a defensive position on the far bank and bombed from the air. The divisional engineers had a wagon carrying about a tonne of explosives, which was parked amid the moving columns and the watering horses in the wadi. Had a bomb hit this target, the resulting explosion would have killed or injured hundreds of New Zealanders and their horses.[45] As it was, bombs killed three men and 30 horses in the Anzac division. At dawn the Anzac Mounted Division was at Shellal, the Imperial Mounted Division at Tel el Jemmi. After watering their horses at Shellal, three of the Anzac division's brigades rode towards Hareira to begin the demonstration.

A hill crowned by a Turkish machine gun post overlooked the ford near Shellal. After the assault troops had moved past, the remains of a 1500-year-old mosaic were found under the post. The 'Shellal Mosaic' was excavated and taken to the Australian War Memorial in Canberra, where it is currently on display. Under the mosaic was a burial chamber containing a skeleton, which an enthusiastic padre thought belonged to Saint George. When he cabled Divisional HQ, 'Have found the bones of a saint', the message

AUTHOR'S COLLECTION

The Jewish Memorial to the Anzacs who fought at Gaza in 1917.

somehow ended up in Cairo. The EEF Records Office replied, 'Send full name, No. and Regiment of Trooper Saint.'[46]

The infantry brigades closed up on the enemy positions in front of Gaza and along the Gaza–Beersheba road without difficulty, although their casualties were not light. They dug in, protected themselves with barbed wire, then bought the artillery forward. Three hundred casualties were sustained in the entire EEF.

Further east the Desert Column also achieved its tasks easily. The Anzac division pushed close up to the Hareira Redoubt but the Turks did not react. Fred Sterling's AMR squadron helped to drive away the Turkish screen, then settled down to outpost duty.

About 1 p.m. we had pushed out as far as was healthful, so took up an outpost line, and sat or slept away the remainder of the day. When my turn on observation post duty came, I could see old Jacko, fairly strong in force, watching us from a high ridge about two miles away. His nearer posts kept sniping away, but all his lead fell short.

Enemy aircraft machine-gunned the New Zealanders during the day but caused no injuries. At dusk the mounted divisions pulled back across Wadi Ghazze, leaving a brigade of Yeomanry cavalry in an outpost line to watch the enemy. As Sterling's squadron rode off, it was fired upon by the Turks. He described seeing the red muzzle flashes from their rifles in the deepening darkness, and watching the bullets striking the ground around the horses' feet.[47]

The next day, the Turkish positions were bombarded from land and sea. The British infantry divisions remained in place, building up their ammunition and water stocks for the next part of the battle, while the mounted divisions repeated the previous day's activities without incident. The enemy was inactive throughout the day, although aircraft hunted, unsuccessfully, for the Anzac horses. So far, all had gone well.

The final phase of the attack began on 19 April. The infantry divisions, reinforced by dismounted men from the ICC Brigade and the Imperial Mounted Division, advanced against the enemy defences along a front of about 10 kilometres. The assaults were preceded by a heavy artillery bombardment, including poison gas shells, and supported by the eight obsolescent tanks. The Anzac Mounted Division was ordered to cover the right flank of the Imperial Mounted Division when it attacked the Atawineh Redoubt. As it marched overnight to be in position at dawn, the New Zealand brigade got itself completely lost: at one point the advance guard caught up with the rearguard.[48]

The infantry assaults were beaten back with heavy losses. Those tanks that did not break down or get stuck were destroyed and the poison gas shells were useless. The artillery fire was wholly inadequate to smash a way through the Turkish defences. Few men in the unsupported infantry battalions made it to the enemy trenches alive. By dusk, all the infantry assaults had ground to a halt in the face of heavy artillery and machine gun fire and fierce Turkish counter-attacks.

The mounted troops enjoyed no more success than the infantry, although their casualties were much lighter. In the Anzac division, the two light horse brigades advanced towards the Hareira Redoubt and to the east. The 22nd Mounted Brigade protected the wells at Shellal and the NZMR Brigade was held in reserve, ready to push through any gap into the Turkish rear areas. The Imperial Mounted Division had a bad day. Hodgson's brigades began a dismounted advance against the Atawineh Redoubt at 6.30 a.m.

> A barley crop, gay with red poppies, covered the slopes; the dew had been heavy, and the men were soon wet above their knees…. with the men of the leading wave about ten yards apart, the light horsemen presented … a painfully slender force for an assault on substantial and strongly garrisoned earthworks; and there was not an officer in the [4th LH] brigade, or in the whole division, who believed that the enterprise had the faintest chance of success.[49]

The thin lines of men made some early progress towards Atawineh, but were held up when Turks on the adjacent Sausage Ridge opened fire on them with machine guns. This ridge had to be cleared before the attack on Atawineh could be completed. The 5th Mounted Brigade made some initial progress there, but at 9.30 a.m. Chaytor had to send the Wellington regiment and some machine guns up to help.[50]

The Turks had sited their redoubts so that each could support its neighbours and heavy fire from the Hairpin Redoubt held up the assault on Sausage Ridge. In the early afternoon, the Canterbury regiment was sent in to block a wadi between the WMR and the 5th Mounted Brigade, along which a strong Turkish force was advancing. As the South Islanders rode into position, they were bombed and shelled heavily. After they had dismounted, their led horses were bombed mercilessly. The animals were 'at times quite obscured from view by the mass of shells and bombs which fell in and around them … The stories told of the escapes of groups of horses from seeming annihilation were little short of miraculous.'[51] Jim McMillan feared that 'many of the troops in the battle line would be without mounts when, and if, they returned to collect them'. Fred Sterling recalled that 'horses were galloping all over the place', although McMillan stated that few animals broke loose. According to Powles, the behaviour of the horses 'under heavy shelling or bombing was amazing, for they seemed to know just what was required of them and, although trembling with fear, would seldom try to break away from the horse holder'. Machine gunner Hedley Green and his horse were hit by one shell. 'Green's leg was blown off and his horse [was] badly smashed. An officer went at once to Green's assistance; his first words were, "Shoot my horse, sir, and end his misery." Green died a short while later.'[52]

Throughout the afternoon, the Turks launched a series of strong counter-attacks against the Imperial Mounted Division and those units of the Anzac division that were supporting them. At 3 p.m. a strong Turkish attack threatened to overwhelm the New Zealanders and the last Wellington squadron and the reserve machine guns were sent in to hold the line. Soon afterwards, 300–400 Turks advanced against the right of the WMR line, 'presenting a splendid target' to two and a half batteries of horse artillery. The guns fired 'with deadly effect', breaking up the assault. Fifteen minutes later, another enemy attack broke upon the Wellingtons. Their request for help was refused so the mounteds had to hold off the enemy unaided until the Turks broke off the attack at 5 p.m. When the WMR was ordered to withdraw at dusk, the commander of the 2nd (Wellington West Coast) Squadron, Captain John Hine, replied that he believed that he could storm the enemy redoubt on Sausage Ridge. Luckily for Hine and his men, permission was denied.[53]

As dusk fell the Turkish counter-attacks faded away and the front stabilised for the night. The infantry dug in where they stood and the mounted men pulled back to the rear, where they dug in to defend themselves against a possible enemy counter-attack. For many of the men, it was their fourth night without sleep.

Fred Sterling's AMR squadron had been lying in a patch of high barley all day, protecting a battery of horse artillery. At 2 p.m. two Taubes flew overhead and dropped smoke near the guns to mark them for the Turkish artillery. A few minutes later 'Jacko opened up with two 9-inch guns'.

Most marvellous exhibition of big gun practice I have ever seen. Shell after shell, as fast almost as one could count, landed around our little battery. They burst like claps of thunder. Bits fell all amongst our horses and the battery … it was covered in dust most of the time. The gunners would flop down as the shells landed. Then up after the burst and at their firing again. Talk about a little Hell…. Gee Whizz those Tommy gunners were game, and lucky too, for every shell that went actually under the guns failed to explode.

By the time the Aucklands were withdrawn, one man had been killed and 17 others wounded. 'We pulled out at dark and after much messing about in the dark getting lost etc. we managed to find water for our horses and camp for the night. The AMR Regiment had quite a few casualties.... Canterbury and Wellington's losses were even greater. Some injuries were hideous to look upon. The Turks were too many for us.' Many men, in Nicol's words, had 'the uncomfortable feeling that very little had been achieved'.[54]

Little had indeed been achieved all along the front and the casualties had been very heavy. In a few places, enemy trenches were occupied, but ferocious Turkish counter-attacks quickly recaptured them. Some infantry brigades lost so any men that they were no longer combat-effective. The mounted divisions were tired and bloodied but still capable of further effort. According to Gullett, 'the Turks with their machine guns and artillery never lost control of the situation. With one single exception ... every attempt by the infantry and the mounted men to reach the enemy trenches was shattered and frustrated.' Guy Powles thought that the reputation of the mounted troops was their undoing: 'Such was the dread the Turk had of the mounted men that, realising their attack would fall on his left flank, he had massed heavy infantry reinforcements and numerous batteries on this portion of his line'.[55]

As the British divisions rested and General Murray pondered what to do next, the Turks reinforced their line and awaited further attacks with well-founded confidence. Nowhere had their line been threatened and they had a counter-attack plan ready. This aimed to pin the British divisions in front of Gaza with two Turkish divisions, then envelop them from the east with two more divisions. Kress wanted to launch this counter-attack on 19 April but a lack of ammunition and the tiredness of his soldiers forced him to abandon it.[56]

Murray called for the attacks to be renewed at dawn the next day. However, radio intercepts on 19 April had revealed that the enemy commander in Gaza did not consider he needed any reinforcements. Air reconnaissance advised that the Turkish front-line troops were easily holding their own and that the enemy reserves had not yet been drawn into the battle. When this was brought to Murray's attention, and after all his subordinate commanders protested that further attacks would only lengthen the casualty lists, he postponed, then cancelled, further attacks.[57]

Over 80 per cent of the 6444 EEF casualties – 509 men were killed – were in the infantry divisions. There were 547 casualties in the Imperial Mounted Division and 196 in the Anzac Mounted Division. The war diary states that the NZMR Brigade lost seven men killed and 81 wounded in three days. The Turks lost just over 2000 men, mostly wounded.[58]

For the first time in the war, the New Zealand horses suffered heavy losses. With enemy aircraft 'sailing about like angry bees' the 'acres of horses, standing while the men were in action, made an easy target for the bombs of hostile airmen, and also for guns, and they were bombed and shelled from early morning till late at night'. One hundred and nineteen horses were killed in the Anzac division, with another 100 wounded. In the New Zealand brigade 40 horses were killed and 60 wounded.[59]

Murray's second attempt to break the Turkish line anchored on Gaza had failed disastrously. He simply did not have the resources to prevail against a well-prepared and alert foe. He lacked sufficient artillery guns and ammunition to suppress the enemy batteries, to destroy the trenches or to cut the barbed wire. The handful of tanks did little but draw fire on the hapless infantry advancing with them; the poison gas was so ineffective that few Turks even noticed it.[60]

General Murray dismissed Lieutenant General Dobell for his part in the attack and Chetwode took over the command of Eastern Force. Chauvel replaced him in command of the Desert Column and Edward Chaytor, with the rank of major general, moved up to command the Anzac Mounted Division. Soon afterwards, William Meldrum was promoted to brigadier general and given command of the New Zealand Mounted Rifles Brigade. Lieutenant Colonel James Whyte took over the Wellington regiment. Charles Mackesy relinquished command of the AMR to Lieutenant Colonel James McCarroll and became the administrator of the Khan Yunis/Deir el Belah area.[61]

Murray decided to retain a bridgehead on the far bank of Wadi Ghazze. He told the War Office that he needed two more full-strength infantry divisions and extra artillery if he was to attack again with any hope of success. The War Office, disappointed by the two failures to break the enemy line, no longer hoped for the early capture of Jerusalem. Instead, Murray was encouraged to defeat the Turks in Palestine 'as and when this became practicable'. When he was told that he could not have the two extra divisions, he replied that he would be unable to resume offensive operations in the foreseeable future.[62]

The Turks steadily improved their already formidable defences and extended them towards Beersheba. They dug new trenches east and south of that Arab village, brought fresh forces south and laid a new railway track from near Junction Station to Gaza. It was obvious to everyone that another frontal assault against the Turkish line between Gaza and Beersheba could not succeed but General Murray could still see no other options. Worse, he had lost the confidence of his subordinate commanders, and the men of the EEF were 'despondent, depressed, and defeated'.[63] A new concept of operations, and a new commander, were needed.

8

When will the war be over?

*It must have come as a surprise to certain of our countrymen … to find out that
our job was not guarding the brothels of Cairo and Alexandria, as some seemed to
imagine, to learn that we fought battles and had many gaps in our ranks.*

EDWIN McKAY

AFTER THE DOUBLE failure of the EEF at Gaza in March and April 1917, both sides began a
period of static warfare that was to last for the next six months. The land now stretching
away in front of the Anzacs was rich in biblical history but quite small in area. Damascus
was less than 300 kilometres from Gaza; the distance from Jaffa to Amman was barely 120
kilometres. The Judean Hills rose north of Beersheba and ran northwards through Hebron
and Jerusalem to Nablus. The western side of this range of rocky hills sloped gradually
down to the fertile coastal plains. To the east, the range dipped more steeply to below
sea level in the Jordan Valley. North of Gaza was a plain of gentle, rolling pastureland,
partly sown in barley and other crops and intersected by many deep wadis. Inland from
the sandy Mediterranean coast, the ground hardened and water became scarcer. The only
roads – a rough rectangle linking Jaffa, Jerusalem, Hebron, Beersheba, and Gaza – were of
limited capacity in the summer and barely passable in the winter.

The Arab village of Beersheba lay 50 kilometres inland, on the banks of Wadi Saba, in
a shallow bowl, overlooked by the Judean Hills to the north and by low hills on all other
sides. The Hebron Road ran northwards into the Judean Hills towards Hebron and Jerusalem.
Beersheba was an important camel-trading centre but its importance to the EEF lay in its
many deep wells.. The village was surrounded by well-constructed trenches, with those to
the east being the weakest. On this side of Beersheba a strongpoint on a hill named Tel el Saba
dominated the flat ground to the south and east. The Turkish defences around Beersheba
were isolated from the Hareira trench system by a weakly defended gap 10 kilometres wide.

In the months after the defeat at Gaza, the Anzac Mounted Division began a long and
tedious period of patrol and outpost work.

A man would be on patrol one day, starting with the usual 'stand to' at about three o'clock in the darkness before dawn, travelling over arid, dusty country all day, and not returning till after dark. Outpost duty would claim him the next night, to be followed, if he were lucky, with a spell of sorts the next day. Then the cycle of duty would commence again, this routine continuing week after week.

Turks often tried to 'scupper' the New Zealand patrols. 'There was a hill nearby, from which the adventures of these small parties of horsemen on the open country below could be watched by their mates; the frequent gatherings there, to watch the patrol encounters on the country beneath them, gave this area of flying shots and galloping horses the nickname of "the racecourse".'[1] On 29 April the NZMR Brigade handed over its outpost duties to the 74th (Yeomanry) Division and moved into reserve on the banks of Wadi Ghazze near Tel el Fara. On 10 May a force of 2500 Turks was reported to be advancing towards Tel el Fara from Beersheba. The NZMR Brigade rode out to face the enemy but found nothing more than a few cavalry patrols. The stunt furnished valuable information on the roads and water supplies in the area and some of the New Zealanders had their first glimpse of the minaret of Beersheba's mosque.[2]

In May 1917 Murray ordered Chetwode to destroy the Turkish railway line between Asluj and Auja. Because there was little water, and the demolition parties would be vulnerable to enemy attacks from Beersheba, speed and surprise were essential to complete this task quickly and at minimum risk. Raiding parties were formed from the ICC Brigade, which would move from Rafah down the border to Auja, and the 1st LH Brigade of the Anzac Mounted Division, which would ride from Shellal to Asluj. The rest of the Anzac Mounted Division was to protect the raiders from Turkish interference and the Imperial Mounted Division was ordered to create a diversion up towards Beersheba. To distract the Turks, Gaza was to be bombarded in the days leading up to the raid.[3]

The Anzac engineers were supplemented by horsemen 'with experience of explosives'. Guy Powles told of one corporal who qualified by 'having just been thrice blown up by shells!' It was estimated that the 500-man demolition parties could destroy 20 kilometres of rails and 30 bridge arches per hour. The horsemen had six hours to cause as much damage as possible. After a week of intensive training, the raid began on 22 May with an all-night march in a khamsin duststorm. It was impossible to see and hard to breathe, and static electricity made the manes of the horses spark when the riders touched them.[4]

Major General Chaytor was ill but he insisted on leading his new command. Medical staff dissuaded him from riding so he was carried in a sand cart. The men admired his

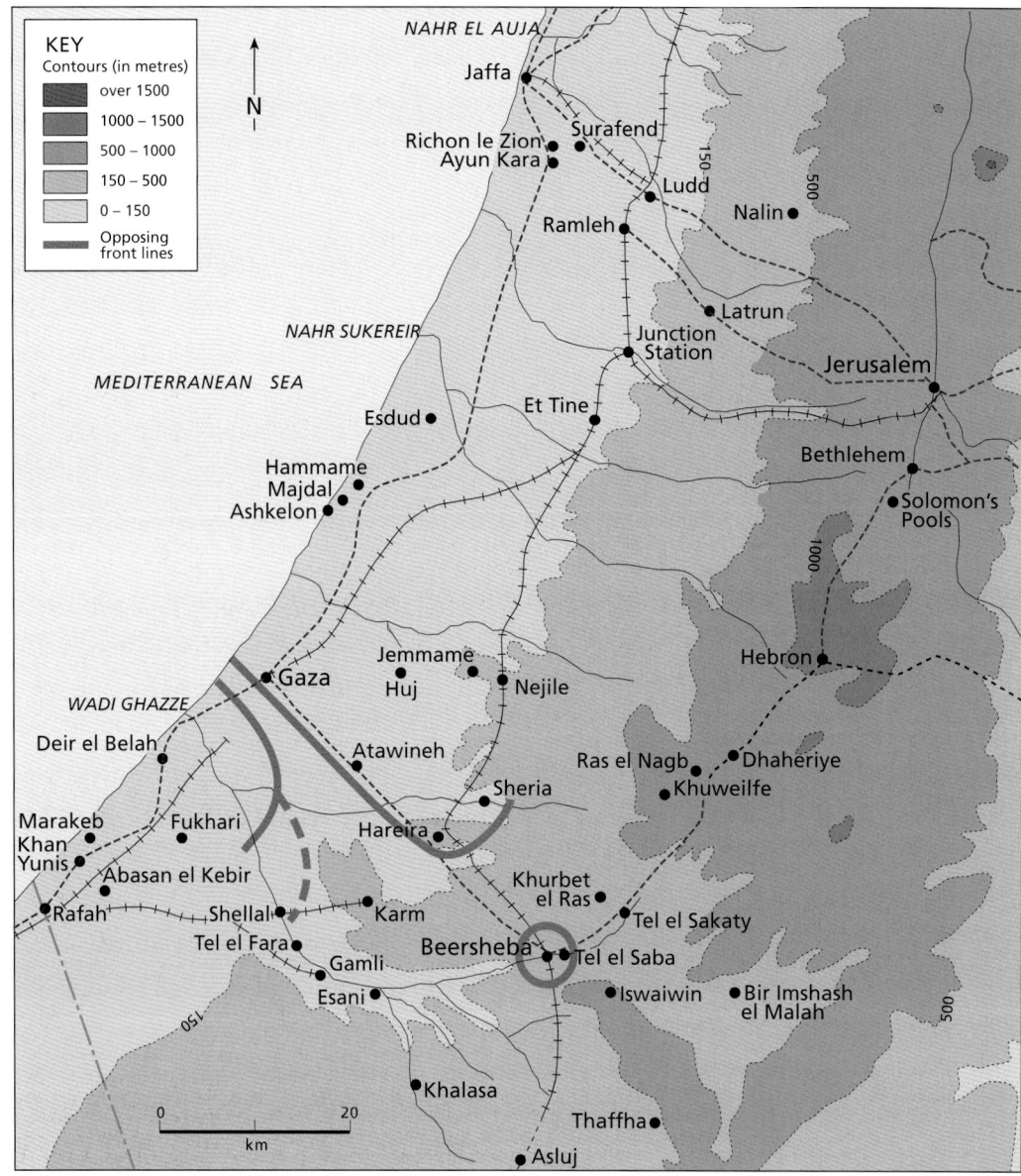

Map 11: Southern Palestine, September 1917.

stubbornness: Ion Idriess thought Chaytor was 'a game old beggar'. The NZMR Brigade deployed in a screen line to the north of Asluj, keeping in touch with the Imperial Mounted Division to its left. Fred Sterling was impressed with the workmanship of the railway bridges: 'Jacko can build all right'. Eleven kilometres of line and five bridges south of Asluj, including one bridge with 18 arches, were blown up by the demolition parties accompanying the 1st LH Brigade. The cameliers destroyed another seven bridges and wrecked a further nine kilometres of line. According to Sterling, 'as one charge after the other exploded on the line, it was like a fireworks show, and old Bedouin, scared out of their wits, could be seen with their families, sheep, goats, etc. going for dear life.'[5]

The Turks reacted sluggishly. Two cavalry regiments advanced towards Asluj from Beersheba in the morning but turned back when fired upon by the screen. After capturing two armed and two unarmed Arabs, the New Zealand brigade withdrew at 5.30 p.m., setting crops on fire as they went. The brigade suffered no casualties. The ride back to camp 'was wearisome in the extreme. For some reason, known only to themselves, the head of the column led into many strange places, such as cactus hedges, wire entanglements and other camps, before the Colonel obtained permission for the [Canterbury] Regiment to find its own way back.'[6]

The ease with which these raids were carried out suggested to General Chetwode that the Turks did not expect any serious attack on the eastern end of the Gaza–Beersheba line. Useful information was gained about water supplies in the Khalasa and Asluj areas and about the suitability of the ground for movement by large mounted forces. This information started Chetwode thinking seriously about the inland option as an alternative for future attacks.[7]

Two British Yeomanry brigades arrived from Salonika in June and July, bringing the total number of mounted brigades in the EEF to 10. Chauvel's Desert Column was renamed the Desert Mounted Corps (DMC). He reorganised his horsemen into three divisions: the Anzac Mounted Division under Chaytor, the Australian Mounted Division and the Yeomanry Mounted Division. The Anzac division lost one cavalry brigade and some of its artillery (see Figure 3, p.183).

The success of the railway raid could not compensate for Murray's double failure at Gaza and he was ordered to return to England on 11 June. His replacement was General Sir Edmund Allenby, the former commander of the British 3rd Army in France. 'Bull' Allenby was a physically impressive man, gruff, forceful and energetic, with 'an intense love of being boss'. Unlike Murray, he knew the value of being seen regularly by the troops under his command. Within a week of his arrival, Allenby went up to the front line in southern Palestine to see it for himself.[8] In an early letter to his wife, he declared himself impressed with the troops under his command: 'All the men and animals are looking well and in good condition and spirits. The men are burnt as black as Arabs. One sees them sitting in the blazing sun, often, with practically nothing on but a helmet; and apparently enjoying it.'[9]

'The Bull' immediately caused 'alarm and despondency' by slashing the number of staff officers in cushy Cairo billets and it was not long before his name popped up in New Zealand letters. George Ranstead wrote that Allenby was 'cleaning a lot of the deadheads out of the bases in Egypt'.[10] Edwin McKay noticed something else.

> We were … NEWS. Home papers reaching us spared an occasional couple of inches of space to note some of our activities. It must have come as a surprise to certain of our countrymen … to find out that our job was not guarding the brothels of Cairo and Alexandria, as some seemed to imagine: to learn that we fought battles and had many gaps in our ranks.[11]

The War Office expected Allenby to quickly break the Gaza–Beersheba line, to capture Jerusalem and finally to expel the Turks from Palestine entirely. He was led to believe that he would get whatever reinforcements he asked for.[12] Allenby would not be rushed and refused to begin his offensive until he felt completely ready. General Chetwode presented Allenby with a detailed proposal to break the stalemate in front of Gaza. Chetwode wanted to destroy the Turks in southern Palestine. If they managed to withdraw intact, they would become stronger as they went north and they were certain to fight desperately for Jerusalem because of its significance to the Muslim faith. Chetwode was sure that the

Anzac demolition parties at work.

STERLING COLLECTION, KAURI MUSEUM

Turks would not abandon the Gaza–Beersheba line without a fight. He thought Gaza too strong to be captured by frontal assault and the centre of the line too open to be attacked. The enemy defences towards Beersheba were less formidable, and the village itself was isolated from the other Turkish defences, but this flank had limited water.

Chetwode envisaged infantry attacks on Gaza and the central part of the enemy line, to hold the Turks opposite them in place while the high ground between Hareira and Beersheba was captured. This would force the Turks to evacuate Beersheba; after that, the rest of the Turkish line should be able to be rolled up towards the coast, aided by the EEF's mounted divisions operating behind the collapsing enemy defences. As the Turks withdrew, the wells would be left for the EEF. Chetwode was confident that his horsemen could slow the withdrawal of the Turks long enough for the British infantry divisions to catch and destroy them; all they needed was water.[13]

After carefully evaluating all the options, Allenby accepted Chetwode's plan and added a few touches of his own: Beersheba became an objective, and several days of shelling against Gaza, and dummy preparations for an amphibious landing on the coast north of Gaza, were added to focus the attention of the Turks on that end of their line. On 12 August, the Eastern Force was abolished. Allenby arranged his forces into three corps: two infantry corps (20 and 21), and the Desert Mounted Corps (DMC). In all, Allenby had at his disposal 75,000 infantrymen, 17,000 horsemen and cameliers and 460 guns.[14]

The DMC and 20 Corps were tasked with the inland operations; 21 Corps had responsibility for the diversionary operations at Gaza. Four days after the commencement of the artillery bombardment of Gaza, Beersheba was to be captured by 20 Corps and the DMC. The four infantry divisions of 20 Corps would attack Beersheba from the south-west, drawing the defenders of Beersheba towards them and capturing the heights overlooking the village to the west and south. At the same time, the Anzac and Australian Mounted divisions would ride in from the east and south-east and capture Beersheba and its vital wells.[15]

With Beersheba and its water secured, 21 Corps (35,000 men) would attack Gaza. At the same time 20 Corps was to break through the other end of the main enemy line at Sheria and Hareira; the DMC's roles were to protect 20 Corps' right flank and threaten the Turkish line of retreat. The horses of the DMC needed to be as fresh as possible for this phase of the operation and Allenby demanded that Chauvel's horses be capable of at least one more day's effort without water after the capture of Beersheba.

The EEF's longer-term objective was the Turkish railway at Junction Station: its capture would isolate the Turkish forces in the Judean hills around Jerusalem. Finally, Allenby

A demolished railway bridge near Asluj. Some of these ruins still stand today.

would try to capture the Holy City itself. Allenby believed there were 46,000 rifles, 250 machine guns and 200 artillery pieces, as well as 2800 cavalrymen, in the Turkish line or close behind it, and reinforcements were thought to be heading south. Against this significant enemy force, Allenby considered that he had sufficient troops to break the Gaza–Beersheba line and perhaps to capture Jerusalem. Nonetheless, he submitted a 'shopping list' of reinforcements that included two new infantry divisions, a great increase in artillery and three squadrons of modern aircraft. The War Office agreed to most of this. (In fact, the Turks in southern Palestine could muster about half the number of rifles above.)[16]

Allenby faced four problems: lack of time, transport and water, and the need for secrecy. If the Turks could hold off the EEF until the winter rains began in October, their chances of defeating it would be greatly improved. Allenby wanted to launch his offensive in September to forestall an expected Turkish spoiling attack, and to give him plenty of time to get to Jerusalem before the rains began. However, it soon became clear that his forces would not be ready in time so Allenby settled on the last week of October. He hoped that the violence and speed of his assault would get him to the Jaffa–Jerusalem line in the fortnight or so before the winter weather was expected to stop him.[17]

None of the EEF's ten divisions could operate away from the railway for long. Unless they somehow increased their mobility, the assault forces would soon come to a halt, allowing the Turks to escape. The tracks leading to Beersheba were not suitable for mechanical transport so Allenby's forces were reliant on 30,000 camels to carry water, ammunition and rations.

Any advance beyond Beersheba depended, above all, on water being found or captured there. The wells of Beersheba were so important to Allenby's plan that he allocated an overwhelmingly strong force to their capture. Four infantry divisions and two mounted divisions (over 55,000 men) were to be employed against a garrison of just 4500 Turks. To avoid premature detection of this enormous force by the enemy, it was kept close to Gaza until the last moment, then quickly moved across the desert to its assembly areas in several night marches. A search of historical documents revealed that Khalasa and Asluj had once been large towns, presumably with ample water supplies. Both locations had been examined by EEF engineers during the railway raid in May. It was established that, with 10 days of uninterrupted work, the engineers could repair the wells sufficiently to water the horses of two mounted divisions. This vital news allowed Allenby to select the route to be followed by the DMC in its march towards Beersheba. The horsemen would cross Wadi Ghazze at Shellal and move south-east through Esani to Khalasa and Asluj, before looping around to the east of Beersheba.[18]

Anything that might disclose Allenby's plan prematurely had to be concealed. Supplies were to be brought forward at the last possible moment and all moves to start lines had to take place at night. 'By day the area was comparatively calm, but as soon as night fell, it was a … buzzing hive of industry, as train followed train, and convoys rolled eastwards in the choking clouds of dust.' Allenby, unable to conceal the movement of men, animals and guns into the desert towards Beersheba, decided to create the impression that the strike force was simply a feint to divert Turkish attention away from Gaza. A variety of deception measures were designed to create this impression and Allenby's new Bristol Fighters swept the skies clear of enemy scout aircraft.[19]

As Allenby developed his plans and gathered his forces, the Turks were working on schemes of their own. When the Bolsheviks withdrew Russia from the war in mid-1917, only the British Empire remained active in the fight against Turkey. With the EEF seemingly safely blocked south of Gaza, the Turks decided to try to recapture the Mesopotamian city of Baghdad. They created a new force called the *Yildirim* ('Thunderbolt') Army Group, made up of two Turkish armies and a German 6500-man infantry brigade group (known to the Turks as Pasha 2), all under the command of the German Marshal Erich von Falkenhayn. While the Yildirim dealt with the British in Mesopotamia, the Turkish 4th Army in southern Palestine was expected to hold its line if attacked; if it had to withdraw northwards, it was to fight all the way.[20]

Falkenhayn considered the recapture of Baghdad impracticable and believed that a renewed EEF offensive in southern Palestine was inevitable under Allenby's forceful leadership. If successful, this would endanger the entire Turkish position in Syria. Falkenhayn wanted to use the Yildirim to attack the EEF first. Cemal Pasha, the 4th Army commander, agreed that the recapture of Baghdad was out of the question, but he wanted the Yildirim to be held at Aleppo as a theatre reserve, not used to attack the EEF.[21]

Falkenhayn eventually got his way. By mid-September, seven Turkish infantry divisions and Pasha 2 were on their way to southern Palestine – but they were too late. Falkenhayn had lost too much time arguing his case and only three divisions had arrived in the south when Allenby attacked. As these troops were unfamiliar with southern Palestine, they were dispatched to the apparently secure Beersheba flank where, at worst, they might have to face a raid from a single British infantry division and a cavalry division.[22]

The Turkish forces in Palestine were reorganised into three armies: the 8th (commanded by Kress von Kressenstein) and the 7th (Fevzi Pasha), both on the Gaza–Beersheba front and under Falkenhayn's command, and the 4th Army, which was east of the Jordan River and commanded by Cemal Pasha. When Falkenhayn toured Palestine, he discovered that the weak divisions of the 7th and 8th armies were nearly all deployed in the forward defences between Gaza and Beersheba. There were no depth positions and few reserves. The trenches were vulnerable to EEF artillery and the Turks' own artillery was 'hopelessly insufficient'. To make matters worse, tonnes of ammunition earmarked for the Palestine front were destroyed in an enormous explosion near Istanbul in September. German attempts to improve the defensive layout failed.

The Turkish soldiers were badly trained, half-starved and poorly equipped. The front-line troops, especially those in and around Gaza, were under almost continuous British shellfire. Many of their own guns could not be moved for lack of horses to pull them. Leave was non-existent and the rates of sickness and desertion were alarmingly high. Despite these handicaps, the Turks possessed a strong defensive position, especially towards the coast. The defences stretching eastwards from Gaza were even stronger than they had been in April and a road and railway network behind the front line

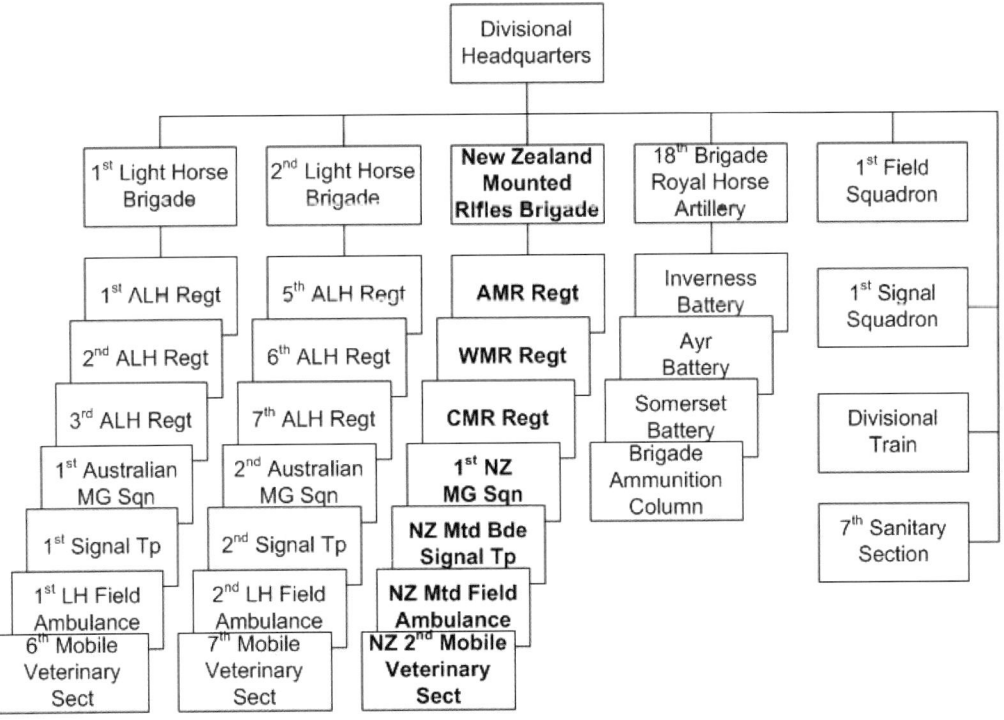

Figure 3: The Anzac Mounted Division in 1917–18.[23]

183

General Allenby, posing with a captured German Albatros aircraft.

permitted the swift movement of Turkish forces.[24]

The hard life in southern Palestine, coupled with boredom and disappointment about the recent defeats, made some Anzac horsemen wish that they had never left Sinai.

> *The conditions under which they lived were dreary and dull; the digging and wiring that began this period were strenuous; the frequent reconnaissances that followed, though less dull, were exhausting, while the days of so-called 'rest' in bivouac were occupied in watering the horses, a task which often involved a ride of several miles two or three times a day, in grooming, in patrols, and in numerous fatigues carried out in a continuous atmosphere of dust. Leave was rare, facilities for recreation few, and at first the future contained little to invite anticipation.[25]*

The spring crops had long since been burnt away to dust. 'The dust was very fine and lifted to every breath of wind and enveloped every moving man, horse or vehicle in a white cloud.... At about 10 o'clock in the morning the sea breeze began blowing from the west or north-west and continued until dark, making life in a "bivvy" a torment, one breathed dust and ate dust and at night wrapped oneself up in dust.[26] Flies swarmed in greater numbers than ever.

A dish of tea set down for a moment would immediately become a swimming bath for as many
as could cover the surface, and if the thirsty owner was not prepared to remain that way the
only thing to do was to skim them off and get outside the liquid at once, even though a few of
the persistent ones were swallowed with it.[27]

Food was plentiful and regular, especially when the men were in camp, but fresh fruit and vegetables rarely featured on the menu. The men often gave precise instructions about what food should be sent from New Zealand. 'Condensed milk is a good thing to send,' wrote William Milliken, 'so always put in a tin or two, and any sort of jam [except] marmalade …biscuits such as gingernuts are good to send, also fruit cake, Wrigleys [chewing] gum and chocolate. Don't send any coffee and milk, socks and handkerchiefs.' He reported that his birthday cake 'arrived in splendid condition; it was nice and moist and not dry like some of them that arrive here. It was the best piece of cake I tasted since I left NZ, [and] the other boys enjoyed it very much.'[28]

These supplements from home were not enough to prevent a slow deterioration in the horsemen's health. Vitamin deficiencies were manifested by weakness, lassitude and by large, open sores on faces, legs and hands. Minor scratches inevitably became infected and the subsequent lesions were difficult to treat and took a long time to heal. Men were often seen swathed in bandages; in July 1917, nearly one man in four in the Anzac Mounted Division suffered from these painful sores.[29]

The horses also suffered, becoming 'jaded and in low condition' after a month in the forward area. On 6 September, the Anzac division's chief veterinarian reported that all of the horses were debilitated and that three-quarters of them were eating sand and their own droppings. Chaytor improved the horse ration slightly in an attempt to improve the animals' health and to stop them eating sand.[30]

At least there was little enemy activity to worry about, apart from almost daily bombing raids by German aircraft. William Milliken described the 'awful feeling' of being bombed with 'those damn things coming down on top of you, you can't tell where they are going to land'. Milliken and his horse had a close call from a bomb that 'fell exactly eight yards from where I was lying, the concussion fairly lifting me off the ground. I don't know how my horse escaped; I could hear the pieces of bomb whistling over me'.[31]

When in the front line, each brigade was allocated an area of operations for reconnaissance and raiding. They were expected to 'make it unsafe for any party of the enemy to be [there] … by day or night …. The methods will be small parties of men moving out by night, either mounted or on foot, armed with some sort of hand-to-hand weapon, a bayonet if nothing else is available, and carrying two or three bombs [hand-grenades] per man.… If any small party of Turks is met, it is to be dealt with at once and as quietly as possible.… The whole idea is to establish a sense of fright in the enemy.' According to George Berrie, 'patrolling … became the old game of going as far as Jacko's outposts would allow and then sitting down and exchanging shots which fell a few hundred yards short.'[32]

> *Many fond parents would have failed to recognize their sons, could they have seen them returning from patrol duty in these times. As the troop rode into bivouac with a jingling of accoutrements, some men would be seen wearing riding breeches, others slacks, with their spurs. Their bodies would be but half covered in sleeveless shirts or singlets, always open at the neck, round which was slung the heavy bandolier. Rifles would be carried across the front of the saddle, or slung over the left shoulder. Many would be unshaven, with red-rimmed eyes peering from faces darkened by sunburn and dust. The horses' coats would be rough and streaked with sweat, and horse and rider would be smothered in the dust of the day's march.*[33]

Whenever a troop, squadron or regiment was away from its usual campsite for longer than a day, it followed a standard procedure at day's end. First, scouts located a likely-looking

Corporal Williams resting with his horse in southern Palestine.

campsite, concealed from enemy observation and near a water supply for the horses. Sentries were posted, and the site was occupied. 'Men slide tiredly to the ground, horses raise drooping heads a little. They wonder: do we drink?' The first job was to secure the horses. The Section No. 3 held the section's horses, while the other three men secured a long 'built-up' rope to the ground, using sandbags or wooden pegs as anchors. Each horse was connected to this using the head-rope looped around its neck. Horses with a reputation for kicking also had a hind leg secured to the ground. As soon as the horses were secure, they were off-saddled, groomed and fed.[34] 'The patient animals always knew the order "feed-up", which was greeted with a chorus of hungry whinnying and much pawing of the ground.'[35] Water for the thirsty animals often had to be hauled up from the depths of ancient wells using canvas buckets. It could take hours for every horse to have its regulation two buckets of water, and it was usually pitch dark before the job was done. Once the horses were taken care of, the men looked to their own comfort. While the officers received their orders for the night and the next day, those men who were not on sentry or horse guard duty erected their bivvies behind the horse lines, cleaned their weapons and lit fires to boil the billy and cook the evening meal. This invariably consisted of biscuits and bully beef, 'reduced to oily string through tossing about in haversacks in the heat of the day'. If their water bottles were empty, they drank the same brackish well water as the horses – usually in the form of hot tea. Dry camel manure, sticks and scraps of wood were used for the fires. Rations and water were issued for the next day if the transport wagons had arrived. Finally, the men turned in.

> By 8.45, with [horse] line guards posted, outlying pickets (poor sods!) set out in front and on flanks, the squadron's men stretch out their weary bones behind the horse lines, and ease puttees and boots. Roll in blankets, a last puff at a cigarette, which is carefully pinched out and saved, and settle down to sleep. About 9.30 a peeping half-moon creeps over the horizon, to show what looks like a camp of the dead, men and horses stretched out sleeping the sleep of exhaustion. Sleep well – reveille is at 3 a.m.[36]

The faintest dawn light revealed a hive of activity.

> Everywhere would be men rolling blankets, strapping gear to saddles, and tying up and securing their horses' canvas nosebags. On the warning 'get ready to move', straps and girths would be finally tightened, and horses bitted up, until punctually at the appointed time the leading squadron would move out mounted.[37]

The availability of three mounted divisions allowed for a regular rotation of forces. A lightly entrenched line extended from the eastern end of the main trench line at Tel el Jemmi to Shellal. Each division spent about a month in this front line, moved back into reserve near Fukhari or Abasan el Kebir to train and then returned to the beach at Marakeb for rest and recreation.

Major General Chaytor was relentless in his drive for greater efficiency. On 30 July, his three brigades received a memo directing various improvements to be made. Chaytor thought that many officers were 'slow in making up their minds and in putting their plans into execution'. He expected them to ride ahead of their troops while on patrol to avoid being surprised. Further, 'men are inclined to dismount and open fire too soon. As long-range fire is usually harmless, it is useless for what we are here for, which is to reduce the enemy's strength on every occasion we can by killing or capturing Turks.' He reminded the brigades that such tactics were 'rather those of mounted infantry than those of mounted rifles.... Our tactics are to get at the enemy's flank.' The security of the force also concerned Chaytor. 'Both by day and night, sentries and patrols should be so disposed as to prevent Arabs passing through, and instructions should be issued to all, that there should be no hesitation in firing at any one who refuses to halt when challenged.' More men were trained to operate the Hotchkiss guns, and gas training was conducted. 'Parties were marched through dense clouds of gas,' Nicol wrote, 'and they felt very sorry for themselves.'[38]

Life in the front line was not all hard work, however. On 12 May, a brigade sports meeting was held at Tel el Fara. Events included foot races, horse races, a sack race, tug-of-war (on foot and on horseback), horseback wrestling, a potato race, tent pegging and a driving competition.[39] Further back, entertainment was provided by the New Zealand Band, which came up from Moascar. Other entertainers also appeared, including the 74th (Yeomanry) Division's 'Palestine Pops'.

The 'Palestine Pops' were talented vocalists and comedians and the 'lady' was inimitable. 'She' was fair, slim, and graceful, and 'with a way with her' that took by storm the hearts of the boys.... Hot discussions followed when the performance was over as to whether 'she' was really a man or a girl, and one reckless man, to settle a heavy wager, stayed behind and boldly invaded [the dressing room], but was met by a good, round sentence full of the expletives that none but a Tommy can use, and so returned a disappointed man.[40] ['She' was killed when the Yeomanry division attacked Sheria in November.]

The 9th (Wellington East Coast) Squadron resting during a stunt 'somewhere in Palestine'.

According to Edwin McKay, there was one common denominator to all the concerts.

> *Everyone nibbled peanuts and the crackling rustle of peanut shells was as much part of the show as the National Anthem. Those who imagine that army concerts would have a large proportion of smutty items should revise their immature ideas. There might be a spicy item or two, but we didn't want too much of that stuff. We wanted the stuff we used to hear with Mum and Dad and the girl friend, and in the main we got it.*[41]

There was a little training at Marakeb in June but most of the time was devoted to doing nothing. Of a later rest period, Alec McNeur wrote, 'we don't work hard. Feed the horses three times a day and groom twice. We take them twice to water and work in pairs so that each man only goes once. The rest of the day is spent as we please.' In Alexander Wilkie's words, 'From the dust, heat, and flies which had infested the camp at Fara, the change to sea-bathing, recreation, and a different diet had an electrical effect, both men and horses benefiting by it. Swimming, rifle shooting, and boxing at the stadium were the principal pastimes of the men, competitions in these being keenly contested.' Jim McMillan certainly enjoyed the break: 'It was a greatly rejuvenated body of troops that rode away from Marakeb at the end of the allotted period. The horses too were in great fettle, having derived as much benefit from the rest and swimming as their riders had.'[42]

In mid-1917 there was talk of home leave for the few hundred Main Body men still in the brigade. But although there were plenty of reinforcements available in Egypt, most Main Body men were senior NCOs and officers, not easily replaced by junior and inexperienced reinforcements, so the proposal was not approved. George Ranstead, a Main Body man, recorded the reaction of the veterans to this hard news: 'Heard the other day that our NZ leave has been knocked on the head and everyone is feeling rather disgusted about it'.[43]

The New Zealand brigade began July in reserve at Fukhari. On 3 July, the mounteds provided a screen near Beersheba while the Australian Mounted Division scouted the Shellal-Asluj-Beersheba area.

> *Here a remarkable incident was witnessed. A British aeroplane landed on open ground between the advanced division and the reserves. In a twinkling the Turkish artillery had the range, and the pilot was forced to bolt on foot. Fully 100 shells burst around the 'plane, which everyone thought must have been damaged. Later the pilot, unseen by the Turks, crept back to his machine, and, starting the engine, careered along the road to safety. He could not rise owing to one wing being broken, but the machine rushed along the road like a motor car, to the great joy of the horsemen.*[44]

On 6 July, the Anzac division took over the front line from the Australians. Their tasks included pushing back the enemy screen to locate main defensive positions and test enemy reactions, providing protection to water, railway and artillery survey parties, and locating and testing water. The horsemen also conducted close reconnaissances of Turkish defensive positions.

> *A small patrol under an officer would go out at night to test or examine some portion of the Turk's line. The party would ride on a compass bearing until close up to the objective. Then a selected few would dismount and spend a few hours on foot in among the Turkish patrols, examining, listening and noting down tracks, movement, trenches and, above all, water.*[45]

Fred Sterling described this work as 'horribly trying at times … out in the front a thin line of men looking for, at night, something they cannot see, and knowing full well that what they are looking for can hear them coming. Some would say that the life of a mounted man in Palestine is safe and a splendid one: seeing the wonders of an ancient country. He takes a tenfold risk though, and often pays a price. A mounted man has no trench, [offers] the best of targets, and what odds he is up against.' Occasional enemy bombing raids took their toll; on 19 July the brigade lost two men and 14 horses killed; 12 men and 11 horses were wounded.[46]

The tedious work continued into August. Turkish working parties were closely observed and enemy artillery and machine gun positions were mapped. During a night attack on a Turkish redoubt on 11 August, one Canterbury squadron got ahead of another in the dark and was fired upon by mistake. Three horses were killed and two men fatally wounded. According to Walter MacFarlane, 'Scotty Cameron had a narrow escape' when his horse was killed under him.[47]

Around this time, Kingston Hull sent some advice to his brother Burton, who was training in New Zealand before sailing to join the brigade.

Keep low in a scrap, and get a 'don't care' feeling into your head, and you will be alright. If the enemy's bullets are making a deadly sort of music – well be sure, yours will do the same to him, so give them all you can. Do not delay firing because you think you cannot hit the mark. It is only a very small majority [sic] of chaps who are hit by shots aimed directly at them…. I will tell you, Burton, that the biggest nerve-racking fright you ever had in your life will be

New Zealanders posing with their new Hotchkiss gun.

1991.1615, QUEEN ELIZABETH II ARMY MEMORIAL MUSEUM

A New Zealander and his trusty mount.

when you first hear the whisk of bullets ... As the affair goes on, you kind of get numbed down to it, but no matter how many scraps one has been in, the opening shots of each fresh one make one's heart go to his boots.... look after your own skin first, for no-one will look after it for you. You will think it funny when I say the best thing to do when things seem hopeless for you is to do nothing – except kill the enemy if you can get a shot in while keeping low. You will perhaps hear chaps talking of Turks they have shot – as a rule you don't know. The only ones I am sure of were about fifty yards off, when there was no mistaking. I am sure more than one Turk thought he had me on several occasions, as when the bullets are coming too persistently to be chance shots. I have shammed dead and then made another bolt for it.[48]

A visit to the Anzac division by Allenby on 28 September was a mixed success and Chaytor sent a scathing memo to the brigades afterwards. In the New Zealand brigade, 'during the tour of the Commander-in-Chief through the Ambulance lines, only natives and one Army Service Corps man stood to attention. The remainder either took no notice of the Commander-in-Chief, or lay about in their tents taking photographs of the party as it passed by.' In one unnamed AMR squadron, Allenby was greeted by its commander casually clad and without a tunic. His 'utter lack of courtesy' was considered inexcusable. A subsequent letter directed that 'officers are at all times to be ready to turn out at a moment's notice, and no officer slouching about in shoes and slacks at midday can be said to be ready to move'.[49]

The forward divisions always had to be ready to move at very short notice and they were tested regularly.

> *The time taken to turn out was noted by Staff officers, and the keenest rivalry sprang up between the divisions and the different units of each division to make the best showing. Rations and store wagons were packed each night, nosebags filled after the last feed and tied on the saddles, and all harness and saddlery laid out in order behind the horses. The men's [saddle] wallets were kept packed permanently, the rations in them being renewed from time to time, when the old ones were consumed.*[50]

After a few weeks of these drills, an entire mounted division could be on the move in less than an hour. In order to prepare them for protracted operations away from supply bases, the riders travelled in 'light order', with no blankets or greatcoats. Each man carried three days' rations and a few items of spare clothing in saddle wallets, and two nose-bags on the saddle carried two days' worth of grain for the horse, with a third day's supply carried on regimental wagons. This allowed the regiments to be self-sufficient, except for water,

The WMR resting on the beach at Marakeb, near Khan Yunis.

A brave New Zealander poses with some unexploded ordnance. The large shell is probably from a naval gun.

for three days. The horses became accustomed to going without water for up to 30 hours, while the riders made do with two water bottles, in country described as 'a desert of blistering rocks and stones [in which] the temperature ranged up to 110 degrees [43°C] in the shade (of which there was none, save that cast by the bodies of men and horses), and the flies were innumerable and persistent'.[51]

Between 4 July and 18 August, the Anzac Mounted Division carried out 62 'minor enterprises' – reconnaissance patrols, ambushes and raids on the railway line. On 19 July, the division fought off a half-hearted Turkish attack on Shellal; the NZMR Brigade, which was in reserve, lost two men killed and 10 wounded from shelling and bombing. A few days later, the New Zealanders went out to verify a report that some of the Turkish trenches around Beersheba had been abandoned. The report was incorrect. At the end of August, the Anzac division was replaced by the Yeomanry Mounted Division and sent back to the beach for rest and training. On 18 September the NZMR Brigade moved back up to Fukhari, where it was greeted by a severe and persistent khamsin.[52]

As the date for Allenby's offensive neared, the commanders of the assault divisions carefully scouted assembly areas and the routes towards their objectives, screened by the mounted regiments. These stunts were unpopular with the horsemen, who referred to them as 'Royal Parties', but they served the useful purpose of making the Turks accustomed to such operations, so that when the real advance occurred, they would think nothing of it until it was too late.

Allenby issued his final attack orders on 22 October 1917.

It is the intention of the Commander-in-Chief to take the offensive against the enemy at Gaza and at Beersheba, and, when Beersheba is in our hands, to make an enveloping attack on the enemy's left flank in the direction of Sheria and Hareira. On Zero-Day 20 Corps ... and the Desert Mounted Corps ... will attack the enemy at Beersheba, with the object of gaining possession of that place by nightfall. As soon as Beersheba is in our hands, and the necessary arrangements have been made for the restoration of the Beersheba water supply, 20 Corps and Desert Mounted Corps ... will move rapidly forward to attack the left of the enemy's main position, with the object of driving him out of Sheria and Hareira and enveloping the left flank of his army.... Desert Mounted Corps ... will move north of the 20 Corps to gain possession of Nejile, and of any water supplies between that place and the right of 20 Corps, and will be prepared to operate vigorously against and round the enemy's left flank if he should throw it back to oppose the advance of the 20 Corps.[53]

9

Tel el Saba

The horses, despite their great loads, were touched with excitement, as they always were when marching in large bodies, and fretted on their … reins as they stepped briskly over the harsh country.

HENRY GULLETT

THE NEW ZEALANDERS spent the first three weeks of October 1917 at Fukhari, practising rifle and Hotchkiss gun shooting, gas drills, bombing and signalling. All leave was cancelled in mid-October 1917 and the baggage was sent to the rear. Alec McNeur noted that 'they are feeding us up in great style, and are seeing that we have all we need'. These signs were clear proof to the men that something big was imminent – but exactly what the plan was, few yet knew. In a few weeks, Allenby's assault troops would be fully equipped, trained and ready to move into their start positions. They would be loaded up with as much water, food and ammunition as they could carry and more would follow them.[1]

As the last days before Z-Day passed, activity increased enormously. The ground between the camps and the assembly areas for the attack was deserted by day.

Hardly had dusk screened the land from view when the whole area swarmed into life like a stirred ant hill…. Huge columns of camels, having picked up the loads stacked ready for them in long rows, filed out across the [Wadi] Ghazze almost in silence, to disappear in the dust raised by their own feet….The transport column of the Desert Mounted Corps alone … was six miles long. By midnight, vast clouds of dust hung over the teeming plain. But by dawn all was still once more.[2]

To many men 'it seemed inevitable that the enemy must learn of the movement. The nights were illuminated by a moon almost at the full, and the dust clouds arising from the columns could be clearly seen for miles.'[3] In fact, the Turks had little idea of what was coming; they believed that the bulk of the EEF was still opposite Gaza, and they positioned their own forces accordingly. There was not enough water for both EEF mounted divisions to move together so they were to move a day apart, with the Anzac Mounted Division leading. Their camps were left standing to deceive the enemy and fires were lit around the empty bivouacs at night. Spare men and horses marched around these camps all day, stirring up dust, to create the impression that the sites were still occupied.

On the night of 21 October, the 2nd LH Brigade rode from Fukhari to Esani (see Map 11, p.176). The engineers of the Anzac Field Squadron carried on to Khalasa and Asluj, where they began repairing the demolished wells. Three days later, the brigade joined them at Asluj. On the same night the New Zealand brigade rode to Esani. While there, the New Zealanders carried out various support tasks, including escorting camel convoys and manning outposts.[4]

General Chauvel's final orders were issued on 27 October. The Anzac Mounted Division was to leave Asluj at 6 p.m. on 30 October, and march, via Thaffha and Iswaiwin, to a position east of Beersheba. From there it was to cut the Hebron road between Tel el Sakaty and Tel el Saba and seize both hills. The Australian Mounted Division was to follow as far as Iswaiwin, where it was to be prepared to advance into Beersheba or assist the Anzac division.[5]

The New Zealanders departed Esani at 5 p.m. on 28 October, bound for Khalasa. The men reached their destination at 9.30. Fred Sterling, whose troop escorted the camels, remembered that 'a sort of mist, mixed with the dust from the passage of thousands of camels, horses, guns, wagons, motors etc., filled the plains. It was beautifully moonlit, nevertheless.' After a day's rest, the New Zealanders rode from Khalasa to Asluj, arriving at 9.30 p.m. on 29 October. Behind them, the Australian division rode to Khalasa. Allenby's great concentration was complete by dawn on 30 October, which

J02836, Australian War Memorial

Anzac engineers repairing demolished wells at Khalasa.

was a rest day for the 10,300 horsemen of the Anzac and Australian mounted divisions. James McCarroll noted that 'we are to have a business interview with the Turk tomorrow.... Everyone was in great spirits, we would have sung if we had been allowed.'[6]

The Anzac horsemen began their final approach march at 5 p.m. on 30 October 1917. The NZMR Brigade's strength that day was 95 officers, 1763 men, 1727 riding horses, 144 packhorses, 243 draught horses, 27 mules and 35 camels. Each rider carried two days' rations for himself, plus one day's horse feed and two days' emergency grain in a sandbag.

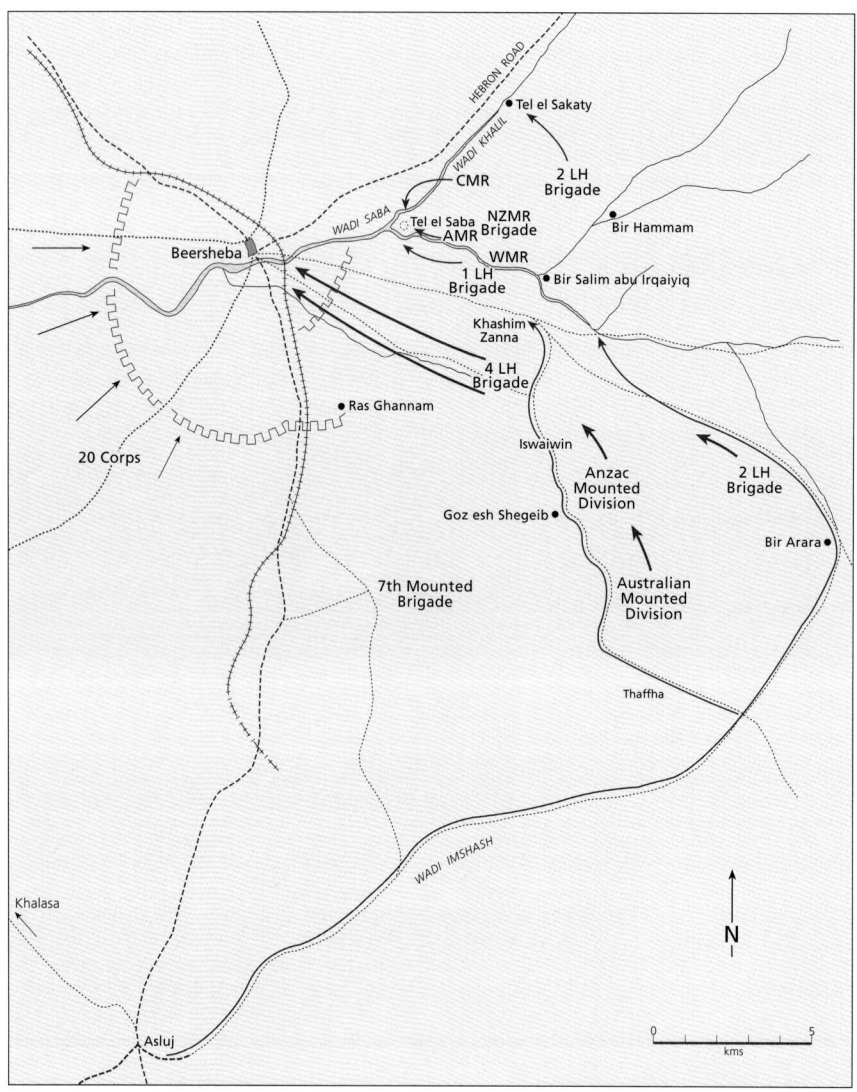

Map 12: Capture of Beersheba.

The horses were 'hard and fit, already inured to long marches and long periods without water, while horsemastership learned in the hard school of Sinai had reached a level so high that sore backs were seldom seen'.[7] Despite their 'great loads', the horses were 'touched with excitement, as they always were when marching in large bodies, and fretted on their bridle-reins as they stepped briskly over the harsh country'.[8]

The only wagons accompanying the combat brigades and the artillery batteries were those carrying the first line of ammunition and watering equipment. The wagons containing rations for the men and the horses, and the rest of the ammunition, were left at Asluj.[9]

A silent march had been ordered but nothing, on this cold, still night, could quieten the sound of thousands of metal horseshoes as they struck sparks from the stones along the way. Ion Idriess wrote: 'A full moon shone silver-white on a metalled road running between the hills. How different to the desert night marches was the hoarse rumble of artillery, transport and ambulances along that hard road!'[10]

By 8 p.m. the last Anzac horseman was clear of Asluj. 'Hardly had the rattle and thud of hooves died away to the north-east, when the camp guard … heard the sound anew from the north-west. It was the head of the Australian Mounted Division, approaching from Khalasa.'[11] At the same time as the DMC rode out of Asluj and Khalasa, the 45,000 infantrymen of Lieutenant General Chetwode's 20 Corps began their shorter approach marches from the railheads at Karm and Gamli.

The Anzac Mounted Division followed a 'splendid' metalled road on the banks of Wadi Imshash for about 15 kilometres. Around midnight, the advance guard of the division reached a crossroads east of Thaffha and halted while scouts rode forward to mark the next part of the route. According to James McCarroll, 'the whole force was asleep [instantly]; except [for] a horse blowing something out of his nose, [there was] not a sound'. After a two-hour rest, the 2nd LH Brigade left the column and rode off north-eastwards along the Bir Arara track. The rest of the force, led by the Wellington regiment, moved directly towards Iswaiwin.

As the route became much more difficult, the transport and artillery columns had to travel on the same track as the regiments. The WMR rode ahead to Goz esh Shegeib, to kill or capture a force of Turkish cavalrymen reported to be there, but when the Wellingtons reached the location at 2.45 a.m. they found no sign of them.[12]

At 6.45 a.m. the New Zealanders made contact with a small force of Turks at Iswaiwin. They drove them off without difficulty and moved forward to their assembly areas near Khashim Zanna. Ahead, the white mosque in the village of Beersheba was plainly visible against a backdrop of bare, brown rolling hills. The 2nd LH Brigade concentrated near

Bir Hammam and the New Zealand brigade assembled at Bir Salim abu Irqaiyiq. The 1st LH Brigade was behind the New Zealanders. The Australian Mounted Division dispersed behind Kashim Zanna. General Chaytor 'hoisted his pennant' on a hill at Kashim Zanna, 'from [where] a birds-eye view of the great Beersheba plain was obtained'.[13]

The Anzac Mounted Division had successfully negotiated nearly 40 kilometres of difficult and largely unknown terrain without loss. It was 'a monument to staff work and skill in the memorizing of almost featureless country by guides – junior officers for the most part – who carried out hasty reconnaissances'.[14] Allenby's greatly superior assault forces were now within a short day's march of their objectives. It seemed certain that Beersheba would be captured but would the vital wells be intact? If the attack took too long, the Turks would destroy the wells and that would spoil everything.

As the EEF's infantry and mounted forces moved into their assault positions around Beersheba, they were belatedly detected by its Turkish garrison. A few reserves were hastily shifted to the eastern defences but little else could be done unless strong reinforcements arrived quickly. Kress refused to send any extra infantry regiments to Beersheba and ordered the commander of the garrison to stay put and defend the village. The 3rd Cavalry Division was moved north to defend the Hebron road and to prevent the encirclement of Beersheba from the north.

At 9 a.m. Chaytor sent the 2nd LH Brigade cantering towards Tel el Sakaty to cut the Hebron road and to protect the division from counter-attack from the north. Although the numerous dry wadis on the plains slowed the Australians' advance, they also provided good cover from Turkish artillery fire. The light horsemen cut the road and captured the lightly defended tel at noon but they were unable to secure the hills to the west.

Tel el Saba proved to be a much more difficult nut to crack. Its flat, boulder-strewn top covered about eight hectares and its steep sides made it invulnerable to mounted attack. Tel el Saba was defended by about 300 Turks, who were better fighters, on the whole, than the Arabs who made up most of the Beersheba garrison. Their main role was to protect a machine gun company, whose eight weapons dominated the wadi and the flat land along its banks. The men and their weapons were well dug in, often with overhead protection against enemy artillery fire. Other machine guns in blockhouses on the banks of Wadi Saba, and on a low knoll to the east, supported the main position on the hill. Enemy artillery in Beersheba could interfere with any attack against Tel el Saba. The ground and these defences made the tel 'a formidable work for horsemen to assault. The open ground prevented a near approach mounted, and the firepower of a brigade of cavalry on its feet is equivalent only to that of an infantry battalion. Moreover, the light shells of the horse

Horses at Asluj, viewed from the minaret of a mosque. A repaired well is in the foreground.

artillery batteries would have little effect on the deeply-protected machine guns on the tel. These same horsemen had already solved similar problems at Rafah and Magdhaba; but the solution required time, as those actions showed. And time was pressing.'[15]

The New Zealand brigade began its assault on Tel el Saba at 9.10 a.m. on 31 October 1917. The Canterbury and Auckland regiments led the advance. Meldrum retained the Wellingtons as his reserve for the time being. The Canterbury regiment was given four machine guns and ordered to cross Wadi Khalil and envelop the hill from the north, while the Aucklands attacked directly from the east.[16] The leading AMR squadron galloped across the open ground under long-range machine gun fire, dismounting 1750 metres from the objective. The other two Auckland squadrons rode up the wadi bed to within 750 metres of the tel, before a hail of rifle and machine gun fire also forced them to dismount. The Aucklands slowly advanced on foot, under covering fire from their own Vickers machine guns. The wadi became a trap, as it was swept by close-range machine gun fire from the heights of the Turkish redoubt on Tel el Saba. The advance slowed to a crawl, and casualties mounted. The gunners of the Somerset Battery did their best to suppress the fire from the tel, but their light shrapnel shells were practically useless against the entrenched Turks and Germans, and the enemy machine guns were difficult to spot.

At 11 a.m. Chaytor ordered the commander of his reserve 1st LH Brigade to send

WMR horses sheltering from bombing raids after the capture of Tel el Saba.

two regiments and the Inverness Battery into the fight. Seeing no covered approaches, the commanders of the 2nd and 3rd ALH regiments decided to make a dash for it. Their stratagem succeeded at little cost to the riders and the men dismounted about 1500 metres from the tel on the south side of Wadi Saba. The Australians advanced on foot, suffering increasingly heavy losses as they closed in on the enemy machine guns.[17] The horse artillery batteries pushed forward and engaged the enemy at increasingly short range, but with no better results. Enemy aircraft now added to Chaytor's worries, bombing the Anzac horses relentlessly. Despite effective covering fire from Australian machine gunners on the south bank, the Aucklands in the wadi bed could not get closer to the tel than 400 metres. At 1.30 p.m. Chauvel ordered Major General Hodgson to place one of his brigades and two artillery batteries at Chaytor's disposal.

The light horsemen of the 1st LH Brigade captured the blockhouses on the southern bank of Wadi Saba and used the machine guns in them against the main enemy position. To the north, the Canterbury regiment crossed Wadi Khalil and threatened Tel el Saba from the north – although long-range fire from the hills overlooking the Hebron road stopped them from reaching the tel. This support allowed the Aucklands to get very close to the first enemy position, on the small knoll to the east of the tel. Second Lieutenant Ernest Picot brought his two machine guns into action at a range of 1000 metres, closing to half that distance as the Auckland troopers advanced. He was soon able to fire along the face of the forward enemy position and this permitted the troopers to charge the first enemy line around 2 p.m. Picot took one Vickers gun in the leading assault wave, then raced ahead to capture single-handedly an enemy machine gun and its crew of six men. Two or three machine guns and 60 prisoners were taken at 2.40 p.m. The guns were immediately turned around and used against the main defensive position.[18]

Twenty minutes later the Aucklands, reinforced by a WMR squadron and a light horse squadron, completed the job by charging the tel itself. As they clambered up the steep slopes, the garrison tried to escape. A number of fleeing Turks were shot down as they ran and 132 prisoners were taken, along with four Maxim machine guns and a camp cooker. Twenty-five Turks lay dead on the tel.[19]

Enemy aircraft and artillery bombed and shelled the tel and its environs for the next two hours. According to James McCarroll, the Turk shellfire was so heavy that the New Zealanders found it 'quite impossible to stay on top'. The horses of the WMR came under accurate shellfire in Wadi Saba. They were quickly moved to better cover against a cliff near the captured tel but 'showers' of shrapnel and aircraft bombs still caused casualties. Eight NZMR Brigade men were killed and 26 wounded on 31 October, almost all from the AMR. Six horses were killed and 19 wounded.[20]

Tel el Saba, viewed from the south bank of the Wadi Saba. Some trenches are visible.

B03068. AUSTRALIAN WAR MEMORIAL

Light horsemen inspecting captured trenches on Tel el Saba, above Wadi Saba.

Chaytor ordered the 1st and 3rd LH brigades (the latter from Hodgson's division) to advance immediately on foot to the northern outskirts of Beersheba to isolate the town and complete its capture, but they were hotly opposed and made little progress.

The capture of Tel el Saba had removed the main enemy position dominating the eastern approach to Beersheba but the day was far advanced and the town and its vital wells were still in Turkish hands. With the sun almost setting, there was little time left to capture Beersheba. The infantry of 20 Corps, watching from the heights to the south and west of the town, could not help. A bolder solution was required if the town and its wells were to be secured before dark. General Chauvel had always intended to use the Australian Mounted Division for the attack into Beersheba. He had planned to conduct a standard dismounted attack with these light horsemen but that was now out of the question.[21]

Brigadier General William Grant's 4th LH Brigade was ordered to lead a mounted charge into Beersheba, followed by the 5th and 7th Mounted brigades. Grant's two leading regiments, deployed on either side of the Iswaiwin–Beersheba track, were ordered to carry their bayonets in their hands as they rode. The horsemen moved up to their start lines, two to three kilometres from the forward enemy trenches. They were ready to go at 4.30 p.m., just before sunset. 'In front of them lay a long, but slight, slope broken occasionally by tracks cut by the rains and totally devoid of cover.' They set off at a trot until the squadrons had spread out and settled, then they increased the pace to a canter. The last two kilometres or so were ridden at the gallop.[22]

To the New Zealanders watching, it was quite a spectacle. James McCarroll watched as 'a great sight suddenly sprung up on our left, lines and lines of horsemen moving. The Turks were on the run and the Aust. Div. was after them. We could see the horses jumping the trenches, dust everywhere.' At the first trench line, the Australians of the 4th ALH Regiment killed 30 to 40 Turks in unusually bitter fighting, before the survivors surrendered. Further south, small groups of men from the 12th regiment killed about 60 Turks, while the rest of the regiment galloped straight on for the town. On the way in, the Australians overtook many fleeing Turkish soldiers, killing those who would not surrender. Several guns were overrun and captured. Their own losses were 31 killed and 32 wounded.[23]

Thirty minutes before this charge, the Turkish commander in Beersheba had ordered his men to blow up the wells and then withdraw, after sunset. Seeing the town invaded by the Australians, the Turks abandoned their defences and attempted to flee without stopping to destroy most of the wells. The New Zealanders moved forward from Tel el Saba to the edge of Beersheba, reaching it by 6 p.m. Half an hour later, Beersheba was firmly in the hands of the Desert Mounted Corps. The AMR was left to guard Tel el Saba overnight; the rest of the brigade withdrew into reserve.[24]

J03177, AUSTRALIAN WAR MEMORIAL

The result of an enemy bombing raid during the Beersheba operations.

The New Zealanders were well pleased with their efforts. Frank Twisleton described the capture of Tel el Saba as 'a very brilliant little action, requiring plenty of nerve and dash and the troops have plenty of it'. [25] Although most Australians would disagree, James McCarroll considered the capture of Tel el Saba to be the key achievement of the day: 'When the Turk lost that, he had to retire. If the Turk had had another week, he would have made the position much stronger. Evidently, they did not expect such a force to attack him in rear.'[26]

The Desert Mounted Corps captured more than 1500 Turks in the day's fighting, mostly by the 4th LH Brigade. More than half the enemy infantrymen in and around Beersheba were killed or captured; only the 3rd Cavalry Division got away more or less intact. The entire DMC suffered 53 men killed and 144 wounded.[27]

Although all the wells in Beersheba were prepared for demolition, the speed of the Australian charge had not given the German engineers enough time to destroy more than two of them before they were captured or chased off. Two reservoirs holding about 410,000 litres of water were taken intact. The water in Beersheba, plus a few pools of rainwater in surrounding wadis, seemed to be enough to meet nearly all of the needs of the forces around Beersheba.[28]

Turkish prisoners captured at Beersheba.

10

In the land of milk and honey

It was worth a month's pay to see old Charley stick his head down,
and drink, and drink, and drink.

BEN HAYMAN

———————————————

THE CAPTURE OF Beersheba was supposed to be followed within two days by 20 Corps' attack on the eastern end of the Turkish main defensive line at Hareira and Sheria. Lieutenant General Chauvel's Desert Mounted Corps was sent northwards from Beersheba to secure the right flank for 20 Corps' attack, and to search for water. There was practically none between Beersheba and the wells and cisterns at Khuweilfe, 17 kilometres to the north in the lower Judean Hills (see Map 11, p.176). Unfortunately, the tel guarding the water was well defended and the barren, stony approaches to it were very exposed.

The men of the Anzac Mounted Division rode into the hills on 1 November 1917. The 2nd LH Brigade advanced north-east along the Hebron road while, to its left, the WMR and CMR regiments rode along two bridle paths. The Anzacs captured 179 prisoners and four machine guns on the first day. The Canterbury and Wellington regiments had heavy fighting against strong Turkish positions that were liberally equipped with machine guns.

The Canterbury regiment … came under fire, but by a brilliant piece of work, in which the 10th [Nelson] Squadron and Lieutenant C.M. Milne's troop in particular made a frontal attack, and the 1st [CYC] Squadron came in on the enemy flank, captured an officer and 12 men with a machine gun.[1]

The New Zealanders withdrew to bivouac at 11.30 p.m., having lost two horses killed, and two horses and two men wounded.[2]

Thus far, the advance had been straightforward but future prospects were less rosy. The Turks believed that the movement of this force along the axis of the Hebron road heralded the start of an advance on Jerusalem, and they sent reserves from their main defensive line into the Judean Hills to block it. The absence of water in the hills meant that each mounted brigade could stay in the front line for only 24 hours before it had to be sent back to be watered. On 2 November, Chaytor dispatched the New Zealand brigade to Bir Imshash el Malah, 17 kilometres east of Beersheba, where good wells had been reported. The rest of the Anzac division, the Imperial Camel Corps (ICC) Brigade and the 7th Mounted Brigade had to try to capture their water from the Turks.[3]

When the New Zealanders arrived at Imshash el Malah at noon, they found only a few scattered pools of muddy water and a couple of wells. According to Fred Sterling, 'the best name for this place is Hell'.

> *It has taken us five hours to get enough water for our neddies. Trekked across to a wadi and found it dry, came back and went out to some ancient wells and baled the water out of them with canvas buckets on the end of 50 feet of bridle reins and head ropes.... Some of the wells here were an enormous depth and every ruined well had a dead camel or beast in it.[4]*

The New Zealanders spent the next two days searching for water. There was no grass for the horses so they had to subsist on emergency grain rations. A hot, dry khamsin

A British horse artillery battery supporting the attacks in the Judean Hills. Horse lines are visible in the background.

wind began blowing on 2 November, evaporating the last pools of water from the recent rainstorm and increasing the thirst of men and horses.

Up in the hills, the 2nd LH Brigade tried to capture the village of Dhaheriye. Lack of water, difficult ground and a tenacious defence by the Turks, who believed they were defending the approaches to Holy Jerusalem against the infidels, defeated the lightly armed Australians. Further west, the 7th Mounted Brigade's advance towards Khuweilfe also enjoyed very limited success.

On 3 November the 53rd Division reinforced the mounted forces in the hills. The infantry made some progress but suffered heavy casualties and captured no water. The Anzac Mounted Division, still without the New Zealanders, went forward again on their right. As they approached Khuweilfe, enemy resistance again stiffened. Further east, the 2nd LH Brigade gained a little more ground and secured some water, but Dhaheriye remained in enemy hands and the Australians were too isolated to remain in place for long. The horses of the 1st LH and 7th Mounted brigades were now in desperate need of water so Chaytor sent both brigades back to the wells in Beersheba.

According to Ben Hayman, the water supply was so poor at Imshash el Malah by the morning of 4 November that the New Zealanders 'were told to go anywhere we thought we'd get water for the horses'.[5] At noon, wrote Fred Sterling, some of the horses returned.

> Poor beggars, they got no water. Our boys paid Bedouin boys to go down the wells and bail the water into buckets, but [there was] not half enough for a quarter of the horses. We are leaving here shortly. I don't know where to, but anywhere is better than this.[6]

When the NZMR Brigade was sent forward that afternoon to relieve the 5th Mounted Brigade in the front line, most of its horses had not had a drink for at least 24 hours.

By 5 p.m. the head of the New Zealand column was within 2000 metres of the main enemy position on Khuweilfe and coming under effective artillery fire. The riders pressed on to Ras el Nagb, a waterless hill on the other side of a valley, 1500 metres north-east of Khuweilfe. Four Vickers guns of the New Zealand Machine Gun Squadron inflicted casualties on several small groups of Turkish infantry. Late in the afternoon a determined Turkish attack was 'practically wiped out by the Squadron's guns'.[7]

The New Zealanders spent nearly two days on Ras el Nagb, enduring 'almost perfect' enemy artillery fire. 'It was estimated that the Turks had fifteen guns firing from three different directions.' The New Zealanders piled stones in front of them, as the ground was too hard to dig trenches in, but exploding Turkish shells turned the rocks into lethal shrapnel. There was no shelter in the low ground behind the front line for the horses, and they suffered heavy losses from relentless artillery fire. The brigade's new 13-pounder horse artillery guns 'could not find the hostile batteries; moreover, they could not have hit hard enough if they had done so…. The new batteries were outranged and outweighted in every fight the brigade was subsequently engaged in.'[8]

The New Zealanders were shelled and machine-gunned on the morning of 5 November as a prelude to a heavy Turkish infantry attack. Four hundred Turks advanced strongly against the left of the Canterbury line and two Wellington squadrons had to be rushed forward in support. 'The Turks got to within two hundred yards of our line, but could not get any closer, and the attack gradually died away.' Lance Corporal Leonard Greenslade, a twenty-seven-year-old Canterbury man, was killed while trying to evacuate a wounded colleague from the firing line. With no trenches to provide cover, Greenslade and another man had to carry the casualty through a hail of bullets and shrapnel. Both rescuers were hit, but Greenslade was the only one to die. He was one of six New Zealanders killed that day; another 81 mounteds were wounded. Thirty-five horses were killed and 84 wounded.[9]

The NZMR Brigade was ordered back to Beersheba on 5 November. After watering there, the New Zealanders were told to support 20 Corps' delayed attack on Sheria the next day. The New Zealanders were supposed to be relieved by the ICC Brigade but the cameliers got lost in the wadis leading up to the hills, and failed to turn up.[10] At 5 p.m. Fred Sterling wrote: 'So far no relief is to hand. Horses are in a bad way…. We got an issue of water ourselves. Most of us gave it to our nags. The machine gun packs have been removed. Horses could not stand up under them.'[11]

The Turkish artillery fire ceased at dusk and the men had a relatively quiet night. Many of the surviving horses were weak from lack of food and water so Brigadier General Meldrum sent most of them back to Beersheba without their riders at 11 p.m. (The Vickers and Hotchkiss gun pack horses had to stay behind in case the weapons had to be moved in a hurry.) According to James McCarroll, 'we felt quite lonely [and doubtless vulnerable] without them'.[12] The men's jackets and greatcoats went back with the horses. 'The result,' as Robert Tuke noted, 'was that our regiment was on the ridge all night in our thin shirts, and it was one of the coldest we have ever experienced. We did curse the Camel Corps.'[13]

Many of the horses had already gone 48 hours without water but there was little relief in Beersheba for most of them.

Ras el Nagb, viewed from near the Turkish position on Tel Khuweilfe.

Seemingly every horse in the Desert Mounted Corps was at Beersheba for water. Camels, donkeys, mules and horses were mixed up in hopeless confusion. The engineers, in an effort to cope with the rush, set a time limit for each unit. This being much too short ... many animals got no water at all.[14]

Some horses rushed forward uncontrollably when they smelt the water, upsetting the troughs and spilling the precious liquid. Ben Hayman's horse did manage to get a drink. 'It was worth a month's pay to see old Charley stick his head down, and drink, and drink, and drink.'[15]

When the ICC Brigade finally turned up at 8 a.m. on 6 November the cameliers generously gave some of their water to the parched New Zealanders. 'Everyone was tempted to gulp the water, but most took only a sip, and boiled the rest for tea.' The exhausted New Zealanders then trudged eight kilometres to Khurbet el Ras. The machine gun packhorses, most of which had been 72 hours without water, staggered back down the wadis with the men. As the men were filling their water bottles, one animal lay down and seemed close to death, until someone gave him a drink of water. 'He struggled to his feet and drank it out of a dixie lid, and we gave him another. He showed his appreciation by walking 12 miles, where he was rewarded with a good drink and a month in hospital.' Another of the packhorses was so weak that 'two of us removed all the ammunition from the [Hotchkiss] gun [ammunition] strips and dumped it to enable the poor brute to carry out the saddle and panniers'. As Fred Sterling wrote, 'It's wonderful what some horses can stand.' The CMR stopped at Khurbet el Ras while the rest of the brigade carried on to a bivouac on the Hebron road six kilometres from Beersheba. Their horses joined them at 9 p.m.[16]

The horses had to make a 10-hour round trip into Beersheba each day to water. Along with the water shortage, there was little food for the men and even less forage for the horses. Many of the men spent hours at night hunting for water for their horses, adding to their own exhaustion. The majority of the brigade remained in reserve for the next four days but one squadron was sent back up into the hills to provide a link between the ICC Brigade and the 53rd Division and the Auckland regiment was temporarily attached to the 53rd Division.[17]

Between 1 and 6 November 1917, 32 Anzac Mounted Division men were killed and 308 wounded; 131 horses were killed. The New Zealanders suffered 87 casualties in this period, including 16 fatalities. Thirty-seven horses in the brigade were killed and 84 others were wounded. Turkish artillery fire was the main cause of these losses. 'Although the country was very rugged, with innumerable deep gullies that normally could be expected to provide good shelter for the animals, they proved to be death traps in many cases. With the heavy howitzers in use by the enemy, their gunners were able to drop the high trajectory shells right into the gullies, or alternatively, to pepper the sheltering men and horses from above with bursts of shrapnel fired from the so accurately ranged high velocity field guns.' Ben Hayman had 'never been under such intense and prolonged shrapnel fire. All back down the gullies the horses lay dead, in heaps in some places.'[18]

It was now time for 20 Corps to attack the Turkish defences at Hareira and to capture the wells at Sheria. The NZMR Brigade was placed under command of the 53rd Division, along with the ICC Brigade, and given the task of pinning down the Turks at Khuweilfe to prevent them from interfering with the main attack against Hareira. The rest of the Anzac division and the Australian Mounted Division waited to push through the enemy line as soon as it was pierced by 20 Corps. All was ready by the morning of 6 November.

The Sheria–Hareira sector of the Turkish line was weakly held as a number of Turkish battalions had been pulled out of the line and sent into the Judean Hills to defend Khuweilfe and the Hebron Road. Consequently the enemy line was cracked in one day and smashed wide open in two.

Up in the hills, the 53rd Division's operation did not go as well. Navigational errors, compounded by early-morning mist, led some battalions to attack the wrong features. Turkish resistance was resolute and fierce counter-attacks were beaten off with difficulty. The situation stabilised at nightfall and the Turks abandoned their positions the next evening and withdrew to the west. The attack had served its purpose: no enemy forces left this sector in time to assist the Turks defending Hareira.

On the morning of 7 November, 21 Corps discovered that Gaza had been evacuated by the Turks. With the Turks finally out of their prepared defences and in the open, this should have been the mounted troops' opportunity to turn their retreat into a rout. Orders were issued for the DMC – without the NZMR Brigade, the ICC Brigade and the Yeomanry division, which were all left behind for lack of water – to advance rapidly to Huj and Jemmame to capture the wells there, before moving west to cut off the retreating Turkish armies. After a late start on 7 November, the two light horse brigades of the Anzac Mounted Division galloped through the gap between Sheria and Khuweilfe and into the Turkish rear area. Initially many surprised Turks were rounded up but reaction quickly stiffened. The Australian Mounted Division was held up briefly by stubborn Turkish resistance at its crossing point.

The opportunity to capture the Turkish main body was quickly passing. Many enemy

New Zealand horses under shellfire in 'Dead Horse Gully' below Ras el Nagb.

213

The NZMR Brigade walking out from the Judean Hills on 6 November 1917.

regiments had already been pulled out of the line when the DMC was launched. They were slowly making their way northwards, protected by determined rearguards which included German machine gunners and Austrian artillerymen. The Turks did not fear being caught by the British infantry, whom they could always outmarch with a few hours' head start. If they could keep the enemy horsemen away from water for just a little longer, they would have to stop, allowing the Turks to make a clean break and complete their withdrawal. This was exactly what Allenby wanted to avoid but he was powerless to prevent it.[19]

As the horsemen advanced towards the coast they captured a few intact wells, but the ancient bores were often 70 metres deep and the retreating Turks had cut the ropes and thrown them and the buckets into the depths. The horsemen often had to use canvas buckets attached to lengths of telephone cable to haul water to the surface. 'The horses were almost unmanageable, and when they saw water they threw themselves on their knees and upset as much as they drank.' Under these impossible conditions, it often took an entire night to water a single squadron of horses. The wells at Jemmame were captured by the 1st LH Brigade on the afternoon of 8 November. This allowed some of the parched horses to be watered.[20]

The Australian Mounted Division pushed on, desperately trying to close the net around the Turks. As the horsemen approached Huj on 8 November, the British cavalry had a rare and irresistible opportunity for mounted shock action. When a column of retreating Turks was spotted beyond a thin flank guard in the hills, the 5th Mounted Brigade was ordered to charge. Opposing the 120 sword-wielding cavalrymen were 200 Turkish infantrymen, two Austrian artillery batteries and four German machine guns. With no artillery or machine guns to suppress these enemy weapons, the British cavalrymen made easy targets as they galloped up to the enemy positions. Few Turks stayed to face the final charge but many brave German machine gunners and Austrian artillerymen stayed with their guns until they were killed with sword thrusts. About 70 prisoners were taken. The British lost 70 men killed or wounded out of the 120 who charged; 100 of their precious horses were killed.[21] Huj was occupied without further fighting but, once again, the Turks had destroyed the wells. Horses had to be sent over to Jemmame to water but few succeeded in getting a drink there either. The water situation was steadily worsening and men and horses were suffering severely from thirst.

Allenby brought the Yeomanry Mounted Division up to rejoin the Desert Mounted Corps, which he ordered to push on towards the Mediterranean coast on 9 November. The exhausted Australian Mounted Division was left behind to rest and water its horses as best it could. Delays in transferring the Yeomanry division, and the continuing lack of water, meant that only the Anzac division, still without the NZMR Brigade, was ready to advance on time. By now, Allenby's pursuit force had been reduced to two weak light horse brigades, fewer than 1000 tired men and parched horses. The 1st and 2nd LH brigades linked up with the leading elements of 21 Corps advancing out of Gaza at Majdal and reached the shore of the Mediterranean Sea near Esdud. The net was finally closed but few Turks from the Gaza garrison were inside it.

Allenby's next objective was Junction Station, 30 kilometres north-east of Majdal. Capturing this railway junction would isolate the Turks in the Judean Hills around Jerusalem from the main Turkish supply line to the north. Before the advance could resume, however, a great deal of reorganisation was required. During this period, most of the NZMR Brigade remained near Beersheba, while the AMR regiment continued to watch the Turks in the foothills near Khuweilfe.

On the morning of 10 November Chaytor was forced to tell Chauvel that the Anzac Mounted Division 'was ridden out, and that it positively must halt till its horses had drunk their fill. They had reached a stage very near collapse.' The Australian Mounted Division was in slightly better condition, having spent the previous day watering its horses. The Yeomanry Mounted Division moved up behind the Australians, before being sent across to Majdal to relieve the Anzacs. The 52nd Division, coming up from Gaza, captured Esdud on the morning of 11 November. Allenby then moved his assault divisions forward for the attack on Junction Station.[22]

On 10 November the NZMR Brigade (less the AMR) moved into Beersheba. The next day, it was ordered forward to rejoin the Anzac division at Hammame. After waiting for the AMR to be relieved in the front line, the New Zealanders rode out from Beersheba at 4.30 p.m., in a blinding duststorm that forced the scouts to use luminous compasses. Some riders and their horses fell down the steep banks of the wadi at Sheria, as they tried to cross it in the dark. 'We trekked all night in a miserable sort of way,' wrote Fred Sterling. 'In and out amongst the gun pits and trenches first walking, then trotting, then halting etc. The dust was that thick we could hardly breathe let alone see. The night was very dark and cold.'[23]

After a brief rest at dawn, the riders were back in the saddle by 7 a.m. on 12 November, heading for Jemmame. According to Guy Powles, 'the dust … was appalling, the route taken … was intersected with deep wadis which could only be crossed in single file, while in some cases the transport and ambulance wagons had to travel many miles extra till they found crossing places'. The riders passed the bodies of dead Turks and animals, abandoned wagons, trains, guns and stores. Some horses drank filthy water from wadi pools or from abandoned wells. 'The horses are horribly tired, and, where possible, we walked.' The

WMR men and Australian light horsemen filling their water bottles.

PA1-Q-605-24-2, POWLES FAMILY COLLECTION, ALEXANDER TURNBULL LIBRARY brigade finally reached Hammame at 9 p.m. that night, having ridden 85 kilometres in 28 hours. Frank Twisleton noted that the exhausted and parched horses 'fairly wobbled at the finish'.[24]

Allenby's infantrymen had marched up to 80 kilometres since 29 October 1917 and most of his horsemen had ridden three times as far. The Turkish 7th and 8th armies had been forced off the Gaza–Beersheba line, losing 10,000 men in the process, but they had escaped 'the complete annihilation that at one time seemed to threaten them. The stout fighting of their rearguards and the hard marching of their infantry would not, however, have availed to save them had not the lack of water so dispersed the pursuing mounted troops and restricted their rate of movement.'[25]

Allenby pressed ahead with his preparations for the capture of Junction Station. The main attack was the responsibility of 21 Corps, with the Australian Mounted Division on its right. The rest of the DMC was to advance along the coast. A bridgehead across Nahr Sukereir was expanded and the assault forces were ready to advance on the morning of 13 November 1917.[26]

11

Gallop for your life!

A few thousand Turks chased as many hundred of us and we escaped by a miracle.
We had two miles to gallop with bullets flying around … and these beggars chasing
us. I just lay flat and wished I were smaller and the old hack Jerry did his best.

ALEC McNEUR

_____

TWO TURKISH ARMIES were withdrawing ahead of Allenby's army. The 8th Army was closest to the Mediterranean coast, while the 7th Army hugged the western edge of the Judean Hills to shield Jerusalem. As long as the Turks held the railway and roads linking Jaffa to Jerusalem, these armies could communicate with each other; once these links were cut, they would be separated and vulnerable to defeat in isolation (see Map 11, p.176). Allenby

Horses waiting for water at Jemmame.

acted quickly to sever both lines of communication. The seizure of the railway at Junction Station on 14 November did not involve the NZMR Brigade but the capture of the high ground in front of the Jaffa–Jerusalem road, on the same day, was a wholly New Zealand affair.

The Anzac Mounted Division was required to cut the road linking Jaffa to Jerusalem, by capturing Ramleh and Ludd. In the first stage of his operation, Chaytor tasked the 1st LH Brigade to take the Jewish village of Rechovot (Deiran in Arabic) on the right, while Meldrum's New Zealand brigade was told to capture Ayun Kara.[1]

The area of Palestine the New Zealanders were entering was starkly different from what they had become accustomed to. They crossed Nahr Sukereir, the 'the first real river' they had seen since leaving Cairo, via 'a fine, old stone bridge … evidently dating from the time of the Crusaders'.[2] As they rode northwards across the fertile and well-watered plains, they began to encounter modern towns inhabited by friendly European Jews and surrounded by vineyards, plantations of olive trees and groves of orange trees.

Ayun Kara was near the northern end of an undulating ridge that extended southwards for about five kilometres to the bank of Wadi Hanein. This ridge (which I shall refer to as WMR Ridge) was composed of sandy, red soil and punctuated by frequent, and very defensible, rocky knolls and plateaus. WMR Ridge was not an impressive geographic feature – nowhere did it rise more than 70 metres above sea level – but it dominated the lower ground to the south and on either side, and that was what mattered. Part-way along WMR Ridge, near a small but prominent hill called Red Knoll, a crescent-shaped ridge curved west (Counter-attack Ridge) towards the coastal sand dunes and south-east (CMR Ridge) to the orange groves and vineyards around another Jewish settlement, Nes Ziyona, in the valley of Wadi Hanein. On the northern side of Counter-attack Ridge, behind Red Knoll, was a cultivated valley (the Basin) that was hidden from view from the south. From near Red Knoll, a lower and gentler spur (AMR Ridge) extended south-westwards from WMR Ridge. These two ridges were separated by a narrow valley containing a dry wadi and the Gaza–Jaffa road. Apart from the cultivations around Nes Ziyona and in the Basin, the terrain was bare and exposed – good defensive ground.[3]

That morning, the jaded horsemen plodding along behind the scouts 'had made up our minds we were to have more or less of a quiet day, and the country and scenery were wonderful'.[4] Since leaving Ras el Nagb three days earlier, the only Turks the New Zealanders had seen were corpses or prisoners. With the start of the rainy season overdue, many of the horsemen must have looked forward to settling quietly into winter quarters.

At 9 a.m. the Canterbury regiment led the NZMR Brigade into Kubeibeh. When the

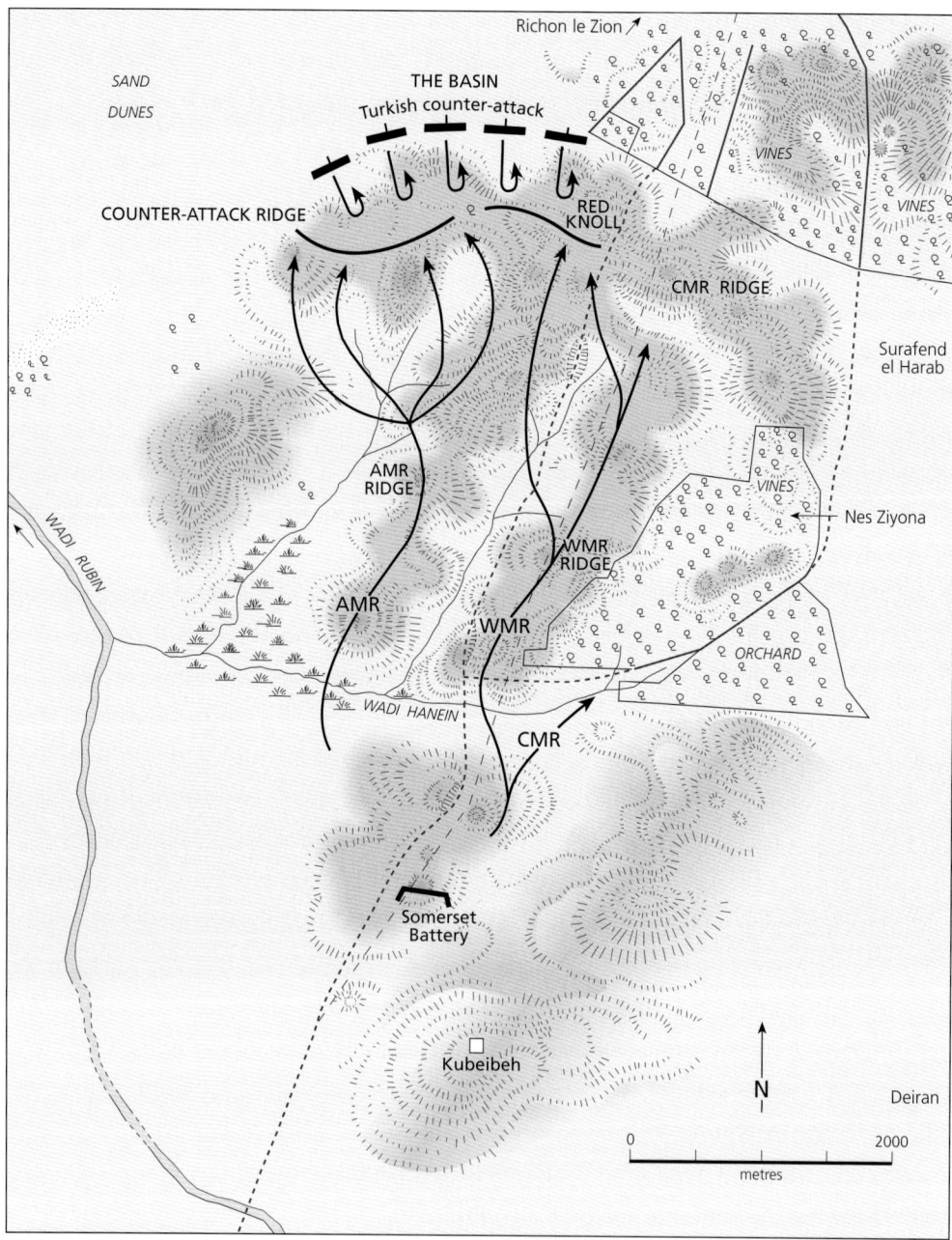

Map 13: Ayun Kara.

main body of the brigade arrived, the Canterburys pushed on north-eastwards towards the Arab village of Surafend el Harab. The South Islanders reached the banks of Wadi Hanein at 11.25 a.m., where they were held up by heavy machine gun and rifle fire from Turkish redoubts in the orchards around Nes Ziyona. The 1st LH Brigade captured Deiran at 9.30 a.m. As the New Zealanders prepared to move on from Kubeibeh, the light horsemen warned Chaytor that they could see enemy troops moving towards the New Zealand brigade. NZMR scouts identified several Turk positions along WMR Ridge and on Counter-attack Ridge but AMR Ridge appeared to be undefended.[5]

Brigadier General Meldrum's orders required the Wellington regiment to attack on foot along WMR Ridge. The Aucklands were to advance on horseback up the adjacent AMR Ridge, protecting the Wellingtons' left flank and looking for an opportunity to outflank the Turks on WMR Ridge. The CMR was to protect the WMR's right flank and clear the orchards around Nes Ziyona, before moving up onto CMR Ridge. The regiments would then concentrate on the ridge short of Ayun Kara which, if it had not been abandoned by then, would be captured by a brigade attack. The Somerset Battery deployed its four 13-pounder guns on a small knoll south of Wadi Hanein and the New Zealand Machine Gun Squadron attached four Vickers guns to each of the North Island regiments. Between them, these two regiments fielded only 700 riflemen – a very slender force with which to assault a defended position, especially with such weak artillery support.[6]

The AMR and WMR regiments rode out from Kubeibeh at 11.30 a.m. The horsemen came under long-range machine gun fire as they crossed Wadi Hanein. The dismounted 9th (Wellington East Coast) Squadron led the way along WMR Ridge, which was only wide enough for one squadron. Supported by covering fire from the machine guns and the 2nd (Wellington West Coast) Squadron, they captured the first enemy position in a bayonet charge at 12.30 p.m., killing 20 Turks and capturing two machine guns. Their own machine guns were then brought forward to the captured trenches, from where they shot up a Turkish counter-attack force and several machine gun posts. Under covering fire from these machine guns and the 2nd Squadron, the 9th Squadron swept on to take the second line of enemy trenches and two more machine guns at 1.30 p.m. They were prevented from securing a hat-trick at the next row of trenches by heavy enemy fire from Counter-attack Ridge and Red Knoll.[7]

According to Lieutenant Colonel James McCarroll, the CO of the AMR regiment, Meldrum's orders to him were simple: 'Find the enemy and smash him'. Major Frank Twisleton's 3rd (Auckland) Squadron galloped up the forward slopes of AMR Ridge to secure an initial fire position on the right. McCarroll then spotted some Turkish cavalrymen to his left front so he sent the 11th (North Auckland) Squadron forward to determine what they were up to. When they were held up, McCarroll sent two troops of the 4th (Waikato) Squadron galloping straight at the enemy. This move seemed to catch the Turks by surprise and the riders reached their objective with few losses. Thinking that the Turks were trying to get around the AMR's western flank, McCarroll reinforced the Waikato men with the North Auckland squadron and two machine guns, before bringing the Waikato men back to join the rest of their squadron.[8]

The Waikato squadron continued to advance along AMR Ridge with the 3rd (Auckland) Squadron in support, keeping pace with the Wellingtons on their right. When he spotted Turks massing to counter-attack the Wellingtons on the neighbouring ridge, McCarroll sent the 3rd Squadron forward to give better support. Although the Aucklands were now encountering few enemy forces on their own ridge, they were subjected to increasingly effective fire from WMR Ridge, Red Knoll and Counter-attack Ridge.[9]

At 2.15 p.m. AMR patrols scouting along the edge of the western sand dunes reported a large number of Turks assembling in orange groves in the Basin behind Counter-attack Ridge. McCarroll immediately ordered the 11th Squadron to send a troop up to the ridge to engage them. These men rode straight into trouble, coming under attack from about 50 Turks. McCarroll sent the 3rd Squadron to help the North Aucklanders. He also assembled all the cooks, signallers, gallopers, horse holders and batmen in his regimental headquarters and sent them into the firing line. Frank Twisleton brought his squadron up at the gallop 'in fine style, dismounting within a few yards of the hard-pressed line'. One of his troops

New Zealand horses watering immediately prior to Ayun Kara.

1986.2089, QUEEN ELIZABETH II ARMY MEMORIAL MUSEUM

briefly occupied a small knoll in advance of the main firing line, where it sustained heavy casualties before the survivors pulled back to a safer position.[10]

The next Turkish counter-attack was launched against the WMR position at 2.30 p.m. but it 'withered away' under massed machine gun and rifle fire from the Auckland and Wellington regiments. With the support of an artillery battery in the gardens of Richon le Zion, the Turkish attack was renewed in greater strength across the entire front at 2.45 p.m. According to the AMR War Diary, several hundred Turks attacked 'very strongly', quickly closing to within 50 metres of the Auckland line. When the knoll mentioned in the previous paragraph was occupied by the enemy, McCarroll ordered the 4th Squadron up to recapture it. The Waikato men took the hill in a bayonet charge, then crept forward until they could fire along the length of the Turks' main line. By now many horse holders were also in the line and signallers were being used to evacuate the many wounded men. Vickers guns on either flank fired point-blank into the lines of advancing Turks, stopping them within 20 metres of the AMR line. As these guns were in the open, several machine gunners were injured by Turkish grenades. When four guns were put out of action, the surviving gunners fought on with rifles and revolvers. With all his squadrons and even his headquarters staff in the firing line, McCarroll asked Meldrum for reinforcements.[11]

With no dedicated brigade reserve to call upon, Meldrum told his old Wellington regiment to do what it could to help the Aucklands. Captain Arthur Herrick led two troops of the 2nd Squadron, at the gallop, across 2500 metres of open ground from WMR Ridge towards Red Knoll. All the riders, and all except two horses, survived the intense machine gun and rifle fire directed at them. The men dismounted 200 metres from the knoll and rushed it on foot. In fierce hand-to-hand fighting, the New Zealanders killed the defenders and captured the machine gun, which they then turned on nearby enemy machine gun posts. Herrick was wounded twice after dismounting; a third bullet killed him. The rest of his squadron quickly galloped forward to Red Knoll to reinforce his success.[12]

With the capture of Red Knoll, the pressure on both regiments eased. The WMR's 6th (Manawatu) Squadron came forward and the 9th Squadron conducted another bayonet charge to capture the final position on WMR Ridge. On the left, two troops from the 3rd (Auckland) Squadron reached a position from where they were able to pour devastating Hotchkiss fire into another Turkish counter-attack force. Reinforced by a couple of Vickers guns, they enjoyed what McCarroll described as 'the machine gunners' dream'. The Turks made a final and 'most determined' attack on the Aucklands and Wellingtons about 4 p.m., closing to within 15 metres and hurling grenades as they came. A counter-charge by the Aucklands stopped the Turks, who were then caught by enfilade machine gun fire from the flanks.[13]

The combined weight of fire from the Auckland and Wellington regiments, and especially from the machine guns, was too much for the Turks, who 'were soon fleeing in all directions'. By 4.45 p.m. the fighting was over, although rifle and machine gun fire and artillery exchanges continued until sunset. According to Fred Sterling, 'the Turks kept up a hellish fire until dark to cover the retirement of their men. Bullets fell like hail everywhere.' Sterling's description of the final Turkish counter-attack is worth quoting at length.

The rifle fire from both sides made up one continual roar.... We could see the Turks mustering like cattle in this orchard, forming up and lying down in lines. Such of our machine guns that were not out of action kept playing into their massed troops. About 2 p.m., Jacko's shelling reached its height, and we were in a sorry way through losses. Ammunition was running short, with no hopes of getting fresh supplies. Jacko attacked, pushing forward his men behind the small ridge in front, which was not more than 200 yards from where we lay. The shooting on our side was simply beautiful, Jacko's ranks at times getting sadly thinned out. After a short spell behind the ridge, during which time we could see their officers getting them in order, Jacko made his final flutter towards our position, yelling 'Allah! Allah' like mad. They staggered in thick lines right up to the base of our ridge, and not 15 yards from where we stood blazing away.... Hundreds of them it seemed to me. They pitched scores of percussion and cricket-ball grenades up at us, which, when they burst, added muchly to the din. The Turks were yelling and calling upon all their saints to help. Our fellows were swearing and cheering, and making sure of everyone that showed up. The fight went on until 4 p.m., and we were about done for – men, officers, batmen, everyone who could be mustered was at it.... The Turkish 'heads' seemed as if they could not make their men make the final charge. Two of their bigwigs came up flash as paint, waving their arms and shouting. They did not last long. [They] fell like wet sacks and then Jacko seemed to throw up the sponge. Like the Devil they ran. Simply went for it, staggering over the soft sand under the raking fire from a big machine gun that our fellows had just got into position.[14]

As McCarroll assembled his squadron leaders to issue pursuit orders, he was shot twice, in the neck and the shoulder. 'I got a smack like a sledge hammer on the shoulder. I was spitting blood.' It quickly became obvious that the brigade was in no fit state for further offensive action, and as there were no fresh troops immediately available, thoughts of pursuing the routed Turks had to be abandoned.[15]

The battlefield graves of the New Zealanders killed at Ayun Kara.

Over to the east, the Canterbury regiment had a relatively quiet day. They cleared the orchards and secured Nes Ziyona by noon but were unable to get up onto CMR Ridge because of heavy fire from the surrounding high ground. The South Islanders held this line until the withdrawal of the Turks allowed them to move forward. During the day, a local Jewish woman asked a troop of South Islanders if they knew her son, who she believed to be serving in the New Zealand brigade. Amazingly, he was located in the Auckland regiment, and mother and son were reunited.[16]

According to the divisional report written after the battle, 162 Turkish corpses were counted on the battlefield and about 250 Turks were wounded. A wounded prisoner 'remarked to an Aucklander, "Inglizee no run", and he seemed to be rather perplexed over the fact that a thin and outnumbered line had refused to budge in the face of what seemed inevitable disaster'.[17]

The New Zealanders gathered in their wounded men and consolidated their positions after dark, bringing all their machine guns up into the line. At 9 p.m. the first reinforcements, a company of cameliers, arrived. As Arthur Moore recorded, 'Throughout that night our thin line of survivors held on to their positions, ready for any renewed attack by the enemy, the darkness being made horrible by the groans and cries of the wounded Turks lying before our line.'[18] According to Ben Hayman 'the ceaseless "Allah, Allah, Allah" of the enemy wounded would give a man the willies'. The brigade stood to between 4 and 6.30 a.m. the next morning, before burying its dead and bringing in the wounded Turks.[19]

Much of the fighting at Ayun Kara was conducted at very close range and because the New Zealanders fought in the open, their casualties were heavy. The exact losses are not known but the Ramleh War Cemetery contains the graves of 49 New Zealand men who died between 14 and 16 November. Moore believed that only about 140 AMR men actually took part in the fight. If the figure is correct, this regiment suffered a casualty rate of nearly two-thirds. Forty-one horses were killed and 22 wounded.[20]

Benjamin Marle considered it 'easily the fiercest fighting we have seen'.

The casualties were something awful, and the most astounding thing is that any of us are left to tell the tale. When we got a view of the Turks retreating we fully realised what we had been up against. I don't think I am exaggerating a bit when I say there were eight Turks to every man of us.[21]

Ben Gainfort recalled years afterwards that Ayun Kara was 'our best scrap…. We lost a lot of good men'. Arthur Harrison wrote that the Turks 'had no heart in the attack and we mowed them down – [there were] enough of them to eat us, but [they] retired in disorder, there were dead and wounded everywhere. Such a mess you never saw. I'm sorry to say we lost a lot of good mates though. I never want to see another day like that one, it was a bit too solid altogether.'[22]

The enemy force at Ayun Kara was thought to number between 1000 and 1500 men, supported by 18 machine guns and an artillery battery. The British official historian stated that 'the bulk of the much-depleted 3rd [Infantry] Division was engaged against the New Zealanders'. If these statements are close to the truth, sending 700 or 800 lightly armed riflemen into battle against that number of Turks could have been a recipe for disaster. However, the Turks had a poor defensive layout, and their counter-attacks were late and badly co-ordinated. It also seems likely that the Turks at Ayun Kara had the limited objective of stopping the New Zealanders, to allow the Turkish main body to achieve a clean break and escape across the next river to the north. With little evidence of any attempt by the Turks to outflank the New Zealanders, it seems clear that the destruction of the NZMR Brigade was not their aim. On the New Zealand side, good links between the assaulting regiments, the use of mounted movement to rapidly exploit fleeting opportunities and the magnificent machine gunners made the difference at Ayun Kara. The efforts of the latter, lugging their heavy Vickers guns and tripods up hill and down dale, mostly on foot and under fire, were quite remarkable, as were those of the support teams who brought ammunition and cooling water forward to the guns all day, while being shot at.[23]

The New Zealanders buried their dead on 15 November before riding to a new bivouac site near Richon le Zion, which Walter Macfarlane described as 'a very pretty little Jewish village' surrounded by gardens. Its chief attraction for Macfarlane and many other men was its wineries.[24]

The successful attacks at Junction Station and Ayun Kara split the Turkish forces. Each army could now be dealt with in isolation without being easily reinforced by the other. After the mauling of its 3rd Division by the New Zealanders, the Turkish 8th Army withdrew to the north bank of a river a few kilometres north of Jaffa called Nahr el Auja. This allowed the Anzacs to cut the Jaffa–Jerusalem road and capture Ramleh, Ludd and Jaffa without further fighting.

At 9 a.m. on 16 November, the Wellington regiments rode into Jaffa, receiving a warm reception from the inhabitants. The town was formally occupied the next day. Guy Powles recalled Major General Chaytor sitting on his horse with 'a happy smile on his face' as the Union Jack was hoisted outside the town hall. Meldrum took over the former German consulate as his headquarters and New Zealanders reportedly took 'great delight in the use

WMR officers inspecting a Turkish machine gun captured at Ayun Kara.

The NZMR Brigade parading at the Jaffa Town Hall, 17 November 1917.

of the impressively headed official stationery, which was found there in large quantities'. William Owers picked up a linen shirt with cut-glass buttons which he wore to dances in New Zealand after the war.[25]

Over the following days, the New Zealanders established an entrenched line along the south bank of Nahr el Auja. The Canterbury regiment occupied Sarona, where a pile of barley straw and a chaff cutter were requisitioned. The hungry horses were soon tucking into excellent barley chaff. This good fodder improved the health of the horses, which had subsisted since before Beersheba on five or six kilograms of barley per day and very little water. Farmers in the CMR regiment appreciated the modern agricultural equipment at Sarona, comparing it favourably with the antiquated Egyptian farming methods. Another attraction at Sarona was what was believed to be the largest number of wine cellars in the world.[26] According to Trooper 'Tap' O'Neill, 'our greatest victory' was the capture of these wine cellars.

We held these against all comers for over a week until the Imperial Infantry caught us up. Of course, they then posted a guard over the entrance to the cellars and then it was 'No Admittance.' However, we knew of a secret entrance through a chaff house over the road. So,

PEF/P/RHODES/91, PALESTINE EXPLORATION FUND, LONDON

for another ten days, we lived like fighting cocks. The Tommies never found out how we got the wine. For that period of rest it was wine and pork. We killed over 200 pigs of all ages and sizes while we were there.[27]

Allenby ordered Chauvel's Desert Mounted Corps to establish several bridgeheads across Nahr el Auja. He hoped that this would convince the Turks that the EEF intended to continue advancing up the coastal plain. This should force them to keep the 8th Army on the coast, away from Allenby's real objective of Jerusalem. The bridgeheads would also put a defensible water barrier between the Turks and the port of Jaffa, which Allenby needed for resupply purposes.

The Auja averaged 15 metres in width, with steep, muddy banks. It was slow-moving but too deep to cross easily except at a few fords, including one at the mouth of the river. Three kilometres upstream at Jerishe, a dam at a flour mill offered a crossing point for men on foot. The main crossing point was a stone bridge on the Jaffa–Nablus track at Hadra, two kilometres further inland. All these crossing points were in enemy hands. The ground on the north side of the river rose gently for 1000 metres, to the village of Sheikh Muwannis and the ruins of Khurbet Hadra. Enemy observers at Sheikh Muwannis could see all the

229

way to Jaffa, while men on Khurbet Hadra overlooked the river nearly all the way to the coast. Bridgeheads were to be established at the coastal ford, at Sheikh Muwannis, and at the Hadra bridge, and the ground to a distance of three kilometres north was to be cleared of Turks by the assault troops.[28]

A troop from the Wellington regiment rode out to reconnoitre the river on 19 November. The troop leader, Lieutenant Robert Sutherland, halted the men near the dam at Jerishe and went forward with two troopers to take a closer look. The men were ambushed at close range; Trooper Austin Curry was wounded and taken prisoner. On the same day, two other New Zealanders were wounded as they scouted the Hadra bridge.[29]

The Anzac Mounted Division received the job of establishing the bridgeheads but only the NZMR Brigade was available; the rest of the division was busy watching the enemy in

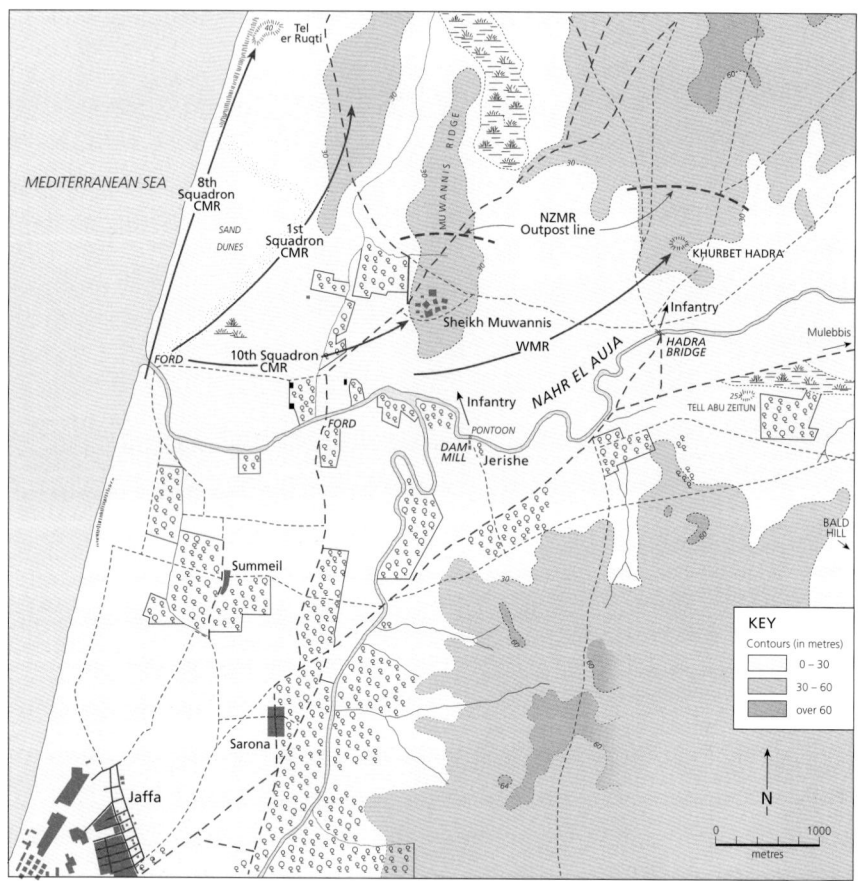

Map 14: Nahr el Auja.

the foothills further east, or resting. Infantry and machine gunners from the 54th Division were to take over the bridgeheads once the NZMR Brigade had established them.[30]

The crossing began at 1 p.m. on 24 November 1917. It should have been preceded by an artillery bombardment of the known enemy positions but the 54th Division's heavy guns were not ready in time. After a light bombardment by the horse artillery, which served only to warn the Turks of an imminent attack, the horsemen of the Canterbury regiment waded across the ford at the river mouth. According to machine gunner Ben Hayman, 'the surprise was complete – a few determined men with a machine gun could have wiped the whole squadron out at that crossing, floundering as we were through the deep water … we crossed without a single casualty'. The 8th (South Canterbury) Squadron galloped for three kilometres along the coastal sand dunes to a knoll at Tel er Ruqti, driving 20 Turks away on its arrival. Two New Zealand machine guns were quickly dug in on this knoll.[31]

The 10th (Nelson) Squadron crossed the ford, wheeled inland and captured Sheikh Muwannis. Turkish cavalry in the village fled to the north, pursued briefly by the New Zealand horsemen. The 1st (CYC) Squadron rode north to reinforce the 8th Squadron.[32]

The Wellington regiment followed the South Islanders across the ford, galloped past Sheikh Muwannis and captured Khurbet Hadra and the nearby stone bridge at 3.30 p.m. The 4th (Waikato) Squadron of the AMR distracted the enemy from the south bank at another ford three kilometres further inland from the Hadra bridge. Twenty-nine prisoners from the 31st Regiment, 3rd Division, and a couple of machine guns were captured, at no cost to the attackers other than one wounded horse.[33]

Two infantry companies from the Essex Regiment of the 54th Division crossed the Hadra bridge and occupied Khurbet Hadra. Another two companies crossed at Jerishe and moved into Sheikh Muwannis. At the request of the infantry commander, the 3rd and 11th squadrons of the AMR established outposts forward of Khurbet Hadra after dark and the 2nd (Wellington West Coast) Squadron of the Wellington regiment deployed an outpost line 500 metres in front of Sheikh Muwannis. The 1st (CYC) Squadron was pulled back from Tel er Ruqti to hold the crossing point at the rivermouth and the rest of the brigade returned to the south bank for the night. The divisional engineers spent the hours of darkness building a pontoon bridge across the river at Jerishe.[34]

All was quiet until the early hours of the next morning. At 2.45 a.m., a Turkish cavalry patrol was chased off by a troop of the 3rd (Auckland) Squadron. Within an hour, a heavy enemy attack had been launched by the Turkish 3rd and 7th infantry divisions. Heavy fire forced the Aucklands to send their horses back. By 5.45 a.m., enemy pressure had forced the mounteds right back onto the supporting infantry line.[35]

The 11th Squadron occupied a stronger position on higher ground and was able to remain in place. In front of Jim McMillan 'the Turks were … coming forward in such numbers that almost suggested a field exercise on their part …. All the fire that we could bring to bear couldn't stop their steady advance, and the position was becoming desperate, for it seemed certain that very soon, if it hadn't already happened, we would be cut off from the crossing and there was surely no chance of holding off the oncoming horde.'[36]

At 8 a.m. the British infantrymen at Khurbet Hadra were ordered back across the river. Kingston Hull was unimpressed, writing that the Essex men 'bolted like sheep when the Turks came near… They are young and small, but have no heart and seem so helpless and ignorant.'[37] The New Zealanders' horses were sent back to the ford at the river mouth.

It was one of the liveliest gallops [the] horse holders ever had. Speed was the one chance of getting the horses out of the closing vice, and speed was secured, notwithstanding the fact that some of the men were leading six horses. Although under fire for most of the way, the horsemen, with their arms almost out of the sockets, reached the ford without serious loss, and plunged through to safety.[38]

According to Charles Nicol, heavy casualties were avoided because the advancing Turks fired as they ran, instead of stopping to take aimed shots.[39]

At 6.10 a.m. the other two squadrons of the Wellington regiment were ordered up to the Hadra bridge to protect the infantry but they were held up by Turkish artillery fire. Some of the British soldiers were killed by enemy machine gun and artillery fire as they crossed the bridge; others who tried to swim the river drowned under the weight of their packs and ammunition.[40]

Once the infantry were clear, the 3rd (Auckland) Squadron crossed the bridge to the south bank on foot. The 11th (North Auckland) Squadron and two Vickers guns from the machine gun squadron covered them from a position immediately north of the bridge. The commander of the machine gunners, Captain Robin Harper, was wounded three times and a section of his guns was knocked out. Harper was carried back across the river by two men. Major Magnus Johnston described how one of Harper's rescuers, Sergeant Sydney Emmerson, 'worked his machine gun until it was disabled, then picked up his wounded officer, ran down the hill and swam with his officer across the river to safety. It was worth a VC, but he got nothing for it. Things like that made me feel pretty sick.'[41]

The ford at the mouth of the Auja today. It is now on the approaches to a municipal and military airport in Tel Aviv.

Once the infantrymen and the 3rd Squadron were clear, the North Aucklanders followed them across the river, covered by the Somerset Battery, which had not fired until then, and by the 11th Squadron from a position on the south bank. A few Aucklands waded the waist-deep stream under fire to rescue wounded men. The bridge was held until 11 a.m., when the Auckland regiment withdrew to higher ground.[42]

The Wellington squadron at Sheikh Muwannis had just as hot a time. The village came under increasingly strong attack from about 6 a.m. and three hours later 2000 Turks forced the Wellington squadron back into the village. The Canterbury regiment recrossed the ford to attack the enemy's right flank, but without effect. Colonel Findlay sent the 1st Squadron back up to Tel er Ruqti, where it immediately ran into 300 Turkish infantrymen. The 8th Squadron was kept close to the ford and the 10th Squadron went across to Sheikh Muwannis to reinforce the Wellington squadron. The latter squadron covered the British infantry as they crossed the river at the Jerishe dam on the new pontoon bridge and by boat. As at Hadra, some heavily laden infantrymen drowned when they tried to swim across the river. As soon as the infantry were safe, the horsemen galloped for the coastal ford, leaving two dismounted Nelson troops as a rearguard.[43]

By 9.30 a.m. 2000 more Turkish infantrymen were advancing down the coast from Tel er Ruqti. Ben Hayman recalled that this 'was a brand new lot of reinforcements, and they meant business'.

They were all dressed in new grey uniforms and carried no packs. They didn't advance in the usual way, laying down to fire, but came on at a lithe dog-trot, firing from the hip, their bayonets … flashing in the sun. There were too many of them for our fire to make the slightest check in their advance. It was what might be called an impressive spectacle.

William Milliken could see that 'we were greatly outnumbered, the Turks were advancing in three lots of four lines each, and just imagine my feelings'. According to Hayman, 'it was quite plain that they meant to get that ford on the beach and cut us all off. So it became a race against time.' Wilkie agreed: 'it was a case of get out or be cut off'.[44]

A section of machine gunners crossed the ford to support the Canterbury squadrons and two Wellington squadrons galloped across to the coast to provide further support from the south bank. As soon as the horsemen from Sheikh Muwannis were across, the South Islanders began their own fighting withdrawal, stepping back through successive fire positions. Lieutenant Alexander Livingston, the commander of the CMR rearguard troop, was killed as he crossed the ford last of all. By noon, the Canterbury regiment was back across the ford and occupying a defensive position on the south bank. The Turks advanced to within 400 metres of the river but made no attempt to cross.[45]

Machine gunner Alec McNeur described the fighting withdrawal of his section.

Orders were 'Every man mount, gallop for your life out of it, Turks [are] coming on in thousands' …. Our L/Cpl was alongside, 'Keep going, Mac', he shouted, but I didn't need much encouragement. It was no place to be hit, as there was no hope of being carried out. Nosebags etc. were flying everywhere, but no time to pick up anything. I looked back once in that gallop, and Turks! Great Scott they just swarmed after us, line behind line, blazing away as they ran … Oh that ford, horses rolling over and over in the current. Men galloping into four feet of water and of course their horses came down, and the men loaded with gear were dragged to land…. A few thousand Turks chased as many hundred of us and we escaped by a miracle. We had two miles to gallop, with bullets flying around … and these beggars chasing us. I just lay flat and wished I were smaller, and the old hack Jerry did his best … We lost some good officers in the fight, and some real good men, but [we] were fortunate to escape at all.[46]

234

Jim McMillan was forced to swim for his life.

> *The murky water certainly looked to be deep, but there was not time for debate about it, and in I jumped, to find it was indeed deep. Luckily, my ammunition had all been expended in that last few hectic minutes on the hill, and though I jumped in with my rifle held above my head, it was not possible to hold on to it and swim, so down it went, leaving me free to put all the effort possible in the endeavour to reach that other shore which seemed to be so far away. The Turks had now reached the crest of the ridge and bullets were popping into the water all around, but incredibly … I reached the far bank untouched and crawled into the undergrowth there.*[47]

The New Zealanders moved back to high ground overlooking the south side of the river and dug in, expecting the enemy, now reported by air reconnaissance to be 5000 strong, to chase them across the river. The Turks, satisfied to have regained the river line, spent the afternoon digging in along the high ground on their side of the river. At 7 p.m. the NZMR Brigade was relieved by several infantry battalions and moved back to bivouac near Sarona.[48]

The NZMR Brigade War Diary states that six New Zealanders were killed, 45 were

The dam and flour mill at Jerishe.

AUTHOR'S COLLECTION

Winter flooding, December 1917.

wounded and three were missing on 25 November, but Commonwealth War Graves Commission records indicate that 10 NZMR men were killed in action that day, with another man dying of wounds two days later.[49]

Guy Powles called this 'a very pretty little action', but Arthur Moore considered that 'the event was nearly a disaster'.

> *The New Zealanders narrowly escaped being cut off by the river and mown down by heavy artillery and machine gun fire. As it was the casualties were heavy enough, but the enemy's object of finally disposing of the dreaded 'death riders', as the Turks called the slouch-hatted Colonial horsemen, was not realized.* [50]

The Turkish 3rd and 7th divisions suffered 437 casualties, including 86 fatalities. A bridgehead across Nahr el Auja clearly required a far larger force than Allenby wanted to use there, so he settled for an entrenched line on the near bank, garrisoned by an infantry brigade, with the Anzac Mounted Division and the ICC Brigade in support. The New Zealanders were withdrawn to Sarona on 1 December.[51]

When the winter rains finally began in December 1917, the temperature plummeted. As the men of the EEF shivered in their thin cotton uniforms, their greatcoats, and covers for the horses, were hurriedly called forward. The plains 'became a sea of mud, through which only donkeys and mules could force a way; camels lay down and died by hundreds; the few roads broke up or disappeared beneath the waters; men and horses exposed day and night to the icy lash of the rains went sick in increasing numbers'.[52]

The New Zealanders took over a section of trenches near Ludd from the ICC Brigade on 5 December (see Map 11, p.176). This was probably the closest the horsemen ever got to experiencing Western Front conditions. 'The trenches,' Powles wrote, 'were simply gaps in the earth, half-full of liquid mud, and fell in as fast as they were dug out.' On 5 December one man was killed when artillery fire blew the trench in on top of him. Fortunately, apart from the intermittent shelling, the Turks were inactive.[53] On the rainy night of 9 December, a Turkish officer stumbled into the CMR headquarters. 'The Turk sat and sobbed bitterly ... Poor devil, he was evidently about the end of his tether, owing to fright and exposure.'[54]

General Allenby's attention was firmly focused on Jerusalem, which surrendered to him on 9 December. Two days later, 34 New Zealand horsemen formed part of a multinational guard for Allenby's formal entry into the Holy City.[55]

A few days earlier, the 52nd Division replaced the Anzacs in the front line. The AMR spent a few days on garrison duty in Jaffa, then went back into the front line on the banks of Nahr el Auja for a week. The WMR was placed under command of the 54th Division from 12 December until Christmas Eve. Both regiments scouted in front of strong British infantry forces on 22 December after a successful crossing of the Auja, before being released to rejoin the NZMR Brigade.

The CMR waded south through the mud to bivouacs at Ayun Kara. A few days later they were sent back to Nahr Sukereir, where they could be supplied directly from the railway. The Canterburys reached the camping site on Christmas Eve but the two other regiments spent the morning of Christmas Day in the saddle, as they had at Magdhaba, a year earlier. The AMR endured 'one of the most severe marches the regiment had ever done'.

Heavy rain fell continuously, and a cold wind raged. The night of December 24 was spent beyond Ayun Kara, the men being drenched to the skin. Pushing on the following morning, the bedraggled column struck seas of mud ... horses going down and being got up with great difficulty. The limbers at some places were right under water. Then the Wadi Sukereir had to be swum.[56]

The march of the WMR was no better. 'Drenching rain, bitter cold, and a quagmire of mud impeded the column's progress, the horses wading belly deep and the transport vehicles almost disappearing at times.' Both regiments rejoined the brigade on Christmas afternoon.[57]

Both the Aucklands and the Wellingtons enjoyed some Christmas cheer when gift parcels from New Zealand were distributed. Otherwise, it was a miserable day: the rain poured down ceaselessly, and the horses and men were drenched and frozen. Mountainous seas and flooded railway lines stopped supplies from getting through and everyone went hungry. An 'inspirational' message from New Zealand's Minister of Defence probably did little to boost morale.

Greetings to all members of the New Zealand Expeditionary Force and Army Nursing Service. The time has come for another Christmas message to go forth from New Zealand to those who are upholding her honour on land and sea. Again we ask you to join with us at 9 o'clock on Christmas morning in prayer for protection and continued success. Heavy as the burden has been, and heavy as it yet may be, we re-assert at this Christmas time our unshaken faith in the righteousness of our cause, and your ability under God to do your country's part to vindicate

A00573, AUSTRALIAN WAR MEMORIAL

The Guard of Honour saluting General Allenby outside Jerusalem's Jaffa Gate on 11 December 1917. The New Zealanders are on the left.

that cause. It is therefore with a stout heart and undimmed pride that we bid you be of good cheer. Next Christmas once more the Divine Message may ring out over the world 'Peace on earth, good will towards men'.[58]

A lengthy respite from operations was needed to restore the combat power of the New Zealand brigade. The New Zealanders and their horses were dead tired and their equipment was worn out. Many of the horses were ill; more than a few were near death from chronic exhaustion.[59]

November 1917 was the worst month of the war for horse casualties in the NZMR Brigade: 108 horses were killed in action, another 33 were so badly wounded that they had to be destroyed and 12 died from sickness. Because the remount depots were nearly empty the remaining horses had to be nursed back to health with prolonged rest, gentle exercise, dry conditions and plenty of wholesome food. Fortunately, all these requirements were met. 'For the first time in many weeks … the horses had clean, dry standings, and the effect of this was soon evident in the improved condition of their legs and coats. At the end of the first fortnight … there was an all-round improvement. Forage was plentiful again, and of fair quality, although everyone would have given a great deal for a few tons of good oats, in place of the eternal barley.'[60]

The men were also in need of a rest after a very trying two months. 'First there had been the long rides, with dust so thick that only the outline of the troop in front could be seen, then the heavy fighting, followed by the long chase, which culminated in the trenches north of Jaffa.' The men suffered from a high sickness rate: enteritis, tonsillitis, pyrexia and septic sores were common ailments.[61] When Chaytor heard that oranges were an effective treatment for septic sores, he requisitioned a supply of the fruit and had it issued to the men. 'The army supply authorities said there was no authority to issue fruit... [but] the General found authority to issue vegetables, and he proved that oranges were vegetables.'[62]

By Christmas 1917, Jerusalem was secure and strong forces were established across the Auja river. It was just in time. 'Rains, such as octogenarian Arabs with wagging white beards asserted they had never seen before, flooded the land and swept away bridges and culverts.' The EEF had lost nearly 19,000 men in the six weeks since the beginning of Allenby's offensive in front of Gaza and Beersheba.[63]

The Turks had lost over 25,000 men in the same period, but their battered divisions still held a continuous defensive line stretching from the Mediterranean to the Dead Sea. Although only 20,000 Turkish troops still faced him at the end of 1917, Allenby decided to postpone any further advance north until the winter was over and his lines of communication had caught up with the fighting troops. In the spring of 1918, Allenby intended to advance north to a line between Haifa and Tiberias. The timing and progress of this advance would depend upon the rate at which the railway could be pushed forward to support it. In the meantime, he decided to occupy Jericho and capture the line of the Jordan River north of the Dead Sea. This would interrupt enemy grain shipments from the east. If he could also cut the Hejaz Railway near Amman, it would isolate the Turks fighting the Hejaz Arabs further south (see Map 8, p.150).[64]

Allenby's conservative plan did not go down well in London, where great things were now expected of the EEF. On 21 January 1918 the War Council decided to remain on the defensive on the Western Front, to preserve their armies until the Americans could join the fight, and to devote maximum resources to the defeat of the Turks in Palestine and Syria. On 7 March Allenby was told that the War Cabinet wanted him to continue operations against the Turks 'with all energy. ... They attach importance to cutting the Hejaz railway as already planned, and desire to know when you can be ready to make a northward advance.' He was promised large numbers of mainly Indian reinforcements from Mesopotamia and from France.[65]

In the past 12 months the combat power of the NZMR Brigade had changed significantly. New weapons and organisational changes had enhanced the combat power of the brigade, and improvements to the communications, engineer, medical and supply units had increased their ability to support the fighting troops. However, the brigade's artillery support was less than it had been at the end of 1916, with four 13-pounder guns supporting the brigade, instead of the 18-pounders. On the plus side of the ledger, each squadron had four Hotchkiss guns instead of the single Lewis gun of a year earlier, air support was much more effective than it had been and the infantry divisions were now an effective fighting force. These changes were vital, as the EEF was now fighting the main force of the Turkish army, instead of the isolated regiments that it had fought in 1916. Commanders had learnt to manoeuvre their units efficiently and to co-ordinate their efforts with flanking units. The men were experienced desert fighters. Their workload had diminished with the addition of extra mounted brigades to the EEF. Lastly, the endurance of both men and horses had been discovered to be significantly greater than expected.

For one New Zealander, the war was nearly over. On 4 December 1917 23-year-old Lawrence Maddison wrote this farewell letter to his mother.[66]

Dear Mum,

Long before this reaches you, I will have left this world for ever. I have known for some time that I can never regain my former health, and I cannot bear to think of the future in my present condition of health. Life is one long headache, with nights of sleeplessness, and I will be far happier where I am going. I do not want you to grieve for me, for it will not be long before we are all united in the land where there is no sickness or pain, and where there is no parting. I have no fear for the future, for I am merely giving back the life I owe. Love to all at home.

Good bye,

Your loving son,

Lawrence

P.S. I leave everything to you.

Lawrence Maddison died of heart failure on 6 January 1918.

12

The road to Jericho

Heavy hail showers all day, with a cold, piercing wind. Everything [is] dirty and miserable.

GEORGE WRIGHT

JIM PARKER SPENT New Year's Day, 1918 near Esdud with the machine gunners. 'It rained today, but nevertheless we made a plum duff, and had a good time to celebrate the occasion.' Most of the DMC had been withdrawn from the front line to rest and to train for future operations. Other New Zealanders camped at the mouth of the Sukereir River, practising rifle and Hotchkiss gun shooting, bombing, signalling and mounted drills. On 12 January the brigade moved back up to Surafend, near Richon le Zion, where training continued until 8 February.[1]

Between December 1914 and October 1918, 8528 men in 42 reinforcement drafts left New Zealand to join the brigade and the other NZEF units in the Middle East. Not all of the new arrivals impressed the veteran New Zealanders. Percy Doherty noted one reinforcement officer who was 'only nineteen, and absolutely unsuitable for this sort of work, he is too young and inexperienced, it is a shame that he should be put in charge of old, experienced war veterans'.[2]

Chaytor described the 19th and 20th Reinforcements as 'a good-looking lot but very poor riders'.[3] As the war dragged on and casualties mounted on the Western Front, some men volunteered as mounted riflemen to avoid being sent to France. Because several could not ride at all, it became necessary to test volunteers for their riding ability when they first arrived at the reinforcement camps in New Zealand.[4]

In New Zealand, mounted rifles reinforcements trained at Featherston Camp, north of Wellington, where there were nearly 300 buildings, including three billiard rooms, a movie theatre, 16 dining halls, six cookhouses and stables for 500 horses. With about 8000 men in the camp at any one time, its post office was the fifth busiest in the country. The

The Aotea Convalescent Home at Heliopolis, outside Cairo.

training programme included eight weeks of dismounted drill, two weeks of shooting, eight weeks of mounted drill and two final weeks of leave. The horses were well used to the training syllabus and many men expressed 'great surprise at the knowledge the animals have of the drill, obeying orders given with little or no effort on the part of the rider'. The men also received lectures on subjects such as 'the soldierly spirit', care of the feet, sanitation, military law and discipline, animal management and stable duties. All mounted reinforcements had to pass confirmatory riding tests before being cleared to go overseas.[5]

After the New Zealand Division had gone to France, reinforcements for the NZMR Brigade were shipped to Sydney or Melbourne, where they embarked on Australian troopships bound for Suez. They did not take horses with them. From Suez the men went by train to the New Zealand Training Centre and Details Camp at Moascar, near Ismailia. The reinforcements still had a lot to learn before they could join the regiments and a final selection took place at Moascar. Soldiers who could not reach the required standard sometimes became disciplinary problems, reacting to the pressure with outbreaks of insubordination, drunkenness and absence without leave.[6]

When reinforcements were needed in the brigade, the required number of men would be sent up the railway line from Kantara. The frequency varied according to the operational situation but one or two small reinforcement drafts usually set off for the front every week. Before the reinforcements left they were medically examined, inoculated for typhoid, paratyphoid and cholera, vaccinated against smallpox, and their shooting records and pay books were checked for completeness.

As the war progressed, officers and men periodically attended training courses to brush up on tactics, techniques and procedures, to learn how to employ new weapons and to prepare for promotion. New Zealanders regularly attended such courses at the Imperial School of Instruction in Cairo. The work was not onerous, the working hours were short and Cairo was a welcome change from the front line. Jim Parker attended a machine gun course in January 1918. He and his fellow students boarded a train at Esdud and took the long ride on the Kantara Military Railway, sleeping on the floor of a carriage for most of the way. On arrival at Kantara, Parker had a good breakfast at Mrs Chisholm's canteen before boarding the afternoon train to Cairo, reaching Zeitoun at 8 p.m. The men had tea in the YMCA tent before bedding down in the tent allocated to them. Course work did

Convalescents (in slippers) and staff at the Aotea Home.

not occupy the whole day, so Parker and his friends were able to visit friends who were on leave, sick in the 27th General Hospital or recovering in the Aotea Convalescent Home. They also visited the zoo and the pyramids, saw movies and shopped for souvenirs.[7]

The Aotea Home was a great boon for the men of the NZEF in the Middle East. Eight women from New Zealand had set up the home in 1915. In November of that year, the 25-bed facility opened in Heliopolis, Cairo.

We have a great variety of amusements, there being a large tennis court, a cricket pitch, a golf course, billiard tables, a ping pong table, and much other material wherewith to pass away the morning and evening hours. Each afternoon, practically everyone who is fit is allowed a pass for Cairo from two to seven.... Almost every week parties are arranged to go to some place of interest, such as the Pyramids or the Barrage du Nil. The parties leave as soon as possible after lunch, go by special tram to the Cairo station, then on by train to the places decided on. Afternoon tea is always arranged, and, after putting in some pleasant hours, the parties return about sunset.[8]

According to George Ranstead, the New Zealand sisters and the matron could not 'do enough for the boys . . . . We have six meals a day (homemade scones and New Zealand butter for afternoon tea), and, really, if a man doesn't get fit here, there is something vitally wrong with him.'[9]

In one respect, the mounteds' countrymen fighting on the Western Front had a better deal. Leave was available to the cities and towns of unoccupied Belgium and France, and to England. Away from the front line, life was recognisable and familiar to the New Zealanders and the local people were Europeans. Leave in the Middle East meant visiting places like Cairo, Kantara, Port Said and, in 1918, Jerusalem and Bethlehem. Leave to England was uncommon, except for a few senior officers, and nobody was granted leave to New Zealand unless for urgent compassionate reasons. Egyptian society offered little for the war-weary trooper on leave and being away from the regiment in such circumstances

WMR and AMR men on the Kantara Military Railway.

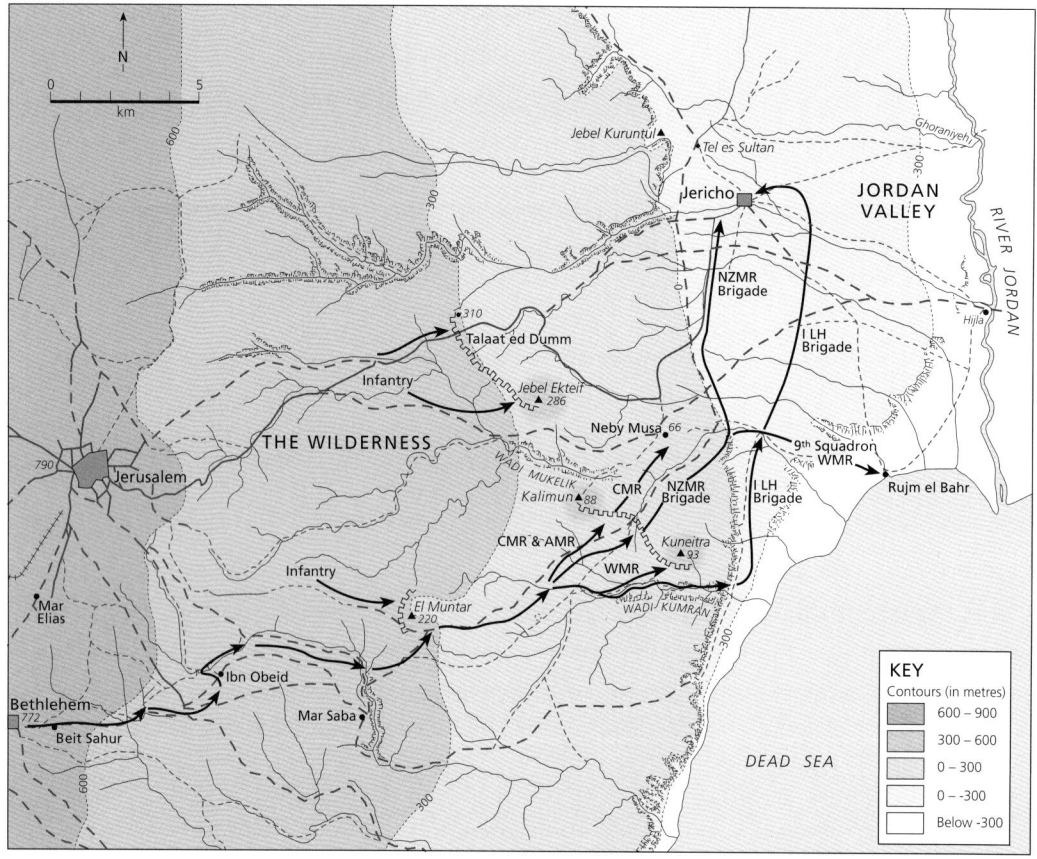

Map 15: Capture of Jericho.

soon lost its appeal for most men, who looked forward to rejoining their friends. Those on leave in Cairo stayed in cheap lodgings and ate frugally in order to maximise their spending money for such things as visiting the YMCA recreation club in the Esbekiah Gardens and going to the pyramids, which they climbed and raced around on camels. Then, for many men, it was off to the brothels of the Wazzir.[10]

The worst aspect of leave was the travel required to get from the front line to the leave destination, and back again.

[Once] you had succeeded in the superhuman task of convincing the orderly room clerk that your name was next on the roster, there came first a long trek across country to railhead. Here you were harassed by an officious person called the RTO [Regimental Transport Officer] who inspected your papers and then scrutinised your person in order to satisfy himself that you were not a criminal escaping from justice. Then you were handed over to an underling

The Wilderness of Judea.

who led you to a glorified cattle truck, whose interior was an amazing jumble of boots, bare knees, helmets, rifles, packs, faces and [cotton] drill clothing, and courteously invited you to step inside. Regardless of the howl of protest from within the truck, you thrust a tentative leg over the side, to be met immediately with a muffled but earnest request that you removed your boot from the speaker's face.... Then came the thirteen-hour journey to Kantara, followed by another four hours on the Egyptian State Railway to Cairo, or seven to Alexandria. If you accomplished the whole journey without going into hospital you could, on your arrival, consider yourself on leave.[11]

The Young Men's Christian Association (YMCA) provided a range of welfare services to all members of the EEF. The YMCA's Anzac Hostel in Cairo provided cheap and clean leave accommodation for the Anzacs, and the YMCA facilities at the Esbekiah Gardens offered reading and writing rooms, regular boxing tournaments and athletic meetings – and the only swimming pool in Cairo. George Ranstead had little time for the clientele of the Egyptian 'Y', describing them as 'a lot of fat, lazy fellows who have never seen anything more dangerous than a native brawl'. Alec McNeur thought that the YMCA was 'a bit of a failure in our brigade, and not a single mounted man will say a good word' for it.[12]

Horse shows and race meetings were popular distractions closer to the front line.

Wherever a meeting was held everybody who could beg, borrow, or steal a horse, a mule, or a camel entered it, entirely indifferent of the feelings of the animal in the matter, or whether its best distance was five furlongs or five miles.... Army horses, except officers' chargers, are notoriously gregarious by reason of their training, and you could generally be sure of a close finish in any race confined to horses belonging to 'other ranks' of the cavalry and artillery.[13]

The system of rotating brigades through rest camps, reserve camps and the front line, and the chance for individuals to take leave back at Kantara, Port Said or Cairo, was a major factor in maintaining the battle readiness of the mounted men and their horses through 1917 and 1918.

While his forces rested and trained, Allenby planned his advance across the Judean Hills and into the Jordan Valley. Beyond Jerusalem, the eastern flank of the Judean Hills plunges steeply into the valley of the Jordan River. This side of the range, known in the Bible as the Wilderness of Judea, is broken up by many deep wadis, making cross-country movement very difficult. The Wilderness descends into the Jordan Valley in a series of small ledges or ridges, separated by steep escarpments. Between Jerusalem and Jericho, the land drops 600 metres in a little over 20 kilometres. The hills rise steeply above the valley floor,

B00059. AUSTRALIAN WAR MEMORIAL

Neby Musa, with the hill occupied by the New Zealanders on 21 February in the background.

creating 'a strange, sinister sense of oppression and confinement. This is increased by the bare, desert aspect of the mountain sides, and especially by the dark, still surface of the Dead Sea, and the steep, rocky and gloomy walls with which it is enclosed. The absence of human life intensifies the sense of desolation.'[14]

The floor of the lower Jordan Valley lies nearly 400 metres below sea level. It averages 15 kilometres in width and the distance from Musallabe to the Dead Sea is about 25 kilometres. The flat plain is intersected by many wadis. Near the meandering Jordan River, a region of bare, white clay mounds and ridges gives way to a belt of swampy mangrove jungle on the banks of the waterway. Although one rather jaundiced observer described it as 'an unpleasant, foul stream running between poisonous banks', the Jordan was clean, fast-flowing and up to 40 metres wide. The only permanent human habitation on the valley floor was Jericho, a small village inhabited by about 500 people. With only a few centimetres of rain falling annually, the valley floor is very dry away from the watercourses. February was an ideal month for the men to acclimatise to the Jordan Valley. 'The whole plain was covered with a short grass, and the hills looked green in every direction ... it was warm, restful and free of the heat, mosquitoes and dust which were to play such havoc with the forces in the summer.'[15]

Lieutenant General Chetwode was put in charge of the coming operation, which was to begin as soon as the weather cleared. Allenby attached the Anzac Mounted Division to Chetwode's corps. The 60th (London) Division, with the Wellington regiment under command, was ordered to capture El Muntar and Jebel Ektief. As soon as the way was clear, the Anzac division's horsemen would make their way past El Muntar and follow tracks to the valley floor, from where they would gallop for Jericho to cut off the enemy's line of retreat from the Wilderness. A number of boats and a grain storehouse on the northern shore of the Dead Sea at Rujm el Bahr were also to be seized, and the Turks were to be pushed back across the Jordan River.[16]

The Turkish 7th Army had between 3000 and 5000 men deployed between Jerusalem and Jericho. They had concentrated their defences on the road between those towns, believing that the broken country to either side would be impassable to the EEF.[17]

The Wellingtons left their bivouac area at Richon le Zion on 9 February 1918. Before long they resembled 'half-frozen rats' in the pouring rain. A number of horses lost shoes in the mud and the drenched horsemen stopped at Latrun for two days to wait for the downpour to stop. They then rode on towards Bethlehem via an old Roman road. As they gained height, the temperatures dropped, promising mild days and cold nights ahead. On 11 February the WMR joined the 60th Division at the Greek monastery of Mar Elias, between Bethlehem and Jerusalem. The next day, the 6th (Manawatu) Squadron took over an outpost at Ibn Obeid and sent patrols towards El Muntar to keep an eye on the Turks until the operation began.[18]

The rest of the New Zealand brigade left Richon le Zion on 15 February. Following a devious route to avoid detection by enemy spies, they passed through many biblical locations, including the spot where David is said to have slain Goliath with a slingshot. According to Fred Sterling, 'there are [certainly] plenty of stones'. The horses took little interest in biblical history as they 'floundered through the heavy going, up to their knees and higher'. The NZMR Brigade arrived at Bethlehem on 17 February. The men watered their horses in the nearby King Solomon's Pools – three large rock reservoirs built in Roman times – and laboured to remove the caked mud from the miserable animals. A few men took the opportunity to visit Jerusalem and Bethlehem. George Wright 'had lunch early and went up in a wagon to Bethlehem to see the Church of Nativity of Christ. Saw the exact spot where he was born, a silver star marks the place.'[19]

The attack into the Wilderness began two days later. The Wellingtons crept forward at night around the southern flank of the Turkish defensive position on El Muntar. They had to be in position by 6 a.m., at which time the infantry would attack the hill. Their path led through a gorge towards another Greek Orthodox monastery at Mar Saba.

It soon became necessary to lead the horses in single file along goat tracks – no other formation being possible, the horses glissading on their haunches down the steep banks of a succession of deep, tortuous and jagged gorges which scarred the country.[20]

Veterans compared the ground they now encountered with the ascent of Table Top on Gallipoli in August 1915. The only differences now were that they were accompanied by the horses, 'and their climb was down the cliffs … instead of up'. By dawn on 20 February, the Wellingtons had reached a valley east of El Muntar. Soon afterwards, the British infantry captured the hill.[21]

At dawn the rest of the Anzac division caught up with the Wellingtons, who had discovered that the Turks were defending a track between Mar Saba and the floor of the Jordan Valley, south of Neby Musa. Two dominating hills called Jebel el Kalimun and Tubk el Kuneitra were the first objectives of the New Zealand brigade. To get into position for the assault, they spent the morning hours winding their way in a 13-kilometre-long single file down a steep, zigzag track descending from Muntar, in full view of the Turks on the hills opposite. They then had to cross a wide flat valley that was covered by enemy machine

New Zealanders galloping into Jericho.

guns and artillery. With no artillery support of their own to call upon – the guns could not travel on the rough tracks – it promised to be a daunting task. An attempt to outflank the enemy position failed and, shortly after noon, the regiments left their horses under cover in a ravine and began their dismounted assault. The WMR closed in on Kuneitra but the CMR missed its objective and had to be recalled.

The AMR was called up from reserve and sent in against Kalimun. The Aucklands made slow progress under heavy fire until a lull in the firing at noon allowed them to rush a forward position. A mounted charge by an AMR squadron captured a second position. The two hills were in New Zealand hands shortly afterwards and this helped the British infantry capture Jebel Ektief. This in turn convinced the Turks still in front of the NZMR Brigade to abandon their positions and withdraw towards Neby Musa.[22]

Effective enemy fire and very difficult ground halted further progress. Strenuous efforts were made to water the horses, but with limited success. That night, the 1st LH Brigade began to descend the precipitous Wadi Kumran below Kuneitra. Before dawn on 21 February, the light horsemen reached the floor of the Jordan Valley. The Canterburys were able to walk onto Neby Musa unopposed after the Turks abandoned it to avoid being cut off.

At 8 a.m. on a foggy, wet morning, the leading troop of the 1st LH Brigade galloped

New Zealanders on guard in Jericho.

into Jericho, followed 10 minutes later by the first New Zealanders. The 9th (Wellington East Coast) Squadron of the WMR rode to the shores of the Dead Sea at Rujm el Bahr, but the boats were gone and the grain stores were empty. The two Anzac brigades pushed east as far as the banks of the Jordan River, leaving several squadrons in Jericho to protect intelligence officers as they arrested a number of suspects and established a stay-behind espionage ring.[23]

No one had a good word to say about Jericho. Fred Sterling described it as

a small, dirty, half-pie modern village containing a church, a mosque, [and] a few fair-sized buildings, including a now-dry hotel . . . .The lot [is] surrounded by dilapidated mud hovels. Some of the houses contain dead Turks etc. Fever is rampant, and of a deadly kind. The streets are littered with all manner of filth, and the Turks, to make the jumble complete, looted the town as they retired.[24]

Guy Powles was even less complimentary, describing Jericho as 'a degenerate city full of loathsome disease. Of all the cities of the east that our men had passed through, Jericho easily led the way as the filthiest and most evil-smelling of them all.'[25]

The state of the Jericho hospital appalled Magnus Johnson. 'On opening the doors

Part of the AMR camp in the foothills, overlooking Jericho in the middle distance.

of the small wards, I found the beds therein were occupied by dead men. Some of them must have died a week [ago], as one corpse was dripping through the mattress.' Doctors and volunteers from the field ambulances, wearing only leather gloves for protection, buried the dead Turks, cared for those who were still alive and cleaned and disinfected the buildings. Fortunately, none of these courageous men contracted typhus.[26]

The Wilderness operation was a complete success. Three New Zealanders were the only fatalities in the Anzac Mounted Division. Seventy-seven British infantrymen died: 'Many little crosses bearing the names of Londoners afterwards marked the road from Jerusalem to Jericho.'[27] The names of Generals Chetwode, Chauvel and Chaytor were nearly added to the casualty list when Turkish artillery fire caught them at breakfast between Jericho and the Judean foothills. 'General Chaytor was sitting on the step of his car and had a very narrow escape, the front of the car being blown in, and he himself covered with glass from the windscreen and half stifled from the fumes of the shell.'[28]

On 22 February the 60th Division left outposts on the cliffs overlooking the valley floor and withdrew to Jerusalem. The Anzac horsemen followed them, leaving the Auckland regiment, a section of machine gunners and a battery of horse artillery in the valley for several weeks. The nervous Turks often shelled the AMR patrols as they rode along the western bank of the Jordan River.

It was a common practice for them to 'snipe' at our patrols with their field guns, often sending shell after shell over at a couple, or even one, of our men. As they often made exceptionally good practice at such moving targets, patrol work under direct observation was most exciting, as one shell crashed before a rider, and another whipped up the dust behind him with its flying fragments.[29]

The rest of the New Zealanders reached Bethlehem just before dawn on 23 February. The weather up on the Judean Hills was still terrible, according to George Wright: 'Very cold, rough day. About the coldest we've experienced this side of the line. Heavy hail showers all day, with a cold piercing wind. Everything [is] dirty and miserable.' He was glad to leave the 'cold wet hole' with the rest of the NZMR Brigade when it rode back to the coastal plain, reaching its old bivouac area at Richon le Zion on 26 February. There, the New Zealanders went back to training and a period of rest. 'A fair amount of leave to Egypt was now being granted to all ranks, and there was no lack of candidates for the leave parties.'[30]

13

More than we can chew

This was the most hellish day of my life.[1]

JIM PARKER

ALLENBY'S NEXT MOVE was to cross the Jordan River and attack the Turks defending the Hejaz Railway at Amman, in order to support the Arabs fighting the Turks further south along the railway. This was to be the first time that the Arabs and the EEF worked together. Arab gains after their capture of Aqaba in July 1917 had alarmed the Turks, who sent a strong force (including a German infantry battalion) south from Amman to help defend the railway and the important town of Ma'an. This weakened the defences of Amman, offering Allenby a fleeting opportunity that he intended to take advantage of.

Beyond a strip of vegetation and a thin band of white clay hills, a wide, flat plain extended from the Jordan River to the foothills of the Gilead and Moab mountains. The road from Jericho crossed the Jordan River at Ghoraniyeh (the bridge was destroyed by the Turks in February), entered the hills at Shunet Nimrin and wound upwards to the towns of Es Salt and Amman. Several rough tracks also entered the hills at other points. Most of these routes were simple bridle paths, accessible to horses but impassable to wheeled transport. From the edge of the valley floor, the ground rises steeply at first before levelling out into a wide, limestone plateau west of Amman, which is more than a kilometre above the valley. The soil of the Amman plateau is fertile but liable to become boggy after rain.

In March, the country is green and pleasant, with numerous streams to sparkle in the sunlight, and patches of dwarf lupins covering whole acres with a sheen of turquoise, with orchards in blossom at Es Salt and Suweile. The midday sun is hot when the sky is cloudless, but winds are chilly and the nights often bitterly cold.[2]

The Hejaz Railway runs just to the east of Amman. Beyond it, sterile desert stretches away

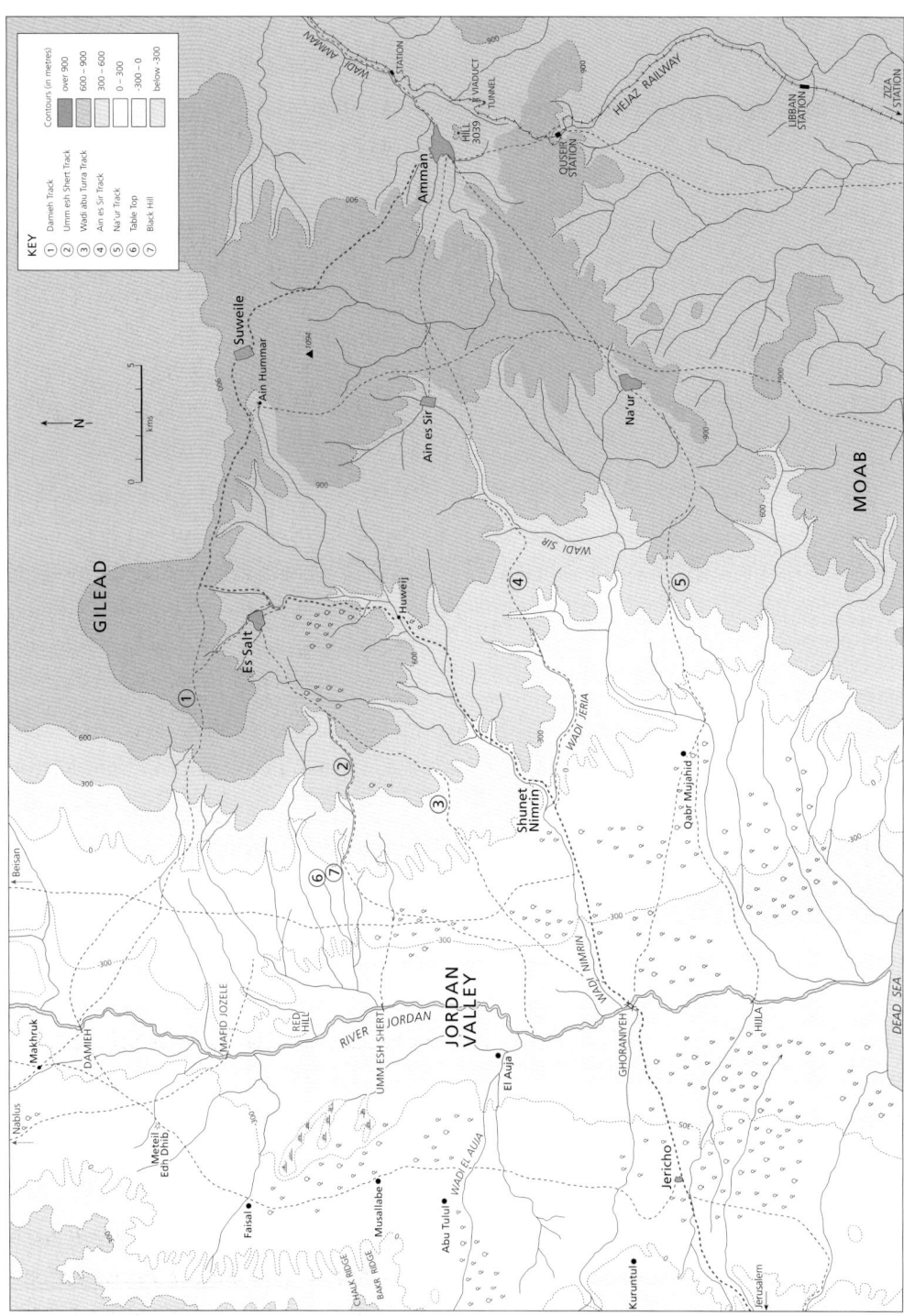

Map 16: Trans-Jordan Operations.

towards Mesopotamia (modern Iraq). In 1918, the railway track crossed a large masonry viaduct and passed through a long tunnel, just south of Amman. Es Salt was the largest town in the area, with a population of about 15,000, including 4000 Christians. Amman was a small village, containing an ancient Roman amphitheatre and a ruined citadel, nestled within steep hills. The population of Amman and some other nearby villages included many pro-Turkish Circassians.[3]

Amman was a long way from the Jordan Valley but Allenby considered it to be within range of his highly mobile mounted troops. Major General John Shea, the commander of the 60th (London) Division, was placed in command of the operation by Chetwode. In addition to his own infantry division, Shea's Force, as it was known, included the Anzac Mounted Division, the ICC Brigade, several artillery batteries and armoured car patrols and some extra bridging troops.[4]

As soon as the weather cleared, Shea's infantrymen were to seize bridgeheads across the Jordan River at Ghoraniyeh and Hijla. The Anzac Mounted Division and the ICC Brigade would then advance into the hills via the Ain es Sir and Na'ur tracks. Their first task was to get behind the Turks in Es Salt in time for the 60th Division – with the 6th (Manawatu) Squadron attached – to advance up the Shunet Nimrin road and capture the town and its trapped garrison. The 1st LH Brigade and the Auckland regiment (the latter only temporarily) were to remain behind in the Jordan Valley to guard the 60th Division's northern flank. Then, leaving Es Salt in the hands of the infantry, the mounted troops were to push on to Amman, where they were to destroy the viaduct and the tunnel on the Hejaz Railway. The force would then withdraw across the Jordan River, leaving a strong infantry detachment at Es Salt to garrison the town and prevent the repair of the railway. The river crossing was scheduled for the night of 19 March 1918.[5]

The Turks were well aware of the vulnerability of Amman and the Hejaz Railway and news of Allenby's impending attack reached them in mid-March. The new commander of the Yildirim Army Group, Marshal Liman von Sanders, sent orders for the weak garrison at Amman to be reinforced. By the time Allenby's troops entered the hills, the Turkish force numbered at least 4000 men, including the German 703rd Battalion, a formidable infantry unit well endowed with machine guns.[6]

The Anzac Mounted Division left Richon le Zion on 13 March 1918. After waiting for two days at Junction Station for the rain to stop, which it did not, the horsemen rode up into the Judean Hills, arriving at Bethlehem on 17 March. Percy Doherty described the ride as 'the roughest trip this brigade has ever had … horses and men [were] hardly recognisable for mud'. Jim Parker wrote that several bivouacs were flooded by rainwater, while James Cameron noted 'mud galore, inside bivvy and everywhere'. The rain continued without let-up, and it was bitterly cold; a number of camels and some of their Egyptian handlers died. Some Wellingtons found shelter in the Mar Elias monastery near Bethlehem. 'Fires were lit to dry out what we could as the baggage camels (with spare clothing) were still miles to the rear.' Major Wilkie recalled that the monks were 'good fellows [who] entertained the Regiment right royally that night'.[7]

Orders for the Anzac division to move to Talaat ed Dumm on 18 March were cancelled because of the atrocious weather. Sightseeing trips into Jerusalem were allowed, but few men enjoyed them in the miserable conditions.[8]

As the heavy rain caused the Jordan to rise, Chetwode wrote to Allenby on 18 March, expressing his concerns about the operation. The flooded river would pose a great threat to the troops once they were across it, especially if more rain fell during the attacks in the hills, and Chetwode had no spare bridges to replace any that were swept away. He also knew that the Turks were being reinforced and was not confident that he could force them back far enough to expose the railway tunnel and viaduct. With no significant reserves of his own, Chetwode feared that the withdrawal of Shea's Force from Amman and Es Salt would be very difficult. By now, the Jordan was so high and turbulent that it could not be

The hills below Amman, viewed from the Jordan Valley.

bridged and Allenby had no choice but to postpone the operation until the river subsided a little. He refused to cancel it outright. [9]

On the evening of 20 March, the NZMR Brigade rode down the Jericho road to a dreary, wet bivouac site at Talaat ed Dumm. Three days later they continued to the Jordan River at Hijla. The racing current defeated the first attempts at bridging the river, but a small party of engineers eventually swam over at Hijla. Two bridges were quickly thrown across by the Anzac Bridging Train but several tries at crossing upstream at Ghoraniyeh failed. It was decided to clear the enemy on the far side of this ford from the rear.[10]

The Auckland regiment was ordered to cross at Hijla and clear the east bank of the river as far north as Ghoraniyeh, a distance of about seven kilometres. With little knowledge of what awaited the AMR on the other side, this was a risky task. Fred Sterling thought 'the prospects were not too bright, as we knew that machine guns were covering a large proportion of the ground we had to pass over'. The Auckland horsemen clattered across the pontoon bridge at 7.30 a.m. on 23 March 1918. As Powles recorded, 'It was a beautiful morning [the rain had stopped], the horses were in great form, and the men [were] eager for a ride.' The country was ' excellent for fast mounted work. Fast work it was to be. Two troops of the 11th squadron were sent eastward, and one to the north-east, while the 3rd and 4th squadrons were ordered to make a dash north to attack … the Turkish garrison defending the crossing at Ghoraniyeh … All pack horses, except those carrying Hotchkiss guns, were left behind.'[11]

A troop from the 11th Squadron, commanded by Lieutenant Ken Tait, intercepted 60 Turkish cavalrymen on a narrow track near Qabr Mujahid. The AMR war diary recorded what happened.

Without a second's hesitation, Lieutenant Tait with his 20 men, armed only with rifles, galloped at the sabres. The Turks showed some spirit, and attempted to ride the North Aucklanders down, but they broke and fled before the troopers, who fired as they galloped forward. The Arab horses of the Turkish cavalry were no match for the swift and powerful mounts of the riflemen, who, within a few minutes, were on the heels and abreast of the Turks, and shooting with deadly accuracy. Numbers of Turks dropped from their saddles, while their comrades spurred on in panic, yelling in fear, and shooting wildly in the air or blindly backwards. No less than 20 of the Turks were shot down during this wild ride, and seven were taken prisoner.

Tait was the only New Zealander killed, shot by the enemy commander. One source claims that when Tait called upon this officer, apparently a German, to surrender, he responded by shooting Tait from his horse. 'Needless to say, that German wasn't taken prisoner.' James McCarroll, the CO of the AMR, wrote with satisfaction that the Turkish cavalry 'will keep away from us in future'.[12]

Meanwhile the 3rd and 4th AMR squadrons galloped north as fast as they could, urged on by cries of 'Faster, faster!' from McCarroll, who was right behind them. At 9 a.m. the leading squadron rode over a post of 17 Turks, capturing it intact and at no loss to themselves. The 4th Squadron then galloped off towards the foothills at Shunet Nimrin but was driven off by artillery and machine gun fire. Other troops captured or chased off other Turks before the regiment concentrated in a wadi for the attack on Ghoraniyeh. The 3rd Squadron seized high ground overlooking the ford, from where a pair of captured machine guns was used on a group of fleeing Turks, killing 11 of them. The Turks abandoned the ford and ran for their lives, allowing the engineers across the river to start building their bridges. In what Charles Nicol described as 'a wonderful day', 50 Turks were killed and 60 were captured, along with four machine guns. Ken Tait was the only Aucklander killed. Two men and six horses were wounded.

The NZMR and 1st LH brigades crossed the pontoon bridge at Hijla in the early hours of 24 March. In Gullett's words, 'the night … was fine and warm, with bright moonlight, and the force was in perfect physical condition and keen for the adventure.' As the horses gingerly made their way across the swaying bridge, the riders strained for a view of the far bank. Tall trees and rushes blocked their view but they saw the unburied bodies of the Turkish and British soldiers who had died fighting for the crossing point and heard the distant stutter of machine guns and the crump of artillery explosions. By 5 a.m. everyone was safely across the river, and the leading battalions of the 60th Division were leading the advance through horse-high barley crops towards the foothills.[13]

As the horsemen neared the hills, Arab horsemen

armed with modern rifles and beautifully-inlaid swords and daggers, rode down to meet us. These fellows chased each other in mimic warfare, slashing with their swords in a dramatic manner, and manoeuvring their weedy horses with some dexterity. One or two remained with us to guide the column up the mountains, but the others soon disappeared.[14]

Enemy opposition was light and by nightfall the leading infantry brigade, led by the 6th (Manawatu) Squadron of the WMR, was halfway up the main track to Es Salt. At the base of the hills the rest of the mounted troops split up into three columns. Divisional headquarters, the 2nd LH Brigade and the cameliers took the Na'ur track. The NZMR

The fertile summit plateau near Es Salt. The Jordan Valley is visible in the distance.

Brigade picked up the Auckland regiment and turned off the main track at Shunet Nimrin to follow the Ain es Sir track up Wadi Jeria. The 1st LH Brigade rode up the valley to take up a flank protection role near the ford of Umm esh Shert, dispatching the 3rd ALH Regiment up a track towards Es Salt. Each brigade had its supporting horse artillery battery with it.[15]

Rain began to fall again in the afternoon and the temperature dropped as the men gained altitude. The column on the Na'ur track began its ascent at 3 p.m. Chaytor had been told that this track was suitable for wheeled transport but it was not. Hours were spent transferring all the explosives and as much small arms ammunition as possible from the wagons onto spare camels. The wagons and the horse artillery battery were then sent back to the valley floor, leaving just the small-calibre mountain guns of the ICC Brigade's camel-mounted Hong Kong and Singapore Battery with the column. The cameliers and light horsemen moved deeper into the hills, halting when the moon set. They struggled on all through the following day, passing through Na'ur that night.

The New Zealanders' climb up the Ain es Sir track was nearly as difficult. After watering the horses in a fast-flowing stream near Shunet Nimrin – the animals, not used to moving water, followed the water downstream in search of a still place to drink from – the riders turned into Wadi Jeria, 'which was knee-deep in grass and ablaze with bright flowers'.

This route also was impassable to wheeled transport so the New Zealanders had to send their supply wagons and field guns back. In many places, the route could be traversed only by men leading their mounts on foot and in single file. They were repeatedly forced to cross roaring mountain torrents where rocks made slippery by moss or lichen meant very insecure footing for the iron-shod horses. The route was nearly impossible for the camels.[16]

> *Our camels were led by Egyptians, bare-footed and only clothed in cotton overalls. We were all wet, it had rained all night and a lot of the [Egyptians] died, and the rest were useless.... the camels could not hold their feet and they came down, doing the splits with their hind legs. They could not stand again, so [they] had to be shot and the loads unpacked and loaded again onto spare mules. Waiting for the camels made the progress very slow.*[17]

Both columns easily could have been stopped by a few Turks with machine guns but the only interference to their progress came from the atrocious weather. 'All night it rained,' Powles recorded, 'and all night the weary columns climbed and slipped and fell. Daylight found them far from the top and the weather if anything became worse.' Sometimes, Richardson wrote, 'no track of any sort was visible and men had to dismount and drag their weary horses over huge boulders'. In the downpour the tracks marked on the maps 'revealed themselves for what they really were, the beds of mountain streams', now rushing torrents 'carrying down rocks and mud'.[18] Each column had with its advance guard a work party armed with picks and shovels to improve the track where necessary. They were very busy.

The New Zealanders rested briefly before dawn. Because fires could not be lit a hot cup of tea was impossible. After spending 90 minutes standing in the pouring rain, 'as miserable as frozen dogs', the horsemen continued. Not long afterwards, the rain finally stopped and a heavy mist descended. As the riders disappeared into the murk, they looked 'more like phantom horsemen than flesh and blood'.[19]

The New Zealanders spent the morning of 25 March struggling upwards towards the Circassian village of Ain es Sir, on the edge of the plateau high above the Jordan Valley. As they approached the village, they met some Hejaz Arabs, who warned them that the Circassians were hostile and advised them to 'cut all their throats or let them do it for us!' Few New Zealanders were impressed by these armed Arabs. Guy Powles described them as 'a poor collection of men ... armed with a variety of rifles, pistols, daggers and wooden clubs, whose declared object was to knock all wounded Turks on the head'. Arthur Harrison called them 'a wild lot … a more bloodthirsty lot you never saw. They hate the Turks, and God help any Turks they get hold of. I saw sights that I'm not going to write about here. Too horrible.'[20]

The advance guard of the NZMR Brigade led the way into Ain es Sir at noon. The accompanying Arabs were very disappointed that the New Zealanders would not let them slaughter the inhabitants.[21] Walter Dawbin watched them plunder the village: 'Bursting doors in and helping themselves…. almost exactly like the Mexican cowboy picture shows…. Some were firing from the hip and using clubs and stones.'[22]

By 1.30 p.m. on 25 March, the exhausted NZMR Brigade was bivouacked at a nearby crossroads. The New Zealanders waited there for divisional headquarters, the 2nd LH Brigade and the ICC Brigade to join them. When some Turks cutting trees nearby were captured, they were very surprised to find themselves prisoners when, as far as they knew, the EEF was still on the far side of the Jordan River. That night, another enemy party was rounded up, this time including six Germans. According to William King, 'one German officer attempted to escape, so they shot him'. He continued: 'The Germans are a bit of a curio to most of us, as we have seen very few of them. They are well-equipped and fitted out. They don't look very shiny now as the curio hunters have been at work.'[23] Some men were so tired that they began hallucinating, as they had after the capture of Magdhaba in 1916, seeing non-existent trees and houses on the side of the track.

The modern town of Es Salt.

The railway viaduct south of Amman, one of the objectives of the March attack.

Further north, the infantry and light horse columns made good progress towards Es Salt on better tracks. The 3rd ALH Regiment occupied Es Salt without difficulty at 6 p.m. that day. The next afternoon, 26 March, the light horsemen and cameliers following the Na'ur track finally reached the rendezvous point near Ain es Sir. The march into the hills had exhausted everybody. The camels had an especially bad time: many slipped and fell to their deaths. The camel convoy carrying grain for the NZMR Brigade's horses was stuck down the track so the horses grazed on fields of oats. Later, 50 horses were led back down the track to meet the struggling camels and bring up their loads.[24]

Chaytor received orders to seize Amman, 10 kilometres to the east. Leaving the camel battalions and the New Zealanders at the crossroads, Chaytor led the Australian 2nd LH Brigade towards Suweile. The Australians captured a convoy of German trucks and a car that were stuck in the mud, and rounded up 61 Turks near Suweile, but they could get no further. Chaytor's men were exhausted after three consecutive night marches and he received permission from General Shea to delay the attack on Amman until the following morning.[25]

While he waited, Chaytor dispatched two raiding parties to attack the Hejaz Railway during the night. A troop from the WMR, riding the freshest horses available, successfully demolished a short section of track south of Amman, but the Australian light horse detachment responsible for the northern raid was driven off by enemy cavalry before they could complete their task. Within hours the Turks had repaired the damage done by the New Zealanders.[26]

The first attack on Amman was launched on the morning of 27 March. The village was already defended by over 2000 rifles, 70 machine guns and 10 artillery pieces, and 2000 enemy reinforcements were on their way towards the village along the still intact Hejaz Railway. The attack was to be conducted by two Anzac mounted brigades and the cameliers (around 3000 rifles), supported by the six mountain guns of the ICC Brigade's Hong Kong and Singapore Battery, known to the Anzacs as the 'Bing Boys'. All the assault troops were dog-tired, freezing cold and wet through before they started, and the Anzac horses, according to Fred Sterling, were 'just about done for. They had tasted no grain for three days. All that was keeping them going was an occasional few minutes grazing now and then.'[27]

The New Zealanders were ordered to cross Wadi Amman south-west of the town and attack the enemy defences on Hill 3039, overlooking Amman from the south. To their right, a battalion from the ICC Brigade was to destroy as much of the railway line as possible, while the rest of the camel brigade attacked Amman from the west. The 2nd LH Brigade was to cut the railway line north of Amman, then attack the village from the north-west. The 2nd (Wellington West Coast) Squadron was posted on high ground five kilometres south-east of Ain es Sir to watch for Turkish reinforcements approaching from the south.[28]

A strong, cold wind was blowing and rain was still falling when the assault troops moved off at 9 a.m. Off-road movement was very slow as the horses sank to their knees in the newly ploughed ground. The steep-sided wadis were difficult to cross except at a few points, and then only in single file. The Turks had piled stones into improvised bunkers covering the approaches to Amman. They held their fire until the attackers were well within range of the machine guns and the artillery. 'Then, as if in instant response to a single order, guns, machine guns, and rifles opened fire together, with a roar and a rattle which echoed and re-echoed from the hills and wadis that covered them.'[29]

The New Zealanders reached Wadi Amman at 10.30 a.m. and spent the next four hours getting across it. As they approached Quseir Station, a patrol from the 9th (Wellington East Coast) Squadron, which was escorting a demolition party from the camel brigade, surprised 300 Turks in a train. After a brief exchange of fire, the train got up steam and escaped towards Amman. Fifty Turks who missed the train were captured by Arab horsemen.[30] Arthur Moore described the scene: 'Dragging their victims out, they quickly stripped them of their possessions, our men arriving just in time to prevent the Arabs murdering them all'.[31]

The Turks' skilfully placed and well-concealed machine guns, many manned by Germans, covered all the approaches to the town. Chaytor lacked the artillery needed to destroy them. Turkish artillery fired with impunity from gun positions far out of range of Chaytor's puny mountain guns. The 2nd LH Brigade made some initial progress towards Amman until it was stopped by a counter-attack. The Turks began to threaten the Australians' left flank and their advance bogged down. The ICC Brigade's attack was stopped by heavy machine gun fire across the open ground west of Amman. The New Zealanders enjoyed no more success to the south. Hill 3039 was 'alive with machine guns' and every attempt to capture it was resisted fiercely. Just before dark, the Canterbury regiment was forced to give ground in the face of a particularly strong counter-attack. The South Islanders regrouped and recaptured the lost ground at bayonet point. Turkish artillery fire was heavy and accurate: when one shell landed in a hollow in the midst of the AMR's 4th (Waikato) Squadron, 'the result of its explosion was a bloody sight, seven men and eight horses being put out of action'.[32]

By dusk, the attack on Amman had stalled everywhere. Chaytor, realising that his

The ground cleared by Ken Tait's Aucklanders on 23 March 1918. The Moab hills are visible in the distance.

mounted force could not capture Amman alone, decided to hold his ground until infantry reinforcements arrived. The assault units were ordered to dig in where they stood. The Anzac division lost 26 men killed and 183 wounded during the day. One New Zealander died of wounds.[33]

No rations reached the New Zealanders that night but the horses chomped happily on the lush grass in the wadi beds. The ground was so wet and muddy that some men had to sleep on piles of stones. The demolition party from the ICC Brigade blew up eight kilometres of track south of Amman during the day and that night the light horsemen did the same 11 kilometres to the north. The Australians also destroyed a bridge across a deep wadi, creating a gap eight metres wide. It was estimated (wrongly) that it would take the Turks 48 hours to repair the damage, by which time Amman should have been captured.[34]

Back down in the Jordan Valley, things were not going well. The 1st LH Brigade, guarding the flank between the foothills and the Jordan River at Umm esh Shert, was coming under increasing enemy pressure from new Turkish units brought down from the north and from across the river. The Jordan was still in flood, threatening the bridges that were the only means of escape for the men fighting up in the hills.[35]

The 28th of March dawned quietly in the hills around Amman but that changed as soon as the Turkish artillery opened up. The British infantry battalions, accompanied by the mountain guns and the WMR squadron, finally arrived. The infantry commander recommended making a night attack on Amman but Chaytor disagreed and ordered the attack to begin at 1 p.m. The infantry battalions joined in the attack, advancing south-east towards Amman, but otherwise the assault plan was similar to that of the previous day, and equally unsuccessful. The British infantrymen ran into heavy machine gun fire from three sides and were 'shot to a standstill'. The ICC Brigade was again held up by heavy machine gun fire to the west of Amman. To their left, the 2nd LH Brigade held off determined Turkish attempts to outflank them, but gained no ground.[36]

An unexpected Turkish counter-attack at 11 a.m. upset the preparations of the NZMR Brigade and it made little subsequent headway against the defences of Hill 3039. The brigade borrowed two mountain guns but one was useless and the other 'erratic and ineffective'. By 4 p.m. the AMR and the 4th Battalion of the ICC Brigade had advanced 500 metres to the lower slopes of Hill 3039 but they could proceed no further. 'Steep rocky faces lay above them, and these were swept by the nest of machine guns which remained intact.'[37] Without effective artillery fire to suppress these weapons, the New Zealanders and cameliers stood no chance of success in daylight. The rain continued to fall in sheets, and the weather was bitterly cold. The downpour and the lack of fuel meant

The entrance to Wadi Jeria, the route followed by the NZMR Brigade. The route quickly steepened and narrowed.

that even a cup of hot tea was impossible. Fred Sterling watched the attacks against Hill 3039 fail: 'Poor devils, it was too one-sided. We had only one small battery of mountain guns, but its shooting was … a farce. With us during the day we had our usual following of Arabs and Bedouin. All armed to the teeth, patiently waiting to plunder. Their chatter nearly drove us mad.'[38]

The Anzac division lost 20 men killed and 137 wounded during the day; another 26 men were listed as missing. Four New Zealanders were killed and one died of wounds. Chaytor called off the attacks and convinced General Shea to let him delay the next attempt until the early morning of 30 March, by which time more infantry reinforcements should have arrived.[39]

Apart from the Turkish artillery fire, 29 March was a relatively quiet day up on the plateau as both sides drew breath for the next round. Additional British infantry battalions and mountain gun batteries arrived from Es Salt and a horse artillery battery was sent up the improved road from the Jordan Valley towards Es Salt.

Enemy reinforcements continued to pour into Amman during the day. The Turkish artillery fire was relentless: 10 horses bringing up ammunition for the New Zealand machine gunners were killed by shelling. Several strong Turkish counter-attacks launched

The Anzacs spent hours climbing flooded ravines, such as this one below Ain es Sir.

during the day against the Australians and the British infantry north of Amman were beaten off with difficulty.[40]

Back towards the Jordan Valley, the situation went from bad to worse. A strong Turkish cavalry and infantry force crossed the Jordan and climbed the unguarded Damieh track north of the Australian flank guard to threaten the British infantry garrison in Es Salt. All but one of the bridges across the Jordan River were washed away and the approaches to the last were under water. If this bridge was lost, Shea's Force would be stranded on the wrong side of the Jordan River. Chaytor had to take Amman quickly. As William King succinctly wrote on 29 March, 'things don't look too good for us. I think we have bitten off more than we can chew this time.'[41]

Apart from its timing, Chaytor's plan of attack was basically the same as for the previous two attempts. The NZMR Brigade and a camel battalion (which included a company of New Zealand cameliers) were to attack Hill 3039, the rest of the ICC Brigade was to attack Amman from the west and the reinforced infantry were to advance on the village from the north-west. The 2nd LH Brigade was too weak and tired to play an active role in this last attack. The Somerset Battery was expected to arrive at Amman during the morning of 30 March. As the assault troops moved into position, the heavens opened again and it rained heavily throughout the night.

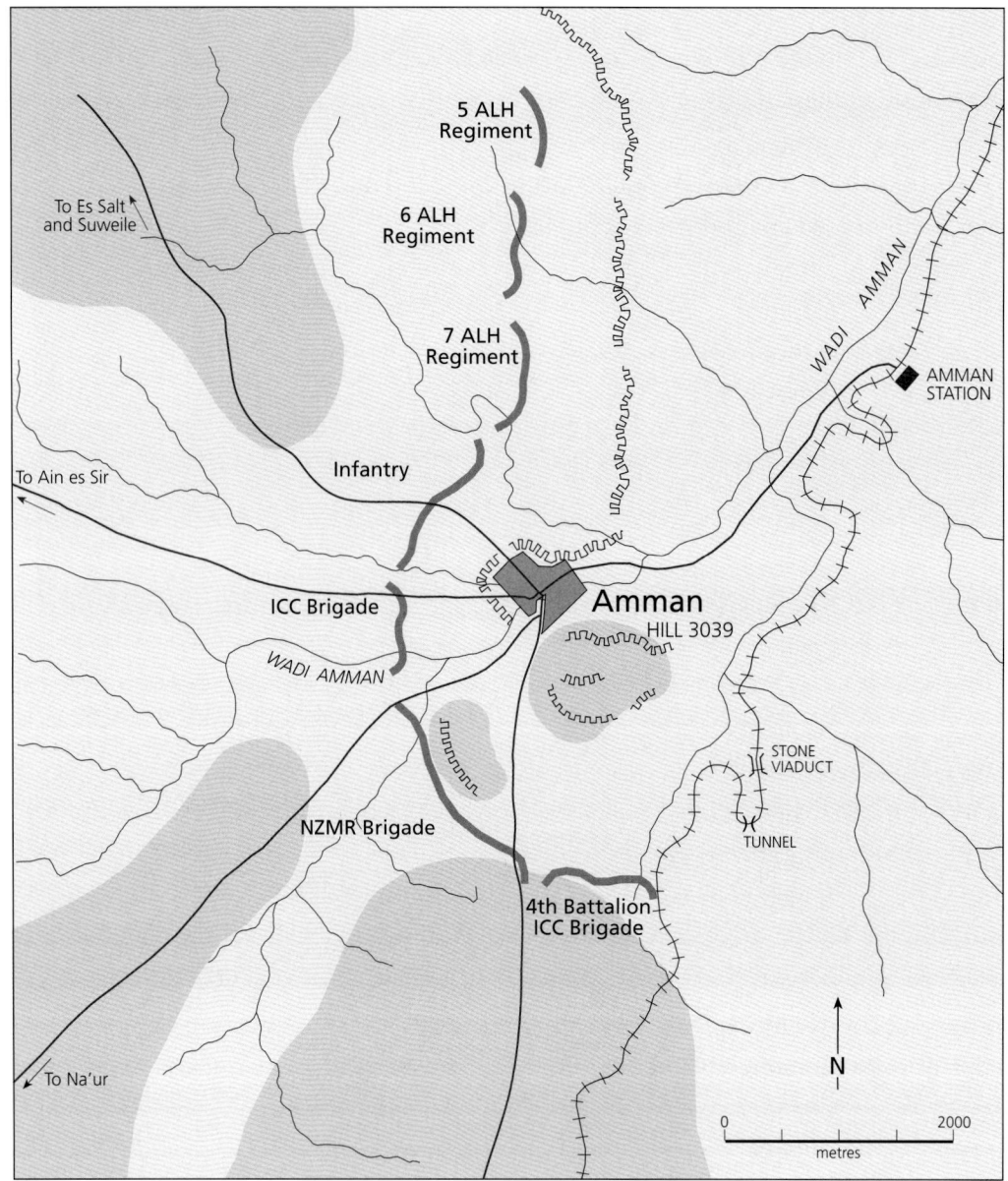

Map 17: First Battle of Amman.

New Zealand officers had spent the previous day conducting a careful reconnaissance of Hill 3039 and its approaches so they had a very good idea of the Turkish defences. These consisted of a central group of trenches and sangars (rock bunkers) on the crest of the hill, and several smaller positions on spurs leading up to the high ground. It was obvious to Meldrum that a frontal attack unsupported by artillery fire would not succeed, even by night. He decided to conduct a silent night attack from the flank. His assault regiments would creep around the forward enemy defences and make for the central group of trenches. Once these defences fell, the rest of the position should become untenable for the Turks. The Aucklands and part of the 4th (Anzac) Battalion of the ICC Brigade were to lead the assault, followed by squadrons of the Canterbury and Wellington regiments. Other troops would guard the flanks of the assault.[42]

The attack was launched in the middle of an overcast night, in driving rain and bitter cold. The men had been without sleep and hot food for days, they were soaked to the skin and weighed down by sodden clothing, and now they had to advance across slippery, rising ground against a heavily armed and determined enemy, using fixed bayonets and unloaded rifles – a single shot would give the game away.[43]

Fred Sterling and the rest of the Aucklands left a wadi at 1.30 a.m. on 30 March, climbed a steep rocky hill, and formed up in a long line (see Map 18, p.275).

All close together, and with our rusty bayonets pointing to the sky. We had hardly got into line when the order came. Move on, no shooting, and no prisoners. The attack, we all knew, simply had to be successful…. We had nothing behind us to fall back upon, so failure and a counter-attack from Jacko meant the finish of things … The Camel Corps' ranks, like our own, were almost disastrously weak, so that it was a thin, tired line that set out upon its desperate errand, in the form of a half circle. A pale moon shone through a leaden sky sufficiently well enough for us to see the way. It was blowing fairly strong, which helped to deaden our footfalls. For an attack, the night was an ideal one.[44]

As the attackers crept forward, a startled Turkish sentry fired a shot and fled but there was no reaction from the enemy up on the hill. By about 4.30 a.m. the leading assault troops were close enough to charge. Nicol recorded what happened next: 'A splutter of flame broke out from the trench, but it was too late. Shrieks and groans echoed through the night as the bayonets went home with a thud…. Within a few minutes the only Turks remaining in the trench were those who had been captured and those who were dead.'[45]

The Canterburys and Wellingtons captured the forward positions just as dawn broke. Then the 8th (Canterbury) Squadron of the CMR and the 16th (New Zealand) Company of the camel battalion occupied the abandoned trenches on the top of the hill, from where the lights in Amman were clearly visible.[46]

Fred Sterling wrote, 'the air was alive with singing bullets, bombs crashed, machine guns ripped out their leaden hail…. The whole hill was lit with a fierce golden light, and to add to the noise, Jacko started to shell.' Sterling and a group of other AMR men crept up on either side of a Turkish machine gun post, taking advantage of a weapon stoppage to get close. The weapon was repaired by the enemy gunners in time to kill William Sutherland, 'twenty bullets passing through the region of his heart'. Then Dick [McLennan] and Sterling 'blasted in through the canvas top of the gun possie, and must have shot the gunner outright. The gun stopped and out, one after the other, ran first an officer, then five men. None of them got three yards from their gun.'[47]

According to Arthur Moore, a New Zealand signaller following the assault regiments lost his way and found himself on the edge of an occupied enemy trench. Deciding to bluff it out, he muttered a few words of Arabic and joined the Turks in the trench. The Turks immediately recognised him as an enemy and he was only saved from being killed by the intervention of an officer. Soon afterwards, when the New Zealanders charged this trench, most of the Turks fled but the signaller grappled with the officer in an attempt to hold him long enough for the New Zealanders to arrive. When they did, they nearly bayoneted the signaller as he fought with the Turkish officer in the bottom of the trench. The Turk then surrendered, handing his ex-prisoner a pair of binoculars. He followed the signaller around for some time, before being sent away with the other prisoners.[48]

As the light grew, the New Zealanders hastened to prepare their new positions for the

Hill 3039, behind the Roman amphitheatre, in modern Amman. The hill was bare rock in 1918.

inevitable enemy counter-attacks. Trenches could not be dug in the rocky ground and most of the captured trenches faced the wrong way. The trenches on top of the hill were too exposed for the camel battalion so they were held by an outpost of 10 men with two Lewis guns. An enemy trench 200 metres away that had been missed in the dark caused problems until concentrated Hotchkiss and Vickers machine gun fire convinced its occupants to give up.[49]

The first Turkish counter-attack caused many casualties until a bayonet charge swept the Turks from the hilltop. At 9 a.m. a few dozen Canterbury men crept into Amman itself but were forced to withdraw by rifle fire from the houses. The New Zealanders and cameliers endured ceaseless artillery fire on Hill 3039, made worse when the exploding shells turned the rocks into deadly shrapnel.[50]

Mid-morning, a large group of Turks was spotted gathering on the north-eastern slopes of Hill 3039. This tempting target could not be engaged because the mountain guns supporting the New Zealanders had only four shells left. When the Turks attacked at 9.30 a.m., they came to within 10 metres of the New Zealand line before they were stopped in their tracks by massed machine gun fire, including from several captured guns. 'The Turks attacked our fellows in mass formation, but were driven off, simply exterminated with machine guns.'[51]

At one point during this counter-attack someone mistakenly ordered a withdrawal. Some New Zealanders had already begun to move back when the order was countermanded. Taking advantage of this opportunity, the Turks recaptured some of the trenches on top of the hill. The position was quickly recaptured by a massed bayonet charge by the CMR and the cameliers.

Our men surged up on to the crest, and there seemed to be a short pause as the opposing lines faced each other at a bare 15 yards; and then our grand fellows hurled them back. It was estimated that from 400 to 500 Turks assembled on the northern slopes of the hill for this attack and went up to the top. But no more than 50 were seen to come back.[52]

Thomas Ireland's WMR troop was sent up the hill to help repel this attack: 'A call came for help, we left one man to hold eight to 12 horses, and up we went. I got up just in time to see a Turk jump up right in front of our machine gun. Percy Joblin gave him the whole blast and made a window right through him.'[53]

After this experience, the Turks stopped sending men up the hill to be killed by the New Zealanders. Instead, they tried to dislodge the cameliers to the right. When this failed too, they contented themselves with shelling the hill. The New Zealanders and the cameliers suffered steady casualties from this fire. 'They shelled us for hours,' Parker wrote, 'and men were going out wounded in a stream.' The Somerset Battery finally arrived to support the NZMR Brigade but it was too little and too late to affect the outcome of the fight. Although the Turks attacked Hill 3039 several more times during the afternoon, each assault was beaten off by intense machine gun fire from the mounted riflemen and the cameliers.[54]

Apart from the success achieved on Hill 3039, Chaytor's last attack failed. The ICC Brigade was held off by machine gun fire from the Citadel in Amman and the British infantry to the north made little progress. The Turks and Germans launched fierce counter-attacks during the day, particularly against the British infantry battalions. 'The weather was intensely cold, and rain continued to fall heavily, the men [were] lying in mud throughout the day.' William King summed up 30 March as 'a sorry day for the NZ Brigade'. Thirty-eight New Zealanders were killed or died of wounds that day.[55]

At 2 p.m. General Shea asked Chaytor if he thought he could capture Amman that day. Chaytor replied that he could not. Turkish reinforcements were still arriving, and Chaytor had hundreds of wounded men to worry about. Behind him, the light horsemen covering the last bridge across the Jordan River were stretched very thin, and Es Salt was under pressure from several thousand Turks who had come up from the Jordan Valley. The chain of resupply was close to breaking. The wet weather made the mountain tracks treacherous for the camels, the horses of the supply columns in the valley were exhausted and the one bridge over the river was creating a bottleneck.[56]

As is often the case in war, the perception of the situation by commanders on the other side was quite different. A German battalion commander in Amman wrote, 'Why the enemy did not follow up the success he gained during the night [on Hill 3039] it is hard to explain. His entry into the town and, from thence, an advance against the rear of our positions could not have been prevented.' On the afternoon of 30 March, the Turkish commander began to have doubts about his ability to hold off the attackers. Marshal Liman gave orders 'for resistance to the last, regardless'. Of course, Shea and Chaytor knew nothing of this. Shea decided that enough was enough, and told Chaytor to break off the action and withdraw.[57]

The withdrawal began after sunset, with the wounded men going first. Many of the New Zealand casualties were already at a Regimental Aid Post a kilometre behind the firing line on Hill 3039. With no camels to carry them out, wounded men were carried in soggy blankets for two or three kilometres to a dressing station. From there, most of them had to ride horses for 15 kilometres to the collecting station at Es Salt, where they were loaded onto horse-drawn ambulances and taken back to the valley floor. Those men who could not ride were strapped to their horses, even if they had broken bones or serious head, chest or abdominal wounds. 'The only alternative was to abandon the wounded to the Bedouin.' One trooper being lashed to his horse said 'a man was lucky to be killed'. Nicol concluded that no one could ever describe the 'sufferings those men endured on that terrible journey, over slippery and dangerous tracks through the hills on a night which

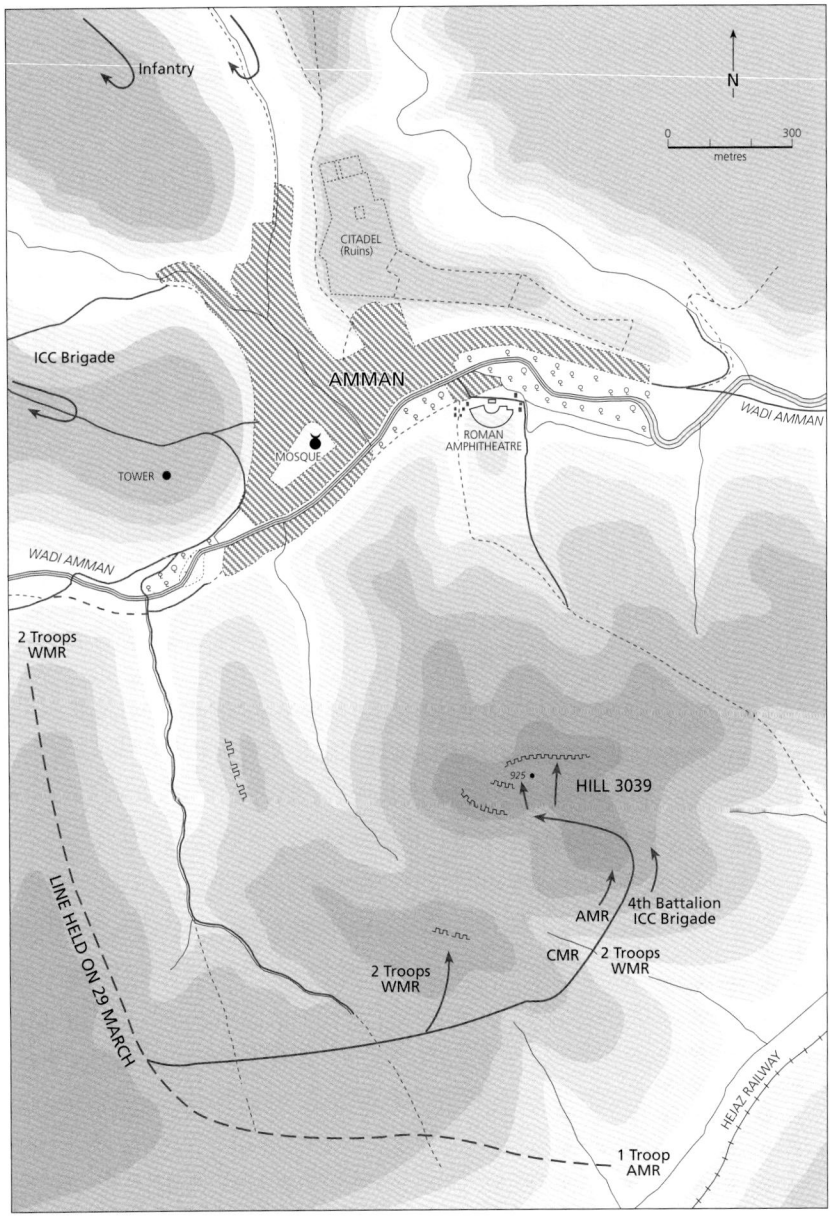

Map 18: Capture of Hill 3039.

Exhausted New Zealanders re-cross the Jordan on 2 April, after the abandonment of the Amman operation.

was piercingly cold'. Alec McNeur believed that 'no badly wounded man had a chance to reach hospital in the cold and wet'. [58]

While the wounded men were being carried away, the men in the trenches buried their dead comrades. Three hours after sunset, the captured machine guns were destroyed and the forward positions were quietly abandoned. 'Care was taken by everyone to avoid even kicking a stone.' When Fred Sterling and his comrades reached their horses about 9.30, they 'found the horse holders … had boiled up and prepared tea for us. Seeing it was the first food we had had since 7 p.m. yesterday we did full justice to it.' The New Zealanders manned a rearguard position in front of Ain es Sir, while the rest of Shea's Force withdrew down the Es Salt road and the Ain es Sir track to the valley floor on 31 March. Thomas Ireland watched 3000 pursuing Turkish infantrymen coming 'like a mob of sheep let out of a paddock'.[59]

When the sun set on 31 March, the New Zealanders picked themselves up, mounted their horses and pulled back to the entrance to a long gorge that descended towards the valley. That night was 'the most bitter yet experienced…. The men … suffered torture from the icy blasts.'[60] For the AMR, it was 'one of the most dreadful nights of its existence'.

A cutting wind blew, and there was no shelter from it. Stiff with the cold, the men lay close together, and prayed that the Turks would be frozen too. The regiment began to retire slowly before dawn.... Daylight was breaking by the time they were clear of the village [Ain es Sir], where the WMR took over the rearguard duties. The column slowly moved down the wadi, along which were scattered the bodies of dozens of camels which had been knocked out by the greasy slopes and the cold, and were now being cut up by the Arabs for food.[61]

As the WMR rearguard passed through Ain es Sir on the morning of 1 April, the 2nd (Wellington West Coast) Squadron was attacked. As Ted Andrews wrote,

those bloody swine of Circassians opened fire on us with firearms of all descriptions. From houses, behind rocks on the hills, and from caves, they poured a murderous fire at close range. Men and horses went down in all directions, wounded horses rearing, bolting and screaming – the most fearful mix-up I ever saw!

Riderless horses galloped around the sides of the hills 'like flies round the walls of a house'. The squadron galloped clear of the village, dismounted, and counter-attacked. The other two WMR squadrons climbed along the ridges above the village, capturing a flour mill and killing its occupants. According to Wilkie, these enemy riflemen were so busy trying to pick off the New Zealand horses as they galloped out of range that they failed to see the mounted riflemen approaching until it was too late. No prisoners were taken. Under machine gun and artillery fire, the surviving Circassians vanished into the hills.[62]

By the time their comrades reached them some of the men who were wounded in the initial ambush had been finished off by the villagers. Others could not be reached and were left behind. The WMR suffered 18 casualties at Ain es Sir, at least five of whom were killed or mortally wounded, including the squadron commander, Major Charles Sommerville. At least 36 of their assailants, mostly Circassian villagers, were killed. Several witnesses, including Harry Judge, criticised the WMR for not clearing the village on foot, as was normally done. 'Whoever is responsible should be made to suffer for that.'[63]

Apart from this incident, the withdrawal of Shea's Force to the Jordan Valley was unopposed. As the men descended, they met a supply convoy bringing food and forage. The riders shared the tracks with hundreds of wretched refugees, mostly Christians, who feared Turkish reprisals after welcoming their supposed liberators a few days previously. The wind dropped, the sunshine was bright and masses of colourful flowers brushed against the horses' legs, but all this did little to lift the spirits of the exhausted and disappointed men, who knew that this was their worst defeat against the Turks since the second battle of Gaza in April 1917. James Cameron hoped that he would never have to go into the Moab hills again.[64]

The NZMR Brigade crossed the bridge at Ghoraniyeh early on 2 April and bivouacked near Jericho. Early the next morning the men were jolted awake by the crash of exploding bombs from eight enemy aircraft. One bomb landed near the Auckland regimental headquarters, killing 18 horses and wounding four or five others, along with eight men.[65]

The Amman operation was a complete failure. The Hejaz Railway tunnel and viaduct were never threatened and the operation did little to assist or encourage the Hejaz Arabs. There were many reasons for the failure, the most important being the delay caused by the flooded Jordan (which gave the Turks time to reinforce the garrison of Amman), the determined defence put up by the Turks and Germans, the weakness of the assaulting force (especially its lack of artillery) and its inability to isolate the battlefield by cutting the Hejaz Railway and blocking the northern tracks from the Jordan Valley to Es Salt.[66]

Fred Sterling described the stunt as 'easily the worst I have as yet experienced'. George Ranstead thought that 'for a hard time, there has been nothing to equal it since the

J02809, AUSTRALIAN WAR MEMORIAL

Refugees, fleeing Turkish retribution, cross a footbridge over the Jordan River.

peninsula [Gallipoli].' Arthur Harrison described it as 'a great stunt for those who got through it safely, but I never want to experience another like it. I never thought human beings could withstand anything like it.'[67] According to Gullett, 'the Australians and New Zealanders … fretted constantly over the men they had left behind among the prowling, ghoulish Arabs on that wild, alien territory'. They had good reason for concern: on 4 April William King noted in his diary that 'our Secret Service reports that all the wounded we left behind at Ain es Sir are lying in the same place with their throats cut'.[68]

More than 1300 EEF men were killed or wounded in the fighting. The Anzac Mounted Division and the ICC Brigade together lost 118 men killed, 551 wounded and 55 missing (mostly captured). CWGC records indicate that 64 New Zealanders died between 27 March and 2 April 1918. Enemy casualties were believed to total 350 killed, 900 wounded and 615 captured.[69]

Shea's Force had performed creditably against near impossible odds. 'The operations had lasted twelve days, and it had rained almost the whole time. The troops were without tents or shelter of any kind, and, for the last ninety hours of the operations, they had been marching and fighting continuously, without sleep or rest.'[70] In Powles's words,

The enemy were fresh troops, well-fed and well-equipped, and were fighting in well-dug trenches supported by artillery; yet our wonderful men, short of sleep, short of rations, wet through, fighting in a strange country which was filled with hostile inhabitants, overcame almost insuperable obstacles, captured impregnable positions in the darkness of night, and carried their wounded for miles over mountain tracks.[71]

A few days after the withdrawal, Chetwode asked Chaytor

to express to your gallant Division and to the ICC [Brigade] my admiration and thanks for the fine work they did east of Jordan…. I do not think they have ever had to overcome such difficulties of ground, or to undergo such fatigue and hardships, as they have had to do in the Mountains of Moab. It was a disappointment to you all, I know, not to be able to complete the destruction of the railway, but as the C. in C. [Allenby] said – if the Anzacs and 60th [Division] could not do it, no-one could.[72]

14

Another disappointment

It isn't nice to … go for a ride towards the hills with a few thousand rifles, about a hundred machine guns, not to mention big guns, all potting at you.

ALEC McNEUR

TWO WEEKS AFTER Allenby received the green light to continue his conquest of Palestine and Syria, and while his Amman operation was still under way, the German Army launched a major offensive against the British and French armies on the Western Front. For a while it seemed that the Allies might be about to lose the war and thousands of reinforcements were urgently summoned to help stop the German onslaughts. On 27 March Allenby was told to adopt a policy of 'active defence' in the Middle East as soon as his Amman operation was completed and to send one of his infantry divisions to France immediately. By the middle of the year 60,000 experienced men – two infantry divisions, 23 infantry battalions, nine Yeomanry cavalry regiments and a number of artillery batteries and machine gun companies – had been transferred from the Middle East to France. Allenby retained his excellent Anzac mounted brigades and most of the Indian Army cavalry and infantry units that he had been promised, but he could no longer advance towards Haifa in the spring as planned. He settled down to rebuild the EEF, in anticipation of renewing the offensive much later in the year.[1]

The EEF held the western side of the Jordan Valley from the Dead Sea as far north as Musallabe and Abu Tulul, opposite the ford at Umm esh Shert, with a small bridgehead across the river at Ghoraniyeh (see Map 16, p.256). Major General Chaytor assumed responsibility for the valley defences on 3 April 1918. Each day his brigades sent mounted patrols out from the Ghoraniyeh bridgehead towards the eastern foothills, where the Turks were busily building fortifications across the road at Shunet Nimrin. Alec McNeur did not enjoy this work.

It isn't nice to … go for a ride towards the hills with a few thousand rifles, about a hundred

A rest period.

machine guns, not to mention big guns, all potting at you. It does not mean a picnic, and, of course, horses make a good target. If we were infantry we could creep along the hollows and amongst the scrub but no, we just jog along as if nothing was happening.[2]

After the bitterly cold Amman operation, the warmth of the Jordan Valley was welcomed for a few weeks, but it became uncomfortably warm when a khamsin began to blow on 17 April, lifting the fine, sulphurous limestone dust from the valley floor into choking and irritating clouds that were much more unpleasant than the Sinai sandstorms of 1916.[3]

On 11 April 2000 Turks attacked the Australian light horse and ICC Brigade troops defending the Ghoraniyeh bridgehead and Wadi el Auja. They were held off by the garrisons with ease and Chaytor did not even bother to order the NZMR Brigade, in reserve near Jericho, to saddle up. A week later, Chaytor conducted a demonstration in the Jordan Valley to support an Arab attack around Ma'an. The Turks reacted so vigorously to the appearance of the mounted troops that they could not even approach the foothills and the force withdrew in the late afternoon.[4]

This minor stunt was the precursor to a much larger operation at the end of April. Allenby decided to send Chauvel's Desert Mounted Corps back up onto the eastern hills to destroy the ripening wheat crops, to make contact with the Hejaz Arabs fighting along

P00339.009, AUSTRALIAN WAR MEMORIAL

A pontoon bridge over the Jordan River. Its sides are covered to prevent horses being frightened by the river.

the railway and to permanently occupy the plateau, thus sparing his troops the ordeal of spending a summer in the Jordan Valley. Allenby gave Chauvel two brigades of the 60th (London) Division, the 20th Indian Brigade and four extra cavalry regiments. Chauvel decided to fix the main enemy force at Shunet Nimrin in place with the infantry and send a mounted force through Es Salt to attack it from behind. The frontal attack on Shunet Nimrin was the responsibility of the 60th Division, supported by the New Zealand brigade.[5]

Major General Henry Hodgson commanded the mobile force, which consisted of his Australian Mounted Division, Chaytor's 1st LH Brigade, a mountain gun battery and several armoured cars. Hodgson was to advance up the eastern side of the Jordan River valley, leaving small detachments along the way to guard several fords. One light horse brigade was to capture and hold the Damieh-Es Salt track where it entered the hills and, if it could, also secure the pontoon bridge at Damieh. Hodgson's other brigades were to climb to Es Salt via the Umm esh Shert and Damieh tracks. After capturing Es Salt and blocking enemy counter-attacks from Amman, these horsemen would move down the Es Salt-Shunet Nimrin track to attack the Turks at Shunet Nimrin from the rear. The Ain es Sir track, the only other known supply route from the Amman plateau to Shunet Nimrin,

was to be blocked by several thousand Bedouin from the Beni Sakhr tribe. Cut off and attacked from two directions, the Turks at Shunet Nimrin would have no choice but to surrender – or so it was hoped. After that, Amman and the plateau would be occupied. Allenby wanted to launch the operation in mid-May, when his third mounted division would be available. However, the Bedouin who offered to help with the attack demanded that it be launched before 4 May, so Allenby settled on 30 April as Z-Day.[6]

After the first British attack at Amman, the Turkish 4th Army east of the Jordan River had been reinforced. Allenby knew this but he did not know that the Turkish 3rd Cavalry Division, the Caucasus Cavalry Brigade and several German infantry units had secretly entered the northern Jordan Valley, that the 24th Division was not far away and that a pontoon bridge had been built and concealed on the Jordan River at Mafid Jozele.[7]

General Chauvel considered the operation impracticable. He believed that he lacked the necessary striking power and that his supply capacity was inadequate. The Turks had been alerted by Chaytor's demonstration on 18 April and Chauvel had no confidence that the Arabs would do their part. Allenby listened, then told him that the operation was to go ahead.[8]

The Australian Mounted Division crossed the Jordan River at Ghoraniyeh in the pre-

The small bridge at Huweij (right) was as far as the EEF forces advancing downhill from Es Salt could reach.

dawn darkness of 30 April. As the 60th Division began its attacks on Shunet Nimrin, Brigadier General William Grant's 4th LH Brigade led the horsemen up the valley. In ninety minutes, they covered 25 kilometres and reached the Damieh track near the foothills. Two light horse squadrons were dropped off at Red Hill, eight kilometres from the rest of the brigade. Grant's brigade was unable to capture the Damieh bridge. Hodgson took three mounted brigades up into the hills on the Damieh and Umm esh Shert tracks. The horsemen took no wheeled artillery into the hills with them, relying once again on a handful of small camel-borne mountain guns. The Australian division's three batteries of British horse artillery were left with Grant's brigade on the river flats.[9]

Marshal Liman heard about the attacks at 8.30 a.m. The 3rd Cavalry Division received orders to cross the river at Damieh, push past the Australians and advance on Es Salt. The 24th Division was told to deal with the forces in the northern valley. The 4th Army was ordered to hold Shunet Nimrin at all costs.[10]

The infantry battalions and guns of the British 60th Division battered away at Shunet Nimrin all day, but achieved little. During the day the Canterbury regiment had 45 of its horses killed by artillery fire. At dusk, the New Zealand brigade withdrew into reserve at the Ghoraniyeh bridge, leaving the WMR forward with the infantry.[11]

In the afternoon, Chauvel ordered Grant to withdraw his regiments from the approaches

The foothills at Shunet Nimrin. The EEF could make no headway against the enemy defences here.

to the Damieh bridge to the foothills. Grant asked for another regiment to help garrison Red Hill but Chauvel replied that no reinforcements were available. Opposite Grant's thin line, the Turkish 24th and 3rd Cavalry divisions, reinforced by two German infantry companies, reached the Jordan River at Damieh at dusk.[12]

The first day of the battle ended with Chauvel's force dangerously extended. The track from the Damieh bridge to Es Salt was threatened by the as yet undetected Turkish force across the river, and the weak Australian position on Red Hill was also vulnerable. The Beni Sakhr failed to block the Ain es Sir track, allowing the Turkish force at Shunet Nimrin to be reinforced at will. If the northern tracks to Es Salt were cut, and if the main road at Shunet Nimrin stayed closed, the mounted brigades up on the plateau would be cut off.

When the sun rose on 1 May, Grant's light horsemen realised that a large enemy force had crossed the river at Damieh in front of them. At 7.30 a.m. 1750 Turks and Germans attacked Grant's 800 light horsemen. At 10 a.m. another enemy force suddenly appeared at Red Hill, having crossed the pontoon bridge at Mafid Jozele. It quickly captured the hill from the two light horse squadrons defending it. Grant's outnumbered brigade was quickly forced away from the Damieh-Es Salt track. Two of his regiments had to escape up the track and the third withdrew down the Jordan Valley. Nine 13-pounder guns from the horse artillery batteries, and many supply wagons and vehicles, were trapped and abandoned after their horse teams were machine-gunned. As soon as the Damieh track was recaptured from the Australians, Turkish cavalry forces set off up it towards Es Salt.[13]

As soon as he heard what had happened, Chauvel placed Chaytor in command of the 4th LH Brigade, a regiment of the 6th Mounted Brigade, a British machine gun squadron and a horse artillery battery, and told him to stop the Turks before they cut all the tracks to Es Salt. It was too late to recapture the Damieh track so Chaytor withdrew his forces to a shorter defensive line guarding the Umm esh Shert track. The Auckland regiment took its place in the line alongside Grant's light horsemen, to be joined later in the day by some armoured cars. The reinforced Turks launched three unsuccessful attacks against Chaytor's line, which was anchored on high ground at Table Top and Black Hill. Table Top was lost, but the vital track to Es Salt remained open.

Meanwhile the 60th Division attacked again at Shunet Nimrin, supported at first by the WMR and the CMR, but the Turks were far too strongly entrenched to be dislodged. 'Our light field guns could make no impression on the rock-hewn trenches of the Turks, and the wire, protected and partly-concealed by the innumerable boulders in front of the positions, could not be effectively cut.' The Canterbury regiment was sent north to bolster

the defences covering the Umm esh Shert track. The Wellingtons followed after a final attack on Shunet Nimrin was cancelled.[14]

By nightfall, three of the four tracks from the valley to Es Salt were under enemy control.[15] The Umm esh Shert track, still covered by Chaytor's forces, was now the only escape route for the four mounted brigades operating around Es Salt. These British and Australian horsemen were not yet aware of the threat to their withdrawal routes. The 2nd and 3rd LH brigades tried and failed to capture the crossroads near Ain Hummar. The 1st LH Brigade secured the junction of the Umm esh Shert and Wadi abu Turra tracks, blocking the latter as an escape route for the enemy down at Shunet Nimrin – who had no intention of escaping. The 5th Mounted Brigade rode down the road leading to Shunet Nimrin but could not get past a well-defended bridge at Huweij. At 4.40 p.m. General Hodgson finally heard what had happened in the valley below. He quickly placed his slender reserve of two light horse troops across the Damieh track to block the enemy cavalry force that was approaching along it. The two Australian brigades to the east were recalled: the 3rd brigade was placed around Es Salt and the 2nd brigade was added to a force that Hodgson had ordered to attack the bridge at Huweij again the following morning.[16]

On 2 May two mounted brigades began their attack down the Shunet Nimrin track but there was still no way through. When Turkish troops attacked the 3rd LH Brigade at Es Salt from east and west, the 2nd LH Brigade was withdrawn from the Shunet Nimrin attack to help defend the town. By dusk the situation was very precarious: with the Damieh-Es Salt track in enemy hands and the Shunet Nimrin route still firmly closed, the only way out of the hills was via the Umm esh Shert track, the eastern end of which was guarded by two regiments of the 1st LH Brigade. The track's exit into the river valley was held by Chaytor's force. That night the 60th Division attacked again at Shunet Nimrin, although with little success.

Throughout 3 May, enemy pressure continued in the hills and in the valley to the north of the Umm esh Shert track, mostly in the form of artillery fire. The Turks held the initiative everywhere, Chauvel's forces in the valley were running low on ammunition and the horsemen up in the hills around Es Salt were reduced to living off the land. With Allenby's approval, Chauvel issued orders for the withdrawal of the mounted brigades from Es Salt at 4 p.m.[17]

The town was abandoned by 2.20 a.m. the next morning. By dawn, everyone was safely past the junction of the Umm esh Shert and Wadi abu Turra tracks. 'The track in many places was worse than going downstairs, and how men managed riding one horse and leading another I don't know. The horses had, however, become like cats.'[18]

An immaculately presented mounted rifleman and his horse in the Middle East.

The last of the horsemen reached the river valley at 10.30 a.m., followed by another straggling column of refugees. The men of the Canterbury regiment climbed into the lower slopes on foot to assist the horsemen as they descended. As soon as the mounted brigades were clear of the hills, the 60th Division withdrew back across the river. The New Zealanders were the last to cross, leaving the Wellington and Auckland regiments temporarily in the Ghoraniyeh bridgehead.[19]

By midnight on 4 May, the withdrawal was complete. Percy Doherty wrote that 'everybody slept all day, excepting when they had to water or feed horses. All dead-tired and worn out'. The next morning, too, as Fred Sterling recorded, 'the camp was very dead … for we slept until the sun and flies really burnt and worried us. The horses look almost wrecks, the men no less.'[20]

The EEF lost 214 men killed, 1298 wounded and 137 missing, mostly from the 60th Division. New Zealand's losses were light: three men were killed on 30 April and two died of wounds in the following two days. About 2000 Turks and Germans became casualties; 44 German and nearly 900 Turkish prisoners were rounded up by the DMC.[21]

General Chauvel's concerns before the battle had been proven to be correct. However, it would have been far worse if the horsemen in the hills around Es Salt had been cut off and destroyed. The determined efforts of the men defending the Umm esh Shert track, perhaps aided by the enemy commander's decision not to try too hard to cut off the horsemen at Es Salt, prevented disaster from befalling the mounted troops of the EEF. Long after the war, Chetwode told Allenby's biographer that 'these two expeditions of Allenby's across the Jordan were the stupidest things he did, I always thought, and very risky'. Two successive failures east of the Jordan caused many Arabs to lose confidence in Allenby and tribes who were thinking of joining the fight against the Turks decided to sit on the fence for a little longer.[22]

15

The valley of desolation

Our boys fight in a very matter-of-fact way,
and one would not know that they were seriously interested.[1]

ALEC McNEUR

LOCAL EXPERTS AND military manuals stated that malaria and the unhealthy climate would kill any European who tried to live in the Jordan Valley during the summer. Allenby considered abandoning the valley temporarily but he did not want to have to recapture it from the Turks in the autumn. He also wanted to keep the Turks guessing about where he would attack them next, and the presence of a mounted force in the valley would have that effect. Allenby left the final decision to General Chauvel, who decided to hold the Jordan Valley throughout the summer, although he intended to minimise the impact on the garrison's health by regularly rotating forces. As the reorganisation of the Yeomanry Mounted Division was incomplete, the Anzac and Australian mounted divisions drew the first short straws.[2]

The temperature in the valley rose steadily as summer approached. The maximum shade temperature of 45°C was recorded on 14 June and 38°C was reached or exceeded on 88 days. The heat was so intense at times that weapons and metal tools had to be wetted before they could be picked up and the horses backs grew too hot to touch.[3] Tom Murray remembered the hot day when some New Zealand machine gunners declared an unofficial truce with the Turks.

At about three in the afternoon … firing got very slack, then stopped altogether, and we saw several Turks show themselves, but it was too hot to bother firing at them, and eventually some of them went down to the stream. Some of us did the same, and before long there was quite a number of us all there together getting water. We couldn't understand them, and I don't suppose they understood what we were saying, but this went on for about an hour, until we went back to our positions, and, after a while, hostilities commenced again.[4]

Looking west through the white clay hills towards the Jordan River.

A typical summer's day in the Jordan Valley began with a hot, northerly wind lifting clouds of fine white dust into the air. This acrid, alkaline powder, which scalded the throats and stung the eyes of men and horses, penetrated everywhere. The wind often died down in the middle of the day 'as if lulled by the fierce heat of the sun, and there is a spell of roasting heat'. In the afternoon, the wind would rise again, this time from the south, creating towering 'dust devils' that ripped tents from the ground and flung them into the air. Any movement stirred up dense clouds of dust, which hung in the air like fog.

> *Men returning from watering their horses were often weird sights – their scanty clothes would be wet with perspiration, which sometimes dripped from the knees of their riding breeches. A white coating of dust would enshroud them, through which their faces could be seen as white masks streaked with sweat.*[5]

The stuffy nights were only a little cooler than the days and the men on outpost duty worked through most of them anyway. Most of the men avoided the enclosed bell tents and slept in low open-sided bivouacs made from sticks and horse blankets.

Outpost duty in the Jordan Valley for a troop of mounted riflemen usually began in the afternoon, with the men loading up with rations and ammunition while the troop leader received his orders. When it was dark, the officer led his men down to the river to relieve the troop already there. The outgoing officer briefed the new arrivals on the sector in front of them before leading his men away. The new troop placed its horses under cover, posted sentries and a listening post in front of the main position and sited the Hotchkiss gun. The men boiled their billies for tea while the horses were fed. Linked together by their head ropes, the horses remained saddled and picquets guarded them continuously. With all these duties to be taken care of, few men got any sleep. Most nights passed uneventfully, with the men hearing nothing more than the odd cough from the horses or the baying of jackals. If the Turks attacked, the listening post pulled back to the main outpost, which was to be defended to the last bullet if necessary. When the sun rose, the listening post was called in, the horses were unsaddled and the troop spent the day with just one or two sentries keeping an eye on the enemy across the river. Any Turks who showed themselves were usually sniped at and the Turks bombarded the posts with artillery if they spotted them. British artillery officers and senior commanders would sometimes visit the post during the day but little else happened until the relieving troop appeared in the late afternoon.[6]

The indigenous valley population was described by Ted Andrews, who had little good to say about anyone who was not a New Zealander, as

F-106310-1/2, ALEXANDER TURNBULL LIBRARY

Men of the 11th (North Auckland) Squadron digging trenches in the Jordan Valley (unusually, in daylight).

a surly, villainous lot of pariahs and outcasts. It wasn't safe to go about without a rifle. I did one day, and was mighty glad to meet one of our patrols. Eventually, our Military Police rounded them all up and moved them out to a barbed wire enclosure.[7]

In addition to the human denizens of the valley, there were poisonous snakes, hairy spiders and centipedes which wriggled and crawled across the ground beneath swarms of flies, mosquitoes and other unpleasant insects. Grasshoppers nibbled the bare toes of sleeping men and new arrivals quickly learned that sleeping with their faces uncovered would result in a mouthful of flies in the morning. It was not unusual for men to wake up and find several large scorpions under their groundsheets. 'When I say "large",' wrote Henry Bostock, 'they certainly were – 4" and 5" long and, with the tail straight out, more than 6" [15 cm] long. They certainly bred monsters in the Jordan Valley.' Staged fights between scorpions and tarantula spiders were still popular and men betted heavily on the outcome. Storks, vultures and wild pigs also inhabited the valley.[8]

B00228. Australian War Memorial

Clearing a stream to prevent malarial mosquitoes from breeding in the stagnant water.

According to Robert Wilson, Jordan Valley mosquitoes were 'big enough to carry bombs'. Edwin McKay explained how the horses dealt with these insects at night.

On outpost they were tethered less rigidly than in the lines, and while all hands but the sentry slept, they would work around until they stood in a circle, each with his head buried in the tail of the animal ahead, for protection from the flying irritants.[9]

By the end of June, as George Berrie explained, 'the irrigated plots had long since been burnt off under the overpowering heat, the Jordan moved sluggishly, and the streams feeding into it from the foothills had shrunk to trickles.' The enervating heat was too

Horses killed by bombs while watering.

much for some men and standards slipped. When Chauvel inspected the outposts manned by the AMR on 3 July, he was not pleased with what he saw. Little recent digging or wiring had been completed, handover procedures were poor, range cards were inadequate and in some places the barbed wire was loose. A few trenches were too narrow to permit the evacuation of casualties or the bringing forward of ammunition, and some emergency rations were stale.[10]

There were a few good points about the valley. There was no lack of clean, cool water in the many wadis feeding into the Jordan River – although poisonous snakes were common near the water. Food was plentiful but the lack of refrigeration meant that it was 'pretty uninspiring' by the time it reached the troops. Bread from Jerusalem bakeries was dry and rock-hard by the time it got to the men in the valley. Fresh vegetables were rarely seen and bully beef remained the staple item of diet. Jaffa oranges were supplied regularly when in season and they were a great help. Swimming in the Jordan River was a popular pastime for men and horses but the use of hand grenades for fishing was prohibited.[11]

The biblical associations of the valley appealed to some men. After the war bottles of Jordan River water were often taken home to New Zealand and used to baptise infants. When men introduced their horses to the buoyant waters of the Dead Sea, they laughed at the perplexed expressions on the animals' faces as they floated high out of the water. A

Solomon's Pools, near Bethlehem.

warped sense of humour helped others to endure the terrible conditions. One Australian practical joker placed a snake inside an officer's bag. When the man reached into the bag, felt the snake and thought he had been bitten, he rushed off to the medical officer, who could find no evidence of a bite. The officer was adamant but, by the time he thought to show the snake to the doctor, it had been replaced with an inoffensive piece of rope.[12]

For the most part, the Turks were content to lob a few shells over the river or drop bombs from aircraft. 'The British gunners, more through politeness than anything else, threw a few back – at least so it seemed to the men on the horse lines or in the trenches.' British anti-aircraft batteries 'were cursed nearly as much as the [enemy] aeroplanes were, owing to their habit of landing spent shrapnel and shell cases among the camps'. Enemy shells or bombs did sometimes find their mark; on 7 May, seven Canterbury horses were killed and eight were wounded by bombs.[13]

Malaria became a serious threat from May onwards and a campaign began to eliminate the stagnant pools of water in which the mosquitoes bred. 'Mosquito Squads' drained swamps and pools of water or covered them with a film of oil. Reeds along the banks of slow-moving streams were removed and their channels were straightened to remove areas of sluggish water. However, it was impossible to eradicate the threat, mainly because the wind blew the mosquitoes across from the Turkish side of the river.

The insects were most active at night, so every man was issued with a mosquito net to sleep under. Mosquito veils were also issued and men were supposed to roll their shirt sleeves down and button them at the wrist, then apply an 'anti-mosquito ointment' to their exposed hands. An average of 80 malarial cases per week were evacuated from the valley in June and August 1918, with 221 in the first week of August alone. The number of cases fell in the first three weeks of September as the preventative measures finally began to pay off.[14]

The men were susceptible to all sorts of illnesses. 'Sand-fly fever' and 'five-day fever' incapacitated thousands of men for days on end and everyone suffered from upset stomachs. Allenby forbade the horsemen to wear shorts on horseback, insisting that they wear breeches and puttees to stop septic sores from developing on their bare legs. This added greatly to the discomfort of the men in the hot valley and eventually he was persuaded to allow the men to ride in 'slacks' without puttees.[15]

Sleep was a precious commodity in the Jordan Valley. The heat, flies and dust-laden wind made it impossible to sleep during the day. The coolest period was the four or five hours between midnight and sunrise but work party duties made sure that few men slept even then. In July Chaytor ordered the brigades in reserve to limit training to officers, NCOs and specialists; the troopers were to have as much rest as possible. A month later, he changed his mind when he realised that men with little to do were liable to become listless, and even sick, through sheer boredom. He directed that there were to be at least two hours of training every day, with lessons covering squad and rifle drill, saluting, bayonet fighting, machine gun shooting and signalling.[16]

Under these conditions, many men lost weight through lack of appetite. They became chronically weak, tired, irritable and, in some cases, clinically depressed. Alec McNeur wrote, 'The worst aspect of the valley is the effect it has on one's spirits. The first week is not too bad but each succeeding week the outlook becomes more gloomy and life less worth living.' The official summary was that 'Heavy and continuous physical exertion, excessive heat, combined with the early stand to arms, which cuts down so largely the hours of rest, are having a very depressing effect on the men's vitality, which is reflected in the sick rate'.[17]

The deterioration in the health of the Anzacs in Palestine in 1918 was similar to that seen on Gallipoli in 1915. The Anzacs in Chaytor's division were in the poorest shape, as the cumulative strain of two years of continuous campaigning made itself felt. Since crossing the Suez Canal in April 1916, they had lived continuously in desert conditions and a few short rest periods were not enough to maintain their health and morale. By mid-1918 many of these veterans had just about reached the limit of their endurance. More and more Main Body men attended the daily sick parades and others 'who could stand it no longer' looked for easier jobs 'in Base Records, the Post Office – even the [Military] Police'.[18]

The horses also suffered, although to a lesser extent. Despite incessant grooming by their riders, they were always covered in a fine layer of dust, streaked by lines of sweat. There was good water for the animals and fodder was plentiful, if somewhat lacking in nutritional value. The horses handled the heat better than the men, and they were spared the endless work parties and the threat of malaria, but their condition still deteriorated. 'After about three weeks in the valley, they became so tired and dispirited, though they had little or no work to do, that they could scarce drag themselves the mile or so to water and back again.'[19] An outbreak of anthrax killed three horses but otherwise they were relatively disease-free.[20]

Allenby and the other commanders, aware that the fighting fitness of the mounted divisions was inexorably declining, did what they could to postpone their inevitable collapse. Everything possible was done to reduce the number of men required in the front line. Instead of a continuous line of trenches along the river, a number of small, strong

This photograph is believed to show Major General Chaytor visiting the Dome of the Rock in Jerusalem.

outposts were built. Each outpost contained several machine guns, manned by a small number of dismounted horsemen. The posts were entrenched and protected by thick belts of barbed wire. The outposts were widely separated and any Turkish advance into these gaps was to be blocked by mobile reserves from further back. Of course, someone had to dig these defensive positions, and that meant men with picks and shovels.[21]

What kept many men going was the knowledge that, after four to six weeks in the valley, they would be relieved and sent to rest camps around Bethlehem or on the Mediterranean coast. According to Jim McMillan, 'had it not been for these periodical brief spells, it is doubtful that many of the troops could have been able to carry on'. Theoretically, each mounted brigade only spent about a month in the Jordan Valley before being rotated out, but the New Zealanders escaped the valley for just two short periods: 1–13 June and 1–15 August.[22]

After handing over their duties to the incoming brigade, the New Zealanders trekked up the winding road through the Wilderness towards Jerusalem. The first night was always spent at Talaat ed Dumm, where 'the camping grounds were in a filthy condition, and the ground was rocky and stony'. The next morning, the horsemen would ride around the

edge of Jerusalem's Old City and along the Hebron Road past Bethlehem to their usual camp site near Solomon's Pools (see Map 11, p.176).[23]

After the oppressive heat of the Jordan Valley, the cool climate of the Judean Hills was very welcome, and 'all ranks breathed again'. With few work parties required, men could sleep right through the nights for a change. The countryside was green and fertile, and the men appreciated the lush vineyards, orange groves and barley fields.

> The hills all rise in narrow limestone ledges and every ledge almost is a garden. The vines are so fresh and green. And the olives darken the hillsides. In the valleys and wide terraces grows the corn…. In the cornfields and on the roadside are poppies and cornflowers lending grace to the beauty with their scarlet and blue. Butterflies of all colours flit about … The valley was depressing and all was languid in man and nature…. [here] the natives laugh and chatter, and our soldiers are different men.[24]

Villagers sold tomatoes, cucumbers, eggs, onions, oranges and mulberries to the men. 'Tomatoes are the chief attraction, and I manage about a shilling's worth a day. We make salads, or fry them, or eat them as they are, but they are good anyway, and a great treat.'[25]

ALBUM 213 P.87, AUCKLAND WAR MEMORIAL MUSEUM LIBRARY

Mounted riflemen meet their Arab allies.

The 11th (North Auckland) Squadron departs Bethlehem for the valley.

Officially the regiments in the rest camps were in reserve but little training went on. The main purpose was to give the men and the horses a decent rest in a more hospitable climate. Of course, there were horse picket duties every so often, water had to be pumped to the horse troughs and guards had to be provided, but nonetheless these periods were greatly appreciated.[26]

There was ample opportunity for the men to visit Jerusalem and Bethlehem. Religiously inclined men, equipped with their *Active Service New Testament* and their *Soldier's Handbook, Palestine and Jerusalem*, sallied forth enthusiastically to view the places they had heard about at Sunday School in New Zealand. Others relied on the biblical knowledge of the regimental padres. Many, perhaps the majority, of the Anzacs were not terribly interested in ancient history and found little to impress them at the historic Holy Land sites: 'The streets … are ill-paved and crooked … and are excessively dirty after rain. Some of them are vaulted over into evil-smelling passages.' Roy McCormack described the inhabitants as 'a low horde, steeped in vice and unfortunately, poverty and all asking for Baksheesh or presents'.[27] Men with time on their hands chatted endlessly about New Zealand.

One of our favourite themes of conversation is what we would do if we were at home, and the comforts we will have. We could picture ourselves stretched on a nice lounge, with someone

The unhappy ride from Bethlehem back to the Jordan Valley.

playing music or talking, while we ate apples, or we could picture ourselves sitting down to a nice tea with just the people we like.[28]

In January 1918, George Ranstead noted that 'some fellows are offering odds [of] six to one that the whole thing will be over in six months, but of course some fellows are fools'. A few months later, Ranstead made a bet with another man 'that the war would be over by Xmas 1925'. Even when the massive German offensives in France were halted and the Allies counter-attacked in August 1918, few men thought that the war was nearing its end. Things looked a little more promising on the Palestine front, although the two recent failures across the Jordan were not encouraging.[29]

In mid-1918, plans were again drawn up to send the few remaining Main Body men home to New Zealand on leave. When these plans were cancelled because of a lack of shipping, Alec McNeur was furious.

Not ships for 80 men! These men have been through Gallipoli and all the campaign here. [They] have had as hard a time as men could have. The men in France are amongst a friendly people who are kind to them, they get to England and have regular rests. Our men here have no friends, and can't get away from the sand and heat wherever they go, and besides are usually short of food and water, and the Government ought to be ashamed.[30]

With next to no chance of overseas leave, mail was the only link to loved ones at home. Letters arrived every two or three months and they were eagerly awaited. In a May 1918 letter to his fiancée, Alec McNeur wrote:

Well, Sweetheart, there is not much to say. A good deal is forbidden, and of course a good deal [is] better left unsaid. We shut our eyes and try to think of home, cool shades, sea beaches, and trickling creeks, but the flies torment [us] and our morning sleep is spoilt by bombs.

And in June:

What a lot of bad habits you will have to break me of. I am quite used to sleeping with boots and clothes on. As for table manners, they are quite neglected, and I will have to practise taking off my hat to a lady, and I really forget which arm to offer her.[31]

Fred Sterling was unimpressed with the quality of many of the reinforcements arriving from New Zealand. Some of them lasted only a few days before being hospitalised, including an 18-year-old, whom Sterling uncharitably described as a 'thin little miserable bugger … Truly those who are responsible for sending these physical little wrecks of lads and old men away from NZ should be made to come and try this game themselves.'[32]

One thing that did not seem to change was the ignorance in New Zealand about the mounteds' war. As Alec McNeur wrote, 'NZ almost forgets that she has troops in Egypt.' When Fred Sterling heard that a Member of Parliament in New Zealand had asked the Minister of Defence 'when the tourists (NZ Mtd Brigade) were to be sent to France to do a little fighting', he decided that 'there is no doubt that NZ harbours many curs'.[33]

A brigade sports meeting was held at Solomon's Pools on 14 August. Events included running races, relays, tug-of-war, hop, step and jump, and horseback wrestling. According to Harry Judge, 'not a great deal of interest [was] taken in them. The men have not enough spare energy in this country for strenuous sports.'[34]

The Canterbury Regimental cricket team won the Brigade tournament, though suffering badly from nerves in the final match. Success was achieved also at the Brigade sports and horse show, the Regiment winning eight events out of the sixteen on the card…. The Colonel forgave the regiment a lot of its sins for the success achieved.[35]

Exhausted or unfit men sent to the Ambulance Rest Station in Jerusalem or to the Desert Mounted Corps Rest Camp at Port Said were replaced in the regiments by reinforcements from Ismailia. At Port Said, men could shop for souvenirs in a nearby Armenian refugee camp, swim in the Mediterranean Sea and enjoy fresh-water showers, soft beds, and deckchairs. They drank endless cups of tea, ate freshly baked cakes and read books and newspapers from the camp library. 'It is just a ripping spell,' according to Walter Dawbin. 'Writing letters galore.'[36]

The New Zealanders were back in the Jordan Valley on 14 July when the enemy launched an attack at Musallabe and Abu Tulul (see Map 16, p.256). Turkish regiments failed to support the three heavily armed German infantry battalions that led the assault and the Germans were stopped in their tracks by the light horsemen of the 1st LH Brigade. An Australian counter-attack rounded up 448 prisoners, including 377 Germans. The WMR took part in the final clearance of one of the Australian positions, capturing 61 prisoners, and the rest of the New Zealand brigade cleared the ground for 1000 metres ahead of the front line. Heavy preparatory artillery fire and a bombing raid on the Wellington regiment contributed to the casualty total for the day: two men and two horses were killed, and seven men were wounded. According to Harry Judge, the 'Germhuns [his spelling] took their defeat very badly, and declared that it was the Turks' fault and that they (the Turks) even fired on them, the Germhuns'. German prisoners claimed that they had been told that the Anzacs in the valley were exhausted 'and that they had only to come and take us. We may be exhausted, but not badly enough to be taken by a pack of huns.' Fred Sterling described the German prisoners as 'fit, well-groomed, but very angry'.[37]

Many of the prisoners were nearly mad with thirst. The heat that day, Fred Sterling wrote, was 'simply terrific.... It actually burned our months-old exposed arms, which clearly shows it was quite out of the ordinary. The sweat is dripping from our horses even when standing still.' Packhorses spent the entire day carrying water to the troops in the firing line, where many men 'were sick and others fainted'. The failure of the attack on 14 July, coupled with increasing losses through desertion, made the future of the Turkish army 'look bleak indeed'.[38]

16

Settling old scores

The sight around the bridge was terrible, horses and men being heaped together ...
The scene of defeat and death ... was one such as one could wish to shut eyes and
nostrils to.

ALEC McNEUR

THE TURKISH GOVERNMENT had lost interest in the Middle East by 1918. They saw rich pickings on offer from the collapse of the Russian Empire and sent forces into the Caucasus to seize as much land and property as they could. The Turkish army in Palestine was effectively abandoned, and it began to fade away through desertion and illness. By September, half a million deserters had gone home or were prowling around in armed gangs behind the front lines. Turkish soldiers had never been particularly well equipped or fed but many of them were now barefoot, dressed in rags and on the verge of starvation. That month the Turkish armies south of Haifa and Nazareth could muster only 32,000 infantrymen, 3000 cavalrymen on emaciated horses and 370 artillery pieces. There was a wholesale changing of the guard in the command echelons of the Yildirim Army Group in 1918. Its commander, Falkenhayn, was replaced by Marshal Liman von Sanders; the 8th Army's commander, Kress von Kressenstein, was replaced by Djevad Pasha; and Cemal handed over the 4th Army to his namesake, Cemal Kucjuk Pasha.[1]

General Allenby realised that the Turkish forces in Syria were qualitatively and numerically weak, immobile, poorly deployed and entirely reliant on their limited railway network. He knew that most of Liman's army group was deployed in front-line trenches, with few mobile reserves and no contingency plans if the front line were ruptured. If the EEF could break through this thin defensive crust, its greater mobility should allow it to wreak havoc in the relatively undefended Turkish rear areas. Allenby also understood that, if he could cut the single railway track linking Dera to southern Anatolia, the enemy would be trapped (see Map 2, p.27).

These considerations led him to abandon the conservative advance along the

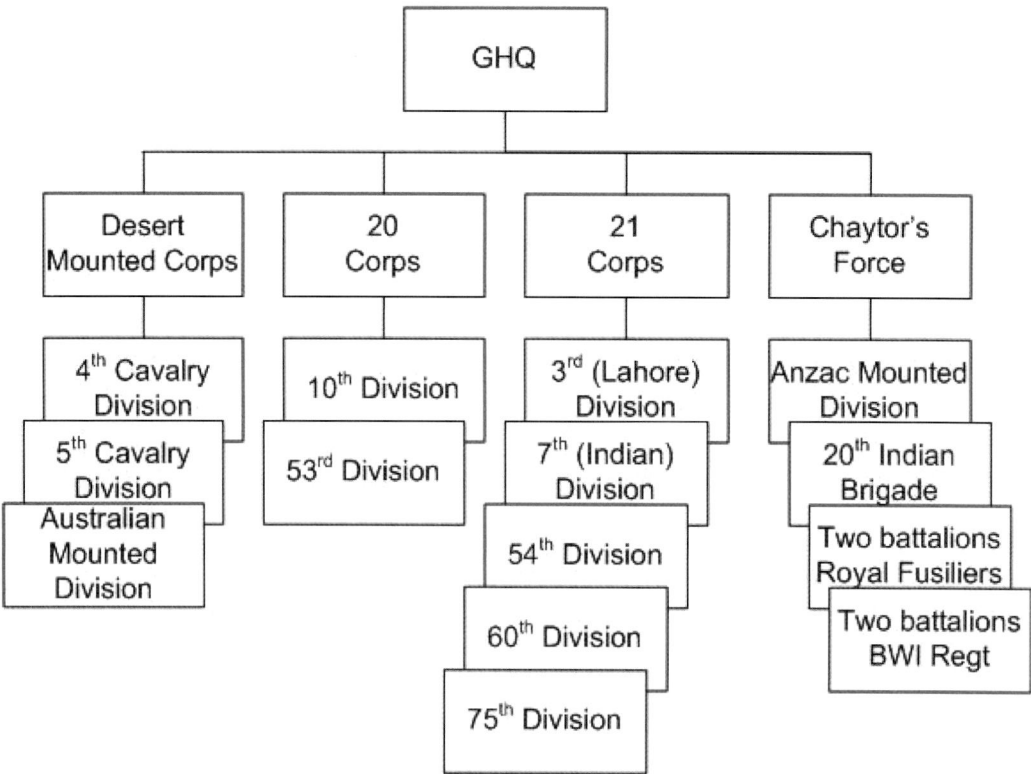

Figure 4: The EEF in September 1918.[2]

Mediterranean coast that he had offered London at the beginning of 1918. Now he aimed at nothing less than the total destruction of the Yildirim Army Group in Syria. Allenby decided to smash open the Turkish defences on the coast, north of Nahr el Auja, using five infantry divisions and massed artillery. Three mounted divisions would ride north towards Haifa, supported by an infantry advance along the spine of the Judean Hills north of Jerusalem (see Map 8, p.150). A smaller force in the Jordan Valley would block the key Jordan River bridge at Damieh, seize Es Salt and cut the Hejaz Railway at Amman. Squadrons of EEF aircraft would bomb headquarters, bridges and other bottlenecks at critical times, and the Hejaz Arabs would attack the Turks along the railway and capture the railway junction at Dera. Allenby hoped to seize the Tulkarm–Nablus line in his first push. In the next phase, mounted troops would seize other key railway junctions, cutting off the only means of escape for the Turkish 4th, 7th and 8th armies.[3]

Chauvel's Desert Mounted Corps was to make the 'great ride', as it was subsequently known, after the infantry of 20 and 21 Corps had broken the Turkish front line on the coast. The DMC now included two new cavalry divisions: the 4th Cavalry Division (formerly the Yeomanry Mounted Division) and the 5th Cavalry Division. The Imperial Camel Corps (ICC) Brigade had been disbanded and the Australian Mounted Division had re-equipped its brigades with swords. By the end of the summer, Chauvel's DMC consisted of three cavalry divisions equipped with swords or lances, and Chaytor's rifle-equipped Anzac Mounted Division. Chaytor's veteran division was to form the core of the force operating from the Jordan Valley.[4]

In order to weight the odds even more in his favour, Allenby carried out a comprehensive deception operation over the summer of 1918. The EEF's two attacks across the Jordan earlier in 1918 had already suggested to the Turks that this was Allenby's preferred area of operations, and he intended to encourage this misperception. He wanted the Turks to strengthen their forces in the east, weakening them on the coast where he really planned to strike. Knowing that the Turks were very wary of the DMC, Allenby created the impression that Chauvel's horsemen were concentrating in the Jordan Valley, when, in fact, the opposite was occurring. Squadrons of horsemen rode quietly away towards Jerusalem at night and some of them returned to the Jordan Valley the next day, stirring up huge clouds of dust as they came. New bivouacs and horse lines containing 15,000 dummy horses made of sandbags, wire, bamboo and straw, sprang up all over the valley floor. Huge piles of horse fodder were dumped near the phony horse lines and teams of mules dragged wooden sleds over the ground to throw up 'regimental-sized' clouds of dust. New infantry camps were also pitched on the river flats and battalions ostentatiously marched down into the valley to occupy them. As soon as it got dark, they were trucked back up into the Judean Hills to repeat the process the next day – over and over again. Engineers built a network of light railways and extended dummy bridges across the lower Jordan River. Larger and more frequent mounted patrols and raids took place, to make the Turks think that the number of horse regiments in the valley was increasing, and also to keep an eye on the enemy's positions.

Any Turkish scout or Arab spy worth his salt would have seen through the deception had he got close enough, so the front line along the Jordan River was sealed by barbed wire and ceaseless patrolling. Enemy aircraft were permitted to fly over the valley when there was something to show them, but never so low that they would see what was actually happening; if they started to get too inquisitive, they were shot down or chased off by new British fighter aircraft.[5]

On 5 September 1918 General Chaytor took over responsibility for the Jordan Valley. Shortly afterwards, the 11,000 troops still in the valley were christened Chaytor's Force. In addition to his own division, Chaytor took command of the 20th Indian Brigade, the untried 1st and 2nd battalions of the British West Indies Regiment and the 38th and 39th (Jewish Volunteer) battalions of the Royal Fusiliers. The combat effectiveness of the new battalions was unknown but Jim McMillan was impressed with the 'splendid physique' of the 'almost-coal-black' West Indians, but less taken with the 'sprinkling' of French Chasseurs d'Afrique and Spahis that he saw. He did not know what role these colonial cavalrymen had but 'to judge by their uniforms, it wasn't a fighting one – their uniforms were much too pretty for that.'[6]

By September 1918 the Anzac Mounted Division was 'a sick and exhausted' force, its 4000 men 'gaunt ghosts'. Men were evacuated from the valley every day, suffering from malaria and a variety of other diseases. Reinforcements arrived from the training camps to replace the evacuated men, but sometimes not quickly enough to fill all the gaps. Despite their weakness, the Anzac horsemen were considered to be 'absolutely dependable'. Their limited endurance would be a problem only if they had to conduct prolonged operations.[7]

Chaytor's 11,000 men faced a similar number of Turks. The enemy had spent the summer busily improving the defences astride the northern part of the Jordan River and in the foothills below Amman and Es Salt. From Shunet Nimrin, the 4th Army's defensive line crossed the river flats to meet the Jordan River south of Umm esh Shert. Across the

Raising dust in the Jordan Valley.

river, their line extended into the western foothills. The 8th Corps garrisoned this line with the 48th Division and the Composite Division. Up on the Amman plateau, the 2nd Corps was responsible for the Hejaz Railway. Seven infantry battalions were down the line at Ma'an and eight others were spread along the track between there and Amman. A rag-tag collection of Circassian irregulars completed the Turkish forces facing Chaytor's Force.[8]

Chaytor's small divisional headquarters was now the HQ of Chaytor's Force. The staff had a great deal of work to do in a very short time to transform the soldiers from New Zealand, Australia, Great Britain, India, the West Indies and elsewhere into an cohesive and effective coalition force. Chaytor split the infantry battalions into mobile and garrison elements. The mobile infantry (rifle companies with extra machine guns) would accompany the horsemen up to Amman while the garrison forces were to stay behind to guard the valley.[9]

Before Z-Day (19 September 1918) Chaytor's Force was required to protect the right flank of the EEF in the Jordan Valley, to mask the departure of the other mounted troops and to prevent the movement of Turkish troops towards the coast by convincing them that another EEF attack towards Amman was imminent. Chaytor's Force was far too weak to evict the Turks from their strong front-line positions so it had to wait for them to move of their own volition. As soon as the EEF's coastal advance began, Chaytor was to watch for any signs of an enemy reaction in front of him. When the Turkish force began to withdraw, as it would have to do to avoid being cut off, Chaytor was to pursue it, snapping up rearguards and baggage convoys as and when opportunity offered.

The first major task for Chaytor's Force was to seize the pontoon bridge at Damieh. This would prevent the Turks transferring troops between the 4th Army and the 7th Army on the Judean Hills around Nablus. Once the bridge was secured, the mobile elements of the force would climb up onto the Es Salt-Amman plateau to deal with the 4th Army. Chaytor's Force was not strong enough to defeat it toe-to-toe but Allenby believed that the 4th Army would try to withdraw as soon as it realised what was happening on the coast. The Turks along the line south of Amman would have to move very quickly if they were to escape before Chaytor blocked the track at Amman. Lastly, Chaytor's Force had to be prepared to advance northwards along the Hejaz Railway towards Dera in the unlikely event that Allenby's coastal advance was held up.[10]

A certain amount of 'housekeeping' took place in the last weeks before Z-Day. Units were brought up to full strength and 30 extra men were added to each regiment as immediate reinforcements. The Turks made little effort to contain the malarial threat on their side of the river, so careful preparations were made to limit the risk of malaria once the advance began.[11]

Attendance at the daily sick parades fell away in early September as rumours of 'a big push' circulated. In Guy Powles' words, 'as soon as a whisper of operations got abroad the [sick] queue dwindled until the last two or three days before the "move" it was with the greatest difficulty that even a seriously sick man could be persuaded to parade sick for fear of missing the "stunt" '.[12] When the doctors starting giving lectures on first aid, the men knew that something was up. 'Little things like this, and the sudden interest shown by troop leaders in everybody having their "field dressings" in possession, could point only to one thing.'[13]

Back in the valley, the Turks occasionally shelled the Anzacs with heavy guns at Shunet Nimrin (known to the men of the EEF as 'Nimrin Nelly') and on the hills north of Jerusalem (known as 'Jericho Jane'). Aside from this desultory shelling, the Turks facing Chaytor's Force were content to remain inside their fortified positions. According to Fred Sterling, the Turks were 'very nervy. They are shelling all hidden ground. Their machine guns rattled almost without interval all night.'[14]

By day, there was nothing obvious to suggest that a great concentration of forces on the coast was under way, although anyone riding through the closely guarded orange and olive groves near Jaffa would have discovered endless lines of tethered horses and camels, and huge truck and wagon parks. Closer to the front line, thousands of infantrymen were concealed in wadis and patches of broken ground. As soon as darkness fell, 'the still countryside awakened miraculously into intense but orderly activity'.

Every metalled highway, every crooked track across the fields, became … crowded with all sorts of transport going west and north. Endless strings of camels, strangely silent and ghostly in the night, followed the native paths; while the prepared roads teemed with motor lorries and horse- and mule-drawn vehicles. So vast and widespread was the movement that all men feared that it must become known to the enemy only a few miles away.[15]

In fact, Allenby's counter-surveillance and deception plans were so successful that the Turks had no inkling about what was occurring opposite them. They believed that the mounted force in the Jordan Valley had actually increased, when in fact it had been halved.[16]

The men in the divisions were kept in the dark about the plan, and their role in it, until the last possible moment. When Harry Judge finally heard that the NZMR Brigade was not to take part in Allenby's coastal offensive, he wrote: 'Well, I think the NZ Brigade has done its bit on this front, and this is the first move of any importance that we have not been in, and … I am quite content to take a back seat. I only wish the whole thing was over.'[17]

B02667, AUSTRALIAN WAR MEMORIAL

Dummy horses. Fifteen thousand of these were built to fool Turkish observers.

The Hejaz Arabs opened what became known as the Battle of Megiddo by attacking the railway between Amman and Dera on 16 September. 20 Corps then attacked along the spine of the Judean Hills. These were precursors to the main event, which began with a massive Western Front-style artillery bombardment in the early hours of Thursday 19 September 1918. The roar of the 400 guns could be plainly heard in the Jordan Valley where, according to Alec McNeur, they sounded like 'great breakers beating on a rocky coast…. The sky was lit by the flashes of the guns.'[18]

The British and Indian infantry quickly broke through the stunned Turkish front-line defenders and the cavalry immediately began their 'great ride' to the north. In the Jordan Valley the horsemen and infantry of Chaytor's Force were placed on three hours' notice to move.

> *We have pulled all our bivvies down and packed them – only the tents are standing. Everything is in readiness. We are to carry nothing except our coats and rations should we move. Six feeds per horse, 48 hours' rations for ourselves.*[19]

The Turkish 4th Army made no move to withdraw for three days and Chaytor's patrols were heavily engaged by artillery and machine guns whenever they ventured too close to the enemy trenches. This activity served a useful purpose by distracting the enemy commander, Cemal Kucjuk, when he should have been withdrawing his army. News of the disaster along the coast was slow in reaching Cemal. When he did hear the reports, he still did not move, despite peremptory orders from Marshal Liman to withdraw immediately towards Dera.[20]

The West Indian infantry 'opened the ball' in the Jordan Valley by capturing Chalk Ridge and Bakr Ridge, overlooking the intended line of advance of the NZMR Brigade (see Map 16, p.256). The Jewish units were less successful down by the Jordan River where, according to Cyril Falls, they 'could not face the Turkish machine guns'. On the night of 20 September, the Aucklands probed northwards from Musallabe along an old Roman road, capturing abandoned Turkish outposts at Fasail and Meteil Edh Dhib. According to Arthur Moore, 'our men came upon dozens of well-prepared entrenched positions from which the Turks had fled before them. In one place, blankets lay on the ground as though their owners had suddenly arisen and fled.' Patrols probing towards the Jordan River crossing at Mafid Jozele were held up by heavy enemy fire and the Aucklands halted to allow the rest of the brigade to join them. It was on this night that Cemal finally obeyed his orders to withdraw the 4th Army. Alert scouts detected 'the unmistakable rattle of transport wheels, and the chase was on'.[21]

The New Zealanders pressed on towards the Damieh bridge. As they rode they came across more abandoned Turkish encampments, in some of which 'numbers of heavy sleepers still lay in the huts etc. They had a very rude awakening.' The pontoon bridge at Damieh was strongly defended and large numbers of Turks were converging on it from Nablus. The Aucklands were ordered to seize the bridge and the Wellingtons were sent to cut the Nablus track at Makhruk.[22]

The WMR surrounded an unsuspecting enemy force at Makhruk, capturing 400 prisoners. They also secured large quantities of stores and equipment from a convoy 'stretching for a mile-and-a-half along the road'. Included in the haul of prisoners was the commander of the Turkish 53rd Division. The general was 'much concerned at being captured, but he was confident he would be released. He knew that large Turkish forces were in the vicinity, and he expected them at any time to overwhelm the little column opposed to them.'[23]

The Aucklands were within sight of the Damieh bridge at dawn on 22 September. A large enemy column was crossing the bridge and an AMR squadron made a dash for the bank to try to stop them. The desperate Turks counter-attacked fiercely, stopping the New Zealanders in their tracks and then driving them back 100 metres. A second Auckland squadron reinforced the first but the Turks threatened to outflank them both. Before long,

Meldrum's brigade was under attack from three directions and Turks were reported to be approaching from the fourth direction. 'Fix Bayonets' Meldrum decided to attack.[24]

A battalion of West Indian infantry and several artillery batteries reinforced the New Zealanders near the bridge. With his flanks and rear secure, Meldrum launched his attack just before 11 a.m. A bold bayonet charge by the West Indians, supported by the Aucklands and two Canterbury squadrons, and covered by artillery and machine gun fire, led to the capture of the vital bridge by noon. According to Harry Judge, the West Indians 'went into the charge laughing, running and jumping just like a lot of school boys just let out of school for the mid term vacation'.[25] Fred Sterling described what followed.

The . . . infantry charged in two waves, straight at the front of the Turkish works, while the CMR men and our 4th [Waikato] Squadron operated upon the flanks. The Turks … held on until the infantry almost gained their trenches, and then broke and made a run for the bridge over the Jordan, their only mode of crossing except for swimming…. As the Turks left their defence works, our men occupied them and caught the thick of the Jackos under a most murderous fire from machine guns and rifles…. I stood with many others up on a hill and watched the slaughter. Men around me laughed aloud … it was not a happy laugh, but a hard grating one. The bullets from our guns simply tore the ground up into dust and whipped

Dead Turks near the Damieh bridge.

PEF/P/Rhodes/122.2, Palestine Exploration Fund, London

Soldiers crossing the pontoon bridge at Damieh after its capture.

> *the waters of the Jordan around the bridge into hundreds of small water spouts. Horses and*
> *men ran like fury but, as a rule, not for long … Few got through that deadly hail.… Our fire*
> *did not cease until not another Turk could be found to fire at.*[26]

Engineers quickly repaired the damaged bridge and the 11th (North Auckland) Squadron of the AMR galloped across in pursuit of the fleeing Turks. Many Turks were captured and the bodies of dozens of less fortunate soldiers and animals littered the bridge and its approaches.[27] For Alec McNeur 'The sight around the bridge was terrible, horses and men being heaped together.… The scene of defeat and death … was one such as one could wish to shut eyes and nostrils to.'[28] Jim McMillan took part in the capture of an enemy post on a hill south of the bridge.

> *The situation became tense as the stalkers neared the place where the quarry was known to be,*
> *but there was no sign of movement or action of any kind. Something had to happen soon and*
> *it did when a German officer rose up with his hands in the air – to the great relief of everyone*
> *concerned, including the German leader of the post, who seemed to be quite happy to hand*
> *over an excellent pair of Zeiss field glasses and his superbly-made Luger pistol – my share of*
> *the booty.*[29]

Anzacs were never shy about stealing the property of prisoners of war. German and Turkish medals, buttons and belt buckles, Luger pistols and Zeiss binoculars were all considered fair game by keen-eyed souvenir hunters. As Ted Andrews recalled, many of the staff officers captured at Makhruk were wearing 'German Iron Crosses, Orders of Medjedie, and large enamel Gallipoli Stars'. By daylight these glittering decorations had changed hands and many Kiwi troopers were wearing foreign orders which had certainly not been granted through the official gazette!'[30] By noon on 22 September all the crossing points on the lower Jordan River had been taken and the New Zealanders had captured 786 prisoners, six artillery pieces, nine machine guns and 200 tonnes of ammunition. Jim McMillan thought that many Turks 'didn't appear to be particularly anxious to escape capture'.[31]

Unwisely, as it turned out, the column bivouacked at the crossing point that night. As soon as the sun set, swarms of mosquitoes rose from the swamps and attacked the men, making sleep impossible. The 4th Army was now in full retreat and as Chaytor's men tried to sleep the Turks abandoned their formidable positions at Shunet Nimrin and elsewhere, and set out for the railway escape route at Amman.

At midday on 23 September the Anzacs and the mobile infantry companies headed up into the hills towards Es Salt. Fred Sterling recalled that this march 'was as hard a trek as we ever did'.

The heat was simply baking, and the march after we left the valley was uphill and continuous. [It] reduced our horses to almost a state of collapse. Our horses got no water after this march and their rations were awfully short.[32]

The men passed the bodies of Turks and horses, lying where they had been killed by RAF bombs and machine gun fire. Harry Judge 'felt sorry for Jacko, as, penned up in those narrow valleys, he had not a ghost of a chance to escape'. The brigade's machine gunners added to the carnage by shooting down an enemy transport and artillery column trying to escape on the Shunet Nimrin-Es Salt road; most of the horses and mules, and many of the drivers, were killed. James Cameron reported seeing 'gruesome sights all over the place'.[33]

The Canterbury regiment led the advance towards Es Salt. A troublesome redoubt on the outskirts of the town was outflanked and captured and by late afternoon Es Salt was in New Zealand hands, along with 538 prisoners. A brass band mounted on ponies and buggies was also captured, providing 'music on tap, whenever we wanted it. This livened things up immensely and all were sorry when we had to hand the band over to a POW camp.' George Berrie remembered that 'Small parties of Turks and Germans were wandering aimlessly about, surrendering to the first comers; the hospitals were full of wounded and sick, and filth and insanitation everywhere reigned supreme.'[34]

Over a period of several days, a number of the brigade's horses died mysteriously. Some men attributed this distressing incident to Germans contaminating abandoned barley with arsenic or strychnine; others blamed a poisonous local weed known as pink laurel, which, according to Fred Sterling, 'acts quickly and surely'.[35]

By the evening of 24 September, the Anzac Mounted Division was assembled near Suweile. Chaytor received orders that night to push on for Amman, to cut the railway north of the town and to make contact with the Arab forces approaching from the south. However, he was slowed by demolitions on the road between Es Salt and Amman, and by Turkish rearguard actions. Chaytor could not afford to let the Hejaz Railway stay open as an escape route for the 4th Army so he decided to take a chance and send 100 men to cut it north of Amman. A section of track eight kilometres north of Amman was completely removed overnight and the raiders were back by 5.30 in the morning, having suffered not one casualty.[36]

The Anzacs knew that Amman was their next objective and orders to attack were eagerly awaited, as Powles explained.

The rest of the NZMR Brigade approaching the Damieh bridge after its capture.

It was felt that of all old scores yet to be wiped off against the Turks, this was the most important. The memory of those four days of bitter fighting in the rain and cold [in March] were yet fresh in everyone's memory.[37]

The situation in Amman was chaotic. Hundreds of desperate Turkish troops converged on the railway station, hoping to board a train to the north. One German officer claimed that he had to use his pistol to assert some degree of control. Wagons containing water earmarked for troops marching on foot towards Dera were attacked and drained by parched Turkish troops in Amman.[38]

The Anzac Mounted Division began its final advance towards Amman at 6 a.m. on 25 September (see Map 17, p.270). The New Zealanders were to attack from the north-west, supported by the 2nd LH Brigade on their right. Artillery support was limited, as most of the guns were held up by a damaged bridge back down the hill. Only a few small mountain guns were immediately available and the British West Indies battalion was not expected to arrive in time to assist. Yet again, Amman was expected to be captured by unsupported mounted regiments. As Wilkie wrote, 'A stubborn defence of the town was anticipated, as its possession was of great importance to enable the Turks to extricate the garrison of Ma'an and the posts along the railway.'[39]

Chaytor's orders emphasised that the horsemen were not to take undue risks. They were to probe the town's defences and attack only if they seemed lightly held; otherwise they were to hold the enemy in place and await the arrival of the Indian and West Indian infantry. As the horsemen moved forward, they continued to pass dead men and animals, and smashed wagons and guns, further evidence of the effectiveness of RAF bombing raids. 'Wounded Turks, who had crawled under the banks of the road, cried piteously for help. It was the hideous side of war.'[40]

The leading New Zealanders came under effective rifle and machine gun fire at 7.45 a.m. The Aucklands were sent up to bolster the line between the Wellingtons and the light horsemen, and the enemy's advanced posts were slowly forced back towards Amman. The attack was a frontal one, with no attempt being made to outflank the defenders lest they abandon the town and escape.[41]

An aircraft dropped a message at 10.40 a.m. stating that the Turks seemed to be evacuating Amman. Chaytor reacted by sending the Canterbury regiment galloping towards the town. They were stopped by the machine guns of an enemy rearguard in a stone tower. Arthur Moore saw the South Islanders 'coming under heavy cross fire from three machine guns'.

The squadron dismounted for action, the horse holders galloping back to the cover of a hill with the led horses. One or two men were shot in the saddle, and their uncontrolled horses set the pace for the rest as they galloped madly back, many with blood streaming from flesh wounds in their sides and legs; their arrival behind the hill with manes and tails flying resembled the finish of some classic race, and was a sight worth seeing.[42]

Once again, the lack of effective artillery support was seriously handicapping the lightly armed horsemen. Under these circumstances, the regiments ought to have waited for infantry support but Chaytor sensed that the enemy resistance was weakening. He decided on an immediate divisional dismounted attack. The Canterburys attacked the stone tower on foot and captured it at 3.15 p.m., taking 119 prisoners (mostly Germans) and six machine guns. The Germans were described by Jim McMillan as 'very youthful-looking soldiers, whose equipment appeared to be brand-new'. The light horsemen pushed forward towards the railway. Troublesome machine gun nests were defeated by rapid mounted gallops to the flanks, from where the enemy gunners were killed by bursts of Hotchkiss gun fire. The CMR men galloped on into Amman, supported by the rest of the brigade, racing the light horsemen for the honour of capturing it. When Hill 3039 and the high ground beyond the town around the railway station were captured by the Australians, the defence collapsed.[43]

Amman was finally in the hands of the Anzacs at 3 p.m. The New Zealanders had taken over half of the 2563 prisoners captured in the town, as well as 300 emaciated horses, 25 machine guns and six artillery pieces. In two 'filthy and verminous' Turkish hospitals, 480 sick and wounded men were found jammed together on the floor.[44]

When General Chaytor entered Amman on the heels of his combat regiments, the light horsemen 'surrounded and cheered "the little red man" again and again…. Chaytor said it was "the proudest moment of his life."' The village was full of food and forage, and piles of abandoned guns, ammunition and transport wagons lay scattered around everywhere. According to Harry Judge, 'Gen. Meldrum went up to the German commander and shook hands with him, and congratulated him on the good fight he had put up'. Bottles of wine, brandy and champagne were 'liberated' from German officers, and Fred Sterling enjoyed 'a large picnic on captured sheep and vegetables'.[45]

The New Zealanders remained at Amman for several days, while stray Turks were rounded up, Bedouin looters were fended off and tonnes of war matériel were collected. James Cameron spent his time 'taking things easy – cooking meat and potatoes and eating vast quantities'. When some New Zealanders went up onto Hill 3039 to fix up the graves

Turkish and German belt buckles, medals, and Mauser ammunition. Anzacs routinely took items such as these from captured prisoners.

of the men who had been killed there six months earlier, they found that many had been opened and robbed.[46]

Once the last Turkish evacuation train had departed from Amman the night before – it was probably the one seen by the AMR demolition party – there was no escape for the remaining Turks, but they fought on through most of the following day to give the 2nd Corps a little more time to join them in the relative safety of Amman. Chaytor was ordered to capture this last enemy force.[47]

On 27 September Australian scouts learned that a large force of Turks was near Ziza Station, 25 kilometres south of Amman (see Map 8, p.150). An aircraft flew over the Turks and dropped a message. The note told the enemy commander that all water sources to the north were in Allied hands and urged him to surrender his force; if he did not comply, his force would be bombed the next day.

Two squadrons of the 5th ALH Regiment, which rode south to destroy the railway and to confront the Turks, found the leading elements of the 2nd Corps at Ziza Station on 29 September. The sight that greeted them was incredible. 5000 Turks, mostly on foot and accompanied by three crowded hospital trains, were surrounded by twice as many Arabs mounted on camels and horses. 'Their patient, watchful attitude suggested the spectacle of vultures attending on a dying man.'[48] The Arabs would not dare to attack the main body of the Turkish force but any stragglers were quickly caught and slaughtered. Over 1000 Turks had already died or been killed on the way from Ma'an to Ziza.[49]

Soon after the arrival of the light horsemen, a trolley came up the railway line carrying

317

a Turkish envoy. He told the commander of the light horse regiment, Lieutenant Colonel Donald Cameron, that the Turkish commander, Colonel Ali Bey Wakaby, wanted to surrender his force. He asked that the actual surrender be delayed until a stronger Allied force arrived to protect the Turks against the Arab mob that was baying for their blood. Cameron later remarked that the Turkish force, despite its overwhelming superiority in numbers, 'was terrified of the Bedouin. Several instances occurred during the day of Bedouin capturing odd Turks. Though armed, the Turks seemed unable to defend themselves, and simply screamed like dying pigs.' Cameron had little choice but to agree to the unusual request. Unsure if the bombing raid had been cancelled, he displayed an aircraft recognition panel (to tell pilots that the location was in friendly hands) in the centre of the Turkish position. When the Turkish commander was warned that the bombing raid might still take place, he said that if it happened it would be the will of God.[50]

As soon as the telephone line linking Ziza to Amman was repaired, Chaytor was informed of the situation. He cancelled the bombing raid and ordered the rest of the 2nd LH Brigade to make a forced march to Ziza to reinforce Cameron's lonely regiment. The New Zealand brigade was told to ride south in support at first light the following day.[51]

While Cameron waited uncomfortably, the Arabs demanded that they be allowed to either attack the Turks if they had not surrendered or to disarm them if they had. Cameron refused and warned them that if they attacked the Turks, his light horsemen would fight them. The 7th ALH Regiment arrived late in the afternoon, covering the last few kilometres at the gallop. Chaytor went ahead of them and told the Turkish commander to be prepared to defend himself all night, as reinforcements were unlikely to arrive before last light. Colonel Ali asked for permission to attack the Arabs, but Chaytor forbade it. He then departed for Amman, taking the Turkish commander with him.[52]

The commander of the 2nd LH Brigade, Brigadier General Granville Ryrie, who remained on the scene to direct operations, decided that he would ally his brigade with the Turks for the night. Just before dark he galloped two regiments through the encircling Arabs and into the Turkish position. Two Arab sheikhs went with them as hostages; they were told that they would be shot if their tribesmen attacked. Ryrie also warned the Arabs that any attempt to attack the Turks would be blocked with force. He even allowed the Turks to keep their weapons that night, to maximise the firepower available to hold off the Arabs. To Charles Nicol, 'it was a rapid change from war to comedy'.[53] As Gullett explained,

The Turks and Australians proceeded, after years of bitter fighting, to bivouac together. They gathered about the same fires, exchanging their food, making chapattis together.... The Turks, demoralised by the swift and complete overthrow of their fortunes, and disconcerted by the presence of the Australians, still feared massacre by the Arabs; all night they stood to arms, and engaged in bursts of machine gun and rifle fire. The light horsemen, revelling in the strange situation, could be heard cheering on their activities.[54]

When the New Zealand brigade arrived at Ziza at 5.30 a.m. on 30 September, it pushed the Arabs back to a distance of 2000 metres and set up Hotchkiss gun posts to keep them there. According to Harry Judge, 'the Arabs … went "crook", as they looked upon the Jackos as their particular prey, and wanted to loot them and incidentally cut their throats!' Fred Sterling described the condition of the sick Turks at Ziza as 'simply awful…. There are dead and dying all over the place' and Percy Doherty recorded that the Turks were 'dying like rabbits for want of attention'. The station yard was in a 'terrible mess, the stench something awful'. The only water, Moore recalled, 'was that from a stagnant reservoir with a dead man and mule lying in it; the boilers of the three engines at the station had already been drunk dry by the sick.'[55]

General Ryrie now felt in a strong enough position to disarm most of the Turks at Ziza. The two strongest battalions of Anatolian Turks were permitted to keep their weapons and ammunition in case the furious Arabs attacked the column during its march to Amman. As 4068 able-bodied prisoners marched off under Australian escort, the New Zealanders remained behind to guard the 534 sick and wounded prisoners and the captured matériel, until the railway to Amman was repaired. The angry and frustrated Bedouin gave up their

This German LP08/14 pistol was taken from a prisoner at Damieh by Sgt Alfred Kemp, WMR.

Turkish artillery captured at Amman.

bloodthirsty designs and disappeared towards Damascus, looking for easier prey.[56]

Chaytor had his engineers repair a damaged railway engine in Amman station so that it could pull water to the parched Turks at Ziza. Bent steel plates were straightened by heating them, then dropping a spare 75-tonne railway engine on them. The damaged steam pipes leaked so badly that, on the first attempt to move the train up a hill, the train stalled and began to run back down into Amman. The brakes did not work so the engineers had to stop it by jamming pieces of firewood into the spokes of the wheels. After more repairs to the engine and the track, the train eventually made it to Ziza late on 30 September. By then 'the prisoners were so famished for water that, when they saw the overflow running away from the injector on the locomotive, they rushed over and cupped their hands and conveyed this practically-boiling water into their mouths'.[57]

The sick and wounded prisoners were loaded onto the first train and sent north to Amman. Their weapons and equipment were gathered up and put on later trains. A total of 150 tonnes of captured stores and 240 tonnes of ammunition were sent into Amman. On 1 October the New Zealand brigade rode back to Hill 3039, leaving the CMR and a section of machine gunners at Ziza to guard the station and some stores. A squadron from the AMR was sent to Madeba (see Map 8, p.150), where a number of prisoners and a large store of grain were captured.[58]

In under two weeks, the 11,000 men of Chaytor's Force captured 10,332 prisoners, 57 artillery pieces, 132 machine guns, 11 train engines, 106 railway trucks, 142 vehicles and a vast amount of ammunition. Of this total, the New Zealanders collected 30 per cent of the prisoners, weapons and vehicles.[59]

The number of casualties in Chaytor's Force was very small. Between 19 September and 3 November, 29 men were killed and 103 were wounded. Most of these casualties were suffered by the Anzac Mounted Division, which lost 16 men killed and 56 wounded in September, and another four killed and seven wounded in October. New Zealand suffered four deaths on 22 September, one each on 23 and 24 September, and five on 25 September. Far more men fell sick than were injured or killed. Between 19 September and 3 November, 6920 men in Chaytor's Force were listed as sick. In the Anzac division, 1088 men were sick in September; the number trebled in the following month.[60]

Nearly all of these men suffered from malaria. On their first night in Turkish territory, swarms of mosquitoes had enveloped the men of Chaytor's Force. Symptoms were delayed for about 10 days as the parasites multiplied in their bodies. The impact of the disease was felt by the end of September, after the conclusion of Chaytor's operations. The epidemic peaked around 9 October, then subsided. Most of the men of the NZMR and 1st LH brigades were infected at the Damieh bridge. These brigades evacuated 360 and 315 sick men respectively before 4 October. The number of New Zealanders who succumbed to the disease is believed to be between 50 and 60. At the same time, the global influenza epidemic arrived in the Jordan Valley, and this also killed a number of men.[61]

It was a tragic sight to see men who had endured so much suddenly stricken, swaying in the saddles and pitching headlong, or lying down for a rest and being unable to rise again. As these [men] were evacuated, their horses were led by their comrades, and by the time [the] Jericho bivouac was reached, there was a long line of horses, but few riders to tend them.[62]

In some regiments, riderless horses were let loose and herded down into the valley like a mob of cattle. According to Fred Sterling, 'our ambulance clearing station now contains most of our brigade, I think. I paid it a visit this afternoon and 200 men were lying sick there. God and some of them are ill. Thin and gaunt and fever-stricken.' Some Main Body men who had survived Gallipoli and the entire Middle East campaign were felled by mosquitoes or influenza when the war was effectively over.[63]

Chaytor's Force achieved spectacular results during its brief existence. The rag-tag collection of disparate units became an effective fighting force that carried out its intended role perfectly, and at very little cost. The destruction of the Turkish 2nd Corps as a fighting force was testament to the effectiveness of the small force.

> *Cool and skilful direction, [and] careful staff work had advanced it step by step on the enemy's heels; every move had inflicted the maximum of damage on the Turks with the minimum of risk to itself. The resistance of the enemy had nowhere been serious, except at ... Damieh and for an hour or two at Amman, but the whole operation would not have had a tithe of the results which it achieved without clever handling, good timing, and the determination of the troops.*[64]

With the Desert Mounted Corps well on its way to Damascus, there was no need for Chaytor's Force to advance northwards along the Hejaz Railway. He received orders to rest, reinforce and re-equip his division, in anticipation of taking it to join the rest of the DMC at Damascus. As soon as the thousands of wretched prisoners were evacuated and the tonnes of captured matériel were sent back to the coast or destroyed, preparations were made for the men to head back to the Jordan Valley. Half of the 10,000 prisoners were too weak to march, so convoys of ambulances and trucks carried them away. Locally conscripted Arabs and Circassian prisoners were released locally, as long as they promised to behave themselves.[65]

B00088. AUSTRALIAN WAR MEMORIAL

Chaytor and the exhausted enemy commander, Colonel Ali Bey Wakaby, at Ziza.

On Thursday 3 October, those horsemen fit enough to ride headed back down into the Jordan Valley for the last time. After spending the night at Ain es Sir, where the WMR rounded up a number of Circassians suspected of involvement in the May attack and escorted them to Jerusalem for trial, the New Zealand brigade reached the Jordan Valley at Shunet Nimrin on the following day. 'The trek was a painfully hard one. Most of us are about done.' They were joined at Shunet Nimrin by the Canterbury regiment and the wheeled transport, and camp was made for the night among more 'swarms of ravenous mosquitoes'.[66]

The New Zealanders crossed the Jordan River on 5 October and rode on to Jericho. Three days later the men of the New Zealand Mounted Rifles Brigade rode out of the Jordan Valley for the last time. 'There were no regrets.' As Fred Sterling noted, 'Our horses look more than jaded. Most of their time between watering they spend lying down, glad of the spell.'[67]

After five days' rest near Jerusalem, the NZMR Brigade arrived at Richon le Zion on 14 October 1918. Equipment and weapons were overhauled, and some training continued, but rest and recuperation were the priorities for the rest of the month. A large draft of reinforcements was welcomed as the workload on the decimated regiments was enormous.[68]

Harry Judge believed 'that the medical authorities had put all [the NZMR] Brigade out of action for three months, wonder if that is really true. If it is, it is a hundred-to-one we shall never see any more fighting, as the war will be over by then it seems.' The report was untrue but it did not matter. When news came in that Damascus had been captured by the DMC, Judge realised that 'we are quite out of the running now as we could never catch up now if we did go across to the coast and the health of the fellows would not permit it'.[69] Burton Hull agreed: 'The war outlook is much better now than it has been, the Allies are getting some of their own back, lots of chaps can see Rangitoto in the distance now'.[70]

While Chaytor's Force was fighting the remnants of the Turkish 4th Army, Chauvel's DMC rode northwards at a great pace. There were few Turkish reserves or depth defensive positions to stop them. On 21 September the railway junctions at Affule, Beisan and Jenin were captured, and part of the 7th Army was bombed and machine-gunned from the air as it tried to make its way down the track to the Jordan River crossing at Damieh. Haifa fell on 23 September (see Map 8, p.150).

By the next day, the Turkish 7th and 8th armies had effectively ceased to exist. The Hejaz Arabs captured the vital railway junction at Dera on 28 September. Seizing the opportunity that his early success presented, Allenby sent Chauvel's horsemen riding

J02247, AUSTRALIAN WAR MEMORIAL

Prisoners being escorted across the Jordan River.

towards Damascus, which fell to the Australians on 30 September. Still not satisfied, Allenby dispatched one of his mounted divisions towards Aleppo, 300 kilometres from Damascus. Aleppo was occupied by the Arabs on 25 October and by the 5th Cavalry Division a day later (see Map 2, p.27).

The 2nd New Zealand Machine Gun Squadron rode with the Australian Mounted Division as part of this great mounted force. After playing a part in the capture of Nablus on 21 September, the machine gunners rode to Jenin. On 27 September they began a long ride through Nazareth, Tiberias and Kuneitra to Damascus. Three days later the New Zealanders reached the cliffs overlooking the Barada Gorge, through which the Damascus–Beirut road ran. The narrow road was packed with fleeing Turkish soldiers, animals and trucks. New Zealand machine guns killed and wounded hundreds of hapless men and animals before 4000 survivors surrendered. The machine gunners finished their war at Homs on 1 November 1918.

Seventy-five thousand prisoners were captured during Allenby's last great offensive, including 3700 Germans and Austrians. The total distance covered in 38 days was more than 500 kilometres. Between 19 September and 31 October 1918 the EEF lost only 853 men killed, 4428 wounded and 385 missing.[71]

By the last week of October, the Turks in Palestine and Syria were soundly beaten and

EEF horsemen were approaching the borders of the Anatolian heartland. However, it was not this threat that forced the government in Istanbul to seek an end to the war. Turkey's ally Bulgaria had signed an armistice on 30 September and this had cut the railway link to Germany and opened an invasion route into western Turkey for the large Allied army at Salonika. With no Turkish reserves to speak of, the road to Istanbul lay open. Germany could offer no more help and the treasury in Istanbul was empty. Further resistance was impossible so the Turks decided to seek their own armistice. This was signed on Wednesday, 30 October 1918 and it came into force on the 31st – 12 months, to the day, since the capture of Beersheba by the Anzacs.

When news of the Turkish armistice reached the New Zealanders at Richon le Zion, it was, in Percy Doherty's words, received 'more or less quietly, being expected … for some time'.[72] There were, Harry Judge wrote, 'a few spasmodic cheers and that was all... fellows are too sick of the whole business and in too low [a] state of vitality to go into [excitement] over anything.' Men began to think about going home, but they knew that Germany and Austria-Hungary were still fighting. 'Everyone talking Home and wondering what will be done with us now … the way Austria is shaping [up], I don't think we will be wanted anywhere.'[73]

Within two weeks, Austria-Hungary and Germany had also signed armistices, and

Anzac horsemen leaving Amman for the last time. Hill 3039 is behind the village.

the war was over. News of the German capitulation on 11 November 1918 was received joyfully in Palestine. 'What a blow-out there was that night,' wrote Ted Andrews, 'Very flares going up, weapons of all sorts being fired, singing and cheering. It's a wonder the thousands of horses didn't stampede!' Charles Nicol: 'Coloured lights lit the town, and singing and cheering filled the air. The veterans of the campaigns frolicked like youngsters.'[74] A congratulatory telegram quickly arrived from New Zealand's Minister of Defence.

> *In their rejoicings at the signing of the armistice which brings to an end the agony of the last four years, the people of New Zealand give thanks to Almighty God for the men living and dead of the deathless New Zealand Division [this mistake must have annoyed the mounted riflemen]. From the landing at Anzac on 25th April 1915, to the surrender of Turkey, you have fought and conquered in battles whose names shall be familiar in our mouths as household words. You have won for New Zealand a fame imperishable. God bless you and bring you safely home to us.*[75]

The last comment must have resonated with the men, who wanted to get home as quickly as possible. George Ranstead wrote,

> *It is hard to say what will happen to us now. We may be about the front for months salvaging military stuff and patrolling the country. It is scarcely likely that we shall get away for some time, owing to the scarcity of shipping.... I won't be home for this Christmas, but next is a good bet.*[76]

He was right.

17

The horses stay behind

The day has come. I lose my horse tonight … [He is] the only thing in this land [that]
I am truly sorry to leave. My very best friend in this land he has been. He left me fat
and in excellent spirits. May he strike a soft job or die soon, for I love him very much.

FRED STERLING

ON WEDNESDAY 13 November 1918 the men of the Canterbury regiment handed in most of their horses and left Palestine for the last time. They were going back to Gallipoli, but not to fight: their role was to monitor Turkish compliance with the terms of the Armistice. After a fortnight at Kantara, where much effort went into improving the appearance of the battle-worn Anzacs, 489 New Zealanders and a similar number of Australians embarked on an old tramp steamer and sailed up the Suez Canal, bound for Turkey (see Map 2, p.27). The ship was unsuitable, the men were overcrowded and the weather on the voyage was dreadful. The sickness rate peaked at 80 men per day during an outbreak of influenza, overwhelming the five-berth ship's hospital. After calling in at Lemnos, the ship arrived at Chanak on 2 December. The men were forced to remain at anchor for four days because the British garrison had not been told they were coming and nothing was ready for them.[1]

After they landed, the Anzacs conducted a reconnaissance of the southern part of the Gallipoli Peninsula. For Percy Doherty,

the most interesting sight … was when we actually reached the Narrows, and the forts on both
sides came into view. 'Gee Whiz! Look at the guns!' was the mildest expression I heard … it
was one of the greatest sights we have seen. Guns were sticking out everywhere, and whoppers
they were too.

When the men stood on the hills above Anzac Cove, they were amazed.

This hill [Baby 700] was one of their strongest positions, and it was almost heartbreaking …

B001158. AUSTRALIAN WAR MEMORIAL

A CMR man sprucing himself up before going back to Gallipoli.

to look from this position down on to the one we held … it is marvellous to think that we hung
on so long, by the skin of our teeth as it were.[2]

A great deal of time was spent in identifying and marking the graves of New Zealanders, and in burying the bones of those who remained above ground. A few graves had been rifled or dug up by dogs and most of their wooden markers had been used by the Turks for firewood. The unburied remains of New Zealanders lying scattered on the slopes of Chunuk Bair and Hill 60, which were recognisable by buttons and scraps of rotted clothing, were collected and interred.[3]

The wintry weather and the influenza epidemic took their toll of the Canterburys. Nearly a quarter of them were hospitalised and 11 died. Coming after the end of the war, these are perhaps the most poignant deaths of all. A planned visit to Istanbul was cancelled and the regiment began its return trip to Egypt on 19 January 1919. Harry Judge thought 'the whole trip has been most ill-timed and badly-arranged. Our own Padre described it as "simply disgraceful".' George Ranstead noted that some doctors said it was 'madness' sending men in less than perfect health to Gallipoli in mid-winter. When he arrived back at Rafah on 23 January, Judge was surprised to see a long line of horses waiting for the men. '[We] thought we had got rid of [the] horses for good.'[4]

The rest of the Anzac Mounted Division remained encamped near Richon le Zion until mid-December 1918 (see Map 11, p.176). On Thursday 14 November a service was held at Ayun Kara to commemorate the New Zealanders who had died there 12 months before. The Jewish residents of Richon le Zion had built a memorial at the little New Zealand cemetery and promised to maintain it in the future. According to George Ranstead, 'the villagers turned out in full force. The graves had been done up beforehand by the schoolchildren here. They take a great interest in our crowd – look on us as their deliverers.'[5] In reply to a speech by the leader of the colony, Brigadier General Meldrum said that 'soldiers are men of few words. If it were left to us to write the epitaph of those who lie buried here, we would say, "They did their bit, and that is all about it." And that is how they would wish it to be written.'[6]

The rest of November and the first two weeks of December were taken up with regimental training, interspersed with sports and shooting competitions.[7] Towards the end of November, several men who had been Turkish prisoners of war returned to the brigade. Captain Frank Allsop, who had been incarcerated in Turkey since his capture at Romani in August 1916, was 'looking very thin and melancholy'.

The treatment they got was very bad. Indians were put over the white prisoners as NCOs. They gave our chaps a very bad spin in order to curry favour with the Turks. Allsop did seven months solitary confinement for attempting to escape. Of the eight men taken with him, five or six have died so you can imagine what sort of a time they had.[8]

On the night of 9–10 December, 21-year-old Trooper Leslie Lowry was sleeping alone in his tent in the Anzac Mounted Division camp near Richon le Zion.[9] Not long after midnight, his kitbag, which he was using as a pillow, was snatched out of his tent. Lowry chased the thief into the sandhills but, as he caught up with him, the man produced a pistol and fired a bullet into Lowry's chest, before disappearing into the darkness. Lowry died about 1.30 a.m. on Tuesday 10 December, having said nothing.[10]

Bare footprints were reportedly found leading to the scene of the struggle, and away from it in two directions: to the blood-stained spot where Lowry was found, and in the opposite direction, as far as a gap in a fence, about 80 metres from the Arab village of Surafend. A kitbag and a small bag containing letters addressed to Lowry, and an Arab skull cap, were found at or near the site of the struggle.

No one seems to have witnessed the chase, seen the fatal shot fired or observed Lowry's assailant running into Surafend or anywhere else. However, the Surafend villagers were already under suspicion for allegedly digging up the graves of New Zealanders killed at Ayun Kara, and for perpetrating 'most of the thieving that was prevalent in all the adjoining camps'. This, plus the trail of footprints reportedly leading towards Surafend, was good enough for the New Zealanders. They threw a cordon around the village to prevent anyone from entering or leaving and waited for 'the heads' to launch an investigation. Major Magnus Johnson, who arrived at first light to conduct a Court of Inquiry into Lowry's death, 'took plaster casts of a big bare foot near where the trooper was killed, and traced it down to the village of Surafend. I retained the bullet that killed the trooper and found from what sort of weapon it was fired, and handed all the information obtained in to the Brigade Headquarters, but no action was taken.' With no eye-witnesses, Johnson could only conclude that Lowry died as a result of a gunshot wound inflicted by 'an unknown person who had been stealing Government Property from No.1 New Zealand Machine Gun Squadron lines'.[11] Under normal circumstances, that would have been an end to it.

As the day passed, however, the men manning the cordon around Surafend became increasingly angry and frustrated. The village headman was ordered to hand over the murderer but failed to do so. Chaytor sent an officer to General Headquarters (GHQ) to register his concern, and another to take command of the cordon. GHQ's only recorded response was to order the immediate removal of the cordon around Surafend. Although

ALAN HALL COLLECTION

The Arab village of Surafend.

Chaytor personally intervened in an attempt to reverse this decision, he had no success. As soon as the cordon was withdrawn in the afternoon, 15 to 20 Arab men left Surafend.[12]

So far, the soldiers had behaved quite correctly but that now changed. Witnesses from a neighbouring light horse regiment stated that New Zealanders arrived in the Australian tent lines as early as 10 a.m. on 10 December, drumming up support for a punitive raid on the village.

We feel very badly about it, these people have given us a very bad spin, and we intend to make an example of them this time…. Don't bring any ammunition, or we will be shooting each other in the dark, but bring a pick handle or some such weapon, or a bayonet will be as good as anything, as we may be attacked ourselves.[13]

According to one source, there was a secret meeting in the sand dunes at 7 p.m. at which the plan was finalised and orders were issued. The old men, women and children in the village were to be taken out of harm's way, then the village was to be searched. Any men found were to receive a beating.[14]

An unknown number of men, armed with pick handles, bayonets and iron strips wrapped in puttees or sacks, quietly encircled Surafend about 8 p.m. Most accounts state that the village sheikh was given one last chance to hand over the murderer. Once again the killer failed to appear so the next part of the plan was carried out. Within 30 minutes, Surafend and a nearby Bedouin camp were on fire, and around 40 male inhabitants were dead or dying. Several sources attribute this high death toll to the resistance put up by the villagers but, with no evidence of any injuries to the attackers, it must have been a very one-sided affair. By around 9 p.m. the raiders were back in their tents and the old men, women, and children were moving back into their wrecked homes to mourn their dead.[15]

When the fires were reported to Brigade HQ, the Auckland and Wellington regiments were each ordered to send a squadron, and the machine gun squadron to send a troop, 'to quell any disturbance, and give any assistance necessary'. When Second Lieutenant Eric Lord arrived at the village soon after 8.45 p.m., he saw 'Bedouin women and children sitting together near the hedges. They were quiet, and no one was interfering with them. There were no troops near the village.' Having decided that 'it was impossible to do anything further', Lord returned to camp with his men. The Wellington squadron placed guards at each corner of the village and patrolled its perimeter. Any soldiers found in the vicinity were to be arrested. No attempt was made to put out the fire and the men withdrew at 10 p.m.[16]

Although most sources state that General Headquarters (GHQ) took immediate action to find out who had participated in the attack, a member of Allenby's staff states that 'The Chief' was away at the time of the attack and that GHQ took no action until his return a few days later. Regardless of who issued the order, the Anzacs were immediately confined to their tent lines, Arabs were banned from the camps and a guard was placed on the ruins of Surafend.[17]

Several further courts of inquiry were convened but none could identify anyone involved in the attack. The men closed ranks and denied any knowledge of the incident and no participants were identified by villagers or by anyone else. With no offenders to prosecute, Chaytor turned his anger on the commanders and officers of the Auckland and Wellington regiments. They had failed in their duty, he decided, by not knowing about the plans for the attack and by failing to stop it once it had begun. This, he wrote, 'can only be due to a very grave lack of knowledge of their duties and responsibilities, or to a deliberate neglect of their duty'. Surprisingly, the only punishment that he imposed was to stop leave for all officers. No one was ever tried or punished for what happened at Surafend: the perpetrators literally got away with murder. The village was rebuilt by the British Army, which was later reimbursed by the governments of New Zealand (£858) and Australia (£515).[18]

Evidence about the leadership, composition and size of the raiding party is inconclusive. Most men interviewed for the inquiries did their best to apportion blame elsewhere. There can be little doubt that Anzacs planned and led the raid but it is unclear whether Australians or New Zealanders were in charge. New Zealanders were certainly not the only nationality involved in the attack, although they were probably in the majority. There is strong evidence that British horse artillerymen and headquarters troops, and Australian light horsemen, were also present, but in what numbers is unknown. Estimates of the size of the raiding party vary from 50 to 200 men. The latter number is probably more accurate: a large force would have been necessary to isolate the village and to carry out the killings and the destruction so quickly, and without any casualties being suffered by the attackers.

General Allenby was furious when he heard what had happened. He ordered the men of the Anzac Mounted Division to be paraded on 16 December so that he could give them a piece of his mind. He galloped up on his black horse Hindenburg, ignored Chaytor's salute and addressed the men. Exactly what he said is not certain, but it was something like: 'There was a time when I was proud of you men of the Anzac Mounted Division. Today I think you are nothing but a lot of cowards and murderers.' The reaction to Allenby's words is also the subject of controversy: several accounts, reportedly from men present at the parade, state that Allenby was 'counted out' but the evidence against it is more convincing. Magnus Johnson wrote that 'no-one made a sound. I was in the middle of the square.' George Ranstead said that the men took the telling off 'without a word'. Others described a sound emanating from the ranks like the hum from 'millions of hives of angry bees'.[19]

An aggrieved Harry Porter called Allenby a 'bastard and son of a bastard'. He claimed that the New Zealanders were placed under 'house arrest' and that guards were ordered to shoot escapers on sight. Whether Porter's claims are true or not, Allenby was wrong to humiliate the entire Anzac division when only a few of its members were guilty of the Surafend attack. Two

The grave of Leslie Lowry.

days later the Anzac Mounted Division was on its way south to a new camp site at Rafah. Many men believed that they were moved as a punishment for Surafend, and to get them away from the wine cellars of nearby Richon le Zion. As the move is first mentioned in the division's War Diary the day before the parade, that conclusion may be correct.[20]

This crime cannot be explained away as an over-reaction by stressed combatants caught up in the 'heat of battle'. The raid was carefully planned and ruthlessly carried out by men who knew that the war was over, and that the victims presented no threat to them. I do not believe that the raiders were looking for evidence or for Lowry's killer, or that the killings occurred only because the villagers fought back. Nor can I accept that a simple beating was intended. Reluctantly, I must conclude that the purpose of the raid was to kill as many Arab men as possible.

Ever since the beginning of the Arab Revolt in mid-1916, the men of the EEF had been ordered to treat the Bedouin with consideration. Bedouin claims of damage to local crops or property by men of the EEF were seemingly always upheld by the authorities and the men had to pay for the damage out of their own pockets. On several battlefields, dead men were dug up and stripped of their clothes, and the failure of the promised Arab support to appear during the second Amman stunt in April 1918 led to many Anzac casualties. The divisional camp near Surafend was the target of ceaseless pilfering so that the men were forced to place armed guards over everything of value. By December 1918 many men considered the Arabs to be cowardly murderers and thieves who could get away with anything. Ben Gainfort made the point that the soldiers who took part in the raid had been trained and expected to kill for the past four years. Edwin McKay believed that 'every army has its toughs. We had our quota, a very very small percentage, but it was there.' Nothing can excuse what happened at Surafend, but perhaps these comments make it somewhat easier to understand. Until reliable eye-witness evidence from a participant surfaces, the full story cannot be known. Unless that happens, it will remain an open and controversial subject.[21]

The NZMR Brigade arrived at Rafah on 22 December. After taking a few days to erect tents and set up the camps, training recommenced. The New Zealanders were addressed by Chauvel a few days after their arrival at Rafah. After expressing his anger and disappointment over Surafend, he told the men that they could expect to be on their way home quite soon. As Powles noted, 'With rest, sports, and good food, the health of the Brigade soon showed much improvement. Malaria had almost gone, and the depleted ranks had been filled up again from reinforcements.'[22]

On New Year's Day the mounted riflemen played the light horsemen at rugby, New Zealand 'winning a great game by eight points to nil... There were thousands of spectators, six to ten deep around the ground.'[23]

While the Anzac brigades were still in Palestine, Chaytor had initiated an Educational Scheme to 'broaden the view, to quicken the intelligence, and to create a desire for study; and to help men in their work after the war by practical instruction in the trade or profession they will follow'. Economics, civics and hygiene lectures were compulsory for all ranks; they could also attend additional classes in motor mechanics, wool classing, stock breeding, veterinary science, bookkeeping, English, arithmetic, electricity, commercial correspondence, shorthand, agriculture, farriery, building and fruit farming. Many of the topics were of little real interest to the men but the scheme helped to keep boredom at bay, and it replaced some drill in the mornings.[24] Even so, some men, like George Ranstead, had little time for the initiative.

If they can teach a man type writing, electrical engineering, architecture or any of the other things they skite [brag] about while he is looking after horses and doing two or more hours drill a day, they are pretty clever. And studying is out of the question. It is hard enough to write a letter.[25]

The scheme, which was compulsory and free of charge, began in earnest after the brigade arrived in Rafah. In addition to attending educational classes each day, the men were also expected to conduct half an hour of physical training and games, and at least two hours of dismounted and mounted training. The men resented the latter requirement, but Chaytor insisted.

Under present conditions, this brigade may be required to move at short notice to any point in this theatre. In addition, should mounted troops be required in any of the neighbouring theatres of operations, this brigade would in all probability be despatched. In view of the above, it is essential that the military efficiency of the Brigade be maintained. This can only be maintained by training.[26]

Despite the urging of senior officers, standards inevitably slipped. Chaytor became

F-106321-1/2, ALEXANDER TURNBULL LIBRARY

New Zealand beating Australia at rugby, 1 January 1919.

CHARLES LONSDALE ALBUM, COURTESY OF MARK RHODES

Aged or unfit horses destroyed at Rafah.

concerned by poor attendance on parades, with many men lying around in tents doing nothing. Hygiene standards were declining, saddlery was poorly maintained and some horses suffered from a lack of attention. Orders went out telling the men to perform their duties properly and to 'smarten up'. They also needed to be reminded of 'the danger of returning clothing, accoutrements, etc., to Ordnance, which have not been searched for matches, bombs, and other explosives'.[27]

The fate of the New Zealand brigade's horses is a sad story. At the end of the war there were nearly 60,000 military horses in Egypt and Palestine, almost 2500 of which belonged to the NZEF, although not all of these horses came from New Zealand. The post-war occupation forces needed only a few thousand of these animals and there were few other options available for the unwanted majority. No country wanted a sudden influx of thousands of surplus animals, there was no shipping available to transport them anywhere and the quarantine regulations of most Western countries, including New Zealand, expressly prohibited the importation of animals from the Middle East.[28]

These hard facts were not widely known in the NZEF and rumours about the likely fate of the horses spread like wildfire in the last months of the war. According to Edwin McKay,

They were going to be returned to New Zealand …they would not be allowed in New Zealand for fear of spreading disease among the NZ livestock; they were going to be sold to the Indian Government; they were going to be sold to the Egyptians. These and other rumours flew from man to man, and a pall of worrying uncertainty brooded over the scene.[29]

It was not long before the actual plan was revealed. The horses were graded by regimental Classifying Boards into four categories. Sound animals aged between five and eight years were graded A. Sound older horses, up to the age of 12, were graded B. These were to be used by the post-war occupation army in the Middle East. Horses that were unsound or were aged over 12 years, but fit for work, were classed C; they were to be sold locally. D-class horses, which were unfit for any work, were to be destroyed. When the New Zealand government was asked if it objected to the sale of surplus horses to 'people of Eastern nationalities', it replied that it did not.[30]

Nearly all the New Zealand horses would have been graded A or B. No horse older than seven years was eligible for war service and a horse aged seven or younger in August 1914 would not have reached the cut-off age of 12 by the end of the war. Also, the horses were nearly all sound and fit for work. When they heard that the C-class horses were to be sold, a few men managed 'to have [their] animals transferred to the class for the kindly bullet'.[31]

The first horses to leave the brigade were those of the Canterbury regiment, before its deployment to Gallipoli. The best animals were transferred to other units and on 13 November 389 CMR horses went to the Imperial Remount Depot at Ludd. Harry Judge was 'glad to get rid of them in one sense, but still, one could not help a sigh of regret at losing such old friends'.[32] A week later, 700 or 800 Anzac horses were shot on the beach near Ayun Kara. According to William King, these were the horses from the CMR and the 7th ALH Regiment. I am not convinced that this is correct since the relevant records are inconclusive.

Regardless of whose horses they were, for the men like Ted Andrews, who took part, it was the 'saddest day of the war.… Each man had to hold two horses, and it was the most sickening job I had during the war.'

It seemed awfully sad that these poor old faithful creatures, after suffering from thirst, hunger and fatigue and carrying heavy loads for hundreds of miles, should have to end their days by being shot down by the very people they had so faithfully served. Thank God they had not the intelligence to realise what seemed like man's ingratitude. Some of the poor old beggars had landed here with the Main Body, and if there is a Heaven for animals, they have earned their place in it!... Better dead than to lead a life of misery at the hands of some gharry [carriage] driver in Cairo, or to be thrashed, starved, and worked to death. But how nice it would have been to be able to turn them all out on some boundless prairie to live out the rest of their lives in peace and comfort … Of course one has to harden one's heart to these sorts of things in warfare, but, I can tell you, it made some of us very miserable for some time afterwards, the memory of those lines of bodies lying stark in the desert, faithful unto death.[33]

The other horses spent a few more months with their riders. In February 1919 the horsemen destroyed their D-class horses at Rafah. The Australians also shot 250 C-class animals to prevent them being sold to the Egyptians. There is no known record of how many New Zealand Brigade horses were graded C or D but it cannot have been many.

No-one wanted the natives ill-treating our faithful old horses, so we saw to it that they very quietly joined the 'C's on their last trip…. There was a bit of bother when no 'B's were found

Bess, the only horse to return to New Zealand from the Middle East after the war.

338

to sell to the natives. There they were, lying dead in rows and not given the decent burial they
so richly deserved. Many of them had more battle scars than the men who rode them.[34]

According to Clifton Bellis, it was 'a hateful job handed over to the latest recruits. So
ended the careers of the soldiers' best friends – the lovely horses. It was a sad parting for
many of the lads who had had only the one horse throughout the campaign.'[35] On 21
February Fred Sterling wrote:

The day has come. I lose my horse tonight at 12 midnight. He goes to Moascar into a general
remount depot. [He is] the only thing in this land [that] I am truly sorry to leave. My very best
friend in this land he has been. He left me fat and in excellent spirits. May he strike a soft job
or die soon, for I love him very much.[36]

Of the 1680 of the NZMR Brigade's A- and B-class horses that went to the Remount Depot
at Moascar, 32 were sold locally, 25 were destroyed and 202 were evacuated to veterinary
hospitals. The remaining 1421 animals were retained 'for War Department purposes'.
Unfortunately, the number of horses in the remount depots soon greatly exceeded the
demand from the occupation forces. From 1919 onwards, many of these horses, including
New Zealand animals, were destroyed or sold as the British garrison in Egypt was reduced
in size. Most of the animals that were sold or given away to Egyptians suffered terrible
cruelty, starvation and neglect for the rest of their lives.[37]

Only one New Zealand horse that served in the Middle East returned home. The lucky
horse was Bess, a mare that left New Zealand with the Main Body in 1914, aged four. After
surviving three years in Egypt and Palestine, apparently without receiving so much as a
scratch, Bess was transferred to France late in 1918. In April 1920, she and three other
New Zealand horses were shipped home from England. Bess died peacefully at the age of
24, at Flock House, near Bulls, in 1934.[38]

Unrest slowly grew in the Anzac ranks as the months passed with no sign of a homeward
move. Some men drew up lists of grievances and submitted them to their officers. According
to Harry Judge, Colonel Findlay received complaints about the decision not to send the
longest-serving men home first, the inability of the men to take leave to England, the lack
of extra pay for occupation army duties, the failure of men holding temporary rank to be
confirmed in that rank, the lack of information in New Zealand about the reasons for the
delay in the repatriation of the brigade, and the poor food.[39]

There were several serious outbreaks of violence in the towns along the Suez Canal. On 8 December a crowd of 200 or 300 men, mostly New Zealanders and Rarotongans from the New Zealand Training Unit and Depot, ransacked shops in Ismailia. On one night in July 1919 a dance in town was cancelled when locals became too frightened to attend and the local bars were closed. When some men saw that the officers' bars were still open, many of them broke into the closed bars. It was determined afterwards that 40 per cent of the offenders were Australian, 40 per cent New Zealanders and 20 per cent British. On 18 July the men were warned that anyone involved in further disturbances would have their repatriation postponed until disciplinary proceedings were completed. That threat quickly put an end to the trouble.[40]

The repatriation of the NZEF from Egypt proceeded slowly as space on ships became available. The first 397 men sailed from Suez on the *Malta* on 15 December, followed 11 days later by 616 more aboard the *Wiltshire*. Most of these men were convalescents recovering from malaria. The next to go were 1059 troopers and corporals from the Main Body up to and including the 6th Reinforcements. Sergeants and above were excluded, prompting George Ranstead to write, 'If they come at the same sort of thing with this next boat I think we'll all chuck our stripes in.'[41]

Harry Mitchell was one of the contingent which sailed for home on the *Kaikoura* on Thursday 6 March 1919. He described the vessel as 'worn out ... [She] wasn't up to speed ... she would stop altogether sometimes.' Food ran out during the voyage and the men were forced to subsist on tea and bread for several days. Clearly, Mitchell felt, 'they don't think much of you on the way home'.[42] As the first veterans departed the brigade, those left behind noticed a change: 'All the old boys going makes one feel like a stranger in this outfit. Somehow the new men are not the same'.[43] Later in March, the longest-serving light horsemen left for Australia and expectations were high that everyone else would soon be on a homeward-bound ship.

There had been pressure for independence in Egypt ever since the British took control of the country in 1882. After the eviction of the Turks in 1916 the British had promised that Egyptian independence would follow the successful conclusion of the war. Egyptians endured considerable hardships during the war years: thousands of them were conscripted into the Egyptian Labour Corps to build roads and railways and dig trenches for the EEF, and thousands of camels and tonnes of food were confiscated for the war effort. Nationalist politicians led by Sa'ad Zaghlul put up with this in the hope that better times lay ahead but when the British arrested Zaghlul and several others on 8 March 1919 and deported them

CHARLES LONSDALE ALBUM, COURTESY OF MARK RHODES

Mounted tug-of-war.

to Malta to prevent them going to London to discuss independence, the Egyptians realised that little had changed.

On Monday 10 March a general strike began in Cairo. Rioting and acts of sabotage quickly spread throughout the country. Railway tracks were torn up, telegraph lines were cut, bridges and railway stations were damaged and European houses and property were looted and burnt. On 16 March, Cairo's railway and telegraph communications with the rest of Egypt were cut and, two days later, eight unarmed British soldiers were killed, and their bodies ritually mutilated, on a train south of Cairo. According to Ted Andrews, Major General Chaytor's brother D'Arcy, and his wife, left this train just before it was attacked. Several sieges took place on the Upper Nile, with small bands of foreigners holding off poorly conducted attacks by large bands of rioters for days. Reportedly the Muslim rioters were promised entry into Paradise if they martyred themselves.[44]

The Acting Commander-in-Chief, Lieutenant General Edward Bulfin, immediately declared martial law. He deployed two EEF divisions south of Cairo and two, including the Anzac Mounted Division, into the Nile Delta to bring the country back under control. The first Anzacs into action were from the 10th Australian Light Horse Regiment. On 16 March these Australians fought off an armed, 'frenzied' mob of 1000 rioters at a village on the Cairo–Ismailia railway line, killing 39 and wounding 25 Egyptians.[45]

Allenby returned from Versailles with the appointment of Special High Commissioner and orders to quell the revolt quickly. In an early conciliatory move, he released the nationalist leaders and allowed them to attend the peace conference at Versailles. This concession led to a cessation of the violence in Egypt. However, the British government refused to negotiate with Zaghlul and the Egyptian delegates were snubbed at Versailles. When, on 13 April United States President Woodrow Wilson announced that Egypt was to be a protectorate of Great Britain, the riots and strikes resumed in Egypt.[46]

At noon on Monday 17 March urgent orders were received at Rafah for the Anzac Mounted Division to move to the Suez Canal to prepare for riot control duties. After a hurried packing-up and burning of non-essential stores, the men boarded two troop trains and headed west that afternoon. The next two days were spent re-equipping on the banks of the Suez Canal.[47] As Arthur Moore wrote, 'Visions of a boat and a quick passage back to New Zealand faded away. ... Disappointment was keen.'[48]

Fortunately, the divisional bivouac was near the remount depot, to which most of the division's horses had been sent the previous month. The best New Zealand horses had already been reallocated, but many others were still there. Fred Sterling and others 'spent a large part of last night stealing … our old horses. I succeeded in getting my fellow after much manoeuvring this morning.' Others 'had to content ourselves with a mixture of draughts, culls and mules, leavened here and there by a lucky find – by moonlight.' Remounting the regiments was a slow process, with many of the horses needing to be reshod.[49]

Most Anzacs already regarded the Egyptians with scorn and contempt. These feelings now grew in intensity, for the rioters were keeping the men from their homes and loved ones. The troublemakers would receive little sympathy or mercy from the Anzacs. The NZMR Brigade first deployed to the Nile Delta town of Tanta (see Map 1, p.23). Regimental columns were formed on arrival, supplemented by machine gunners, signallers, medical, transport and supply teams, and sometimes by armoured cars and armoured trains. Squadron patrols did the bulk of the work, riding along railway tracks and searching villages for offenders and concealed weapons. Boats and carts were stopped and checked for hidden weapons.[50]

The Egyptians rarely took on the military forces openly. Shots were sometimes fired at patrols and government officials, and lone sentries were occasionally assaulted and robbed of their rifles. Their main weapon was the strike: Egyptian railway men, soldiers and policemen all downed tools at various times and places. Egyptians who wanted to work were threatened with beatings, or worse. Government buildings and schools were burnt down, telephone lines cut. Railway tracks were interfered with but the damage was quickly repaired – often by the offenders themselves after they were caught. Threatening crowds often gathered, brandishing sticks and shouting at the military forces, but were usually reluctant to go any further. If the mobs came too close, a few bursts of overhead machine gun fire generally dispersed them.

The 9th (Wellington East Coast) Squadron joined a composite regiment in Cairo, where some of the worst violence took place. On one occasion a mob of Egyptians was looting Armenian shops. When the New Zealanders arrived to restore order, 'it was found that they had erected barricades of carts and furniture, behind which they evidently considered themselves safe. The WMR horses, however, jumped the obstacles, and our men belaboured the natives with batons.' Ted Andrews told the following, possibly apocryphal, tale. An armoured car 'was patrolling a dangerous quarter when those on board noticed a single Australian trooper leaning against a lamp post. They immediately pulled up and told the Australian that it was not safe to be alone. "That's all right," drawled the Australian, "I'm the bait, and my mates are waiting round the corner."'[51]

The work was not arduous and there were long rest periods between patrols. As most patrols were small, many of the men had little to do. When large-scale operations were required, such as searches of large villages, several columns were combined under a single commander. Typically, the troublesome towns were surrounded at first light.

New Zealanders on the bank of the Suez Canal in 1919, waiting for their ship home.

PEF/P/RHODES/123, PALESTINE EXPLORATION FUND, LONDON

Guided by informers and Egyptian police, soldiers then arrested suspects for trial by courts-martial.[52]

As the *New Zealand Herald* reported, commanders were required to establish control of areas and administer martial law 'entirely at their own discretion. They had no code of law to work on, the system apparently being to use fairness, justice, and commonsense. They could not impose the death penalty without the decision being confirmed by a higher authority, but in almost every other respect they had autocratic power.' Commanders often had to deal with very unfamiliar situations: for example, one young officer was petitioned by a local woman to grant her a divorce.[53]

Offenders convicted of rioting by courts-martial received public floggings (10 to 30 lashes), fines or short terms of imprisonment. By 31 March Percy Doherty's unit had 'flogged several hundred natives and we are still going strong.... the job is certainly a unique one, but the novelty of flogging … niggers is wearing off, although our determination is still strong, as we never forget that if the natives had not revolted, we would now have been embarking for NZ'.[54]

According to Ted Andrews, two Wellington men were on sentry duty in a village when 'an unruly mob … led by a huge, coal black native' advanced on them.

We had loaded rifles but were told not to fire except in a last resort. So we fixed bayonets, when the big black fellow was almost upon us, and that stopped him short. He turned to run, but I gave him half an inch of it in his left ham and did he take off? Fought and yelled his way into the mob with them all running with him. In a few seconds the street was clear and … [we] mopped our sweating brows. Then we heard laughter and saw the Hotchkiss gun crew on the barracks wall grinning at us. They were just about to fire a burst over the mob, when our bayonets did the trick![55]

It did not take long for the novelty of patrolling and arresting strikers and rioters to wear off. Commanders did everything they could to keep the tired and homesick men busy, with regular sports events being especially welcome. Cricket, tennis and horse racing were popular pastimes. Regimental and brigade horse races were followed by divisional meetings. These culminated in the EEF race meeting at Heliopolis, near Cairo, on 24 May 1919, where NZMR Brigade riders won five out of the six horse events, including the premier trophy, the Allenby Cup.

But horse races were not enough to satisfy the bored and increasingly resentful soldiers. Some Anzacs apparently told Allenby that they were 'ready to fight enemies of the Empire, but are not prepared to remain to deal with internal troubles'. Some were concerned that they would miss out on jobs at home if they were still away when the troops from Europe arrived home; others had simply had enough. There were still a number of men in the ranks who had left home in 1914 or 1915, and they believed that they had well and truly done their share. Allenby realised that, unless demobilisation recommenced, 'the troops will mutiny'. He wanted all of the 1914 men gone by the end of May, with the 1915 and 1916 men on their way home by the end of June and August 1919 respectively. To replace them, he demanded fresh troops from elsewhere. Fortunately, after three months, the risk of a general uprising had passed and by early June life was nearly back to normal in Egypt. The New Zealand brigade did not sustain a single battle casualty during 1919. About 20 light horsemen were among the 36 EEF men killed; around 800 Egyptians also died.[56]

It was nearly time for the New Zealanders to go home. On 17 June orders were received for the NZMR Brigade to hand in its horses and move to the Demobilisation Camp at Ismailia. 'After the great disappointment at Rafah ... the move to the Canal was welcomed with quiet thankfulness.'[57] Ted Andrews wrote, 'Home seems to be coming nearer.'[58] The New Zealanders were told that the first 1000 men could expect to be on a ship at the start of July. Weapons, bandoliers, spurs and saddlery were all cleaned and handed in. There was plenty of local leave available and parties visited Alexandria and Cairo. Some time was also spent moving the bodies of New Zealanders from isolated graves into a central cemetery at Ismailia.[59]

In a special order dated 27 June 1919, Chaytor thanked the Anzacs 'for their gallantry and endurance which has enabled the Division to remain true to [the] Gallipoli tradition and to establish a fresh record in Sinai, Palestine and Syria' and sincerely hoped that every member would 'have a speedy voyage home and meet with every success in his future life'.[60] The following day, General Allenby, who had apparently reconciled himself to the Anzacs, issued his own tribute to the horsemen.

They have borne with cheerful endurance the thirst and glare of the desert, the heat and dust of the Jordan Valley, and the fatigue of long and exhausting marches. They have responded to every call, and have fully earned the welcome which will reward them on their long deferred return to their homes. I send my congratulations, my thanks, and my best wishes.[61]

The Anzac Mounted Division – and the New Zealand Mounted Rifles Brigade – officially ceased to exist at noon on Monday 30 June 1919.

A man's chances of securing an early berth on a ship home were determined not by his length of service, but by the likelihood of his securing a job when he arrived in New Zealand. Men with businesses or other employment in New Zealand, even if they had been in the NZEF for only a short time, had priority over those who could not point to a waiting job. A lot of long-service veterans had to watch recent arrivals, many of whom had never seen a shot fired in anger, leave before them. They were also disgusted with the complaints of the newer arrivals. As Fred Sterling wrote, 'It's a beggar being left here with this crowd. All growling etc and over nothing compared to what the old fellows had to put up with.'[62] On 30 June 1919 1089 men sailed for New Zealand on the *Ulimaroa* and the *Ellenga* embarked 1094 men on 23 July.[63] It was, in Ted Andrews' words, 'farewell at last to the land of sun, sand, sin and sorrow. No one was in tears about it!' Aboard the *Ulimaroa* on the night of 4 July, Andrews 'lost sight of the North Star, but, glory be, saw a wonderful sight on the starboard horizon, the Southern Cross. It made home seem so much nearer.' According to Tom Murray, many men slept on the decks under a couple of blankets and with a haversack as a pillow, as a real bed was foreign to them.[64]

When the *Ulimaroa* entered Auckland's Waitemata Harbour at dawn on Saturday 9 August, she met 'a great reception, the guns in the forts firing salutes, hooters screeched and large numbers of people on ferries and launches circled the ship, cheering and yelling greetings'.[65] According to a *New Zealand Herald* reporter, 'no soldiers deserve a warmer welcome than these mounted men, who count their campaigning in years and their conquests by countries.... the soldiers who served in Egypt and Palestine have had a peculiarly trying experience, unrelieved by many of the relaxations which softened the hardships of the infantry in France. For them there was little pleasant relief behind the lines, no leave in England and no contact with European civilisation. ... Theirs was the rigorous campaigning of the desert and the torment of the sands.'[66]

When the *Ellenga* berthed in New Zealand in September, another *Herald* reporter wrote:

> These are the last of the Mounted Rifles Brigade, and the story of New Zealand's share in the Egyptian and Palestine campaigns is closed.... These men of ours played a glorious part in the smashing of Turkey, and their name will ever be associated with one of the most brilliant campaigns in history.... the Mounted Brigade has never had from the public the credit that was its due. Few war correspondents watched the Palestine campaign ... and for that reason much of the glory won by the New Zealand Mounted Rifles Brigade has been lost to history.

... The men of this brigade are, as a rule, extremely reticent about their achievements. Some of them, who have memories of insulting messages about the 'Cold footed Mounteds', placed by ignorant people in parcels, decline to speak of their experiences for fear that people may imagine that they have some charge to reply to. But in the case of the majority it seems that the sentiment and silence of the East have possessed them. When they are asked to talk they simply shrug their shoulders and say, 'Maleesh' – 'What matter.'[67]

Conclusion

With fear and trembling, but with an outward show of indifference, we rode to what
seemed like certain death. Those wonderful New Zealand horses, how they toiled to
move us. They could always be depended upon.[1]

ALEC McNEUR

————————————————

THIS CHAPTER BRINGS to an end the story of the men and horses of the New Zealand Mounted
Rifles Brigade in the First World War. Theirs was a very different war from that experienced
by the majority of the NZEF in France and Flanders. The New Zealanders who served in
the Middle East had a much greater chance of surviving the war than did their compatriots
fighting on the Western Front. After Gallipoli, these men never lined up below a trench
parapet with fixed bayonets, waiting for the artillery barrage to cease and for an officer to
send them into no man's land in the face of massed German machine gun fire. As a result,
the total number of casualties suffered by the New Zealanders in three years in the Middle
East was often exceeded in as many days by our 'poor bloody infantry' on the Western
Front.

Five hundred and twenty-two mounted riflemen lost their lives after May 1916. Added
to the 599 Gallipoli fatalities, the total number of deaths in the brigade between 1914
and 1920 was 1120. Battle casualties accounted for 821 of those deaths: 515 on Gallipoli,
306 in the Middle East. Disease took the lives of 177 mounted riflemen during the war,
mostly on Gallipoli and during the malaria and influenza outbreaks in late 1918. Another
123 men died from accidents, injuries and so on. During the war 2113 mounted riflemen
were wounded: 951 on Gallipoli, 1162 in the Middle East. Adding this to the fatalities, and
105 men listed as missing, gives a total of 3338 NZMR casualties in the First World War.
Thousands of other men suffered from non-fatal illness but the official casualty records
do not include them. Figure 5 shows the fatalities in the NZMR Brigade throughout the
war.[2]

Horse losses are difficult to determine. I have calculated that the New Zealanders lost
1416 horses between April 1916 and December 1918: 211 died, 184 were destroyed, 383
were killed in action, 559 were evacuated to hospital with wounds, exhaustion or sickness,
and 79 were listed as missing.[3]

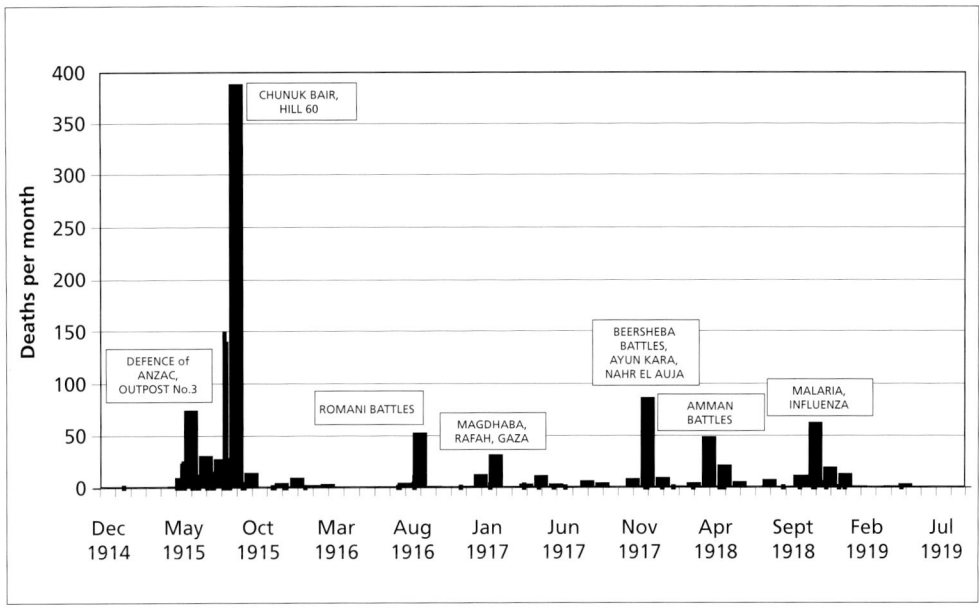

Figure 5: NZMR Brigade Fatalities 1914–19.

More men were killed or wounded by bullets than by any other cause in the Middle East, unlike the Western Front, where artillery was the great killer. The likelihood of a man surviving a wound from a Turkish rifle or machine gun bullet depended largely upon which part of his body was hit. If he were shot in the head, chest or abdomen, he would usually die on the battlefield or soon afterwards; if hit in a limb, he would probably survive the immediate wounding. Whether he lived depended on the ability of the doctors to deal with infection.[4] According to camelier Beethoven Algar,

> *There were no medicines in those days, you know, the only thing was iodine, and they used to bare all the wounds to the open sun and just [let them] heal naturally…. they were very crude as far as operations went… they used to come along and roll me over and the doctor used to put his fingers in and work around in the wound, you know, to try and find this foreign body that was causing the trouble.*[5]

It was not quite that bad: improved surgical techniques, diagnostic bacteriology, X-ray machines, anaesthetics, morphine, intravenous saline drips and blood transfusions all helped to reduce wound mortality. Even though antibiotics were unknown in the First World War, a high percentage of wounded men who were admitted to medical units survived, and many returned to duty after a period of convalescence.[6]

Of the 16 mounted riflemen who became prisoners of war, six died in captivity. The Turks themselves were often starving and dressed in rags, so it should come as no surprise to learn that their prisoners suffered equally, if not more. Brutal guards and hard labour made life hell in some prison camps, and health care was practically non-existent, except in those parts of Palestine where charities ran hospitals.[7]

It proved difficult to account for all the men and horses who served in the brigade. My research indicates that 11,832 mounted riflemen went away to war. Godley took 2050 of these men to France in 1916, 1164 died at Gallipoli and in the Middle East, and 4541 were demobilised and sent home in 1919. The remaining 4077 were probably discharged from the NZEF – they were mainly wounded and sick men who were unfit for further service, but included a number of disciplinary discharges – and sent home during the war. To the best of my knowledge, 5049 horses left New Zealand for service with the NZMR Brigade. Losses account for 1416 of these animals and 2350 were disposed of after the war. The other 1283 horses were probably transferred to the New Zealand Division and shipped to France in 1916.[8]

When the men of the New Zealand Expeditionary Force sailed away to war in October 1914, most of them expected to fight a European rerun of the South African War. That was what the small, lightly equipped NZEF was most suited to. With no heavy artillery and only a few machine guns, it was unprepared for an 'industrial' war fought between mass conscript armies using machine guns, trenches, barbed wire, tanks, heavy artillery and poison gas. It took several years for all combatants to adjust to these realities and they suffered terrible casualties in the process. In contrast, the war fought in the Middle East quite closely resembled what the NZEF had been designed for. Although trench warfare was a part of the Middle East campaign, the decisive fighting usually took place in the open, behind or on the flanks of static defences. Battles lasted for hours or days, not weeks or months, and they were on a relatively small scale, resulting in far fewer casualties.[9]

Doctrinally, mounted riflemen supported the infantry. In the Sinai campaign they became the main strike force, assuming that responsibility when the immobile and poorly acclimatised infantry divisions proved unequal to the task. The horsemen were able to succeed in this unaccustomed new role only because the Turks they fought in the desert were in small, unsupported units. A single Turkish infantry regiment was about all that the Anzac Mounted Division could take on by itself, and even that was a challenge at times. The mounted troops prevailed at Magdhaba only because the isolated Turkish regiment lacked sufficient machine guns and artillery. Whenever the mounted brigades encountered a determined and well-planned Turkish defence with adequate artillery and machine gun support (as at the Second Battle of Gaza and the First Battle of Amman), or were counter-attacked in strength (as they were at Nahr el Auja and during the second raid across the Jordan), they could do little other than withdraw to save themselves.

Historian Christopher Pugsley has described the New Zealand Mounted Rifles Brigade as 'one of the finest fighting bodies that New Zealand has ever raised.'[10] I cannot fault his judgement. The mounteds fought bravely and intelligently on Gallipoli, and their commanders were some of the best on the peninsula. From 1916 until the end of the war, the New Zealand brigade fought in every battle that the Anzac Mounted Division took part in. They were defeated by the Turks on many occasions, but never because of a lack of courage or poor leadership. According to Lieutenant Colonel Peter Wood, 'the NZMR Brigade concluded the campaign as an accomplished fighting formation. They were able to fight mounted and dismounted, and proved [as] capable of advancing over difficult terrain in atrocious weather as they were at conducting a dismounted silent attack at night.'[11]

There are a number of reasons for the success of the brigade. The leaders of the regiments, squadrons and troops were, by and large, very capable men. The three brigade commanders, Russell, Chaytor and Meldrum, were highly proficient leaders and tacticians. Many of the older officers and men had fought in the South African War at the turn of the century. The veldt was not as harsh an environment as the Egyptian desert but the terrible losses of horses in South Africa taught these New Zealanders how to manage horses under active service conditions. Many of the mounted operations in South Africa were conducted over long distances, on short rations and with limited support from infantry or artillery. This experience was of great relevance and value when the fighting began in Egypt in 1916.

Unlike the Western Front, there was a place for horses in the Middle East; indeed, it can be argued that the campaign could not have been won without them. The horses were a critical factor in the success of the brigade. Before the Middle East campaign began it was believed that, unless horses were watered twice daily, they would lose condition and quickly become useless. One of the lessons of the desert war was that this was an ideal, not an absolute requirement. In a post-war report to Parliament, Chaytor wrote:

The horses at times had to go for thirty-six hours without water – and on two occasions from forty-eight to sixty hours – with a day temperature of from 110° to 120° [43° to 49°C]. At the end of October 1917, after nearly three years' service, of which twenty months were occupied in hard active warfare in the desert, one squadron had with it 96 Main Body horses out of an original total of 156. When actual casualties in action are allowed for, the percentage lost or unfit for work as a result of sickness or preventable causes was remarkably small. This may be taken as the fair average experience of the other squadrons in the brigade.[12]

New Zealand's mounted riflemen entered the First World War with an enviable reputation. Many senior British and New Zealand officers considered the mounted rifles regiments to be the best-trained troops in the Territorial Force. The one weakness of the men without South African experience was in the area of horse management. The mounted riflemen quickly had to learn how to keep their horses fit and healthy in desert conditions, with filthy water and barely adequate rations. The long-distance marches that were such an important feature of their war were possible because these lessons were learned, and learned well.

One of the reasons for the high wastage of horses in South Africa was that the animals were committed to battle within days of arriving in the country, with no time for acclimatisation. In 1916 the slow tempo of the campaign gave the men and horses plenty of time to learn how to live in the desert.[13] The stop-start pace of the Middle East campaign also meant that there were ample opportunities for officers and men to train. The low losses throughout the campaign, and the fact that the men were in the war for the duration, meant that hard-won experience was retained in the regiments. Junior officers and senior NCOs became 'craftier fighters and better leaders of men as they gained experience'.[14]

The disciplinary record of a unit is usually a good indication of its morale and effectiveness. With a few exceptions, the record of the New Zealanders in the Middle East was good. The most serious offences occurred when the men were on leave, resting, training or waiting to go home. No New Zealanders were sentenced to death by courts-martial in the Middle East, even though several were found guilty of desertion and sleeping on guard duty (capital offences on the Western Front). Drunkenness and absence without leave feature most frequently in the disciplinary records.[15]

Allenby's victorious EEF did not force Turkey out of the war, and it did nothing to shorten the overall duration of the conflict. Although it kept the Turks occupied, it took very little German effort away from the Western Front. The campaign did provide the victorious Allies with bargaining chips in the post-war territorial carve-up and its morale-boosting successes often came at opportune times during the war. The decision to bring Turkey into the war at its side was undoubtedly the correct one for Berlin. Large Allied forces were diverted to Gallipoli and the Middle East that would otherwise have been used against Germany on the Western or Eastern fronts; the price to Germany was trifling. For Turkey, the decision was a disaster. The Turkish Empire was destroyed by the First World War and its sway over the Muslim world was ended. When the empire was succeeded by the secular Republic of Turkey in 1922, all that remained was the Anatolian heartland and a small area on the European side of the Dardanelles. Turkish war casualties were heavy: 785,000 were killed or died of wounds or sickness; between 400,000 and 640,000 were wounded.[16]

It is quite amazing that the Turks, with all their disadvantages, stayed in the fight for the duration of the war. Part of the explanation lies in the conservative strategy adopted by the British in the Middle East, which one strategist likened to 'swallowing [the Turk] from the feet upwards, like a python dragging its endless length across the desert'. Also, for much of the war the demands of the Western Front starved the EEF of troops and equipment and the climate forced long operational pauses on the EEF every winter. Another important factor was the extraordinary ability of the Turkish soldiers to fight under conditions that would have driven any Westerner to mutiny in a matter of months.[17]

The grudging respect and sympathy for the Turks many Anzacs had developed on Gallipoli continued throughout the Middle Eastern campaign. According to Harry Mitchell, the Turks were 'decent blokes … once they're taken prisoner you never have any trouble with them…. They're just as happy when they're prisoners as when they're not prisoners … You can't help liking an enemy like that, because they're … human beings…. You always felt sorry for the Turks … they're a good enemy.'[18]

A former Governor General of New Zealand, speaking at Gallipoli, said that the fight against Turkey was 'someone else's war. Turkey was not [New Zealand's] enemy.'[19] In fact, Turkey became our foe in November 1914 when it goaded the Allies into declaring war on it. Revisionist statements such as this help to perpetuate the misconception that the war fought by New Zealand's mounted riflemen (and by the NZEF on Gallipoli) was a pointless waste of effort.

The men of the NZMR Brigade played a small part in shaping the modern Middle East. The First World War led to the transformation of this part of the world: most of the countries that exist there today came into being soon after the end of the war. The Hejaz Arabs had been led to believe that they would win independence if they joined in the fight against Turkey. They did their bit and were bitterly disappointed after the war when Britain and France retained control of Syria and Palestine in their own hands and, even worse, gave much of Arab Palestine to the Jews as their homeland. The states of Iraq, Jordan, Syria and Lebanon were all created in the 1920s, but not initially as fully independent nations. The state of Israel came into being in 1948. The destruction of the Turkish Empire, and the failure to address legitimate Arab aspirations afterwards, set the stage for the violent and unstable situation that still exists in the Middle East today. It is significant to note that modern-day Islamic extremists such as Osama bin Laden frequently refer to the 'betrayal' of the Arabs after the First World War as justification for their actions.[20]

Had Turkey stayed out of the First World War, there would have been no Gallipoli campaign and no Middle Eastern war. Turkey probably would have held onto its Middle Eastern territories, at least for a few more years. The map of the Middle East would not have been redrawn by the Allies after the war and that would have had immense strategic consequences. There would be no Israel, no Iraq, no Kuwait and perhaps no Saudi Arabia, at least as we know them today. Had the Allies been able to concentrate all their strength against the Germans and Austro-Hungarians, instead of diverting significant resources to the 'sideshows' of Gallipoli and the Middle East, the First World War might have ended earlier and more decisively. That might have avoided the post-war denial and bitterness in Germany that Adolf Hitler exploited with disastrous results. Russia might have survived the First World War – no Bolshevik revolution, no Stalin, no Cold War – and the United States might not have entered it.

Taken as a whole, New Zealand's mounted riflemen were not natural soldiers or heroes, but nor were they victims or villains. The majority were brave, hard-working soldiers, although some of them neither enjoyed military life nor longed for combat. Some men complained to anyone who would listen, did what they could to avoid work, committed crimes, got drunk and shied away from danger. This became more prevalent as the war dragged on, with veterans becoming jaded and as unwilling conscripts began to join the brigade.

Whether courageous fighters or idle shirkers, very few of the mounted riflemen had any wish to stay in the army for a single day longer than was necessary. By November 1918 their job was done and they were more than ready to shed their uniforms and get back to their real lives in New Zealand. Brigadier General Meldrum summed them up well when he wrote: 'They were wonderful fighters, but they were not great talkers, and they didn't want any heroics about their work. What they did was part of a day's work to be got through and done well, but that was enough.'[21]

A significant number of mounted riflemen signed up to fight the Germans again in 1939, although this time they went to war without horses. Their preferred unit in the

2nd NZEF was the 2nd New Zealand Divisional Cavalry Regiment. Some men with First World War combat experience in the North African desert fought there again in the next war, in the 'Div Cav' and the Long Range Desert Group (LRDG). For the first two years of this war, horses were used in New Zealand in the mounted rifles regiments of the Home Defence Force. Then, as armoured vehicles arrived in the country, the horsed regiments were gradually transformed into Light Armoured Fighting Vehicle regiments and the horses were retired. Independent Mounted Rifles Squadrons patrolled the back blocks of New Zealand on horseback for another year or so but few horses were used in any New Zealand units by the end of the war. There was plenty of fighting ahead for the men, but the day of the New Zealand war horse had finally passed. For that small mercy, I am profoundly thankful.[22]

Bibliography

Unpublished Sources

Archives New Zealand/Te Rua Mahara o te Kāwanatanga, Wellington
Military Personnel Files, Series 18805.
Army Department Series 1.
Army Department Series 10.
War Archives Series 1.
War Archives Series 2.
War Archives Series 9.
War Archives Series 22.
War Archives Series 24.
War Archives Series 40.
War Archives Series 41.
War Archives Series 42.
War Archives Series 43.
War Archives Series 46.
War Archives Series 196.
War Archives Series 235.
War Archives Series 242.
War Archives Series 252.

Alexander Turnbull Library, National Library of New Zealand, Wellington
Cameron, A.E., diary, MSX-2853.
Colbran, B.C., diaries, MS-Copy-Micro-1431.
Dawbin, W., diary, Micro-MS-0004.
Eccles, M.A., diary, MSX-4964.
Gambrill, R.F. (compiler), 'The Russell Saga: Volume 3, World War 1', qMS-0822.
Harper, G., letters, MS-Papers-1444-3.
Judge, H., 'Papers Relating to Service in Palestine', MS-Papers-4312.
Macfarlane, W.A., papers, MS-Papers-3871.
McNeur, A., letters, MS-Papers-4108.
Moore, A.B., 'A Night Stunt of the Auckland Mounted Rifles during the final big operations in Palestine immediately preceding the armistice with Turkey', 80-057.
Ranstead, G., letters, MS-Papers-4139.
Rhodes, A.E.T., papers, 76-123.
Tuke, R., letters, MS-Papers-1547.
Twisleton, F.M., letters, MS-Papers-1705.
Wright, G.F., papers, MS-Papers-1512.

World War I Oral Archive Collection, OHColl-0006, interviewers Jane Tolerton and Nicholas Boyack, Oral History Centre, Alexander Turnbull Library, Wellington
Algar, B., OHInt 0006/01.
Dill, F.G., OHInt 0006/23.
Gainfort, B.S., OHInt 0006/28.
Mitchell, J.H., OHInt 0006/56.
Owers, W.H., OHInt 0006/64.
Porter, W.H., OHInt 0006/62.

Auckland War Memorial Museum Library, Auckland
Harrison, A.C., Papers, MS 2004/5.
Law, J.O., Papers, MS 90/20.

Kauri Museum, Matakohe, Northland
McCarroll, Lieutenant Colonel J.N., diary.
The Wartime Diary of Sgt F. Sterling, 13291, 11th NAMR, 13th Reinforcement, New Zealand Expeditionary Force, 29th May 1916 to 9th September 1919.

Kippenberger Military Archives and Research Library, Queen Elizabeth II Army Memorial Museum, Waiouru
Doherty, P.G., diaries, 1991.2000.
Doherty, P.G., letters, 1989.944.
Hayman, B.F., diaries, 1993.1661.
Hull, G.B., letters, 2001.1035.
Hull, J.K., letters, 1993.1039.
Ireland, T.W., 'Raid Over the Jordan', 2002.187.
Marle, B., letter of condolence to parents of Tpr W. J. Lunnon, dated 29 November 1917, 2000.325.
Masterman, J.W.V., 'Memoirs', 1998.1936.
McCormack, R. D., diaries, 1999.2619.
McKay, E.C.M., 'The Years Unfold: Memoirs', 1998.31.
Meldrum, Brigadier General W., 'Notes on Campaigns of NZMR'.

The Warkworth and District Museum, Warkworth
Maddison, L.D., letter dated 4 December 1917.

The Trustees of the Liddell Hart Centre for Military Archives, King's College, London
Allenby Papers.
Robertson Papers.

Imperial War Museum, London
PP/MCR/C1, Chetwode, Field Marshal Lord, Papers.
99/55/1, King, W.A., diary, January–December 1918.

Australian War Memorial, Canberra
AWM4 Unit War Diaries 1914–18 War, 1/60/1–1/60/40, General Staff, Headquarters Anzac Mounted Division War Diary.
AWM4 Unit War Diaries 1914–18 War, 1/61/1–1/61/42, Administrative Staff, Headquarters Anzac Mounted Division War Diary.
AWM25 385/3, Report on Machine Guns with Mounted Troops and Infantry during Actions in Egypt, November 1916.
AWM25 455/69, Desert Mounted Corps, Report on Operations East of the Jordan, April–May 1918.
AWM45 7/12, EEF Special File, August 1916.
AWM45 7/13, Romani, Report on Operations from 19/7/16 to 12/8/16.
AWM45 7/31, EEF Special File, March 1918.
AWM45 12/7, Chetwode, Lieutenant General P.W., 'Notes on the Palestine Operations', dated 21 June 1917.

Private Collections
Hull, G.B. and J.K., letters, property of Hull family, Waiuku.
McMillan, J., 'Forty Thousand Horsemen: being the Memoirs of 7/1322 Cpl Jim McMillan, Canterbury Mounted Rifles, First NZEF, on Service in Gallipoli and Palestine, WW1', unpublished manuscript, property of C.B. McMillan and family, Whangarei.
Milliken, W.T., letters.
Parker, J.H., diary, property of Parker family, Auckland.
Peed, E.S., diaries, property of Peed family, Taihape.
Smith, L.J., diaries, property of G.R. Smith and family, Wellington.

Johnson, Major M.E., 'Memoirs of a Soldier', property of Mrs R.T. Bruce and family, Auckland.

Manuscripts, Research Papers etc.

Davidson, A.M., 'The New Zealand Mounted Field Ambulance: a History of its Activities from the Outbreak of the Great War to the Conclusion of the Sinai Campaign, August 4 1914–January 12 1917, University of Otago, 1938.

Jones, I. *Who Are the Blokes in the Black Hats? Australian Light Horse and the Egyptian Rebellion of 1919*, Proceedings of the Australian War Memorial History Conference, July 1989.

Chauvel and Royston at Romani: a Study in Command and Leadership, Proceedings of the Australian War Memorial History Conference, November 1991.

Milnes, D.J., 'Imperial Soldiers? The New Zealand Mounted Rifles Brigade in Sinai and Palestine 1916–1919', thesis for Master of Arts (History), University of Otago, 1999.

Smith, M., unpublished manuscript on Major General Sir E.W.C. Chaytor.

Wood, Lieutenant Colonel P., 'Tackling the Turk: an Examination of Tactics Employed by the New Zealand Mounted Rifles Brigade during the Sinai Palestine Campaign of World War I', thesis for Master of Philosophy, Massey University, 2004.

Published Sources

Official Publications

Annual Reports on the Defence Forces of New Zealand, Government Printer, Wellington, 1910–1922.

Journal of the House of Representatives of New Zealand, Wellington, 1919.

Bean, C.E.W., *The Official History of Australia in the War of 1914–1918, Volume 3, The Australian Imperial Force in France 1916*, 6th edition, Angus & Robertson, Sydney, 1938.

Blenkinsop, Major General Sir L.J., and Lieutenant Colonel J.W. Rainey, *History of the Great War Based on Official Documents, Veterinary Services*, His Majesty's Stationery Office, London, 1925.

Branch of the Chief of the General Staff, *New Zealand Expeditionary Force, its Provision and Maintenance*, Government Printer, Wellington, 1919.

Downes, Colonel R.M.G., 'The Campaign in Sinai and Palestine', *The Official History of the Australian Army Medical Services in the War of 1914–1918, Volume 1, Gallipoli, Palestine and New Guinea*, Australian War Memorial, Canberra, 1930, pp. 547–777.

Falls, Captain C., *Military Operations, Egypt and Palestine, from June 1917 to the End of the War*, His Majesty's Stationery Office, London, 1930.

Gullett, H.S., *The Official History of Australia in the War of 1914–1918, Volume 7, The Australian Imperial Force in Sinai and Palestine 1914–1918*, University of Queensland Press edition, 1984.

Macmunn, Lieutenant General Sir G. and Captain C. Falls, *Military Operations, Egypt and Palestine, from the Outbreak of War with Germany to June 1917*, His Majesty's Stationery Office, London, 1928.

Murray, General Sir A., *Sir Archibald Murray's Despatches (June 1916–June 1917)*, J.M. Dent & Sons, London, 1920.

New Zealand Expeditionary Force, Alphabetical List of Casualties, Books 1–14, Government Printer, Wellington, 1916–1919.

Studholme, Lieutenant Colonel J., *Records of Personnel Services During the War of Officers, Nurses and First Class Warrant Officers, and Other Facts Relating to the NZEF, Unofficial but Compiled from Official Sources*, Government Printer, Wellington, 1928.

War Office, His Majesty's Stationery Office, London:

Animal Management, 1908.

Field Service Regulations, Part 2, Organization and Administration, 1909.

Yeomanry and Mounted Rifles Training, Parts 1 and 2, 1912.

Remount Regulations, 1913.

Field Service Pocket Book, 1914 (Reprinted with Amendments), 1916.

A Brief Record of the Advance of the Egyptian Expeditionary Force under the Command of General Sir Edmund H.H. Allenby, GCB, GCMG, July 1917 to October 1918, Compiled from Official Sources, 2nd edition, 1919.

Statistics of the Military Effort of the British Empire during the Great War, 1914–1920, 1922.

Manual of Horsemastership, Equitation and Driving, 1929.

Books

Aaronsohn, A., *With the Turks in Palestine*, 1st World Library Literary Society edition, Fairfield, 2004.

Adam-Smith, P., *The ANZACs*, Thomas Nelson, Melbourne, 1978.

Amber and Black: the Journal of the Queen Alexandra's (Wellington West Coast) Mounted Rifles, New Zealand Military Forces, Hawera, 1934–1938.

Andrews, T., *Kiwi Trooper: the Story of Queen Alexandra's Own*, Wanganui Chronicle, Wanganui, 1967.

Anglesey, the Marquess of, *A History of the British Cavalry 1816 to 1919, Volume 5, Egypt, Palestine and Syria, 1914 to 1919*, Leo Cooper, London, 1994.

Annabell, Major N., *Official History of the New Zealand Engineers During the Great War, 1914–1919*, Evans, Cobb & Sharpe, Wanganui, 1927.

Austin, Lieutenant Colonel W.S., *The Official History of the New Zealand Rifle Brigade (The Earl of Liverpool's Own)*, L.T. Watkins Ltd, Wellington, 1924.

Baker, P., *King and Country Call: New Zealanders, Conscription and the Great War*, Auckland University Press, Auckland, 1988.

Bean, C.E.W., *Anzac to Amiens: a Shorter History of the Australian Fighting Services in the First World War*, Australian War Memorial, Canberra, 1946.

Berrie, G.L., *Morale: a Story of Australian Light Horsemen*, Holland & Stephenson, Sydney, 1949.

Blackwell, F. and D.R. Douglas, *The Story of the 3rd Australian Light Horse Regiment*, Adelaide, 1950.

Bluett, A., *With Our Army in Palestine*, Andrew Melrose Ltd, London, 1919.

Bostock, H.P., *The Great Ride: the Diary of a Light Horse Brigade Scout, World War 1*, Artlook Books, Perth, 1982.

Bourne, Lieutenant Colonel G.H., *The History of the 2nd Light Horse Regiment, Australian Imperial Force, August 1914–April 1919*, John Burridge Military Antiques edition, Swanbourne, 1994.

Bourne, J., P. Liddle and I. Whitehead. (eds), *The Great World War 1914–45, Volume 1, Lightning Strikes Twice*, HarperCollins, London, 2001.

Bowman-Manifold, Major General Sir M.G.E., *An Outline of the Egypt and Palestine Campaigns, 1914 to 1918*, 4th edition, Institution of Royal Engineers, Chatham, 1928.

Boyack, N. and J. Tolerton, *In the Shadow of War: New Zealand Soldiers Talk about World War One and their Lives*, Penguin Books, Auckland, 1990.

Buckshee: a Pictorial Record of the Work of the New Zealand YMCA on Active Service, London, 1919.

Burton, O.E., *The Auckland Regiment: Being an Account of the Doings on Active Service of the First, Second and Third Battalions of the Auckland Regiment*, Whitcombe & Tombs, Auckland, 1922.

Carbery, Lieutenant Colonel A.D., *The New Zealand Medical Service in the Great War 1914–1918*, Whitcombe & Tombs, Auckland, 1924.

Cecil, H. and P.H. Liddle (eds), *Facing Armageddon: the First World War Experience*, Leo Cooper, London, 1996.

Cooper, J., *Animals in War: Valiant Horses, Courageous Dogs, and Other Unsung Animal Heroes*, Lyons Press, Guilford, 2002.

Crawford. J. (ed.), *No Better Death: the Great War Diaries of William G. Malone*, Reed Books, Auckland, 2005.

Crawford, J. and I. McGibbon (eds), *New Zealand's Great War: New Zealand, the Allies and the First World War*, Exisle Publishing, Auckland, 2007.

Drew, Lieutenant H.T.B. (ed.), *The War Effort of New Zealand: a Popular History*, Whitcombe & Tombs, Auckland, 1923.

Erickson, E.J., *Ordered to Die: a History of the Ottoman Army in the First World War*, Greenwood Press, London, 2001.

Falls, C., *Armageddon 1918: the Final Palestinian Campaign of World War 1*, University of Pennsylvania Press edition, Philadelphia, 2003.

Finkel, C., *Osman's Dream: the History of the Ottoman Empire*, Basic Books, New York, 2006.

Fox, F., *The History of the Royal Gloucestershire Hussars Yeomanry: the Great Cavalry Campaign in Palestine*, Philip Allen & Co., London, 1923.

Fromkin, D., *A Peace to End All Peace: the Fall of the Ottoman Empire and the Creation of the Modern Middle East*, Henry Holt, New York, 2001.

Gabriel, R.A. and K.S. Metz, *A History of Military Medicine, Volume 2, From the Renaissance through Modern Times*, Greenwood Press, New York, 1992.

Gammage, B., *The Broken Years: Australian Soldiers in the Great War*, Penguin Books, Harmondsworth, 1975.

Harper, B. (ed.), *Letters from Gunner 7/516 and Gunner 7/517*, Anchor Communications Ltd, Wellington, 1978.

Harper, G. (ed.), *Letters from the Battlefield: New Zealand Soldiers Write Home 1914-18*, HarperCollins, Auckland, 2001.

Haythornthwaite, P.J., *The World War One Source Book*, Arms and Armour Press, London, 1996.

Henderson, J. *Soldier Country*, Millwood Press, Wellington, 1978.

Hill, A.J., *Chauvel of the Light Horse: a Biography of General Sir Harry Chauvel, G.C.M.G., K.C.B.*, Melbourne University Press, Melbourne, 1978.

Holden, D., *The New Zealand Horseman*, A.H. & A.W. Reed, Wellington, 1967.

Horner, D.M., *The Commanders: Australian Military Leadership in the Twentieth Century*, George Allen & Unwin, Sydney, 1984.

Hughes, M., *Allenby and British Strategy in the Middle East 1917–1919*, Frank Cass, London, 1999.

Hughes, M. (ed.), *Allenby in Palestine: the Middle East Correspondence of Field Marshal Viscount Allenby June 1917–October 1919*, Sutton Publishing Ltd/Army Records Society, Thrupp, 2004.

Idriess, I., *The Desert Column: Leaves from the Diary of an Australian Trooper in Gallipoli, Sinai and Palestine*, Angus & Robertson, Sydney, 2nd edition, 1951.

James, L., *Imperial Warrior: the Life and Times of Field Marshal Viscount Allenby 1861–1936*, Weidenfeld & Nicolson, London, 1993.

Keogh, Colonel E.G., *Suez to Aleppo*, Wilke & Co., Melbourne, 1954.

The Kia Ora Coo-ee: the Magazine for the Anzacs in the Middle East 1918, facsimile edition, Cornstalk Publishing, Australia, 1981.

King, M., *New Zealanders at War*, Heinemann, Auckland, 1981.

Kinloch, T., *Echoes of Gallipoli: in the Words of New Zealand's Mounted Riflemen*, Exisle Publishing, Auckland, 2005.

Kress von Kressenstein, F., *Mit den Türken zum Suezkanal*, Dorhut-Derlag Otto Schlegel, Berlin, 1938.

Liddell Hart, B.H. *History of the First World War*, Cassell edition, London, 1970.

_____*Strategy*, 2nd revised edition, Penguin Group, New York, 1991.

Liman von Sanders, O., *Five Years in Turkey*, The United States Naval Institute, Annapolis, 1927.

Luxford, Major J.H., *With the Machine Gunners in France and Palestine*, Whitcombe & Tombs, Auckland, 1923.

Lyttelton, C.G., *The Yeomanry Cavalry of Worcestershire 1914–1922*, Mark & Mordy Ltd, Stowbridge, 1926.

Mackenzie, C.N. (ed.), *Chronicles of the NZEF*, NZ Contingent Association, London, 1917–1919.

Massey, W.T. *The Desert Campaigns*, G.P. Putnam, New York, 1918.

_____*How Jerusalem was Won: being the Record of Allenby's Campaign in Palestine*, Constable & Co. Ltd, London, 1919.

McGibbon, I. (ed.), *The Oxford Companion to New Zealand Military History*, Oxford University Press, Auckland, 2000.

Millen, J., *Salute to Service: a History of the Royal New Zealand Corps of Transport and its Predecessors, 1860–1996*, Victoria University Press, Wellington, 1997.

Moore, Lieutenant A.B., *The Mounted Riflemen in Sinai and Palestine: the Story of New Zealand's Crusaders*, Whitcombe & Tombs, Dunedin, 1920.

Murray, T., *A Collection of Memories: Recollections of Otau, Ness Valley, Clevedon and World War One*, Fraser Murray, Clevedon, 1989.

Nicol, Sergeant C.G, *The Story of Two Campaigns: Official War History of the Auckland Mounted Rifles Regiment, 1914–1919*, Wilson & Horton, Auckland, 1931.

Olden, Lieutenant Colonel A.C.N., *Westralian Cavalry in the War: the Story of the Tenth Light Horse Regiment, AIF, in the Great War, 1914–1918*, Melbourne, 1921.

O'Sullivan, B. and M., *New Zealand Army Personal Equipment, 1910–1945*, Willson Scott Publishing Ltd, Christchurch, 2005.

Phillips, J., N. Boyack and E.P. Malone (eds), *The Great Adventure: New Zealand Soldiers Describe the First World War*, Allen & Unwin, Wellington, 1988.

Powles, Lieutenant Colonel C.G., *The New Zealanders in Sinai and Palestine*, Whitcombe & Tombs, Wellington, 1922.

Powles, Colonel C.G. (ed.) and Officers of the Regiment, *The History of the Canterbury Mounted Rifles, 1914–1919*, Whitcombe & Tombs, Auckland, 1928.

Preston, Lieutenant Colonel the Honourable R.M.P., *The Desert Mounted Corps: an Account of the Cavalry Operations in Palestine and Syria 1917–1918*, Constable & Co. Ltd, London, 1921.

Pugsley, C.*On the Fringe of Hell: New Zealanders and Military Discipline in the First World War*, Hodder & Stoughton, Auckland, 1991.

_____*The Anzac Experience: New Zealand, Australia and Empire in the First World War*, Reed Books, Auckland, 2004.

Reid, F., *The Fighting Cameliers*, Angus & Robertson Ltd., Sydney, 1934.

Richardson, Lieutenant Colonel J.D., *The History of the 7th Light Horse Regiment, AIF*, Radcliffe Press, Sydney, 1923.

Robertson, J., *With the Cameliers in Palestine*, A.H. & A.W. Reed, Wellington, 1938.

Sheffy, Y., *British Military Intelligence in the Palestine Campaign 1914–1918*, Frank Cass, London, 1998.

Scripture Gift Mission and Naval and Military Bible Society, *The New Testament of Our Lord and Saviour Jesus Christ*, London, 1914.

Stanbrook, Sergeant G.L. (ed.), *Featherston Military Training Camp: the Record of a Remarkable Achievement*, Brett Publishing and Printing Co., Auckland, 1917.

Stevens, K.M., *Maungatapere: a History and Reminiscence*, Whangarei Advocate, 1973.

Stewart, Colonel H., *The New Zealand Division 1916–1919: a Popular History based on Official Records*, Whitcombe & Tombs, Wellington, 1921.

Strachan, H., *The First World War, Volume 1, To Arms*, Oxford University Press, Oxford, 2001.

Sykes, Reverend H., *A Soldier's Handbook, Palestine and Jerusalem: Salient Points in the Geography, History and Present-Day Life of the Holy Land*, Hodder & Stoughton, London, 1917.

Teichman, Captain O., *The Diary of a Yeomanry Medical Officer*, T. Fisher Unwin Ltd, London, 1921.

Thomas, M. and C. Lord, *New Zealand Army Distinguishing Patches, 1911–1991*, Part 1, Wellington, 1995.

Thompson, Lieutenant Colonel R.R., *The Fifty Second (Lowland) Division, 1914-1918*, Jackson & Co., Glasgow, 1923.

The Times History of the War, Volume 13, The Times, London, 1917.

Tolerton, J., *Ettie: a Life of Ettie Rout*, Penguin Books, Auckland, 1992.

Tucker, S.C. (ed.), *The Encyclopedia of World War 1, Volumes 1 to 5*, ABC CLIO, Santa Barbara, 2005.

Tuke, R.C., *Letters to Trixie: a Collection of Letters Written 1914–1919, Predominantly Penned by Robert Clive Tuke*, Te Rau Herald Print, Gisborne, 1997.

Wavell, Lieutenant General Sir A.P., *The Palestine Campaigns*, Constable, London, 3rd edition, 1941.

Wavell, General Sir A., *Allenby: a Study in Greatness, The Biography of Field Marshal Viscount Allenby of Megiddo and Felixstowe, GCB, GCMG*, Oxford University Press, New York, 1941.

Wilkie, Major A.H., *Official War History of the Wellington Mounted Rifles Regiment, 1914–1919*, Whitcombe & Tombs, Auckland, 1924.

Wilson, J., *Lawrence of Arabia: the Authorized Biography of T.E. Lawrence*, Atheneum, New York, 1990.

Wilson, Brigadier General L.C. and Captain H. Wetherell, *History of the Fifth Light Horse Regiment (Australian Imperial Force), from 1914 to October 1917, and from October 1917 to June 1919*, Motor Press of Australia, Sydney, 1926.

Wilson, R.H., *Palestine 1917*, Costello, Tunbridge Wells, 1987.

Woodward, D.R., *Hell in the Holy Land: World War 1 in the Middle East*, University Press of Kentucky, 2006.

Young, Lieutenant Colonel J., *With the 52nd (Lowland) Division in Three Continents*, W. Green & Son Ltd, Edinburgh, 1920.

Articles

Anon, 'The Surafend Incident: Why Allenby Ignored the Anzacs, a Trooper's Story', *Quick March*, 10 January 1920, pp. 63–4.

Browne, Lieutenant Colonel J.G., 'Operations of the Mounted Troops of the Egyptian Expeditionary Forces', *Cavalry Journal*, Volume 2, 1921, pp. 223–44.

Bruce, A., 'Strange Events at Ziza: Aussies Protected Turks against Allies', *Reveille*, Volume 31, 1 April 1958, pp. 23–4.

Foster, Lieutenant Colonel W.J., 'Operations of the Mounted Troops of the Egyptian Expeditionary Forces', *Cavalry Journal*, Volume 2, 1921, pp. 3–32, 127–61.

Hopkins, Major General R., 'Chaytor's Force: a Personal Account', *Australian Defence Force Journal*, Number 13, November/December 1978, pp. 29–33.

Kress von Kressenstein, Baron F., 'The Campaign in Palestine from the Enemy's Side' (translation), *Journal of the Royal United Services Institute*, Volume 67, 1922, pp. 503–13.

Meldrum, Brigadier General W., 'Impressions of Romani', *Reveille*, 1 August 1933, pp. 20–1, 46–7.

Mousa, S., 'Unrest in Egypt', *Purnell's History of the First World War*, pp. 3, 325–8, 329.

Muhlmann, C., 'Battle of Romani: German Staff Officer's Record', *Reveille*, 1 March 1938, pp.14–16.

Newell, J.Q.C., 'Learning the Hard Way: Allenby in Egypt and Palestine, 1917–19', *Journal of Strategic Studies*, Volume 14, September 1991, pp. 363–87.

Osborne, Lieutenant Colonel R., 'Operations of the Mounted Troops of the Egyptian Expeditionary Force', *Cavalry Journal*, Volume 12, 1922, pp. 41–58, 113–42, 344–74 ; Volume 13, 1923, pp. 138–56.

Powles, Colonel C.G., 'Major-General Sir Edward Chaytor; a New Zealand Appreciation', *Reveille*, 1 September 1939, pp.10, 15.

Robertson, Major H.C.H., 'The 10th Australian Light Horse Attack at Magdhaba, 23rd December 1916', *Cavalry Journal*, Volume 25, 1935, pp. 228–33.

Robertson, Lieutenant Colonel H.C.H., 'The N.Z.'s at Rafa', *Reveille*, 1 April 1938, p. 42.

Sheffy, Y, 'The Origins of the British Breakthrough into South Palestine: the ANZAC Raid on the Ottoman Railway, 1917', *Journal of Strategic Studies*, Volume 22, Number1, March 1999, pp. 124–47.

_____'The Chemical Dimension of the Gallipoli Campaign: Introducing Chemical Warfare to the Middle East', *War in History*, Volume 12, Number 3, July 2005, pp. 278–317.

Skander Bey, 'The Battles of Es Salt, Amman and Jordan from Turkish Sources', *Journal of the Royal United Services Institute*, Volume 69, 1924, pp. 334–43, 488–98.

Thalacker, Lieutenant, 'The Hijaz Railway 1918', *The Journal of the T.E. Lawrence Society*, Volume 12, Spring 2003, pp. 15–33.

Wilson, Brigadier General L.C., 'From Dueidar to Salmana', *Reveille*, 1 August 1933, p. 9.

Newspapers
New Zealand Herald, 1919.
The Times, 19 May 1964.

Internet Material
Cenotaph Database, Auckland War Memorial Museum, URL: http://www.aucklandmuseum.com/
Commonwealth War Graves Commission (CWGC) fact sheets, 2001, URL: http://www.cwgc.org/cwgc/task.htm
Dictionary of New Zealand Biography, URL: http://www.dnzb.govt.nz
Mallett, R., *The Interplay between Technology, Tactics and Organisation in the First AIF*, University of New South Wales Australian Defence Forces Academy, 1999, URL: http://www.unsw.adfa.edu.au/~rmallett/
Shaine, G., *Action of Ayun Kara*, URL: http://anzac-israel.com
War Memories of Robert Ellwood, URL: http://www.jcu.edu.au/aff/history/net_resources/ellwood/016.html

Discussion Forums:
The Australian Light Horse Association Forum, URL: http://www.lighthorse.org.au/forum
The Great War Forum, URL: http://1914-1918.invisionzone.com/forums/index
The New Zealand Mounted Rifles Association Forum, URL: http://www.nzmr.org/
The UP Forum, URL: http://www.militaryhorse.org/forum/forum/

Other
New Zealand Society of Genealogists Inc., *New Zealand WW1 Service Personnel and Reserves Index*, Version 2, Auckland.

Notes

Abbreviations

ANZ	Archives New Zealand, Wellington.
ATL	Alexander Turnbull Library, National Library of New Zealand, Wellington.
AWM	Australian War Memorial, Canberra.
AWMML	Auckland War Memorial Museum Library, Auckland.
IWM	Imperial War Museum, London.
KM	Kauri Museum, Matakohe, Northland.
KMARL	Kippenberger Military Archives and Research Library, Waiouru.
LHCMA	Liddell Hart Centre for Military Archives, King's College, London.
OHC	Oral History Centre, Alexander Turnbull Library, Wellington.

Author's note

1. War Diaries vary widely in content, reliability and accuracy. Glyn Harper notes that 'there is a tendency … to focus on positive events. Unit loyalty, and the scrutiny of commanding officers, may induce diary compilers to gloss over unit failures…. Censorship by higher authority is not unknown, with sections of unit diaries blacked out or removed altogether.' Harper, G., in McGibbon, I. (ed.), *The Oxford Companion to New Zealand Military History*, Oxford University Press, Auckland, 2000, p. 548.
2. Fred Sterling wrote in his diary that 'the descriptions of our war life out here have had nothing added but much left out'. Diary entry dated 20 May 1918, *The Wartime Diary of Sgt F. Sterling, 13291, 11th NAMR, 13th Reinforcement, New Zealand Expeditionary Force, 29th May 1916 to 9th September 1919*, KM.
3. Even the *Oxford Companion to Military History* errs by discussing the charge of 'Australian and New Zealand Light Horse' at Beersheba, and by implying that the word 'Anzac' is synonymous with 'Australian'. Holmes, R., (ed.), *The Oxford Companion to Military History*, Oxford University Press, Oxford, 2001, pp. 188, 62–3.
4. The old Sinai battlefields are not usually accessible to foreigners, and those in Israel and Jordan are not always easy to find. I was unable to visit the battlefields and CWGC cemeteries in the Gaza Strip and the West Bank, or the cemeteries in Haifa, Damascus and Beirut.
5. Nearly all the available records are from men who fought in the combat units. I found little on record from New Zealanders in the engineer, signals, veterinary, medical and logistics units that supported the combat regiments.
6. The government in Istanbul considered itself to be Turkish, not Ottoman. Anatolian Turks made up the majority of the soldiers in the Turkish Army and they had the reputation of being the best fighters. I have usually spelt place names as they are written in the British official history. Although current spellings may differ slightly, readers looking for the locations on modern maps should have little difficulty in finding them. Some statistics quoted in this book differ slightly from those in my first book. The additional two years of research should, I hope, make the statistics in this book more accurate.

Introduction

1. McNeur, A., letter dated 6 Aug 1918, MS-Papers-4108, ATL.
2. See Moore, Lieutenant A.B., *A Night Stunt of the Auckland Mounted Rifles during the final big operations in Palestine immediately preceding the armistice with Turkey*, 80-057, ATL. Sterling diary entries dated 24 and 25 Sep 1918; Powles, Lieutenant Colonel C.G., *The New Zealanders in Sinai and Palestine*, Whitcombe & Tombs, Wellington, 1922, pp. 249–50.
3. Branch of the Chief of the General Staff, *New Zealand Expeditionary Force, its Provision and Maintenance*, Government Printer, Wellington, 1919, pp. 18, 58.

4. Not included are casualties in the Otago Mounted Rifles (OMR) Regiment, which was attached to the NZMR Brigade on Gallipoli. This part of the NZMR Brigade's story is told in my first book, *Echoes of Gallipoli: in the Words of New Zealand's Mounted Riflemen*, Exisle Publishing, Auckland, 2005.

5. At the time of writing, the two CWGC cemeteries in the Gaza Strip are inaccessible to sensible tourists, but New Zealanders are free to visit the cemeteries in Cairo, Alexandria, Port Said, Suez, Ismailia, Kantara, Beersheba, Jerusalem, Ramleh, Haifa, Beirut and Damascus. The CWGC cemeteries in Egypt also contain the graves of many Gallipoli casualties.

6. Findlay, Lieutenant-Colonel J., in Moore, Lieutenant A.B., *The Mounted Riflemen in Sinai and Palestine: the Story of New Zealand's Crusaders*, Whitcombe & Tombs, Dunedin, 1920, p. 5.

7. Even the graves of long-dead soldiers are not safe from the present troubles in the Middle East. In November 2006 several CWGC headstones and memorials in the Gaza War Cemetery were reportedly destroyed or damaged by Israeli artillery and helicopter fire or by bulldozers.

8. Bellis, C., 'The Role of the Horse in the Sinai and Palestine Campaign during the 1914–18 War', in Holden, D., *The New Zealand Horseman*, A.H. & A.W. Reed, Wellington, 1967, p. 56.

Prologue

1. The Turkish Empire in 1914 encompassed the modern nations of Turkey, Israel, Lebanon, Jordan, Kuwait, Egypt and Syria, and parts of Iraq, Saudi Arabia and Yemen. The British occupied Egypt in 1882 over concerns about international access to the Suez Canal.

2. Erickson, E.J., *Ordered to Die: a History of the Ottoman Army in the First World War*, Greenwood Press, London, 2001, pp. 10, 15; Haythornthwaite, P.J., *The World War One Source Book*, Arms and Armour Press, London, 1996, pp. 299–305.

3. Kaiser Wilhelm II saw Turkey as a useful ally in the event of a war with Russia. Thirteen hundred km of railway track were laid between Damascus and Medina by 1908, but the last 400 km to Mecca were never completed. Two sections of the Hejaz Railway remain in operation today. Liman became a Marshal in the Turkish Army.

4. The Germans hoped that Turkey would distract the Russians and the British, giving Germany time to deal with France. It would be even better if the caliph declared a Holy War against the Allies. A group of young, ambitious, secular nationalists, the Young Turks, led Turkey's ruling Committee of Union and Progress (CUP).

5. Finkel, C., *Osman's Dream: the History of the Ottoman Empire*, Basic Books, New York, 2006, p. 529.

6. Strachan, H., *The First World War, Volume 1, To Arms*, Oxford University Press, Oxford, 2001, p. 683.

7. Zurcher, E., 'Little Mehmet in the Desert: the Ottoman Soldier's Experience', in Cecil, H. and P.H. Liddle (eds), *Facing Armageddon: the First World War Experience*, Leo Cooper, London, 1996, p. 235; Maunsell, Colonel E.B., quoted in Anglesey, the Marquess of, *A History of the British Cavalry 1816 to 1919, Volume 5, Egypt, Palestine and Syria, 1914 to 1919*, Leo Cooper, London, 1994, p. 21.

8. Haythornthwaite, pp.301–04.

9. Aaronsohn, A., *With the Turks in Palestine*, 1st World Library Literary Society edition, Fairfield, 2004, pp. 42–3.

10. See *Echoes of Gallipoli*, pp. 64–70.

11. New Zealand infantrymen took part in the battle, but the mounted riflemen did not.

12. Most Turkish units were withdrawn from Syria in 1915 to reinforce the Gallipoli front, but Kress launched several small and ineffective raids against the Suez Canal throughout the year.

13. After being wounded in South Africa, Chaytor was medically downgraded in 1904 by a medical board that decided he was 'totally incapacitated' and 'not fit for active service'. Eight years later he was regraded as 'fit for active service'. Between 1902 and 1914, Chaytor held a number of command and staff appointments and was the first New Zealander to attend the prestigious Camberley Staff College course in England. Chaytor File, Base Records, HQ New Zealand Defence Force, Wellington.

14. When Brigadier General Russell left the NZMR Brigade, General Godley offered the command to Chaytor, saying that 'it would give you a definite and good command sooner than having to wait for the formation of the Rifle Brigade, and I want you to have the first brigade that is going and likely to be in action'. WA Series 252/6, Semi-Official Letters by Godley, ANZ.

15. Wicksteed, M., 'Chaytor, Edward Walter Clervaux 1868–1939', in *Dictionary of New Zealand Biography*, updated 7 Apr 2006, URL: http://www.dnzb.govt.nz; Powles, Colonel C.G., 'Major-General Sir Edward Chaytor: a New Zealand Appreciation,' *Reveille*, 1 Sep 1939, p. 10.

16. Mackesy was reputedly the oldest New Zealander on Gallipoli. He was sent back to Egypt after a few weeks on the peninsula to look after the reinforcements and horses. In 1917 he took command of the New Zealand training units in Egypt. Mackesy was disappointed not to receive the command of the NZMR Brigade after Chaytor's promotion. AWMM Cenotaph Database record; Green, D., 'Mackesy, Charles Ernest Randolph 1861–1925', *Dictionary of New Zealand Biography*, updated 7 Apr 2006, URL: http://www.dnzb.govt.nz

17. Meldrum was a good cricketer and rugby player at provincial level and the New Zealand chess champion in 1896. He was believed to be the second-oldest New Zealander on Gallipoli, after Mackesy. Godley described Meldrum as 'exceptionally good … cool and fearless in the hottest of action [on Gallipoli]'. Meldrum died in 1964, at the age of 98. Grover, R., 'Meldrum, William 1865–1964', *Dictionary of New Zealand Biography*, updated 7 Apr 2006, URL: http://www.dnzb.govt.nz; AWMM Cenotaph Database record; letter dated 6 Sep 1916, WA Series 252/6, Semi-Official Letters by Godley, ANZ.

18. Milnes, D.J., 'Imperial Soldiers? The New Zealand Mounted Rifles Brigade in Sinai and Palestine 1916–1919', thesis for Master of Arts (History), University of Otago, 1999, p. 127.

19. War Office, *Field Service Regulations, Part 2, Organization and Administration*, HMSO, London, 1909, p. 54; *NZEF Provision and Maintenance*, p. 7; Allen Papers, AD Series 1, ANZ; Baker, P., *King and Country Call: New Zealanders, Conscription and the Great War*, Auckland University Press, Auckland, 1988, p. 55; McGibbon, p.118.

20. Half of the horses died of wounds, disease, overwork or exposure. Although this death toll is dreadful, it was a vast improvement over the South African War (1899–1902), in which more than 90% of the horses died. Over 8000 horses went to South Africa from New Zealand; only one returned. Efficient military remount and veterinary services were the main reason behind the improved survival rates for horses during the First World War. Cooper, J., *Animals in War: Valiant Horses, Courageous Dogs and Other Unsung Animal Heroes*, Lyons Press edition, Guilford, 2002, pp. 15, 21; Tucker, S.C. (ed.), *The Encyclopedia of World War 1*, (Volume 1), ABC CLIO, Santa Barbara, 2005, p. 103.

21. A 'hand' is 10 cm; a 15.2 hand horse was 1.55 m tall, measured at the shoulder. Fifty thousand of New Zealand's 400,000 horses were considered suitable for war use. Defence Council Report dated 14 Oct 1912, *Annual Reports on the Defence Forces of New Zealand*, 1910–1922, Government Printer, Wellington, p. 35; War Office, *Remount Regulations*, HMSO, London, 1913; War Office, *Manual of Horsemastership, Equitation and Driving*, HMSO, London, 1929, p. 138; War Office, *Animal Management*, HMSO, London, 1908, pp. 29–30.

22. Remount Depot horses were used to train reinforcements in New Zealand. New Zealand and Australian remounts were handled in Egypt by the Australian Remount Squadron at Heliopolis (later at Moascar). The depot prepared horses for field conditions by getting them used to hard rations and limited water and by regularly exercising them. At times, they did not perform their job to the satisfaction of the mounted brigades. Some remounts arrived unbroken, unacclimatised, not used to hard feed, too small or weak, unsafe to ride or unshod. Some horses that had been evacuated with injuries or lameness months before turned up again as remounts with exactly the same problems. Veterinarian Major John Stafford wished that some of the horse buyers could be forced to ride the 'angular brutes' they bought for six months, in order to make them more careful in their selections. WA Series 1/3, XFE 566, Remounts Supplied to NZMR Brigade and Training Regiment for Quarters Ending Jan/March and April/June 1917, ANZ; Stafford, 'The Thoroughbred, Racing and Remounts', in Powles, Colonel C.G. (ed.), and Officers of the Regiment, *The History of the Canterbury Mounted Rifles 1914–1919*, Whitcombe & Tombs, Auckland, 1928, p. 256; Moore, p. 45.

23. It could have been worse: New Zealand horses in the Middle East were seldom required to drag themselves through mud and shell holes, and they never suffered the agonies of mustard gas blisters on their delicate skin or eyes or choked on poisonous chlorine gas. War Office, *Field Service Pocket Book, 1914 (Reprinted with Amendments, 1916)*, HMSO, London, 1916, pp. 206–9; *Manual of Horsemastership, Equitation and Driving*, pp. 39–48.

24. When horses were discharged from a veterinary hospital or convalescent depot, they were sent to the nearest remount depot for subsequent reissue. Their former riders did not usually get them back.

25. *Animal Management*, p. 304.

26. About 30 minutes twice daily was the minimum requirement, but many men spent much longer grooming their animals. Two fitted horseshoes were carried on the saddle and another set was carried in the regimental transport wagons. *Manual of Horsemastership, Equitation and Driving*, pp. 13–14, 21–2.

27. Dhoura is the Egyptian name for millet, berseem is a type of fresh green fodder, and tibbin is chopped barley straw. The authorised daily ration at first was 4–5 kg of barley and 680 grams of bran, but this was soon increased to 5.5 kg of barley, the same of hay, 30 g of salt and 11 kg of compressed rations (pressed oats, beans, maize, bran, or chaff). Blenkinsop, Major General Sir L.J. and Lieutenant Colonel J.W. Rainey, *History*

of the Great War Based on Official Documents, Veterinary Services, HMSO, London, 1925, pp. 167–8; *Manual of Horsemastership, Equitation and Driving*, pp. 5–6; Cooper, p. 60.

28. Few troops or squadrons were at full strength except at the beginning of an operation. After taking out horse holders and other details, a troop could put about 20 men into a firing line. A small administrative HQ in Cairo looked after postings, reinforcements, casualty notifications, pay and postal arrangements for the NZEF in the Middle East (the NZMR Brigade, divisional troops, training units, two New Zealand camel companies, several Convalescent Homes, a Rarotongan labour force and a Pack Wireless Troop in Mesopotamia). It was also responsible for keeping New Zealand informed of NZEF activities in the Middle East, for monitoring New Zealanders in hospital or prison and for arranging the return to New Zealand of men who were discharged or dismissed from the NZEF.

29. The No. 3 (horse holder) was usually an older man, a man recently returned from hospital and not yet fully fit, or a new reinforcement.

30. Regiments were usually allocated local interpreters and a number of local children were 'employed' for menial duties. In August 1917, a Divisional Train (supply unit) was formed in the Anzac Mounted Division. It consisted of a HQ Company, No. 2 and No. 4 companies (Australian) and No. 3 Company (New Zealand). AWM4, 1/61/18, Unit War Diaries 1914-18 War, Administrative Staff, HQ Anzac Mounted Division War Diary, AWM.

31. Adapted from Powles, p. 5.

32. In military terminology, an ambulance was a medical unit, not a vehicle. Sand carts needed up to six horses to move two stretcher cases. The camel section comprised 140 camels and 81 handlers from the Egyptian Labour Corps (ELC). Davidson, A.M., *The New Zealand Mounted Field Ambulance: a History of its Activities from the Outbreak of the Great War to the Conclusion of the Sinai Campaign, August 4 1914–January 12 1917*, University of Otago, 1938, pp. 4, 8, 33–5; Carbery, Lieutenant Colonel A.D., *The New Zealand Medical Service in the Great War 1914–1918*, Whitcombe & Tombs, Auckland, 1924, p. 450.

33. In the meantime, Chaytor formed an ad hoc Pioneer Troop, which did what it could with shovels, axes and sandbags. Smith, M., unpublished manuscript on Major-General Sir E.W.C. Chaytor; WA 46/1, War Diary of New Zealand Engineer Field Troop, ANZ.

34. A heliograph was a tripod-mounted arrangement of moveable mirrors which used reflected sunlight to transmit messages.

35. Powles, p. 12. Mounted brigades were normally supported by lighter 13-pounder guns and this became standard in the EEF mounted divisions later in the war. Shrapnel shells, which burst in the air above the target and lashed it with hundreds of small metal balls, were deadly against unprotected men and horses, but useless against dug-in troops and fortifications, and little better at cutting barbed wire.

36. War Office, *Yeomanry and Mounted Rifles Training, Parts 1 and 2*, 1912, HMSO, London. Mounted infantry were different again. They were fully trained infantrymen who used horses or camels only to move around the battlefield. They always fought on foot and did not conduct security or reconnaissance operations. Mounted infantry units had disappeared from the British Army by 1914.

37. By August 1917, each mounted rifleman carried up to 280 rounds of rifle ammunition on his body or on the horse (90 rounds in each of two bandoliers, 40 in the saddle wallets and 60 in pouches on the belt). A regimental reserve of 24,000 rounds was maintained and the brigade supply section carried another 30,000 rounds. Each regiment also carried four boxes of hand grenades. Non-combatant specialists such as signallers often used rifle buckets. Wood, Lieutenant Colonel P., 'Tackling the Turk: an Examination of Tactics Employed by the New Zealand Mounted Rifles Brigade during the Sinai-Palestine Campaign of World War I', thesis for Master of Philosophy, Massey University, 2004, p. 36; O'Sullivan, B. and M., *New Zealand Army Personal Equipment 1910–1945*, Willson Scott Publishing Ltd, Christchurch, 2005, pp. 81–3.

38. The Vickers Mark I machine gun, with a full water jacket, weighed about 18 kg. Its tripod weighed another 23 kg, and a box of belted .303 inch ammunition (250 rounds) weighed 10 kg (total weight 51 kg). Each gun crew carried 7500 rounds of ammunition and a reserve of 8,000 rounds per gun was held in reserve. Wood, *Tackling the Turk*, p. 37.

39. On 29 Mar 1917, all troops in the Anzac Mounted Division were ordered to wear felt slouch hats instead of Wolseley helmets. AWM4, 1/61/15, HQ Anzac Mounted Division War Diary, AWM.

40. Reinforcements usually arrived in Egypt wearing distinctive reinforcement badges (see endpapers), but these were replaced by regimental badges when the men were sent to the brigade. Non-regimental units, such as the NZMGS, usually wore their own badges. From August 1916, a man who had been wounded was entitled to wear a gold braid wound stripe on the lower left sleeve of his jacket. From September 1918, embroidered service chevrons (one per year of service: red for 1914, blue for 1915 and onwards) were

allowed to be worn on the lower right sleeve. Thomas, M., and Lord, C., *New Zealand Army Distinguishing Patches 1911–1991*, Part 1, Wellington, 1995, p. 26.

41. McMillan, J., *Forty Thousand Horsemen: Being the Memoirs of 7/1322 Cpl Jim McMillan, Canterbury Mounted Rifles, First NZEF, on Service in Gallipoli and Palestine, WW1*, property of C.B. McMillan and family, Whangarei, pp. 266–7.

42. Officers usually used the Saddle, Officer, Mark IV. Sand muzzles were used to stop the horses eating sand. The 1912 UP Saddle, with hinged arches, was also in service, but relatively few New Zealanders used it. *Field Service Pocket Book*, p. 184. With such heavy weights on the horses, the riders were encouraged to dismount and walk whenever possible. War Office, *Yeomanry and Mounted Rifles Training, Parts 1 and 2*, p. 45.

43. Metal chains were sometimes used instead of head-ropes.

Chapter 1: Return from Gallipoli

1. The Anzac infantry battalions moved by rail to camps at Moascar and Tel el Kebir, close to the Suez Canal.

2. Wilkie, Major A.H., *Official War History of the Wellington Mounted Rifles Regiment, 1914–1919*, Whitcombe & Tombs, Auckland, 1924, p. 77; Mitchell, J.H., interview, OHInt 0006/56, OHC.

3. Weak riders were posted to regimental 'details squadrons' for extra training, while hopeless cases were transferred to the infantry. Nearly all of the 2100 horses that had reached Egypt with the brigade in December 1914 were still alive and another 1400 remounts had arrived from New Zealand during 1915. Remount shipments were suspended between June 1915 and Jan 1916. Many of the NZMR remounts went to France with the New Zealand Division. Powles, *CMR*, pp. 80–3; WA Series 40/1, HQ NZMR Brigade War Diary, ANZ; *NZEF Provision and Maintenance*, pp. 58–9; McKay, E.C.M., 'The Years Unfold: Memoirs', 1998.31, KMARL, p. 96.

4. The extreme heat of the Egyptian summer, when shade temperatures routinely exceeded 40°C, was still months away. Carruthers, W.G., letter dated 10 Jan 1916, in Phillips, J., N. Boyack and E.P. Malone (eds), *The Great Adventure: New Zealand Soldiers Describe the First World War*, Allen & Unwin, Wellington, 1988, p. 266; Powles, p. 3.

5. The Turkish railway and a metal road had reached the Egyptian border near Beersheba by May 1916. Britain ruled half of the world's Muslims, including 70 million in India. Macmunn, Lieutenant General Sir G. and Captain C. Falls, *Military Operations, Egypt and Palestine, from the Outbreak of War with Germany to June 1917*, HMSO, London, 1928, pp. 83, 90.

6. WA Series 252/9, Letters of General Sir William Birdwood, Commanding 1 AIF and 1 ANZAC Corps and General Sir Alexander Godley, Commanding 1 NZEF, 1915, ANZ.

7. Cemal had an excessively high opinion of his own military ability.

8. Horses will usually drink water with a salt content of up to 8000–9000 parts per million, but unless they are carefully introduced to this water, they will quickly lose condition. Blenkinsop and Rainey, p. 139.

9. Sabkhet means 'salt lake' or 'marsh'. This one is named after the Crusader King Baldwin I. The Darb el Sultani had been an invasion route for thousands of years. Egyptians, Babylonians, Assyrians, Persians, Greeks, Romans, Crusaders, Saracens, Napoleon Bonaparte's French army and Israelis all used it. The second route, which passed through the central highlands from Kossaima to the Great Bitter Lake, was passable for wheeled transport and water was found in rock cisterns that filled up during the winter rainy season. This was the main route used by the Turks in their unsuccessful attack on the Suez Canal in February 1915. The most southerly route crossed the peninsula from Aqaba to Suez via Nekhl. It had limited capacity even for camels, and was impassable for wheeled vehicles.

10. Instructions from the Secretary of State for War to Lieutenant General Sir A. Murray, KCB, appointed General Officer Commanding in Chief, Mediterranean Force, dated 29 Dec 1915, quoted in Macmunn and Falls, p.99. The EEF was created from a merger of the MEF with base units in Egypt. Lieutenant General Maxwell effectively removed the Senussi threat by conducting a successful pre-emptive campaign in the Western Desert in late 1915 and early 1916. The NZMR Brigade was not involved. By July 1916 General Murray had transferred nearly a quarter of a million troops to Europe. All he had left were his mounted brigades (which were not needed in France) and four British Territorial Army infantry divisions.

11. General Murray hedged his bets by emptying the water cisterns and pools along the central route at Jifjaffa and Moiya Harab, and by placing a sizeable force at Suez to deter any Turkish advance by the southern route. This allowed him to concentrate most of his troops on the coastal route.

12. Despite British promises that the Egyptian people would not be called upon to take part in the war, thousands of them were used as camel drivers in the Camel Transport Corps (CTC) or as labourers in the Egyptian

Labour Corps (ELC). This broken promise would have serious consequences after the war.

13. Camels were used to carry food, water and ammunition, and to evacuate casualties. The CTC was formed to carry out these essential roles for the EEF. It was never possible for camels to carry enough drinking water for the horses (each of which consumed 25–35 litres every day), so local water was the only option for them.

14. The Austro-German force was named Pasha 1. Kress von Kressenstein, Baron, 'The Campaign in Palestine from the Enemy's Side' (translation), *Journal of the Royal United Services Institute*, Volume 67, 1922, p. 505.

15. McCarroll, J.N., diary entry dated 24 Jan 1916, KM; Doherty, P.G., diary entry dated 23 Jan 1916, 1991.2000, KMARL; Peed, E.S., diary entry dated 27 Jan 1916, property of Peed family, Taihape; Andrews, T., *Kiwi Trooper: the Story of Queen Alexandra's Own*, Wanganui Chronicle, Wanganui, 1967, p. 138.

16. Peed diary entry dated 25 Jan 1916; WA Series 252/6, Semi-Official Letters by Godley, ANZ; WA Series 40/1, HQ NZMR Brigade War Diary, ANZ.

17. Peed diary entry dated 18 Feb 1916; Nicol, Sergeant C.G., *The Story of Two Campaigns: Official War History of the Auckland Mounted Rifles Regiment, 1914–1919*, Wilson & Horton, Auckland, 1931, pp. 96–7.

18. Burton, O.E., *The Auckland Regiment: Being an Account of the Doings on Active Service of the First, Second and Third Battalions of the Auckland Regiment*, Whitcombe & Tombs, Auckland, 1922, pp. 88–9.

19. Alexander Godley commanded the NZEF on Gallipoli in 1915. He was gifted organiser and administrator, but a less-capable tactical commander. A proposal to combine the two corps and the Anzac mounted brigades to form an 'Australian and New Zealand Army' for service in France was rejected in London. General Murray supported the idea but wanted to retain all the mounted troops in Egypt. Bean, C.E.W., *The Official History of Australia in the War of 1914–1918, Volume 3, The Australian Imperial Force in France 1916*, 6th edition, Angus & Robertson, Sydney, 1938, pp. 35–9.

20. The number of men transferred from the NZMR seems high, but the following references suggest that it is probably correct. A memo from HQ NZ Division to HQ 1st ANZAC Corps dated 4 Mar 1916 lists 41 officers (seven from the AMR, 14 from the WMR, and 20 from the CMR) who were transferred from the NZMR Brigade to artillery and infantry units, and Guy Powles lists 19 CMR officers who transferred to other units. WA Series 2 Item 1 Box 2 Item 14/3, ANZ; Powles, *CMR*, p. 86; Studholme, Lieutenant Colonel J., *Records of Personnel Services During the War of Officers, Nurses and First Class Warrant Officers, and Other Facts Relating to the N.Z.E.F., Unofficial but Compiled from Official Sources*, Government Printer, Wellington, 1928, pp. 16–17; Powles, p. 7.

21. Harper letter dated 17 Mar 1916, MS-Papers-1444-3, ATL; Smith, L.J., diary entries dated 1, 2, and 6 Mar 1916, property of G.R. Smith and family, Wellington; Russell, A., diary entry dated 11 Feb 1916, Gambrill, R.F. (compiler), 'The Russell Saga, Volume 3, World War 1', qMS-1822, ATL.

22. Godley had used newly arrived, inexperienced reinforcement officers and NCOs to fill gaps in the ranks caused by deaths or injuries several times on Gallipoli. Russell, then commanding the NZMR Brigade, had wanted to promote experienced men into these vacancies but Godley would not allow it. Only when Godley was too far away in France to interfere, were men in the NZMR Brigade promoted in the field to replace casualties. Harper letter dated 17 Mar 1916, MS-Papers-1444-3, ATL; Colbran, B.C., diary entry dated 11 Mar 1916, MS-Copy-Micro-1431, ATL; WA Series 252, Letters of Colonel the Honourable James Allen, Minister of Defence and General Sir Alexander Godley, Commanding 1 NZEF, 1st World War, 1916, ANZ; *NZEF Provision and Maintenance*, p. 14; Powles, p. 5.

23. WA Series 40/1, HQ NZMR Brigade War Diary, ANZ; Austin, Lieutenant Colonel W.S., *The Official History of the New Zealand Rifle Brigade (The Earl of Liverpool's Own)*, L.T. Watkins Ltd, Wellington, 1924, p. 58.

24. Powles, *CMR*, p. 86; McMillan, p. 45.

25. Powles, *CMR*, pp. 88–9.

26. See *Echoes of Gallipoli*, p. 87.

27. Mallett, R., 'First AIF Order of Battle', URL: http://www.unsw.adfa.edu.au/~rmallett/index.html

28. Chaytor had been another contender for the command. In 1915, Birdwood had suggested to Godley that Russell would be the best commander for an Anzac mounted division, should one be formed. In his opinion, Russell was 'by far the best man for the job, and I should be very glad to have Chaytor in command of the NZ&A [Division]'. Hill, A.J., *Chauvel of the Light Horse: A Biography of General Sir Harry Chauvel, G.C.M.G., K.C.B.*, Melbourne University Press, Melbourne, 1978, p. 66; Anglesey, p. 56; WA Series 252/9, Letters of General Sir William Birdwood, Commanding 1 AIF and 1 Anzac Corps and General Sir Alexander Godley, Commanding 1 NZEF, 1915, ANZ.

29. No. 4 Company, New Zealand Army Service Corps, was part of the Divisional Train from July 1917. Until the New Zealand Field Troop was reformed in July 1917, the Field Squadron was entirely Australian manned.

A Sanitary Section was soon created to co-ordinate the disposal of refuse. Mallett, R., *The Interplay between Technology, Tactics and Organisation in the First AIF*, University of New South Wales, Australian Defence Forces Academy, 1999, URL: http://www.unsw.adfa.edu.au/~rmallett/

30. Godley, General Sir A., *Life of an Irish Soldier*, John Murray, London, 1939, p. 206; Doherty diary entry dated 21 Mar 1916; McMillan, pp. 48–9.

31. Powles, p. 11; Moore, p. 19; Harris letter dated 10 Mar 1916, in *Letters from the Battlefield*, pp. 79–80; Peed diary entry dated 23 Mar 1916.

32. Powles mentions 'a feeling of being "left"', but this was a far cry from the anguished reaction to the Gallipoli decision. Powles, p. 13; Andrews, p. 138; Algar, B., in Boyack, N. and J. Tolerton, *In the Shadow of War: New Zealand Soldiers Talk about World War One and their Lives*, Penguin Books, Auckland, 1990, p. 114.

33. Moore, p. 17; WA Series 40/1, HQ NZMR Brigade War Diary, ANZ. The Training Regiment moved to Tel el Kebir soon afterwards.

34. The 2nd LH Brigade, the NZMR Brigade, and divisional HQ were at Salhia by 10 April. The 3rd LH Brigade remained at Serapeum, and the 1st LH Brigade was away patrolling the Upper Nile. Nicol, p. 99; Idriess, I., *The Desert Column: Leaves from the Diary of an Australian Trooper in Gallipoli, Sinai and Palestine*, Angus & Robertson, Sydney, 2nd edition, 1951, p. 54; Hull, J.K., letter dated 10 Apr 1916, 1993.1039, KMARL; Moore, p. 21; Powles, *CMR*, p. 90.

35. Foster, Lieutenant Colonel W.J., 'Operations of the Mounted Troops of the Egyptian Expeditionary Force', *Cavalry Journal*, Volume 11, 1921, p.14; WA Series 40/1, HQ NZMR Brigade War Diary, ANZ.

Chapter 2: The cold-footed mounteds

1. Four hundred and twenty-five British horses were killed. A British Mobile Veterinary Section was caught up in the fighting, losing one man and 17 horses killed. Macmunn and Falls, p. 170; Anglesey, pp. 42–3; Blenkinsop and Rainey, p. 164.

2. The Army Service Corps, NZMFA and NZMVS were left behind. WA Series 40/1, HQ NZMR Brigade War Diary, ANZ.

3. Powles, *CMR*, p. 92.; Law, J.O., diary entry dated 23 Apr 1916, MS 90/20, AWMML.

4. The South Islanders named their Romani campsite 'Canterbury Hill'. Berrie, G., *Morale: a Story of Australian Light Horsemen*, Holland & Stephenson, Sydney, 1949, pp. 106–7; Foster, p. 14; Doherty diary entry dated 23–26 Apr 1916.

5. Powles, *CMR*, p. 97.

6. Entry dated 27 Apr 1916, AWM4, 1/60/1-1/60/40, HQ Anzac Mounted Division War Diary, AWM; Harper letter dated 1 May 1916, MS-Papers-1444-3, ATL; Hull, J.K., letter dated 10 Jun 1916, 1993.1039, KMARL; Doherty diary entry dated 12–20 May 1916; Rhodes, A.E.T., diary entry dated 30 Apr 1916, 76-123, ATL.

7. Murray to War Office, June 1916, quoted in Anglesey, p. 44. Despite its tactical success, the raid failed to produce any long-term benefit for the Turks and Germans, and the flow of Allied reinforcements to Europe was not interrupted. Never again in the campaign was a British force surprised and overwhelmed.

8. McKay, pp. 97–8.

9. Harper letter dated 19 Jun 1916, in Harper, B., (ed.), *Letters from Gunner 7/516 and Gunner 7/517*, Anchor Communications Ltd, Wellington, 1978, pp. 43–4.

10. Foster, p. 16; Moore, p. 64; Doherty diary entry dated 28–30 Apr 1916. There was no religious element to this negative attitude. Both Bedouin and Turks were Muslims, but the two groups were regarded quite differently by the Anzacs.

11. Hughes, M. (ed.), *Allenby in Palestine: the Middle East Correspondence of Field-Marshal Viscount Allenby June 1917–October 1919*, Sutton Publishing Ltd/Army Records Society, Thrupp, 2004, p. 312; Gullett, H.S., *The Official History of Australia in the War of 1914–1918, Volume 7, The Australian Imperial Force in Sinai and Palestine 1914–1918*, University of Queensland Press edition, 1984, p. 103; Nicol, p. 101; Idriess, p. 65.

12. Mitchell interview.

13. The maximum recorded shade temperatures in Sinai in mid-1916 were: April 41°C, May 45°C, June 47°C, July 46°C and August 43°C. Blenkinsop and Rainey, p. 163; Doherty diary entry dated 12–20 May 1916; Masterman, J.W.V., *Memoirs*, 1998.1936, KMARL; Powles, p. 19.

14. Powles, p. 24; McKay, p. 99; Idriess, p. 68. A spear-point pump was a perforated metal tube that was hammered into the sand far enough to reach the sub-surface water table. It was then connected to a manually operated pump.

15. Moore, p. 26.

16. Johnson, Major M.E., *Memoirs of a Soldier*, property of Mrs R.T. Bruce and family, Auckland, pp. 33, 39.

17. Powles, p. 20; Moore, p. 27; Idriess, p. 63; Anglesey, p. 53.

18. Wilson, Brigadier General L.C. and Captain H. Wetherell, *History of the Fifth Light Horse Regiment (Australian Imperial Force), from 1914 to October 1917, and from October 1917 to June 1919*, Motor Press of Australia, Sydney, 1926, p. 157; Davidson, p. 59; Andrews, p. 139; McKay, p. 108.

19. Moore, p. 48.

20. *Manual of Horsemastership, Equitation and Driving*, pp. 30–2. Horses are helpless in the desert, and any animal that broke free and escaped was doomed unless it was found within one or two days.

21. Named after the temporary commanders of the 1st and 2nd LH brigades at the time of the Battle of Romani.

22. The 1st LH Brigade was returned to Chauvel in late May, but the 3rd LH Brigade remained outside of his control until after the Battle of Romani. The absence of these brigades imposed a heavy extra burden on the others. The shaken and depleted 5th Mounted Brigade was also under General Chauvel's command, but it was of little immediate use.

23. Wilkie, pp. 87–8.

24. Powles, *CMR*, pp. 95–7. These concentration camps were guarded compounds where the Bedouin were forced to wait out the war. They were nothing like the infamous Nazi concentration camps of the Second World War.

25. Lyttelton, C.G., *The Yeomanry Cavalry of Worcestershire 1914–1922*, Mark & Mordy Ltd, Stowbridge, 1926, p. 69; Murray letter to Robertson dated 14 May 1916, Robertson 8/1/27, Robertson Papers, LHCMA.

26. Moore, pp. 25–6; Judge, H., diary entry dated 9 Jun 1916, *Papers Relating to Service in Palestine*, MS-Papers-4312, ATL.

27. Moore, p. 24.

28. NZMR Brigade Operation Order No. 3 dated 14 May 1916, WA Series 40/4, HQ NZMR Brigade Unregistered Files, ANZ.

29. Carbery, p. 451; Blenkinsop and Rainey, p. 163; Rhodes papers; Moore, p. 22.

30. Powles, *CMR*, p. 98; WA Series 40/1, HQ NZMR Brigade War Diary, ANZ.

31. Harper letter dated 19 May 1916, *Letters from Gunner 7/516 and Gunner 7/517*, pp. 41–2.

32. Rhodes diary entry dated 16 May 1916.

33. There were 160 cases of heat exhaustion in all and 70 men were evacuated to hospital. Carbery, p. 451; Blenkinsop and Rainey, p. 163; Rhodes papers; Judge diary entry dated 17 May 1916; quoted in Powles, p. 22.

34. Powles, p. 22.

35. The New Zealanders were supported by two ALH regiments. Nicol, pp. 102–3; Rhodes diary entry dated 30 May 1916; WA Series 242/1: 1st Australian Light Horse Brigade War Diary March 1916 to April 1918, ANZ.

36. Rhodes diary entry dated 30 May 1916; Nicol, p.102.

37. Judge diary entry dated 29 May 1916.

38. Nicol, pp. 102–3.

39. WA Series 40/1, HQ NZMR Brigade War Diary, ANZ; Rhodes diary entry dated 31 May 1916.

40. Powles, *CMR*, p. 100.

41. Doherty diary entry dated 6–12 May 1916; Idriess, pp. 63–4; Bellis, p. 54.

42. The WMR issued an order that stated 'In the event of aircraft passing over the camps officers must identify the machine as being "Hostile" before giving the order to fire'. McMillan, p. 70; Wilson, R.H., *Palestine 1917*, Costello, Tunbridge Wells, 1987, p. 43; recorded by William Peed and preserved with his diaries.

43. Doherty diary entry dated 10–16 Apr 1916; Hull, J.K., letter dated 10 Jun 1916, 1993.1039, KMARL.

44. Fatigue duties included watering the horses, loading ammunition belts, peeling vegetables and chopping firewood, loading wagons and camels with stores, serving as mess orderlies, collecting remounts, guarding stores and horse lines, and pumping water for the horses. WA Series 196, 2a, Unit Records, New Zealand Machine Gun Squadron, ANZ; WA Series 40/4, HQ NZMR Brigade Unregistered Files, ANZ.

45. Peed diary; Masterman, *Memoirs*; McKay, p. 105.

46. Peed diary; Wilkie, pp. 85, 88.

47. Lyttelton, pp. 69–70; Moore, p. 22; McKay, p. 109; Masterman, *Memoirs*; Peed diary entry dated 14 Jun 1916.

48. Nicol, p. 104; Bellis, p. 54. A charger is a superior, well-bred horse of thoroughbred extraction.

49. The 15th (New Zealand) Camel Company was raised on 24 July 1916, followed on 17 October by the 16th

Company. Studholme, p. 17; *NZEF Provision and Maintenance*, p. 4. In December, the ICC became the ICC Brigade.

50. The Maxims were gradually replaced by Vickers machine guns. The 12 guns were arranged in six two-gun sections. Each section was commanded by a sergeant and manned by eight gunners, two signallers and four packhorse leaders. One packhorse carried the gun and its tripod, and other horses carried ammunition (six to eight 250-round ammunition boxes per horse), rangefinders, heliographs, field telephones and signalling lamps, and spare parts. The packhorses were usually used to carry the guns to within about 2000 m of the enemy; after that, the gunners carried the heavy weapons forward. The Lewis machine gun was an American design that was lighter and cheaper than the Vickers machine gun. It fired 600 rounds/minute from a circular drum magazine holding 47 rounds, to an effective range of about 750 m. It could not provide sustained or accurate automatic fire, it was a complex weapon to master and it was prone to jamming in sandy conditions. WA Series 196, 1a, NZMR Brigade Machine Gun Squadron, Establishment Papers 1916, ANZ; Murray, T., *A Collection of Memories: Recollections of Otau, Ness Valley, Clevedon and World War One*, Fraser Murray, Clevedon, 1989, p. 111; Luxford, Major J.H., *With the Machine Gunners in France and Palestine*, Whitcombe & Tombs, Auckland, 1923, pp. 179–80; Gullett, p. 120; Beaven, N.W.H., 'With the Machine Guns', *The Kia Ora Coo-ee: the Magazine for the Anzacs in the Middle East*, facsimile edition, Cornstalk Publishing, Australia, 1981, p. 3.

51. The revolt was encouraged by the British to counter the jihad that Turkey's caliph had declared in 1914. In return for fighting the Turks, the Arabs were led to believe that they would be granted independence after the war. The revolt was purely local at first, with the tribes north of the Hejaz sitting on the fence until they could see some likelihood of Arab success. The British provided money, weapons, armoured cars, and advisers (including T.E. Lawrence, 'Lawrence of Arabia') to the Hejaz Arabs. Only in late 1917 and 1918 did the revolt become a significant factor in the war. I found no mention of the insurrection, or of Lawrence, in any New Zealand letters or diaries. Few New Zealanders would have cared who controlled Syria after the war, unless it interfered with their desire to win the war quickly and go home.

52. Jones, I., *Chauvel and Royston at Romani: a Study in Command and Leadership*, Proceedings of the Australian War Memorial History Conference, November 1991, p. 5; quoted in Anglesey, p. 55; Murray letter to Robertson dated 10 May 1916, Robertson 8/1/26, Robertson Papers, LHCMA; Murray, General Sir A., *Sir Archibald Murray's Despatches (June 1916–June 1917)*, J.M. Dent & Sons, London, 1920, p. 35; quoted in Powles, *CMR*, p. 102.

53. Thompson, Lieutenant Colonel R.R., *The Fifty Second (Lowland) Division 1914–1918*, Jackson & Co., Glasgow, 1923, p. 269.

54. Gullett, p. 126; Foster, pp. 20–1; Eccles, M.A., diary entry dated 19 Jul 1916, MSX-4964, ATL.

Chapter 3: The Battle of Romani

1. Hull, J.K., letter dated 16 Aug 1916, 1993.1039, KMARL.

2. 'Romani, Report on Operations from 19/7/16 to 12/8/16', AWM45, 7/13, AWM; Peed diary entry dated 19 Jul 1916; Eccles diary entry dated 20 Jul 1916; Andrews, p.140; Macmunn and Falls, p.179.

3. The Turks also wanted to stop work on Murray's railway across the desert. The Turkish infantry belonged to the 31st, 32nd and 39th regiments of the 3rd Division. According to Oskar Teichman, 4000 men from the 81st Regiment, 27th Division were also present. Macmunn and Falls, p. 202; Teichman, Captain O., *The Diary of a Yeomanry M.O.*, T. Fisher Unwin Ltd, London, 1921, p. 67.

4. Lawrence knew that the Turks had much greater endurance in the heavy sand than his own relatively soft infantrymen, so he decided to let the Turks exhaust themselves coming to him.

5. Chauvel asked for the entire ridge as far west as Mount Royston to be defended by the infantry, but his request was refused. Gullett, p. 142.

6. Gullett, p. 132; WA Series 40/1, HQ NZMR Brigade War Diary, ANZ. According to Teichman, the EEF counter-attack was to be launched when the Turks crossed a line between Romani and Dueidar. Teichman, p. 60. If Bedouin scouts told Kress about the mounted troops lurking at Hill 70 and elsewhere, he must have dismissed them as a threat because they were so far away from Romani, or possibly because of the poor performance of the British cavalry in April.

7. However, the infantry which made up the majority of this force (the 42nd and 52nd divisions, and one brigade of the 53rd Division) took little active part in the battle. Nearly all the fighting was done by Chauvel's three Anzac mounted brigades, totalling fewer than 5,000 men. Macmunn and Falls, p. 181; Bowman-Manifold, Major General Sir M.G.E., *An Outline of the Egypt and Palestine Campaigns, 1914 to 1918*, 4th edition,

Institution of Royal Engineers, Chatham, 1928, p. 22; Gullett, p. 140.

8. According to Macmunn and Falls, the Turkish force included two 100 mm, four 150 mm, and two 210 mm howitzers (all German), as well as five lighter mountain gun batteries (Turkish and Austrian). Liman von Sanders omits the 210 mm weapons from his account. Macmunn and Falls, p. 202; Liman von Sanders, O., *Five Years in Turkey*, The United States Naval Institute, Annapolis, 1927, p. 142.

9. Berrie, pp. 122–3; Macmunn and Falls, p. 181.

10. A troop of the 6th ALH Regiment also took part in this attack. Powles, p. 28; Macmunn and Falls, pp. 181–2; Tuke, R., letter dated 29 Jul 1916, MS-Papers-1547, ATL.

11. WA Series 40/1, HQ NZMR Brigade War Diary, ANZ; Nicol, p. 107; Foster, p. 32.

12. Chauvel had 1600 rifles, less than two infantry battalions' worth, available for dismounted action. The third regiment of the 1st LH Brigade was in reserve. Foster, p. 32; Anglesey, p. 64; Gullett, p. 140; WA Series 242/1: 1st Australian Light Horse Brigade War Diary March 1916 to April 1918, ANZ.

13. Gullett, p. 143.

14. The 31st Regiment advanced towards the infantry defences in front of Romani. GHQ EEF Special File dated August 1916, AWM45, 7/12, AWM; WA Series 242/1: 1st Australian Light Horse Brigade War Diary March 1916 to April 1918, ANZ; Idriess, pp. 98, 101; Macmunn and Falls, p. 185; Gullett, pp. 143–7.

15. Powles, p. 30; Stevens, K.M., *Maungatapere: a History and Reminiscence*, Whangarei Advocate, 1973, p. 119; Idriess, pp. 97–8.

16. WA Series 242, Box 8, 5th Australian Light Horse Regiment War Diary July/August 1916, ANZ; Foster, p. 131. The 5th ALH Regiment was then ordered to withdraw to the west to await further orders. After picking up the AMR squadron at Bir el Nuss, the riders halted to await those orders. According to the regimental commander, the orders (to move to Canterbury Hill) were issued, but never received by the light horsemen. After trying to make contact for hours without success, the regiment returned to Dueidar, missing the day's fighting. Wilson, Brigadier General L.C., 'From Dueidar to Salmana', *Reveille*, 1 Aug 1933, p. 9.

17. Two Royal Navy warships off the coast fired on these heavy guns, reducing their effectiveness. 'Romani, Report on Operations from 19/7/16 to 12/8/16', AWM45, 7/13, AWM. The Royal Flying Corps did not attempt to fight the superior enemy aircraft.

18. Gullett, p. 151.

19. Aldred, M., quoted in King, *New Zealanders at War*, p. 149.

20. Wilkie, p. 96; Gullett, pp. 151–2.

21. The first brigade of the 42nd Division should have been at Pelusium but its move by rail was delayed. Thompson, pp. 286–7; Gullett, p. 152.

22. Powles, pp. 31–2; Macmunn and Falls, p. 187; Rhodes diary entry dated 4 Aug 1916. Canterbury Hill was not actually in Turkish hands. Lawrence ordered the 3rd LH Brigade to ride from Ballybunion to Hill 70 and to send one regiment to Dueidar. General Murray directed the Mobile Force to move towards Bir Mageibra soon after 7 a.m., and ordered the 42nd Division to move forward along the railway.

23. The brigade commander refused because he was expecting orders from 52nd Division to take part in a counter-attack towards Katia (which did not eventuate). A nearby battalion commander did take over part of the light horsemen's line. Gullett, p. 154; Macmunn and Falls, p. 188.

24. Gullett, p. 156; Teichman, p. 66. According to Macmunn and Falls, the Composite Regiment was reinforced by the rest of the 5th Mounted Brigade before this attack. Macmunn and Falls, p. 189.

25. WA Series 40/1, HQ NZMR Brigade War Diary, ANZ. The two battalions of the 42nd Division arrived from Pelusium Station in time to play a minor role in this attack.

26. Anglesey, p. 68; Wilson, *Palestine 1917*, p. 52.

27. Thompson, p. 287; Luxford, pp. 181–2.

28. Rhodes diary entry dated 4 Aug 1916.

29. McMillan, p. 83; Powles, *CMR*, p. 108. The POWs had their weapons, horses and military papers confiscated. After being warned that anyone resisting the escort or attempting to escape would be shot, they were fed and watered by their captors until they could be turned over to supporting troops.

30. Tuke, R., letter dated 7 Aug 1916, in *Letters to Trixie: a Collection of Letters Written 1914–1919, Predominantly Penned by Robert Clive Tuke*, Te Rau Herald Print, Gisborne, 1997, p. 70; Nicol, p. 110.

31. Aldred, M., quoted in King, *New Zealanders at War*, p. 150.

32. WA Series 40/4, HQ NZMR Brigade Unregistered Files, ANZ; entry dated 4 Aug 1916, AWM4, 1/60/1-1/60/40, HQ Anzac Mounted Division War Diary, AWM. Each man wore two identity discs (one red, one green) around the neck. When a man was killed, the lower, red, disc was removed from his body. The other disc remained with the corpse and was buried with it. Bodies in shallow temporary graves were occasionally

dug up and robbed by Bedouin or eaten by wild dogs.

33. Foster, p. 134 ; McMillan, pp. 84–5.
34. Teichman, p. 72.
35. Gullett, p. 160.
36. The topography of the battlefield between Romani and Bir el Abd is almost unchanged 90 years later. There are no fortifications to be seen, but Mount Meredith, Mount Royston and Wellington Ridge are easy to find, as is the swamp at Katia. They all lie to the south of the coastal road between Kantara and El Arish. The railway was torn up by Israelis and Egyptians for use in later wars. There is a new railway and freshwater canal extending through the middle of the Romani battlefield.

Chapter 4: A terrible day

1. WA Series 42/1, War Diary of Wellington Mounted Rifles Regiment, ANZ; Gullett, p. 165; Richardson, Lieutenant Colonel J.D., *The History of the 7th Light Horse Regiment, AIF*, Radcliffe Press, Sydney, 1923, p. 30; Macmunn and Falls, p. 191. According to a German officer, this force (which included a German machine gun company) should have withdrawn overnight but the necessary orders did not arrive. Muhlmann, C., 'Battle of Romani: German Staff Officer's Record', *Reveille*, 1 Mar 1938, p. 15.

2. Wilkie, pp. 98–9; WA Series 42/1, War Diary of Wellington Mounted Rifles Regiment, ANZ; Meldrum, Brigadier-General W., 'Impressions of Romani', *Reveille*, 1 Aug 1933, p. 20.

3. 5th Australian Light Horse Regiment, War Diary, ANZ.

4. Powles, *CMR*, p. 108.

5. WA Series 42/1, War Diary of Wellington Mounted Rifles Regiment, ANZ.

6. McMillan, p. 87. This swamp is marked as 'Marsh' on maps available to the Anzacs and they must have ridden across it often during the weeks of scouting before 5 August. When I visited Katia in 2001, I found that this swamp has a thin salt crust that a walking or trotting horse might not break through. This may have led commanders to dismiss it as an obstacle. However, a galloping horse exerts a greater ground pressure, enough to crash through the crust.

7. 5th Australian Light Horse Regiment War Diary July/August 1916, ANZ; Nicol, pp. 111–12.

8. Hull, J.K., letter dated 16 Aug 1916, 1993.1039, KMARL.

9. Wilkie, p. 101; Nicol, p. 112. The 3rd brigade's regiments had never fought as a complete brigade and they were not fully equipped for desert fighting. They were unfamiliar with the ground and their commander, Brigadier General John Antill, seems to have been lacking in aggression and initiative. After capturing 425 prisoners at Hamisah, he inexplicably withdrew his brigade out of the fight at 5.15 p.m., exposing the NZMR Brigade's right flank.

10. Lyttelton, p. 64. Some of the NZMR Brigade's new Lewis guns were only able to fire a few rounds before sand got into the mechanisms and jammed the weapons.

11. Idriess, pp. 104–8.

12. Nicol, pp. 112–13.

13. WA Series 40/1, HQ NZMR Brigade War Diary, ANZ; Powles, p. 34; Macmunn and Falls, p. 194.

14. Rhodes diary entry dated 5 Aug 1916.

15. Powles, *CMR*, p. 109; Rhodes diary entry dated 5 Aug 1916.

16. Idriess, p. 112; WA Series 40/4, HQ NZMR Brigade Unregistered Files, ANZ.

17. In one brigade of the 42nd Division, 800 men became casualties from heat illness that day. Gullett, p. 175; Macmunn and Falls, p. 195; Davidson, p. 48.

18. Rhodes diary entry dated 7 Aug 1916; Nicol, pp. 114–15; WA Series 40/3, HQ NZMR Brigade Operational Records, ANZ.

19. Frank Alsopp and seven other men were captured south of Romani in the early hours of 4 August. Rhodes diary entry dated 8 Aug 1916; Nicol, p. 115; WA 41/1, War Diary of Auckland Mounted Rifles Regiment, ANZ; WA Series 40/3: HQ NZMR Brigade Operational Records, ANZ.

20. Entry dated 8 Aug 1916, AWM4, 1/60/1-1/60/40, HQ Anzac Mounted Division War Diary, AWM.

21. WA Series 42/1, War Diary of Wellington Mounted Rifles Regiment, ANZ; Powles, *CMR*, p. 110; Macmunn and Falls, p. 196; Gullett, p. 176.

22. Gullett, p. 177; Powles, *CMR*, p. 111; Macmunn and Falls, p. 196; Hill, *Chauvel of the Light Horse*, p. 81.

23. WA Series 40/3, HQ NZMR Brigade Operational Records, ANZ; Macmunn and Falls, p. 197.

24. WA Series 42/1, War Diary of Wellington Mounted Rifles Regiment, ANZ; Gullett, p. 178; Wilkie, p. 103.

25. Nicol, p. 117; Gullett, pp. 177–8.

26. WA Series 40/1, HQ NZMR Brigade War Diary, ANZ; Macmunn and Falls, p. 197.
27. Muhlmann, p. 16; Macmunn and Falls, p. 202.
28. Rhodes diary entry dated 9 Aug 1916.
29. Idriess, p. 127.
30. Powles, *CMR*, p. 113.
31. Powles, 'Major-General Sir Edward Chaytor; a New Zealand Appreciation', p. 10; Luxford, p. 185; Macmunn and Falls, p. 198. The CMR withdrawal was cleverly executed, with two squadrons mounting their horses and galloping off to opposite flanks simultaneously to reduce the effect of the enemy machine guns.
32. WA Series 40/3, HQ NZMR Brigade Operational Records, ANZ; Dill, F.G., interview, OHInt 0006/23, OHC; Porter, W.H., interview, OHInt 0006/62, OHC.
33. Rhodes diary entry dated 9 Aug 1916.
34. Hull, J.K., letter dated 14 Aug 1916, property of Hull family, Waiuku; Hull, J.K., letter dated 16 Aug 1916, 1993.1039, KMARL.
35. Idriess, p. 131; Foster, p. 139; entry dated 9 Aug 1916, AWM4, 1/60/1-1/60/40, HQ Anzac Mounted Division War Diary, AWM; WA Series 40/3, HQ NZMR Brigade Operational Records, ANZ; Macmunn and Falls, p. 198; Gullett, p. 184.
36. Hull, J.K., letter dated 16 Aug 1916, 1993.1039, KMARL.
37. Rhodes diary entry dated 11 Aug 1916.
38. Powles, *CMR*, p. 115; Rhodes diary entry dated 11 Aug 1916.
39. Macmunn and Falls, p. 199; Gullett, p. 184; entry dated 31 Aug 1916, AWM4, 1/61/6, HQ Anzac Mounted Division War Diary, AWM; Blenkinsop and Rainey, p. 165. The CWGC lists 54 New Zealanders who were killed in action or died of wounds between 24 July and 10 Sep 1916. Most of them are buried or commemorated in the Kantara War Memorial Cemetery.
40. Powles, *CMR*, p. 115; Powles, p. 37. Gordon Harper lies in the Cairo War Memorial Cemetery. Herbert Hammond is buried in the Kantara War Memorial Cemetery.
41. Stretcher-bearers were unarmed and wore a Red Cross arm band. Fighting troops were usually forbidden to carry casualties out of the firing line. War Office, *Field Service Regulations, Part 2*, p. 101.
42. Downes, Colonel R.M.G., 'The Campaign in Sinai and Palestine', The Official History of the Australian Army Medical Services in the War of 1914–1918, Volume I, Gallipoli, Palestine and New Guinea, Australian War Memorial, Canberra, 1930, pp. 563–5; Powles, p. 41; Wilkie, pp. 106–7. The sleds consisted of sheets of corrugated iron with double runners underneath them, a simple frame to carry a single stretcher and a lightweight sunshade fitted on top. Two horses could pull one stretcher case quite easily and the ride was far smoother and more comfortable than that provided by cacolets. As there were few sleds in each field ambulance, they were only used for the most serious cases.
43. Keogh, Colonel E.G., *Suez to Aleppo*, Wilke & Co., Melbourne, 1954, p. 58; Teichman, pp. 79–80. The last man Teichman described was almost certainly Captain George Wood, RMO of the WMR.
44. Liman, *Five Years in Turkey*, p. 144; Muhlmann, p. 16; Lyttelton, p. 65; Wavell, Lieutenant General Sir A.P., *The Palestine Campaigns*, Constable, London, 3rd edition, 1941, p. 50. According to Beethoven Algar, one Turk killed at Romani remained unburied for months and his body was used as a route marker (known as 'Dead Turk'). Algar, B., interview, OHInt 0006/01, OHC.
45. 'Report on Machine Guns with Mounted Troops and Infantry during Actions in Egypt', dated 17 Nov 1916, AWM25, 385/3, AWM.
46. Hull, J.K., letter dated 16 Aug 1916, 1993.1039, KMARL.
47. Murray, *Despatches*, p.73; Andrews, p. 142.
48. Quoted in Gullett, pp. 191–2; WA Series 252/6, Semi-Official Letters by Godley, ANZ.
49. Powles, p. 28; Idriess, p. 126; Tuke letter dated 14 Aug 1916, in *Letters to Trixie*, p. 72.

Chapter 5: El Arish by Christmas

1. Davidson, p. 53.
2. Davidson, p. 56.
3. McMillan, p. 104.
4. Peed diary entries dated 19 Aug and 2 Sep 1916.
5. Peed diary entry dated 20 Sep 1916; Berrie, p. 133; Judge diary entry dated 14–19 Sep 1916; Eccles diary entry dated 11 Sep 1916.
6. Hull, J.K., letters dated 11, 21, and 26 Sep 1916, 1993.1039, KMARL.

7. Tolerton, *Ettie: a Life of Ettie Rout*, Penguin Books, Auckland, 1992, pp. 132–6.

8. Tolerton, pp. 138–9. Ettie Rout returned to Egypt in 1917, hoping to set up a new club at El Arish, but with no success. After opening another club at Moascar, she left Egypt for the last time in mid-1917.

9. Tolerton, pp. 141, 137.

10. The force was unable to make any impact on the 700 enemy troops at Mazar. Seven hundred camels carried water to a rendezvous 15 km east of Salmana, but the first brigade to arrive took all of the water, so later regiments missed out and had to ride on without water for a long distance. The railway advanced at about 25 km per month. Gullett, pp. 197–9; Macmunn and Falls, p. 245.

11. Nicol, pp. 121–2.

12. Powles, *CMR*, p. 120.

13. McMillan, p. 111.

14. Nicol, p. 122.

15. Teichman, p. 81.

16. Powles, *CMR*, pp. 121–2.

17. Ranstead, G., letter dated 29 Nov 1916, MS-Papers-4139, ATL; Wavell, *The Palestine Campaigns*, p. 59. Around this time, the men heard that Germany had proposed a peace conference. Harry Judge was in two minds about the news. 'Well, I'm sick enough of this life, Goodness knows, but I'd rather stay here another year than think that there should be any peace till Germany has been made to suffer at least some for the horror that she has caused France and Belgium to suffer. But Oh God, what a blessing peace would be.' Judge diary entry dated 15 Dec 1916. Germany's offer, which was supported by the United States, was unacceptable to the Allies and the war went on.

18. Macmunn and Falls, pp. 246–51; Gullett, pp. 205–6. The ICC Brigade consisted of four battalions; the 4th Battalion included two New Zealand companies. The ICC Brigade could put as many rifles (about 1700) into a firing line as two light horse or mounted rifles brigades. It was supported by a machine gun squadron and by six 9-pounder mountain guns in the Hong Kong and Singapore Battery. The ICC Brigade gave the Desert Column what it sorely needed: a strong force that could be used in support of the more mobile, but weaker, horse-mounted brigades. Murray told the War Office that he was prepared to advance to Rafah with his current force, but that he would need two more infantry divisions for any progress into Palestine to be possible. On 15 December, the War Office advised him that his primary responsibility was still the defence of Egypt. While he waited for them to make up their minds, Murray decided to press ahead and secure the Egyptian border. The essential first step was the capture of El Arish.

19. This number was far fewer than the initial estimate of 10,000 defenders. German aerial reconnaissance detected the EEF build-up near El Arish on 8 December. A request by Kress for reinforcements was refused and El Arish was abandoned on the night of 17 December. Wilkie, p. 111; Sheffy, Y., *British Military Intelligence in the Palestine Campaign 1914–1918*, Frank Cass, London, 1998, p. 206.

20. Moore, pp. 50–1.

21. McMillan, p. 118.

22. Macmunn and Falls, p. 252.

23. Powles, p. 49; Powles, *CMR*, p. 123.

24. Young, Lieutenant Colonel J., *With the 52nd (Lowland) Division in Three Continents*, W. Green & Son Ltd, Edinburgh, 1920, p. 56; Mitchell interview; Macmunn and Falls, p. 252; WA Series 40/3, 49, Box 8, Account of Battle of Magdhaba, ANZ.

25. WA Series 40/3, 49, Box 8, Account of Battle of Magdhaba, ANZ; Sheffy, *British Military Intelligence in the Palestine Campaign 1914–1918*, p. 207.

26. WA Series 40/3, 49, Box 8, Account of Battle of Magdhaba, ANZ; Murray, *Despatches*, p. 101; Macmunn and Falls, pp. 252–3.

27. Olden, Lieutenant Colonel A.C.N., *Westralian Cavalry in the War: the Story of the Tenth Light Horse Regiment, AIF, in the Great War, 1914–1918*, Melbourne, 1921, p. 111; Gullett, p. 216.

28. McMillan, p. 120; Eccles diary entry dated 23 Dec 1916. The brightness of the fires made the position appear closer than it really was and this is why Chauvel halted the column so far from the objective.

29. WA Series 196, 1b, Machine Gun Squadron Summary of Actions, ANZ; Powles, p. 51; WA Series 40/3, 49, Box 8, Account of Battle of Magdhaba, ANZ. The aircraft also dropped bombs on the enemy position, annoying General Chauvel, who wanted the bombs to be saved until his attack began.

30. When Kress visited Magdhaba on 22 December, he found it garrisoned by 'seven raw companies' of infantry, a camel squadron and four 'outdated' cannon. There were no wire obstacles. Kress does not mention the order to withdraw mentioned by Sheffy. Kress von Kressenstein, F., *Mit den Türken zum Suezkanal*, Dorhut-

Derlag Otto Schlegel, Berlin, 1938, pp. 206–7.

31. Gullett, p. 218.

32. The 10th ALH Regiment was part of the 3rd LH Brigade, the rest of which Chaytor retained as his own reserve. Macmunn and Falls, p. 254; Powles, p. 52.

33. It was later found that a number of Arabs had decided to leave Magdhaba without permission. WA Series 40/3, 49, Box 8, Account of Battle of Magdhaba, ANZ; Gullett, p. 219; Anglesey, p. 81; Sheffy, *British Military Intelligence in the Palestine Campaign 1914—1918*, p. 196.

34. Wilkie, p.117; WA Series 40/3, 49, Box 8, Account of Battle of Magdhaba, ANZ. According to Gullett, General Chauvel actually issued orders for the withdrawal to his brigadiers. When the message was handed to Brigadier General 'Fighting Charlie' Cox, he was about to assault the redoubt to his immediate front. Apparently his response was, 'Take that damned thing away, and let me see it for the first time in half-an-hour.' Gullett, p. 221.

35. Gullett, pp. 225–6.

36. Powles, p. 53; Wilkie, pp. 117–18. Lieutenant Maurice Harding, who was 26 years old when he died, is buried in the War Memorial Cemetery at Kantara.

37. Quoted in Andrews, pp. 143–4. Reginald Gamlin (aged 23 when he died) and Alan Morgan (aged 20) are buried in the War Memorial Cemetery at Kantara.

38. Robertson, Major H.C.H., 'The 10th Australian Light Horse Attack at Magdhaba, 23rd December 1916', *Cavalry Journal*, Volume 25, 1935, p. 232; WA Series 40/3, 49, Box 8, Account of Battle of Magdhaba, ANZ.

39. Gullett, p. 226.

40. Some enemy equipment which could not be collected in time was lost when darkness fell. Murray, *Despatches*, p. 104; Macmunn and Falls, p. 257; WA Series 40/3, 49, Box 8, Account of Battle of Magdhaba, ANZ; 'Operations December 20th to December 24th, including the Occupation of El Arish and the Attack at Bir el Magdhaba', AWM4, 1/60/10, HQ Anzac Mounted Division War Diary, AWM. CWGC records list 10 NZMR Brigade men who were killed or died of wounds on 23 December, and one who died of wounds on the following day. All are buried in the War Memorial Cemetery at Kantara.

41. WA Series 40/3, 49, Box 8, Account of Battle of Magdhaba, ANZ. It seems that only one broken Turkish machine gun was captured at Magdhaba. One machine gun and a single mountain gun battery were never going to cause much damage, and this supports the suggestion that the troops at Magdhaba were under orders to move when the EEF caught them.

42. WA Series 40/3, 49, Box 8, Account of Battle of Magdhaba, ANZ. It took until the following afternoon for all of the wounded to be found and brought in to Magdhaba, where they were treated in a captured Turkish field hospital.

43. Wilkie, p. 118; Powles, *CMR*, p. 127; Powles, p. 55.

44. Powles, p. 54.

45. Luxford, p. 191; McMillan, p. 122. An Italian liaison officer, whose hat was a little different in appearance to those worn by the Anzacs, was arrested as a spy three times by bleary-eyed troopers when his horse wandered into the regimental columns. Powles, pp. 54–5.

46. Bourne, Lieutenant Colonel G.H., *The History of the 2nd Light Horse Regiment, Australian Imperial Force, August 1914–April 1919*, John Burridge Military Antiques, Swanbourne, 1994 edition, p. 45.

47. Powles, p. 55; Judge diary entry dated 23 Dec 1916; Andrews, p. 144.

48. Johnson, *Memoirs of a Soldier*, p. 45; Nicol, p. 126.

49. Gullett, p. 227.

50. WA Series 47/1, War Diary of New Zealand Mounted Field Ambulance, ANZ; Davidson, p. 66; Downes, pp. 592–3; Carbery, pp. 457–8.

51. Quoted in Powles, p. 57. Chetwode's statement has been taken to suggest that he did not know the difference between cavalry and mounted riflemen. He certainly did know this; his point was that it was very unusual for mounted troops of any type to attack and capture heavily defended and fortified infantry positions. Magdhaba is little changed today. Several stone buildings built by the Turks still stand in the midst of a small Egyptian village. The locations of several of the redoubts can be determined quite easily. Being well away from the coastal road, Magdhaba is inaccessible to non-Egyptians without special permission.

Chapter 6: A damned good scrap

1. Masaid proved to be a very comfortable camp when the weather improved, especially after a few tents arrived for the men. Nicol, p. 128; Powles, *CMR*, p. 128.

2. Macmunn and Falls, p. 262; Gullett, p. 230. The last-named unit was commanded by a New Zealander, Lieutenant William McKenzie.

3. According to Sheffy, orders for the garrison at Magruntein to withdraw were issued, but the 31st Regiment had not received them when the EEF attacked. Sheffy, *British Military Intelligence in the Palestine Campaign 1914–1918*, p. 208.

4. Macmunn and Falls, pp. 262–3.

5. Teichman, p. 98.

6. Robertson, Lieutenant Colonel H.C.H., 'The N.Z.'s at Rafa', *Reveille*, 1 Apr 1938, p. 42; 'Report on Operations of the NZMR Brigade, on the 8th/10th January, 1917', dated 11 Jan, 1917, Rhodes papers. A daylight start was risky but the distance to be covered was too far to permit an after-dark start.

7. Powles, pp. 67–8.

8. Reid, F., *The Fighting Cameliers*, Angus & Robertson Ltd, Sydney, 1934, p. 66; Powles, p. 68; Nicol, p. 129; 'Battle of Rafa, January 9th, 1917', *Amber and Black: the Journal of the Queen Alexandra's (Wellington West Coast) Mounted Rifles, New Zealand Military Forces*, Hawera, 1934–1938, p. 213.

9. Wilkie, p. 123; Macmunn and Falls, p. 264; Powles, *CMR*, p. 132; Gullett, p. 231. William Harris, who was 36 years old when he died, is buried in the War Memorial Cemetery at Kantara.

10. Report dated 10 Jan 1917, WA Series 40/4, HQ NZMR Brigade Unregistered Files, ANZ. According to Arthur Moore, the thief knocked out the trooper with his sword, then leapt on his horse and galloped away. A nearby marksman levelled his rifle and took careful aim. 'At a range of nearly eight hundred yards, he fired at the galloping horseman. The horse fell in a cloud of dust, throwing his rider clear. Being unhurt, the Bedouin commenced to run, when the marksman, deliberately reloading and aiming, brought him to his end with his second shot.' Moore, pp. 62–3.

11. Powles, p. 69; Lyttelton, p. 76; Downes, pp. 593–4.

12. Gullett, p. 233.

13. Reid, p. 69.

14. Chetwode to Dobell, quoted in Gullett, p. 233.

15. The New Zealanders, accompanied by a political officer, were ordered to search the Police Post and huts at Rafah for secret documents. Massey, W.T., *The Desert Campaigns*, G.P. Putnam, New York, 1918, p. 107; Powles, *CMR*, p. 133.

16. McCarroll diary entry dated 9 Jan 1917.

17. Powles, Colonel C.G., 'Peeps at Palestine', *Amber and Black*, p. 56.

18. Powles, p. 73.

19. Andrews, p. 146; Nicol, p. 131.

20. Massey, *The Desert Campaigns*, p. 109.

21. Wilkie, p 124; Powles, *CMR*, p. 134.

22. Reid, p. 76.

23. 'With the Mounted: Humours of the Desert War', Mackenzie, C.N. (ed.), *Chronicles of the NZEF*, NZ Contingent Association, London, 2 May 1917, p. 108.

24. Powles, *CMR*, pp. 134–5.

25. Davidson, p. 77; Luxford, p. 194. Robert Reid is buried in the War Memorial Cemetery at Kantara.

26. Gullett, p. 235.

27. The ground was so exposed that heavy, continuous fire was needed to keep the Turks' heads down. 'Report on Operations of the NZMR Brigade, on the 8th/10th January, 1917'; Macmunn and Falls, p. 271.

28. Macmunn and Falls, p. 267; 'Report on Operations of the NZMR Brigade, on the 8th/10th January, 1917'; Bourne, p. 46.

29. 'Report on Action at Rafa, January 8th, 1917'; 'Report on Operations of the NZMR Brigade, on the 8th/10th January, 1917'; Wilkie, p. 128.

30. Nicol suggests that, by this stage of the battle, there was as much danger to the New Zealanders in a withdrawal as in an advance, as the ground was completely without cover in either direction. Nicol, p. 132; Gullett, p. 240; Wilkie, p. 128.

31. McCarroll diary entry dated 9 Jan 1917.

32. 'Report on Operations of the NZMR Brigade, on the 8th/10th January, 1917.'

33. Davidson, p. 82; Hull, J.K., letter dated 19 Jun 1917, Hull family; 'Report on Operations of the NZMR Brigade, on the 8th/10th January, 1917'; Nicol, pp. 132–3. One hundred and sixty-two wounded Turks were captured in the Reduit. Davidson, p. 82.

34. Gullett, pp. 240–1; Owers, W.H., interview, OHInt 0006/64, OHC; Andrews, p. 147.

35. Masterman, *Memoirs*.

36. McCarroll diary entry dated 9 Jan 1917; Nicol, p. 134; Wilson, *Palestine 1917*, p. 63.

37. Powles, *CMR*, p. 136.

38. Carbery, p. 460; Downes, p. 596; Davidson, pp. 83–5.

39. Dill stayed at El Arish for 11 days, then went by hospital train to Kantara and on to Cairo, where he spent a month convalescing before being sent home. Dill interview.

40. Hull, J.K., letter dated 17 Feb 1917, 1993.1039, KMARL.

41. Gullett, p. 242. Most of the Turkish bodies were buried in their trenches.

42. Four mountain guns, seven machine guns, 1610 rifles, 83 camels, 19 horses and 35 mules were captured. Macmunn and Falls, p. 270; Wilkie, p. 130; Powles, p. 79; Algar interview.

43. CWGC records show that 23 New Zealanders were killed or died of wounds on 9 Jan 1917. All of them are buried or commemorated in the War Memorial Cemetery at Kantara. Clarence Gordon Abercrombie was 25 years old when he died. Ewen Elmslie died on 13 Jan 1917. Ewen's brother, Major Jim Elmslie, was killed on Chunuk Bair in August 1915. 'Report on Action at Rafa, January 8th, 1917'; Woodward, D.R., *Hell in the Holy Land: World War 1 in the Middle East*, University Press of Kentucky, 2006, p. 54; 'Report on Operations of the NZMR Brigade, on the 8th/10th January, 1917'; Gullett, pp. 240, 242; Andrews, p. 147.

44. Tuke letter dated 28 Dec 1916, MS-Papers-1547, ATL. A total of 46 horses were killed, and 144 were wounded, at Rafah. Blenkinsop and Rainey, p. 182; 'Report on Operations of the NZMR Brigade, on the 8th/10th January, 1917'.

45. Andrews, p. 145; Macmunn and Falls, p. 270; Powles, pp. 75–6.

46. Chaytor report on Rafah dated 19 Jan 1917, WA Series 40/4 Box 5 Item 32, ANZ.

47. Bourne, p.47. This criticism is ill founded. Magdhaba had shown that the Turks would not surrender without a fight. To have attacked Rafah without careful reconnaissance in daylight would have been extremely risky. The operation was conceived as a raid, with the aim of 'cutting out' the enemy garrison and then withdrawing. There was no intention to 'fight it out' if the defence proved to be stronger than expected, or if enemy reinforcements arrived.

48. The grazing enabled the horses to get rid of some of the sand which was clogging their intestines, so that by the end of March 1917 the horses were much fitter and healthier than they had been during 1916. Bellis, p. 55; Blenkinsop and Rainey, p. 183. Rafah is now a large town and Palestinian refugee camp straddling the border between Egypt and the Gaza Strip. The battlefield has been altered significantly as a result of this recent population growth.

Chapter 7: Someone has blundered

1. Wilkie, p. 131.

2. Berrie, pp. 141, 144; Powles, *CMR*, p. 145.

3. Gullett, pp. 244–5; Nicol, p. 130; Bowman-Manifold, p. 29. The supply wagons were brought up from Kantara, where they had been since the beginning of the Sinai campaign, to supplement the camel convoys. Millen, J., *Salute to Service: a History of the Royal New Zealand Corps of Transport and its Predecessors 1860–1996*, Victoria University Press, Wellington, 1997, p. 100.

4. Olden, p. 125.

5. As far as is known, no New Zealand horse ever fell victim to a horse trap. Macmunn and Falls, pp. 276–8; Powles, *CMR*, pp. 141–3; Nicol, p.136; WA Series 40/3, HQ NZMR Brigade Operational Records, ANZ; Wilkie, p. 132; Judge diary entry dated 22–3 Feb 1917.

6. Macfarlane, W.A., diary entry dated 9 Mar 1917, MS-Papers-3871, ATL. On 13 March, news arrived that the British had captured Baghdad from the Turks. This ancient city, the capital of Mesopotamia, was of great importance to the Turks, and its capture after the disasters of Gallipoli in 1915 and Kut el Amara in 1916 was a welcome boost to the Allied cause. A Taube was an early German reconnaissance aircraft. The Anzacs referred to all enemy aircraft as Taubes.

7. Hill, *Chauvel of the Light Horse*, p. 100.

8. Powles, p. 84.

9. Murray was promised some infantry from India and East Africa during the coming summer, as well as some tanks and a supply of poison gas shells from France. In Feb 1917, the 42nd Division was sent to France. Macmunn and Falls, pp. 259, 272–3; Hughes, M., *Allenby and British Strategy in the Middle East 1917–1919*, Frank Cass, London, 1999, p. 18.

10. Because the EEF intended to occupy Gaza after its capture, and because strong Turkish reserves were known

to be nearby, Murray needed to use infantry as well as mounted troops in the attack. By mid-March, the desert railway was approaching Khan Yunis, which had unlimited water supplies. These two logistic factors were essential pre-requisites for the use of the EEF's infantry divisions against Gaza.

11. Gullett, p. 265; Macmunn and Falls, p. 284; WA Series 40/1, HQ NZMR Brigade War Diary, ANZ.

12. Sheffy, *British Military Intelligence in the Palestine Campaign 1914–918*, p. 211; Kress, *The Campaign in Palestine from the Enemy's Side*, p. 506.

13. 'First Attack on Gaza', in Sterling diary.

14. Gullett, p. 266; WA Series 40/1, HQ NZMR Brigade War Diary, ANZ.

15. Sterling, 'First Attack on Gaza'; Berrie, pp. 146–7.

16. Idriess, p. 187.

17. Gullett, pp. 267–8; Macmunn and Falls, p. 291.

18. Idriess, p. 189; Gullett, pp. 269–70.

19. Powles, p. 89.

20. Kress, *The Campaign in Palestine from the Enemy's Side*, pp. 506–7.

21. 'Account of Action of Anzac Mounted Division from 24th March to 27th March 1917', dated 4 Apr 1917, AWM4, 1/60/13, HQ Anzac Mounted Division War Diary, AWM; Macmunn and Falls, p. 299; WA Series 40/1, HQ NZMR Brigade War Diary, ANZ. General Chauvel received the 3rd LH Brigade from Hodgson's division to bolster his attack.

22. The Imperial Mounted Division had not finished relieving all of the outlying patrols, so only three troops of the Auckland regiment took part in the Gaza fighting. The CMR squadron remained in the Ali Muntar redoubt until the brigade withdrew from Gaza. Wilkie, p. 135; Powles, *CMR*, p. 148; Judge diary entry dated 26 Mar 1917; Gullett, pp. 281–2; Macmunn and Falls, p. 299; 'Report on Operations at Gaza on 26th March 1917', dated 4 Apr 1917 [excerpts], WA Series 40/1, HQ NZMR Brigade War Diary, ANZ.

23. One hundred and eighty prisoners were captured in the hospital, half of whom were unwounded Turkish soldiers who had taken refuge there. According to Gullett and Wilkie, all 32 Turks in the trench were killed. Lieutenant Cecil Allison died of wounds on 9 Dec 1917, aged 27. He is buried in the Ramleh War Cemetery. Powles, p. 93; Gullett, p. 281; Wilkie, p. 136; WA Series 40/1, HQ NZMR Brigade War Diary, ANZ.

24. According to Anglesey, these guns had already been put out of action by British horse artillery. Anglesey, p. 99.

25. Andrews, p. 152.

26. According to Gullett, the WMR suffered one fatality and 19 men wounded in these fights. Claude Rouse was killed on 14 Nov 1917, probably at Ayun Kara, aged 30. He is buried in the Ramleh War Cemetery. Wilkie, pp. 137–8; Powles, pp. 92–3; 'Account of Action of Anzac Mounted Division from 24th March to 27th March 1917'; Macmunn and Falls, p. 299; Gullett, p. 281.

27. Wilkie, p. 138.

28. Sterling, 'First Attack on Gaza'.

29. Powles, *CMR*, p. 148. The EEF had yet to learn that horses could survive without any water for at least two days without suffering long-term ill-effects.

30. Idriess, p. 201, Gullett, p. 282; Andrews, p. 152.

31. The field ambulances had not been able to keep up with the regiments but there were only a few dead and wounded men to be evacuated. The NZMFA evacuated 34 casualties, 31 of whom were New Zealanders. 'Account of Action of Anzac Mounted Division from 24th March to 27th March 1917'; Carbery, p. 462; Wilkie, p. 138.

32. The NZMR Brigade lost its way, missing the divisional rendezvous and bumping into Hodgson's headquarters. Sterling, 'First Attack on Gaza'; Olden, p. 133; Andrews, pp. 152–3; Anglesey, p. 102.

33. Sterling diary entry dated 27 Mar 1917; McCarroll diary entry dated 26 Mar 1917; Gullett, p. 284; Nicol, pp. 138–9.

34. Almost all the casualties occurred in the 53rd Division. One hundred and thirty EEF horses were killed or destroyed as a result of the Gaza battle. The Desert Column took 645 prisoners, including four Austrian and five German soldiers. Kress, *Sinai*, quoted in Macmunn and Falls, p. 322; Macmunn and Falls, p. 315; 'Account of Action of Anzac Mounted Division from 24th March to 27th March 1917'; Blenkinsop and Rainey, p. 185.

35. Fitzherbert had been offered promotion and a transfer to clerical duties, but he preferred to remain as a fighting man. Two New Zealand horses were killed and six were wounded in the fighting. CWGC records indicate that three NZMR men (including Fitzherbert) were killed in action or died of wounds on 26 March, and one man died of wounds the next day. Three of the New Zealanders are buried in the Deir el Belah War

Cemetery; one lies in the Gaza War Cemetery. WA Series 40/1, HQ NZMR Brigade War Diary, ANZ; Gullett, p. 284; Wilkie, pp. 139–40; Powles, pp. 95–6.

36. Chetwode letter to Chauvel and Hodgson dated 29 Mar 1917, PP/MCR/C1, Chetwode, Field Marshal Lord, Papers, IWM.

37. Macmunn and Falls, p. 319; Teichman, pp. 124–5.

38. Macmunn and Falls, p. 322.

39. The Hotchkiss was lighter (12 kg), more robust, and simpler than the Lewis gun. Single shots or automatic fire were effective at ranges out to about 1000 m. The Mark 1 weapon fired .303 inch rounds from a 10-round metal strip, six of which were carried in a special bandolier. The gun, a spare barrel and another 900 rounds were carried on a packhorse. Each squadron also had another two ammunition pack horses, each carrying 2400 rounds. Once dismounted, the Hotchkiss could be carried into action slung over the shoulder like a rifle. Mallett thesis, p. 147.

40. Powles, *CMR*, p. 149.

41. There were about 8500 Turks in Gaza and 4500 were positioned nearby. Two thousand Turks manned the Atawineh Redoubt and several thousand more were dug in at Hareira and Sheria. Macmunn and Falls, pp. 331, 349; Powles, p. 97.

42. In order to support the fighting troops and get their supplies forward, the railway and pipeline were extended and large water reservoirs were dug into the bed of Wadi Ghazze.

43. The Turks never used gas in this campaign but Allenby used it in the bombardment of Gaza at the end of October 1917. 'Anzac Mounted Division Order No.80' and 'Special Instructions to BGC, NZMR Brigade', dated 14 Apr 1917, AWM4, 1/60/14, HQ Anzac Mounted Division War Diary, AWM; Mallett thesis, p. 149; Sheffy, Y., 'The Chemical Dimension of the Gallipoli Campaign: Introducing Chemical Warfare to the Middle East', *War in History*, Volume 12, Number 3, July 2005, pp. 316–17.

44. Macmunn and Falls, p. 379; Chetwode to Murray dated 9 Apr 1917, Chetwode Papers.

45. Wilkie, p. 143; 'Second Attack on Gaza 24.03.17', in Sterling diary; Idriess, p. 207.

46. Powles, pp. 99, 114–16.

47. Nicol, p. 142; 'Second Attack on Gaza 24.03.17', in Sterling diary.

48. Wilkie blames this error on a British guide. Powles, *CMR*, p. 153; Wilkie, p. 143.

49. Gullett, p. 319. Chauvel's earlier instructions to not conduct a dismounted assault were cancelled as Murray's battle plan fell apart.

50. Gullett, pp. 329–30; Macmunn and Falls, p. 345.

51. Macmunn and Falls, p. 345; Wilkie, p.144; Powles, *CMR*, pp.153-4; WA Series 40/1, HQ NZMR Brigade War Diary, ANZ.

52. The CMR suffered one man killed and another wounded. Five horses were killed, and seven were wounded. Hedley Green died at the age of 20. He is buried in the Deir el Belah War Cemetery. McMillan, pp. 153–4; Sterling, 'Second Attack on Gaza 24.03.17'; Powles, p. 104; Luxford, p. 203.

53. Wilkie, pp. 145–6.

54. Sterling, 'Second Attack on Gaza'; Nicol, p. 143.

55. Gullett, pp. 306–7; Powles, *CMR*, p. 152.

56. Sheffy, *British Military Intelligence in the Palestine Campaign 1914–1918*, pp. 234–5.

57. Ibid., p. 232.

58. Browne, Lieutenant Colonel J.G., 'Operations of the Mounted Troops of the Egyptian Expeditionary Force', *Cavalry Journal*, Volume 2, 1921, p. 239; Gullett, p. 334; Powles, p. 105; Macmunn and Falls, pp. 348, 350. CWGC records indicate that six NZMR men were killed in action on 19 April, and four others died of wounds between 19 and 22 Apr 1917. They are buried in the Deir el Belah War Cemetery (two) and the Gaza War Cemetery (four) or commemorated on the memorial in the Jerusalem War Cemetery (four). In 1968 a memorial to the Anzac troops was erected in Israel at Be'eri, 9 km south-east of Gaza City, paid for by Jewish communities in Israel, Australia and New Zealand. Gaza City is now a sprawling urban area housing 400,000 inhabitants. It is often the scene of armed clashes between Palestinian militants and Israeli soldiers. With a population approaching 1,500,000, many of whom live in sprawling refugee camps, the Gaza Strip is one of the most crowded places on Earth. The part of the old Turkish front line that lies in Israel today is in rural land and quite easy to locate.

59. Sterling diary entry dated 21 Apr 1917; Browne, p.239; WA Series 40/1, HQ NZMR Brigade War Diary, ANZ; Powles, p.104. Between 17 and 26 Apr, 357 EEF horses or mules were killed, died, or were destroyed, another 80 were missing and 510 were wounded. Blenkinsop and Rainey, p. 186.

60. Murray's artillery density of one gun to every 100 m of front was less than one-tenth of what was considered

acceptable in France. Woodward, p. 77.

61. Nicol, p. 144. Chaytor became the first – and, so far, the only – New Zealander to command an Anzac division.

62. Macmunn and Falls, p. 355. Murray's response was similar to Hamilton's after the failed August battles on Gallipoli. Like Hamilton then, Murray was now working on borrowed time.

63. Hughes, *Allenby and British Strategy in the Middle East 1917–1919*, p. 15.

Chapter 8: When will the war be over?

1. Moore, pp. 71–3.

2. WA Series 40/1, HQ NZMR Brigade War Diary, ANZ; Nicol, p. 146.

3. Sheffy, *The Origins of the British Breakthrough into South Palestine: the ANZAC Raid on the Ottoman Railway, 1917*, Volume 22 Number 1, March 1999, p. 138.

4. WA Series 40/1, HQ NZMR Brigade War Diary, ANZ; Thomas, R.S., 'A Day's Outing Towards Beersheba', in *Chronicles of the NZEF*, 11 Jul 1917, p. 228; Powles, *CMR*, p. 158; Sheffy, *The ANZAC Raid on the Ottoman Railway*, p. 139; Idriess, p. 227.

5. Powles, p. 111; Idriess, p. 228; Sterling diary entries dated 22 and 23 May 1917; 'Report on Operations to Blow Up the Asluj Auja Railway', dated 25 May 1917, AWM4, 1/60/15, HQ Anzac Mounted Division War Diary, AWM; Sheffy, *The ANZAC Raid on the Ottoman Railway*, pp. 141. Some of the demolished bridges and buildings can still be seen south of Beersheba, as can an intact and beautifully constructed Turkish railway viaduct on the outskirts of the city.

6. Powles, *CMR*, p. 159.

7. WA Series 40/1, HQ NZMR Brigade War Diary, ANZ; Sheffy, *The ANZAC Raid on the Ottoman Railway*, p. 144.

8. Falls, C., *Armageddon 1918: the Final Palestinian Campaign of World War I*, University of Pennsylvania Press edition, Philadelphia, 2003, p. 12. Soldiers will forgive many failings in a commander if he wins battles. Murray's cautious tactics and his lack of charisma and leadership ability, coupled with his galling failures at Gaza, meant that few men in the EEF regretted his departure.

9. Allenby letter dated 9 Jul 1917, in Hughes, *Allenby in Palestine*, p. 29.

10. Wavell, General Sir A., *Allenby: a Study in Greatness. The Biography of Field Marshal Viscount Allenby of Megiddo and Felixstowe, GCB, GCMG*, Oxford University Press, New York, 1941, p. 187; Ranstead letter dated 17 Jul 1917.

11. McKay, pp. 131–2.

12. The campaign on the Western Front was achieving little. The collapse of Russia was expected to result in the freeing of large numbers of Turkish troops who were likely to attack Baghdad. A large-scale offensive against the Turks in southern Palestine would, London thought, divert the Turks from attacking in Mesopotamia. With luck, it might be enough to force the Turks out of the war entirely. Soon after he arrived Allenby was asked what extra forces he needed to be certain of gaining the Jaffa–Jerusalem line. He replied that 13 extra divisions would be required. In the end, higher priorities elsewhere meant that he received just two new infantry divisions and extra artillery – and these proved to be enough. Robertson telegram to Allenby dated 5 Oct 1917, in Hughes, *Allenby in Palestine*, pp. 63–4; Wavell, *Allenby: a Study in Greatness*, p. 204.

13. Chetwode, Lieutenant General P.W., 'Notes on the Palestine Operations' dated 21 Jun 1917, AWM45, 12/7, AWM. An infantry division was allocated 250,000 litres of water per day and a mounted division received twice as much. Thirty thousand camels were needed to ferry this water forward from railhead. James, L., *Imperial Warrior: the Life and Times of Field Marshal Viscount Allenby 1861–1936*, Weidenfeld & Nicolson, London, 1993, p. 122.

14. Wavell, *The Palestine Campaign*, pp. 112–13. 20 Corps: 10th, 53rd, 60th and 74th divisions. 21 Corps: 52nd, 54th and 75th divisions.

15. The Yeomanry Mounted Division and the ICC Brigade were detached from the DMC and used to cover the wide gap in the line between the two infantry corps.

16. Falls, Captain C., *Military Operations, Egypt and Palestine, from June 1917 to the End of the War*, HMSO, London, 1930, pp. 12, 15, 35; Hughes, *Allenby and British Strategy in the Middle East 1917–1919*, p. 49.

17. On the positive side, a late start should increase the chances of early winter storms providing water for the EEF horsemen.

18. Gullett, p. 376; James, *Imperial Warrior*, p. 122. By taking all of 21 Corps' transport, 20 Corps and the DMC could be supplied with rations and ammunition as far as Beersheba and one day beyond – except water,

which could only be provided as far as Beersheba. 21 Corps was left with practically no transport, but seven days' supplies were dumped near their trenches in front of Gaza. The Sinai water pipeline was extended to Shellal, from where camel convoys carried water forward. The capacity of the Sinai railway was increased, the main track was extended across Wadi Ghazze and branch lines were built to Karm and Gamli. Kantara was expanded into a huge port and supply base. Allenby ordered his commanders to accustom their men to 4 pints of water per day. This was no problem for the veteran mounted troops.

19. Australian Army, *Operations of the Egyptian Expeditionary Force in Palestine, from 28th October, 1917, to 31st December, 1917*, Army HQ, Melbourne, 1924, p. 36. The Anzacs were used to the old British 'string-bag' biplanes being shot down or chased away by German fighters. Allenby's state-of-the-art Bristol Fighters quickly turned the tables on the complacent enemy aviators.

20. Sheffy, *British Military Intelligence in the Palestine Campaign 1914–1918*, p. 266. The German force consisted of three infantry battalions, three cavalry platoons and strong machine gun, artillery, mortar, communications, medical and transport elements, plus modern aircraft. The troops were hand-picked and thoroughly trained in Germany. Falkenhayn had commanded the invasion of France and Belgium from mid-September 1914, and the Verdun offensive in 1916. He fought a successful campaign in Romania before moving to Syria.

21. Erickson, p. 168.

22. Sheffy, *British Military Intelligence in the Palestine Campaign 1914–1918*, p. 267; Gullett, pp. 373, 384.

23. Mallett, R., 'First AIF Order of Battle', URL: http://www.unsw.adfa.edu.au/~rmallett/index.html The brigades making up the other divisions were as follows: Australian Mounted Division – 3rd and 4th LH brigades, 5th Mounted Brigade; Yeomanry Mounted Division – 6th, 8th and 22nd Mounted brigades. The 7th Mounted Brigade was retained under Lieutenant-General Chauvel's direct command. Two new infantry divisions (60th and 75th) joined the EEF, as did token Italian and French contingents (mainly as a visible reminder of their governments' interest in the future carve-up of the Turkish Empire). Macmunn and Falls, pp. 357–8; Mallett thesis, p. 151.

24. Wavell, *The Palestine Campaigns*, p. 113. Mustafa Kemal had refused the command of the 7th Army, stating that he would not work under Falkenhayn. Cemal also took the title of Governor of Syria.

25. Downes, pp. 630–1.

26. Powles, p. 113.

27. McMillan, pp. 169–70.

28. Milliken, W.T., letter dated 11 Jun 1917.

29. Gammage, B., *The Broken Years: Australian Soldiers in the Great War*, Penguin Books, Harmondsworth, 1975, p. 134; Wilkie, p. 149; Blackwell, F. and D.R. Douglas, *The Story of the 3rd Australian Light Horse Regiment*, Adelaide, 1950, p. 92; Downes, p. 641.

30. Gullett, p. 345; Mallett thesis, p. 152.

31. Milliken letters dated 11 Jun and 24 Jul 1917.

32. WA Series 40/4, HQ NZMR Brigade Unregistered Files, ANZ; Berrie, p. 163.

33. Moore, pp. 71–2.

34. Henderson, J. *Soldier Country*, Millwood Press, Wellington, 1978, pp. 25–6.

35. Moore, p. 80.

36. Henderson, p. 23.

37. Moore, p. 81.

38. WA Series 40/4, HQ NZMR Brigade Unregistered Files, ANZ; WA Series 40/1, HQ NZMR Brigade War Diary, ANZ; Nicol, p. 146. New Mark 3* rifles and more powerful ammunition were issued in June. The Mark 3* rifle was a simplified version of the pre-war Mark 3.

39. WA Series 40/1, HQ NZMR Brigade War Diary, ANZ.

40. Powles, p. 117.

41. McKay, p. 164.

42. McNeur letter dated September 1917; Wilkie, p. 154; McMillan, p. 163.

43. Ranstead letter dated 8 Oct 1917.

44. Nicol, p. 148.

45. Powles, pp. 122–3.

46. Sterling diary entry dated 15 Aug 1917; WA Series 40/1, HQ NZMR Brigade War Diary, ANZ.

47. WA 47/1, War Diary of New Zealand Mounted Field Ambulance, ANZ; Macfarlane and Sterling diary entries dated 12 Aug 1917; Wright, G.F., diary entry dated 12 Aug 1917, MS-Papers-1512, ATL. The two fatalities are believed to be William Gold and Patrick Sheehan. Gold is buried in the Kantara War Memorial Cemetery; Sheehan lies in the Beersheba War Cemetery.

48. Hull, J.K., letter dated 26 Sep 1917, 1993.1039, KMARL.

49. WA Series 196, 3b, 1st NZMG Squadron Miscellaneous Correspondence, ANZ.

50. Preston, Lieutenant Colonel the Honourable R.M.P., *The Desert Mounted Corps: an Account of the Cavalry Operations in Palestine and Syria 1917–1918*, Constable & Co. Ltd, London, 1921, p. 13.

51. Preston, pp. 12–15.

52. Browne, p. 244; Powles, p. 123; WA Series 40/1, HQ NZMR Brigade War Diary.

53. EEF Order dated 22 Oct 1917, Massey, W.T., *How Jerusalem was Won: being the Record of Allenby's Campaign in Palestine*, Constable & Co., London, 1919, p. 278. The balance of forces was heavily in favour of the EEF and senior German officers knew it. They tried unsuccessfully to convince the Turks to either reinforce or abandon Beersheba.

Chapter 9: Tel el Saba

1. WA Series 40/1, HQ NZMR Brigade War Diary, ANZ; McNeur letter dated Oct 1917.

2. Falls, *Military Operations*, p. 40.

3. Gullett, p. 380.

4. WA Series 40/1, HQ NZMR Brigade War Diary, ANZ; Moore, p. 83.

5. Falls, *Military Operations*, p. 52. The 7th Mounted Brigade was ordered to establish an outpost line on the Asluj–Beersheba road, and to be prepared to pursue the Turks if they withdrew. The commander of the Australian Mounted Division ordered his light horsemen to sharpen the points of their bayonets and to carry them as swords in any charge that might eventuate. Anglesey, p. 140.

6. WA Series 40/1, HQ NZMR Brigade War Diary, ANZ; Sterling diary entry dated 29 Oct 1917; McCarroll diary entry dated 30 Oct 1917.

7. Falls, *Military Operations*, p. 53.

8. Gullett, p. 385.

9. Camel convoys carrying a small reserve of drinking water for the men were also left at Asluj. The ammunition column was under orders to follow the division at daylight on 31 October. WA Series 40/1, HQ NZMR Brigade War Diary, ANZ; Powles, p. 134.

10. Idriess, p. 246.

11. Falls, *Military Operations*, p. 42.

12. McCarroll diary entry dated 30 Oct 1917; WA Series 40/1, HQ NZMR Brigade War Diary, ANZ; Nicol, p. 155.

13. Olden, p. 168; Gullett, p. 388; Powles, p. 137. The 7th Mounted Brigade also reached its initial objective successfully and established contact with 20 Corps cavalry to its left and the Australian Mounted Division to its right. While these preliminary moves were completed, another small, independent force was moving quietly around Beersheba towards the Hebron Road. Seventy camel riders, under the command of British Lieutenant Colonel Stewart Newcombe, cut the telegraph line and the road at dusk on 31 October.

14. Falls, *Military Operations*, p. 39.

15. Falls, *Military Operations*, p. 55; WA Series 40/1, HQ NZMR Brigade War Diary, ANZ; Wavell, *Allenby: a Study in Greatness*, p. 211; Wavell, *The Palestine Campaigns*, p. 120.

16. WA Series 242/1, 1st Australian Light Horse Brigade War Diary March 1916 to April 1918, ANZ.

17. Falls, *Military Operations*, pp. 56–7. 'So rapidly were the galloping horses [of the 3rd ALH Regiment] checked, cleared, and rushed back by the horse holders, and so quickly did the dismounted men resume their advance on foot, that the Turks, under the impression that the regiment had retired on the horses, shelled the galloping animals, while for a time the riflemen were not fired upon.' Gullett, p. 391.

18. Luxford, p. 206; Falls, *Military Operations*, pp. 56–7.

19. Wilkie, p. 161; WA Series 40/1, HQ NZMR Brigade War Diary, ANZ; WA 41/1, War Diary of Auckland Mounted Rifles Regiment, ANZ. Tel el Saba is crowned today by a viewing platform overlooking partially excavated ruins.

20. McCarroll diary entry dated 31 Oct 1917. According to war diaries, six Aucklanders were killed in action, one died of wounds and 21 were wounded. The Wellingtons lost one man killed and five wounded. Nicol, p. 158; WA 41/1, War Diary of Auckland Mounted Rifles Regiment, ANZ; WA Series 42/1, War Diary of Wellington Mounted Rifles Regiment, ANZ; WA Series 40/1, HQ NZMR Brigade War Diary, ANZ. The Beersheba War Cemetery contains the graves of nine New Zealanders who were killed in action (seven) or who died of wounds (two) on 31 Oct 1917.

21. Chauvel had already reduced the striking power of the Australian division by detaching its 3rd LH brigade to assist the Anzac division at Tel el Saba.

22. Anglesey, p.150.
23. McCarroll diary entry dated 31 Oct 1917; Gullett, pp. 397–401; Falls, *Military Operations*, p. 60.
24. WA Series 40/1, HQ NZMR Brigade War Diary, ANZ.
25. Twisleton, F.M., letters, MS-Papers-1705, ATL.
26. McCarroll diary entry dated 31 Oct 1917.
27. Falls, *Military Operations*, pp. 59–60. Allenby wrote that 'Kress von Kressenstein, for the third time in his war, left out an isolated detachment. He had done it at Magdhaba, and at Rafa; and, each time, it was snapped up by Chetwode's horsemen.' Allenby letter dated 20 Nov 1917, Hughes, *Allenby in Palestine*, p. 88.
28. Enough water could not be made available immediately, but Allenby was confident that his men and horses could survive long enough on reduced water for the capacity to be fully developed. According to Hughes, the German officer in charge of the demolitions in Beersheba happened to be away on leave on 31 October. Hughes, *Allenby and British Strategy in the Middle East 1917–1919*, p. 57.

Chapter 10: In the land of milk and honey

1. Powles, *CMR*, p. 170.
2. The lack of water forced Chauvel to send the Australian Mounted Division right back to Karm. Gullett, p. 412; Falls, *Military Operations*, p. 79; WA Series 40/1, HQ NZMR Brigade War Diary, ANZ.
3. The sudden appearance of Lieutenant-Colonel Newcombe's 70 cameliers on the road near Hebron helped convince the Turks that a serious threat was developing on the road to Jerusalem. Newcombe's detachment did not last long in such a vulnerable forward position. On 2 November Newcombe surrendered his force to greatly superior German and Turkish forces.
4. Sterling diary entry dated 3 Nov 1917.
5. Hayman, B.F., diary entry dated 6 Nov 1917, 1993.1661, KMARL.
6. Sterling diary entry dated 4 Nov 1917.
7. Six horses were killed by Turkish artillery fire and seven men and 21 horses were wounded. A bombing raid killed one man and wounded another. WA Series 40/1, HQ NZMR Brigade War Diary, ANZ; Luxford, p. 207.
8. Powles, *CMR*, pp. 170–1. The 18-pounders had been replaced by the lighter weapons in September.
9. Twenty-three of the dead horses belonged to the CMR. WA Series 40/1, HQ NZMR Brigade War Diary, ANZ; WA 43/1, War Diary of Canterbury Mounted Rifles Regiment, ANZ.
10. Wilkie, p. 164.
11. Sterling diary entry dated 5 Nov 1917.
12. 'The Advance to Jerusalem', *Chronicles of the NZEF*, 30 Jan 1918, p. 281; WA Series 40/1, HQ NZMR Brigade War Diary, ANZ; McCarroll diary entry dated 5 Nov 1917.
13. Tuke letter dated 22 Nov 1917, in Harper, G., (ed.), *Letters from the Battlefield: New Zealand Soldiers Write Home 1914–18*, HarperCollins, Auckland, 2001, p. 83.
14. Powles, *CMR*, p. 172.
15. WA Series 40/1, HQ NZMR Brigade War Diary, ANZ; Teichman, p. 180; Hayman diary entry dated 6 Nov 1917.
16. Many horses needed a spell with intensive veterinary care to recover from this trying time. A dixie was a cooking pot. WA Series 40/1, HQ NZMR Brigade War Diary, ANZ; Nicol, p. 160; McCarroll diary entry dated 6 Nov 1918; Sterling diary entry dated 7 Nov 1917; Powles, *CMR*, p. 173.
17. Powles, pp. 141–2.
18. 'Account of the Operations Carried out by the Australian and New Zealand Mounted Division from October 21st to December 7th 1917', AWM4, 1/60/22, HQ Anzac Mounted Division War Diary, AWM; Falls, p. 91; Powles, p. 141; Powles, *CMR*, p. 172; McMillan, pp. 178–9; Hayman diary entry dated 8 Nov 1917. CWGC records list 11 men killed between 5 and 8 Nov 1917 (nine on 5 November). Six others died of wounds between 1 and 8 November. They lie in the Beersheba War Cemetery (13), the Jerusalem War Cemetery (two) and the Kantara War Memorial Cemetery (two). Many of the horses were killed in the aptly named Dead Horse Gully.
19. Preston, p. 50.
20. *Operations of the Egyptian Expeditionary Force in Palestine, from 28th October, 1917, to 31st December, 1917*, p. 117; Wavell, *Allenby: a Study in Greatness*, p. 219.
21. Falls, *Military Operations*, pp. 121–3. Another cavalry charge at El Mughar on 13 November was less costly, as it employed proper fire support.
22. Falls, *Military Operations*, p. 143.

23. Sterling diary entry dated 12 Nov 1917.
24. Powles, *CMR*, p. 174; Nicol, p. 161; Wilkie, p. 166; WA Series 40/1, HQ NZMR Brigade War Diary, ANZ; Twisleton papers. The AMR covered nearly 100 km from the vicinity of Tel el Khuweilfe. On 11 November, the Australian Mounted Division was attacked by about 5000 Turks from the direction of Et Tine. The division was driven back a few kilometres, but sustained few casualties.
25. Blenkinsop and Rainey, p. 205; Wavell, *The Palestine Campaigns*, p. 156. There is a school of thought that Allenby should have ignored the inland flank and focused his attack on Gaza instead. With his great superiority in men and matériel, he could have destroyed the Turkish 8th Army completely, perhaps shortening the war in the Middle East as a result. See Hughes, *Allenby and British Strategy in the Middle East 1917–1919*, pp. 56–9.
26. Junction Station was captured on 14 November. Good wells and working pumps were captured intact, and, for the first time in weeks, unlimited water was available for the EEF. The Turks had lost their railway link to Jerusalem and withdrew up the plain towards Jaffa and inland towards Jerusalem, splitting their forces into two in the process.

Chapter 11: Gallop for your life!

1. The 2nd LH Brigade was detached to work with the under-strength Australian Mounted Division in the Junction Station operation, leaving the Anzac division with only two brigades. Ayun Kara is actually a spring or swamp near Richon le Zion.
2. Powles, p. 145; Powles, *CMR*, p. 175.
3. I am indebted to Israeli Colonel (Retd) Itzhak Brenner, who showed me this battlefield in 2001, and to Gal Shaine, for his detailed description of the battlefield on his website. I have adopted Shaine's method of naming the battlefield features. Shaine, G., *Action of Ayun Kara*, URL: http://anzac israel.com
4. Marle, B., letter of condolence dated 29 Nov 1917, 2000.325, KMARL.
5. 'Account of the Operations Carried out by the Australian and New Zealand Mounted Division from October 21st to December 7th 1917.'
6. According to Wilkie, two CMR squadrons were held in reserve at the foot of WMR Ridge, but other sources do not support this. According to Powles, the AMR was the brigade reserve, but this must be incorrect. No other source mentions a reserve. It seems that the entire Canterbury regiment was committed to the right flank, and that no brigade reserve (typically a squadron with added machine guns) was formed. Wilkie, p. 167; Powles, *CMR*, p. 176; McCarroll, J., Lieutenant Colonel, 'The Battle of Ayun Kara – 14/11/17', WA 41/1, War Diary of Auckland Mounted Rifles Regiment, ANZ; Powles, p. 147; Luxford, p. 208.
7. Luxford, p. 208; Wilkie, p. 168.
8. McCarroll diary entry dated 14 Nov 1917.
9. WA 41/1, War Diary of Auckland Mounted Rifles Regiment, ANZ; Powles, pp. 145–6.
10. McCarroll, 'The Battle of Ayun Kara – 14/11/17'. Frank Twisleton was seriously wounded, and died the next day. Twisleton was a veteran of the South African War and a skilled horsemaster. He fought with the Otago Mounted Rifles Regiment on Gallipoli, winning the Military Cross and a Mention in Dispatches. He served with the New Zealand Division on the Western Front before returning to the NZMR Brigade in October 1917 to take command of an AMR squadron. Twisleton, who was aged 44 when he died, is buried in the Ramleh War Cemetery. Crawford, J.A.B., 'Twisleton, Francis Morphet 1873–1917', *Dictionary of New Zealand Biography*, updated 7 Apr 2006, URL: http://www.dnzb.govt.nz/
11. Falls, *Military Operations*, p. 177; Powles, p. 149; WA 41/1, War Diary of Auckland Mounted Rifles Regiment, ANZ; Luxford, pp. 209–10; Sergeant Maurice Malone, the son of Lieutenant Colonel William Malone of Chunuk Bair fame, fought off a Turkish attack against his machine gun section, shooting down several Turks with his revolver. Crawford. J. (ed.), *No Better Death: the Great War Diaries of William G. Malone*, Reed Books, Auckland, 2005, p. 334.
12. Two squadrons from the 1st LH Brigade and a company of the ICC Brigade were also ordered forward but they did not reach the battlefield until after the battle had ended. Chaytor cobbled together a reserve 'troop' from every spare man at Divisional HQ, but it was not needed. Captain Arthur Herrick reportedly was recommended for the Victoria Cross for his gallantry on 14 November; he received the Military Cross instead. Herrick, who was 38 years old when he died, is buried in the Ramleh War Cemetery. WA Series 42/1, War Diary of Wellington Mounted Rifles Regiment, ANZ; Powles, pp. 148–9.
13. WA Series 42/1, War Diary of Wellington Mounted Rifles Regiment, ANZ; McCarroll, 'The Battle of Ayun Kara – 14/11/17'; 'Account of the Operations Carried out by the Australian and New Zealand Mounted

Division from October 21st to December 7th 1917'.

14. McCarroll, 'The Battle of Ayun Kara – 14/11/17'; Sterling diary entry dated 14 Nov 1917.

15. McCarroll, 'The Battle of Ayun Kara – 14/11/17'; McCarroll diary entry dated 15 Nov 1917; Powles, pp. 149–51.

16. WA 43/1, War Diary of Canterbury Mounted Rifles Regiment, ANZ; Powles, pp. 154–5.

17. The NZMR Brigade War Diary gives figures of 160 enemy dead and 122 wounded. 'Account of the Operations Carried out by the Australian and New Zealand Mounted Division from October 21st to December 7th 1917'; WA Series 40/1, HQ NZMR Brigade War Diary, ANZ; Nicol, pp. 165–6.

18. Moore, pp. 89–90.

19. According to Wilkie, the cameliers and a squadron from the 1st LH Brigade did not arrive until 11 p.m. WA 41/1, War Diary of Auckland Mounted Rifles Regiment, ANZ; Wilkie, p.170; Hayman diary entry dated 15 Nov 1917.

20. According to CWGC records, 23 New Zealanders were killed in action on 14 Nov 1917. Another 13 died of wounds and 13 of unspecified causes between 14 and 16 November. Most of the horse casualties occurred when troops and squadrons galloped across open ground under machine gun fire. WA Series 40/1, HQ NZMR Brigade War Diary, ANZ; Moore, p. 90.

21. Marle letter.

22. Gainfort, B.S., interview, OHInt 0006/28, OHC; Harrison, A.C., Papers, MS 2004/5, AWMML.

23. By the time Meldrum appreciated the size of the enemy force, it was probably too late to refuse battle. According to Nicol, the counter-attack force comprised fresh Turkish troops from the Romanian front.. Wounded Turkish prisoners told interrogators that Kress personally directed the counter-attacks. The site of the Ayun Kara battlefield is now a cultivated semi-urban area front immediately south of the Israeli city of Richon le Zion. WA Series 40/1, HQ NZMR Brigade War Diary, ANZ; Powles, p. 146; Nicol, p. 165; Falls, *Military Operations*, pp. 177–8; see Shaine, *Action of Ayun Kara.*

24. Macfarlane diary entry dated 18 May 1918.

25. Powles, p. 156; WA Series 40/1, HQ NZMR Brigade War Diary, ANZ; Powles, *Reveille*, p. 10; Moore, p. 95; Owers interview.

26. Reakes, 'New Zealand Veterinary Corps', in Drew, Lieutenant H.T.B. (ed.), *The War Effort of New Zealand: a Popular History*, Whitcombe & Tombs, Auckland, 1923, p. 157; Wilkie, p. 173.

27. Andrews, pp. 160–1.

28. Falls, *Military Operations*, p. 267; Powles, pp. 161, 164.

29. Andrews, pp. 161–2. Curry spent the rest of the war in captivity. He was released in November 1918.

30. The 2nd LH Brigade demonstrated towards Mulebbis, but did not cross the river.

31. There was one Turkish machine gun post sited near the ford but Hayman and a few others chased the gunners away. 'Account of the Operations Carried out by the Australian and New Zealand Mounted Division from October 21st to December 7th 1917'; Hayman diary entry, undated.

32. WA 43/1, War Diary of Canterbury Mounted Rifles Regiment, ANZ.

33. The Wellingtons were supported by several armoured cars. WA Series 40/1, HQ NZMR Brigade War Diary, ANZ; Falls, *Military Operations*, p. 215; Nicol, pp. 168–9; Powles, p. 161.

34. Powles, pp. 161, 179; Falls, *Military Operations*, p. 215.

35. Powles, p. 162; WA 41/1, War Diary of Auckland Mounted Rifles Regiment, ANZ.

36. McMillan, p. 195.

37. Falls, *Military Operations*, p. 214; Hull, J.K., letter dated 26 Dec 1917, Hull family.

38. Nicol, p. 170.

39. Nicol, p. 170.

40. WA Series 40/1, HQ NZMR Brigade War Diary, ANZ.

41. Luxford, p. 213; Johnson, *Memoirs of a Soldier*, p. 55; Powles, p. 162. Sergeant Sydney Emmerson died of sickness (probably malaria or influenza) in October 1918, aged 28. He is buried in the Jerusalem War Cemetery.

42. The battery commander remained on the northern bank directing the artillery fire, before swimming to safety at the last moment. His battery was shelled heavily and accurately and it had to be withdrawn at the gallop. Falls, *Military Operations*, pp. 214–7; Nicol, p. 171.

43. The Nelson men later crossed the river by boat. Wilkie, p. 176; WA Series 40/1, HQ NZMR Brigade War Diary, ANZ.

44. Milliken letter dated 31 Dec 1917; Hayman diary entry, undated; Wilkie, p. 176.

45. Lieutenant Alexander Livingston was aged 22 when he died. His body was lost and his name appears on the

memorial wall in the Jerusalem War Cemetery. 'Account of the Operations Carried out by the Australian and New Zealand Mounted Division from October 21st to December 7th 1917'; Wilkie, p. 176; Powles, p. 165; WA 43/1, War Diary of Canterbury Mounted Rifles Regiment, ANZ.

46. McNeur letters, undated and dated 3 Jan 1918.

47. McMillan, pp. 196–7.

48. WA 43/1, War Diary of Canterbury Mounted Rifles Regiment, ANZ.

49. Other than two men whose bodies were lost (and whose names appear on the Jerusalem Memorial), all the dead New Zealanders lie in the Ramleh War Cemetery. The infantry lost 120 men, 45 of whom were captured by the Turks. WA Series 40/1, HQ NZMR Brigade War Diary, ANZ; Falls, *Military Operations*, p. 216.

50. Powles, p. 161; Moore, pp. 95–6.

51. On 27 November the Turks captured the nearby Bald Hill from the ICC Brigade. Intermittent fighting continued for several days before the front line stabilised again. The NZMR Brigade was not involved. The area between Jaffa and Nahr el Auja is now part of Tel Aviv, and Nahr el Auja is now known as the Yarkon River. A power station and the Sde Dov municipal airport occupy the coastline immediately north of the river, and Tel Aviv University occupies the site of Sheikh Muwannis. The Jerishe Mill dam is in the Yarkon Park.

52. The horse covers finally arrived from Cairo in mid-Jan 1918. Powles, *CMR*, p.189; Hill, *Chauvel of the Light Horse*, p. 134.

53. WA Series 40/1, HQ NZMR Brigade War Diary, ANZ; Powles, *CMR*, pp. 183, 185; WA 43/1, War Diary of Canterbury Mounted Rifles Regiment, ANZ.

54. Powles, *CMR*, p. 185.

55. The EEF advance into the Judean Hills began on 18 November but the rough ground, stubborn resistance and the winter weather soon brought the advance to a halt. After a Turkish counter-attack on the plains was beaten off and the roads were repaired, the attack was renewed on 8 December. Under orders not to fight in Jerusalem, the Turks evacuated the city that night. Allenby entered the Old City on foot, in deliberate contrast to the ostentatious arrival of Kaiser Wilhelm II in 1898, when a hole was smashed through the walls of the Old City to allow him to enter on horseback. WA Series 40/1, HQ NZMR Brigade War Diary, ANZ; Powles, p. 170.

56. Nicol, p. 176.

57. WA Series 40/1, HQ NZMR Brigade War Diary, ANZ; Wilkie, pp. 178–9.

58. Cablegram from Minister of Defence dated 12 Dec 1917, WA Series 40/4, HQ NZMR Brigade Unregistered Files, ANZ.

59. In response to a query from HQ EEF, General Chaytor reported that the horses of the Anzac Mounted Division went without water for continuous periods of up to 84 hours during November and December 1917. The longest period that NZMR Brigade horses went without water was 72 hours, although much of that time was spent in one location. It was also reported that, after going about 36 hours without water, the horses usually refused to eat. Chaytor commented that the horses started to lose condition quickly after going 36 hours or more without water, but that they recovered quickly when watered and then fed. Powles, pp. 152–3; Powles, *CMR*, p. 189.

60. WA Series 40/4 HQ NZMR Brigade Unregistered Files, ANZ; Preston, pp. 123–4.

61. Powles, *CMR*, p. 189; WA Series 47/1, War Diary of New Zealand Mounted Field Ambulance, ANZ.

62. Nicol, p. 172.

63. About 2500 EEF men were killed, 14,700 were wounded, and 1700 were listed as missing. Falls, *Armageddon 1918*, p. 15; Falls, *Military Operations*, p. 262.

64. Falls, *Military Operations*, pp. 262, 293–4.

65. He was also promised two Canadian railway construction battalions from France, other railway construction personnel from Mesopotamia, locomotives and railway stock and four additional aircraft squadrons. Robertson message to Allenby dated 7 Mar 1918, Allenby 2/5/7, Allenby Papers, LHCMA.

66. Maddison, L.D., letter to mother dated 4 Dec 1917, Warkworth and District Museum. Laurence Maddison is buried in the Kantara War Memorial Cemetery.

Chapter 12: The road to Jericho

1. Entry dated 15 Mar 1918, in Parker, J.H., diary, property of Parker family, Auckland; WA Series 40/1, HQ NZMR Brigade War Diary, ANZ. One mounted division was kept in, or near, the front line between 20

and 21 Corps. The Canterbury regiment spent two weeks in the front line near Nalin, before rejoining the brigade on 4 February.

2. This is in addition to the 2048 Main Body and First Reinforcement men who left New Zealand in October 1914. It is difficult to be certain of the exact numbers because the composition of some reinforcement drafts is not detailed enough. I have assumed that all men on the drafts listed as 'Mounted Rifles Reinforcements' were destined for the NZMR Brigade. The 40th–43rd Mounted Rifles Reinforcements missed the war, arriving at Suez on 22 Dec 1918. *NZEF Provision and Maintenance*, pp. 7, 18–39; Allen Papers, AD Series 1, ANZ; Studholme, p. 376; Doherty, P.G., letter dated 12 Feb 1918, 1989.944, KMARL.

3. 'Report on Operations of the NZMR Brigade on the 8th/10th January, 1917'.

4. From November 1917 most recruits completed a basic training course at Trentham Camp, after which they were allocated to the various arms and services based on individual aptitudes. AD Series 1, 29/236, Box 964, Mounted Rifles Reinforcements, ANZ.

5. *The Times History of the War*, Volume 13, The Times, London, 1917, p. 149; Stanbrook, Sergeant G.L. (ed.), *Featherston Military Training Camp: the Record of a Remarkable Achievement*, Brett Publishing and Printing Co., Auckland, 1917, pp. 71–2.

6. Pugsley, C., *The Anzac Experience: New Zealand, Australia and Empire in the First World War*, Reed Books, Auckland, 2004, p. 128. The Moascar training camp was moved to the banks of Lake Timsah near Ismailia in 1918.

7. Parker diary entries dated 2-26 Jan 1918.

8. 'The Aotea Convalescent Home', *Chronicles of the NZEF*, 5 Jul 1918, p. 251.

9. Ranstead letter dated 5 Apr 1917, in Harper, *Letters from the Battlefield: New Zealand Soldiers Write Home 1914-18*, p. 87. The Aotea Home had room for more than 200 men by 1918. An Auxiliary Home was opened at Port Said in 1917 and a Convalescent Camp near Ismailia in late 1918.

10. Porter interview.

11. Bluett, A., *With Our Army in Palestine*, Andrew Melrose Ltd, London, 1919, pp. 232–3.

12. *Buckshee: a Pictorial Record of the Work of the New Zealand YMCA on Active Service*, London, 1919, p.12; Ranstead letter dated 19 Jan 1917; McNeur letter dated 18 Dec 1918.

13. Bluett, pp. 229–31.

14. Gullett, pp. 543–4.

15. Lyttelton, p. 162; Powles, p. 181; Powles, *CMR*, p. 197. The Jordan Valley is heavily cultivated now, and the Palestinian town of Jericho has a population of around 20,000. The drawing off of 90% of the Jordan River's water for irrigation has led to a drastic lowering of the water level in the Dead Sea. The river is now a heavily polluted, sluggish, brown stream no more than 4 or 5 m wide – much as Lyttelton described it 90 years ago. The Allenby Bridge crosses the river at the site of the Ghoraniyeh ford.

16. Chetwode received the 1st LH and the NZMR brigades and the headquarters of the Anzac division. Falls, *Military Operations*, p. 304; Powles, p. 173.

17. Falls, *Military Operations*, p. 305.

18. Sterling diary entry dated 9 Feb 1918; Wilkie, pp. 181–2.

19. Sterling diary entry dated 16 Feb 1918; Andrews, p. 166; Wright diary entry dated 20 Feb 1918.

20. Wilkie, p. 183.

21. They were fired on by a group of Turkish cavalrymen during the night but suffered no casualties. Wilkie, pp. 182–3. See *Echoes of Gallipoli*, pp. 196–7.

22. Powles, pp. 177–8. Neby Musa is believed by Muslims to be the tomb of Moses.

23. According to Tom Murray, this was the only fog or rain ever experienced by the New Zealanders in the Jordan Valley. Jericho remained in EEF hands until the end of the war, so the stay-behind agents could have had little spying to do. McCarroll diary entry dated 21 Feb 1918; Murray, *A Collection of Memories*, p. 133; Falls, *Military Operations*, p. 308; Sheffy, *British Military Intelligence in the Palestine Campaign 1914–1918*, p. 303.

24. Sterling diary entry dated 21 Feb 1918.

25. Powles, p. 181.

26. Johnson, *Memoirs of a Soldier*, p. 58; Powles, pp. 181–2.

27. Falls, *Military Operations*, p. 309; Gullett, p. 542. The bodies of the three New Zealanders were lost. Their names are listed on the Jerusalem Memorial.

28. Powles, p. 179.

29. Moore, p. 103. AMR activity along the banks of the Jordan River resulted in the Turks demolishing their bridge at Ghoraniyeh. The Aucklands also took part in an infantry advance up the Jordan Valley in early

March but saw no action. The regiment remained in the valley until the start of the Amman operation in March.

30. Wright diary entries dated 22 and 24 Feb 1918; Powles, p. 188; Powles, *CMR*, p. 201.

Chapter 13: More than we can chew

1. Parker diary entry dated 30 March 1918.
2. Falls, *Military Operations*, p. 329.
3. Gullett, p. 568. The Circassians were Muslims from the Caucasus region of Russia. The Turks encouraged the establishment of Circassian communities in areas where Christian settlements existed. Inevitably, Ghoraniyeh was known to the troops as 'Gonorrhoea'.
4. All supplies except water had to be carried forward on trucks from the terminus of the railway at Jerusalem to the banks of the Jordan River. Divisional transport wagons would then carry supplies forward to Shunet Nimrin, from where camel convoys would bring them up to the forward troops. The Anzac Mounted Division employed three camel trains, each of 550 camels; one would carry supplies between Shunet Nimrin and Es Salt, while the other two would carry them from Es Salt to Amman. Casualties would be carried on camels as far as Es Salt, from where horse-drawn ambulances would take them back to the valley floor.
5. The AMR had discovered that the river was not fordable at any point and that Hijla and Ghoraniyeh were the only sites suitable for pontoon bridges. If the raid succeeded in destroying the bridge and tunnel, it would take the Turks weeks or months to repair the damage, and this might compel them to recall their forces from Tafila and Ma'an. Once the main force had withdrawn, mounted troops would maintain a link between the Es Salt garrison and the western Jordan Valley. Powles, pp. 193–4; Falls, *Military Operations*, pp. 310, 331.
6. Marshal Falkenhayn was replaced by Marshal Liman von Sanders (who had been the commander of the Turkish forces on Gallipoli in 1915) on 1 Mar 1918. According to Wilkie there were 4850 infantry troops, 650 cavalrymen, 118 machine guns and automatic rifles, and 40 field guns in the area. Bean, C.E.W., *Anzac to Amiens: a Shorter History of the Australian Fighting Services in the First World War*, Australian War Memorial, Canberra, 1946, p. 501; Erickson, p. 194; Falls, *Military Operations*, pp. 330–1; Skander Bey, 'The Battles of Es Salt, Amman and Jordan from Turkish Sources', *Journal of the Royal United Services Institute*, Volume 69, 1924, p. 338; Wilkie, p. 190.
7. Doherty diary entry dated 17 Mar 1918; Parker diary entries dated 15–16 Mar 1918; Cameron, A.E., diary entry dated 17 Mar 1918, MSX-2853, ATL; Andrews, p. 170; Wilkie, p. 190.
8. WA Series 40/1, HQ NZMR Brigade War Diary, ANZ; Powles, p. 191. Talaat ed Dumm is believed to be the site of the biblical parable of the Good Samaritan.
9. EEF Special File dated Mar 1918, AWM45, 7/31, AWM.
10. WA Series 40/1, HQ NZMR Brigade War Diary, ANZ.
11. Sterling diary entry dated 23 Mar 1918; Powles, p. 196. Much of the following narrative is taken from Nicol, pp. 190–4.
12. 'Record of Operations Carried Out by Auckland MR Regiment on 23rd March 1918', WA 41/1, War Diary of Auckland Mounted Rifles Regiment, ANZ; 'With the Mounteds: the Humour, the Joy and the Interest of Campaigning in Palestine', *Chronicles of the NZEF*, 24 May 1918, p. 172; McCarroll diary entry dated 23 Mar 1918. A burial party found that Tait's body, and those of the dead Turks, had been stripped by Bedouin. According to Fred Sterling, 'God will need to save the Bedouin should we ever catch them at this ancient practice of theirs.' Sterling diary entry dated 23 Mar 1918. Ken Tait's body was lost. His name is listed on the Jerusalem Memorial in the Jerusalem War Cemetery.
13. Gullett, p. 557; Robertson, J., *With the Cameliers in Palestine*, A.H. & A.W. Reed, Wellington, 1938, p. 161.
14. Richardson, p. 82.
15. Falls, *Military Operations*, p. 336.
16. Nicol, p. 195; McMillan, p. 222.
17. Ireland, T.W., 'Raid Over the Jordan', 2002.187, KMARL.
18. Powles, p. 198; Richardson, p. 83; Preston, p. 137.
19. Nicol, p. 196.
20. Andrews, p. 171; Powles, *CMR*, p. 205; Harrison papers.
21. Between 50 and 100 Turks were captured in the village. Wilkie, pp. 194–5; Powles, p. 198; WA Series 40/1, HQ NZMR Brigade War Diary, ANZ.
22. Dawbin, W., diary entry dated 27 Mar 1918, Micro-MS-0004, ATL.

23. King, W.A., diary entry dated 26 Mar 1918, 99/55/1, IWM.

24. McMillan, p. 222; WA Series 40/1, HQ NZMR Brigade War Diary, ANZ; Powles, pp. 198–9; Nicol, p. 197.

25. Gullett, p .563; Falls, *Military Operations*, pp. 337–8.

26. Wilkie, p. 195; Falls, *Military Operations*, p. 338.

27. A 'flying column' of two infantry battalions, four mountain gun batteries and the 6th (Manawatu) Squadron was ordered to march towards Amman from Es Salt to support Chaytor. This column was held up by a fight between Christians and Circassians near the village of Suweile. About 20 deaths had already occurred before the WMR squadron commander separated the factions and convinced them to talk. The British commander ordered the release of some Christian prisoners and told the Circassians to feed them. The flying column did not reach Amman until the following morning. Reid, pp. 27–8; Falls, *Military Operations,* pp. 338–40, 348; Gullett, p. 564; Sterling diary entry dated 27 Mar 1918.

28. Wilkie, p. 195. Hill 3039 dominated Amman, and its capture would outflank the other defences of the village.

29. 'Operations of the A&NZ Mounted Divn, East of Jordan, from March 23rd to April 2nd including Action of Amman', dated 11 Apr 1918, AWM4, 1/60/26, HQ Anzac Mounted Division War Diary, AWM; Powles, p. 200; Gullett, p. 566.

30. Wilkie, p. 196; Powles, pp. 200–1. The WMR squadron later rejoined the NZMR Brigade for its attack on Amman.

31. Moore, p. 108.

32. According to Nicol, two men were killed, but CWGC records list only one New Zealand fatality on 27 March. Nicol, pp. 198–9; Gullett, p. 566; Moore, pp. 109–10.

33. 'Operations of the A&NZ Mounted Divn, East of Jordan, from March 23rd to April 2nd including Action of Amman'. On 27 and 29 March, Cemal awarded the defenders 1000 Turkish pounds in total as a reward for their efforts. Skander Bey, p. 491.

34. Nicol, p. 199; Powles, pp. 200–1; 'Operations of the A&NZ Mounted Divn, East of Jordan, from March 23rd to April 2nd including Action of Amman'.

35. The river rose nearly three metres on 28 March. War Office, *A Brief Record of the Advance of the Egyptian Expeditionary Force under the Command of General Sir Edmund H.H. Allenby, GCB, GCMG, July 1917 to October 1918, Compiled from Official Sources*, 2nd edition, 1919, p. 18.

36. Falls, *Military Operations*, pp. 340–1; Gullett, pp. 569–70.

37. Wilkie, p. 196; Nicol, p. 200.

38. Sterling diary entry dated 28 Mar 1918.

39. Falls, *Military Operations*, p. 341; Wilkie, p. 197; Nicol, p. 200; 'Operations of the A&NZ Mounted Divn, East of Jordan, from March 23rd to April 2nd including Action of Amman'.

40. Luxford, p. 222. Jim Parker wrote, 'Things are all upset with all our horses being killed.' Parker diary entry dated 29 Mar 1918. There are no New Zealand fatalities listed for 29 March. In ordering Chaytor to make another attempt to capture Amman, Shea was influenced by intelligence reports suggesting that the Turks were planning to evacuate Amman, and by Arab promises to guard the railway demolitions north and south of Amman. Both of these reports proved to be overoptimistic. Falls, *Military Operations*, pp. 342–3.

41. King diary entry dated 29 Mar 1918.

42. To bolster the number of troops in the assault, every second horse holder joined in, leaving the others to look after eight horses each. Wilkie, p. 198.

43. Nicol, pp. 202–3. This scheme was similar to that employed by the mounteds on Gallipoli on 6 Aug 1915.

44. Sterling diary entry dated 30 Mar 1918.

45. Nicol, p. 203.

46. A total of 78 prisoners and 11 machine guns were captured. Powles, p. 207; Wilkie, p. 201; WA Series 40/1, HQ NZMR Brigade War Diary, ANZ.

47. Sterling diary entry dated 30 Mar 1918. William Sutherland's body was lost. He is commemorated on the Jerusalem Memorial in the Jerusalem War Cemetery.

48. Moore, p. 111.

49. Powles, p. 207; Wilkie, p. 201; Moore, p. 112.

50. 'Operations of the A&NZ Mounted Divn, East of Jordan, from March 23rd to April 2nd including Action of Amman'; Powles, p. 208.

51. Wilkie, p. 202; Sterling diary entry dated 30 Mar 1918.

52. Powles, p. 209. According to Wilkie, about 400 Turks attacked and they were 'almost wiped out'. Wilkie, p. 202.

53. Ireland, 'Raid Over the Jordan'.

54. Parker diary entry dated 30 Mar 1918; Wilkie, p. 203. By now, some Turkish battalions had been reduced to 50 men and the hospitals in Amman were full of wounded men. Skander Bey, p. 491.
55. Wilkie, p. 203; King diary entry dated 30 Mar 1918. According to CWGC records, 26 New Zealand mounted riflemen lie in the Damascus Commonwealth War Cemetery, one is buried in the Jerusalem War Cemetery and 11 are commemorated on the Jerusalem Memorial. Others undoubtedly died of wounds later.
56. Falls, *Military Operations*, p. 345.
57. 'Account of the Battle from German and Turkish Sources', in Falls, p. 349; Sanders, p. 213.
58. Powles, p. 211; Carbery, pp. 477–8; Powles, *CMR*, p. 214; Nicol. p. 206; McNeur letter dated 20 Apr 1918. In addition to the losses on 30 March, five wounded New Zealanders died on 31 March.
59. Nicol, p. 207; Sterling diary entry dated 30 Mar 1918; Ireland, 'Raid Over the Jordan'.
60. Powles, *CMR*, p. 214.
61. Nicol, pp. 208–9.
62. Andrews, p. 172; Wilkie, p. 206.
63. WA Series 42/1, War Diary of Wellington Mounted Rifles Regiment, ANZ; 'Operations of the A&NZ Mounted Divn, East of Jordan, from March 23rd to April 2nd including Action of Amman'; Gullett, p. 580; Judge diary entry dated 1 Apr 1918. Fifteen New Zealanders were killed on 1 April or died of wounds on 1–2 April. They are buried (four) or commemorated (11) in the Jerusalem War Cemetery.
64. Falls, *Military Operations*, pp. 346–7; Cameron diary entry dated 2 Apr 1918. According to Liman, a pursuit was ordered, but there were no cavalry available for the task. Liman, *Five Years in Turkey*, p. 214.
65. Wilkie, p. 207; Sterling diary entry dated 3 Apr 1918; WA 41/1, War Diary of Auckland Mounted Rifles Regiment, ANZ; WA Series 40/1, HQ NZMR Brigade War Diary, ANZ.
66. Also, on 26 March intercepted EEF wireless messages revealed the plan in detail to the Turks. Memo dated 26 Mar 1918, AWM45 7/31, EEF Special File dated March 1918, AWM.
67. Sterling diary entry dated 1 Apr 1918; Ranstead letter dated 10 Apr 1918; Harrison papers.
68. Gullett, p. 585; King diary entry dated 4 Apr 1918.
69. Falls, *Military Operations*, p. 347; 'Operations of the A&NZ Mounted Divn, East of Jordan, from March 23rd to April 2nd including Action of Amman'; WA Series 40/1, HQ NZMR Brigade War Diary, ANZ; Carbery, p. 478; Nicol, p. 210; Gullett, p. 584.
70. Preston, p. 151.
71. Powles, p. 197.
72. 20 Corps letter dated 3 Apr 1918, AWM4, 1/60/26, HQ Anzac Mounted Division War Diary, AWM. Amman is now the capital city of Jordan. The Roman Citadel and amphitheatre are still in existence (a New Zealand tourist was shot and wounded at the amphitheatre in 2006). Hill 3039 is now part of the residential suburb of Al Yarmouk.

Chapter 14: Another disappointment

1. The Allies were pushed back 60 km in two weeks, losing over 250,000 men. French, Jewish and West Indian units also arrived in the EEF over the summer. Jewish volunteers from Europe and America were enlisted into the 38th, 39th and 40th battalions of the Royal Fusiliers (Jewish Volunteers) and the West Indians formed the 1st and 2nd battalions of the British West Indies (BWI) Regiment. In June, Allenby asked London (unsuccessfully) for light Whippet tanks and Japanese infantry divisions. War Office telegram to Allenby dated 27 Mar 1918, in Hughes, *Allenby in Palestine*, p. 138; Falls, *Military Operations*, p. 421; Allenby letters to Wilson dated 5 and 11 Jun 1918, in Hughes, *Allenby in Palestine*, pp. 161–2.
2. McNeur letter dated 16 Apr 1918.
3. Powles, pp. 216–7.
4. AWM4, 1/60/26, HQ Anzac Mounted Division War Diary, AWM; Falls, *Military Operations*, p. 361; Gullett, p. 596.
5. Allenby letter to Wilson dated 20 Apr 1918, in Hughes, *Allenby in Palestine*, p. 144; Falls, *Military Operations*, p. 365. This operation seemed to fit Allenby's definition of the 'active defence' that the War Office had demanded of him.
6. Falls, *Military Operations*, p. 364.
7. These forces were brought into the Jordan Valley as part of a plan to attack the EEF in May 1918. Falls, *Military Operations*, pp. 392–4; Gullett, p. 637.
8. Hill, in Horner, D.M., *The Commanders: Australian Military Leadership in the Twentieth Century*, George Allen & Unwin, Sydney, 1984, p. 76.

9. The 2nd LH Brigade was also sent up into the hills. Es Salt was captured by the 3rd LH Brigade. According to Falls, the 4th LH Brigade was denied the Damieh bridge by several companies of the German 146th Infantry Regiment. Falls, *Military Operations*, p. 393.

10. Falls, *Military Operations*, p. 393; Keogh, p. 221; Sanders, pp. 222–31.

11. Powles, *CMR*, p. 221; Powles, p. 221.

12. Falls, *Military Operations*, pp. 372–3.

13. In addition to the cavalry, the assault force included the Turkish 143rd Regiment and a storm battalion, two German infantry companies and a German machine gun company. The Turkish 2nd Regiment, which crossed the river at Mafid Jozele on the night of 30 April, was ordered back across the river to cross at Damieh. This kept it out of the fight on 1 May. The enemy cavalry on the way to Es Salt were followed by the 2nd Regiment once it crossed at Damieh. The nine guns were the only British artillery pieces captured by the Turks in the entire campaign. Falls, *Military Operations*, pp. 375–7, 393; Gullett, p. 615.

14. Preston, p. 164.

15. The Damieh, Wadi abu Turra and Shunet Nimrin tracks.

16. Falls, *Military Operations*, pp. 379–80.

17. According to Falls, the Turkish force in the valley was too exhausted to capture the Umm esh Shert track. In approving the withdrawal, Allenby reportedly remarked 'I can't lose my mounted troops'. Falls, *Military Operations*, p. 394; James, *Imperial Warrior*, p. 151.

18. Diary quote in Fox, F., *The History of the Royal Gloucestershire Hussars Yeomanry: the Great Cavalry Campaign in Palestine*, Philip Allen & Co., London, 1923, p. 229. A German officer named Major Franz von Papen fought with the Turks at Es Salt. He survived the war to become Adolf Hitler's vice-chancellor in 1933.

19. Powles, p. 222.

20. Doherty diary entry dated 5 May 1918; Sterling diary entry dated 6 May 1918.

21. Falls, *Military Operations*, pp. 389, 394; 'HQ Desert Mounted Corps Report on Operations East of the Jordan April–May 1918', AWM25, 455/69, AWM. The New Zealanders are buried (two) or commemorated (three) in the Jerusalem War Cemetery.

22. It turned out that the Arab envoys, who promised 20,000 fighting men, could actually speak for only about 400. Even those few failed to put in an appearance, choosing instead to go south to attack Ma'an. According to Liman, the Turks deliberately left the Umm esh Shert track open to give the enemy horsemen an escape route. Chetwode letter to Wavell dated 28 Mar 1939, Allenby 6/9/18, Allenby Papers, LHCMA; Newell, J.Q.C., 'Learning the Hard Way: Allenby in Egypt and Palestine, 1917–19', *Journal of Strategic Studies*, Volume 14, September 1991, p. 376; Liman, *Five Years in Turkey*, p. 230.

Chapter 15: The valley of desolation

1. McNeur letter dated 3 Jan 1918.

2. Gullett, pp. 638–9.

3. Downes, p. 699.

4. Murray, *A Collection of Memories*, p. 135.

5. Diary quote in Fox, p. 233; Moore, p. 146.

6. Moore, pp. 118–24.

7. Andrews, pp. 176–7.

8. McNeur letter dated 16 May 1918; Bostock, p. 141; Moore, p. 118.

9. Wilson, *Palestine 1917*, p. 111; McKay, p. 114.

10. Berrie, p. 199; WA Series 40/4, HQ NZMR Brigade Unregistered Files, ANZ.

11. Richardson, p. 93; Keogh, p. 228; Gullett, p. 644.

12. The biblical site of the baptism of Jesus is believed to be located between the Ghoraniyeh and Hijla crossings. Owers interview; Moore, p. 117; Reid, pp. 218–19.

13. Although Allenby had many squadrons of aircraft, it seems that few of them operated above the Jordan Valley. Nicol, p. 219; Powles, *CMR*, p. 224; WA Series 43/1, War Diary of Canterbury Mounted Rifles Regiment, ANZ.

14. Some Anzacs thought that the nets were 'effeminate and unsoldierly', so close supervision was needed. WA Series 40/4, NZMR Brigade Unregistered Files, ANZ; Falls, *Military Operations*, p. 425; Downes, p. 707; Carbery, p. 479.

15. In June 1918, the NZMFA dealt with two men who had been wounded in action and 158 cases of sickness. The incidence of sexually transmitted infections was highest in the Anzac contingents, but not by much.

Efforts were made to keep native women away from EEF camps and the brothels in Jerusalem and Bethlehem were placed out of bounds. Treatment stations were established in all leave destinations (the names of men receiving treatment were not to be recorded). WA 47/1, War Diary of New Zealand Mounted Field Ambulance, ANZ; Gullett, p. 644; NZMR Brigade Routine Orders 3308 and 3483 dated 23 Jul and 1 Sep 1918, WA Series 40/4, NZMR Brigade Unregistered Files, ANZ.

16. HQ Anzac Mounted Division memo dated 21 Jul 1918, and HQ NZMR Brigade memo dated 26 Aug 1918, WA Series 40/4, HQ NZMR Brigade Unregistered Files, ANZ.

17. McNeur letter dated 6 Aug 1918; WA Series 40/4, HQ NZMR Brigade Unregistered Files, ANZ.

18. Berrie, p. 206.

19. Falls, *Military Operations*, p. 424; Preston, p. 180.

20. The veterinary historian attributes the loss of condition to the lack of sufficient men to groom, feed, exercise and water all the horses. Sickness and other duties meant that there was, on average, one man to look after every seven horses. Blenkinsop and Rainey, p. 228; Reakes, p. 157.

21. Osborne, 'Operations of the Mounted Troops of the Egyptian Expeditionary Force', *Cavalry Journal*, Volume 12, 1922, p. 138. Enemy artillery fire ruled out the use of work parties from the Egyptian Labour Corps.

22. This became possible once the two new cavalry divisions joined the duty roster. Downes, p. 712; McMillan, p. 254; WA Series 40/1, HQ NZMR Brigade War Diary, ANZ.

23. Powles, *CMR*, p. 228.

24. Berrie, p. 144.

25. McNeur letters dated 4 and 27 Jun 1918.

26. Moore, pp. 126–7.

27. Moore, p.130; McCormack, R.D., diary entry dated 6 Apr 1918, 1999.2619, KMARL. To the few Jewish men in the brigade, Jerusalem was as important as it was to the Christians.

28. McNeur letter dated 18 Jun 1918.

29. Ranstead letters dated 18 Jan and 22 Apr 1918.

30. NcNeur letter, undated [August or September 1918].

31. McNeur letters dated 13 May and 27 Jun 1918.

32. Sterling diary entries dated 15 and 28 Jun 1918.

33. McNeur letter, undated; Sterling diary entry dated 14 Jun 1918.

34. Judge diary entry dated 14 Sep 1917.

35. Powles, *CMR*, p. 229.

36. Dawbin diary entry dated 4 Jul 1918. The trip to Port Said was long and involved. The men rode 15 km to Jericho, where they boarded trucks for the trip up the hill to Jerusalem. They then faced a long and uncomfortable train ride in open trucks all the way to Kantara on the Suez Canal. After a refreshing cup of tea at Alice Chisholm's canteen there, they boarded another train for the short trip to Port Said.

37. Wilkie says that four New Zealanders were killed and nine were wounded. Eight horses were killed and seven were wounded. The shade temperature on 14 July was 46°C. Allenby later stated that about 200 'Boche' were killed. While the attack on Abu Tulul was under way, newly arrived Indian cavalrymen charged into a Turkish cavalry force on the eastern bank of the Jordan River, spearing 90 fleeing Turks with their lances. Falls, *Military Operations*, pp. 429–38; Allenby letter to Wilson dated 24 Jul 1918, in Hughes, *Allenby in Palestine*, p. 169; Preston, p. 186; Powles, p. 231; Wilkie, pp. 215–16; Sterling diary entries dated 14 and 15 Jul 1918; WA Series 40/1, HQ NZMR Brigade War Diary, ANZ; Judge diary entry dated 15 Jul 1918.

38. Sterling diary entry dated 14 Jul 1918; Wilkie, p. 215; Hill, *Chauvel of the Light Horse*, p. 160.

Chapter 16: Settling old scores

1. Six thousand of these troops were deployed along the southern Hejaz Railway, where they posed no threat to the EEF at all. Zurcher, 'Little Mehmet in the Desert: the Ottoman Soldier's Experience', pp. 234–5; Falls, *Military Operations*, p. 452.

2. Falls, *Military Operations*, pp. 666–73.

3. Allenby letter to Wilson dated 24 Jul 1918, in Hughes, *Allenby in Palestine*, p. 169.

4. The two New Zealand camel companies became the 2nd New Zealand Machine Gun Squadron, part of the new 5th LH Brigade. The War Office had wanted the New Zealanders from the ICC Brigade to make up the third regiment of the brigade (to be known as the Otago Mounted Rifles Regiment). The New Zealand government was supportive until General Godley protested. In July, Wellington approved the formation of the machine gun squadron instead. An earlier War Office proposal to disband the Australian Mounted

Division and send its men to France as reinforcements for the Australian infantry was rejected by the War Cabinet. Powles, p. 232; Mallett thesis, p. 158; *NZEF Provision and Maintenance*, p. 4; Anglesey, p. 222; Wilson letter to Allenby dated 21 Jun 1918, in Hughes, *Allenby in Palestine*, p. 164; Gullett, p. 678; Wilkie, p. 219; Osborne, 'Operations of the Mounted Troops of the Egyptian Expeditionary Force' *Cavalry Journal*, Volume 13, 1923, pp. 150–1.

5. Allied air superiority was decisive in maintaining operational security. In June, 100 enemy aircraft flew over EEF positions; by September that number had diminished almost to zero.

6. Chaytor also received an assortment of extra artillery, as well as 17 tractors, 64 trucks and 300 donkeys to carry combat supplies. The Anzacs referred to the Jews as 'the Jordan Highlanders', while the West Indians, who wore slouch hats, called themselves 'the Black Anzacs'. Falls, *Military Operations*, p. 466; Johnson, *Memoirs of a Soldier*, p. 67; McMillan, p. 270. The Frenchmen were part of the newly raised 5th LH Brigade.

7. In six months 230 men were evacuated to hospital from the NZMGS with malaria – the equivalent of its entire strength. Most of these cases occurred after the commencement of the 'big push' in September. Gullett, pp. 678, 686; Luxford, p. 225; Falls, *Military Operations*, p. 466.

8. On 29 Sep 1918, Chaytor's Force comprised 8000 British and Anzac soldiers, 3000 Indians and 500 Egyptians, as well as 11,000 horses and mules, 70 donkeys and 110 camels. According to a German officer in Amman, 10,000–12,000 soldiers were stationed east of the Jordan River in 1918, including 1500 Germans and Austrians. However, sickness, malnutrition and Turkish 'unreliability' meant that the actual fighting strength was never more than about one-third of that. Further north, part of the Turkish 7th Army also faced Chaytor's Force. Thalacker, Lieutenant, 'The Hijaz Railway 1918', *The Journal of the T.E. Lawrence Society*, Volume 12, Spring 2003, p. 17; Falls, *Military Operations*, pp. 547–8.

9. The Jewish battalions included volunteers from Great Britain, Russia and the United States.

10. Powles, p. 236; Nicol, p. 223.

11. Troopers were trained to operate specialist equipment, and signallers and Hotchkiss gunners received extra training to allow them to fight in the troops if casualties made it necessary. Powles, p. 236; entry dated 8 Sep 1918, AWM4, 1/60/31, HQ Anzac Mounted Division War Diary, AWM.

12. Powles, p. 234.

13. Powles, *CMR*, p. 230.

14. Sterling diary entry dated 19 Sep 1918.

15. Gullett, pp. 690–1.

16. During the summer, two mounted divisions were stationed in the Jordan Valley. By the night of 18 September, only the Anzac Mounted Division was left; HQ DMC, the 4th and 5th Cavalry divisions, and the Australian Mounted Division were all hidden in the orange and olive groves on the coast north of Jaffa. A German intelligence map captured just before Z-Day showed one EEF cavalry and two infantry divisions on the coastal plain, when there were three cavalry and five infantry divisions there. According to a German air reconnaissance report dated 17 September, 'far from there being any diminution in the cavalry in the Jordan Valley, there are evidences of twenty-three more squadrons there.' Preston, p. 198.

17. Judge diary entry dated 19 Sep 1918.

18. McNeur letter dated 21 Oct 1918.

19. Sterling diary entry dated 18 Sep 1918. Marshal Liman's Yildirim Army Group HQ at Nazareth was raided on 20 September and he barely escaped in his pyjamas.

20. Sanders, pp. 286, 289. Presumably, Cemal wanted to give the 2nd Corps, which was withdrawing northwards from Ma'an along the Hejaz Railway, the best chance to escape before the railway was cut at Amman. In the event, his hesitation doomed his entire army.

21. The ford at Mafid Jozele was captured by a Jewish battalion on 21 September. Falls, *Armageddon 1918*, p. 90; Moore, p. 148; Nicol, pp. 223–4; Hopkins, Major General R., 'Chaytor's Force: a Personal Account', *Australian Defence Force Journal*, Number 13, November/December 1978, pp. 29–33.

22. McNeur letter dated 21 Oct 1918. The British cavalry had cut off all other escape routes by capturing the railway junction at Affule, and a number of fords on the upper Jordan River. The only way out was to cross the Jordan River at Damieh and reach the Hejaz Railway at Amman.

23. Wilkie, pp. 224–5. This was the second commander of the Turkish 53rd Division to be captured by the Anzacs; the first was caught at Gaza in March 1917.

24. The New Zealanders were threatened by Turkish forces attacking along the Nablus track, from the direction of Mafid Jozele, at the Damieh bridge itself, and from the Judean Hills to their left rear. The Wellingtons and a reserve CMR squadron stopped 500 Turks that were advancing towards the bridge along the Nablus track, the enemy in the Judean Hills withdrew and shelled the New Zealanders intermittently through the day,

and the 1st LH Brigade dealt with the threat at Mafid Jozele. Falls, *Military Operations*, pp. 550–1; Wilkie, pp. 224–5; Powles, p. 246.

25. Judge diary entry dated 22 Sep 1918.

26. Sterling diary entry dated 22 Sep 1918.

27. Powles, p. 247; Falls, *Military Operations*, p. 551.

28. McNeur letter dated 21 Oct 1918.

29. McMillan, p. 273.

30. Andrews, p. 180. The Mecidi Order and the War Medal (incorrectly referred to as the 'Gallipoli Star') were Turkish bravery and merit awards.

31. WA Series 40/1, HQ NZMR Brigade War Diary, ANZ; Powles, p. 247; Falls, *Military Operations*, p. 552; McMillan, p. 274. Two of the horse artillery guns captured from the 4th LH Brigade in May were recaptured. RAF reports suggested that only about 600 Turks from the 53rd Division succeeded in crossing the Damieh bridge before its capture.

32. Sterling diary entry dated 23 Sep 1918.

33. Judge and Cameron diary entries dated 24 Sep 1918; Luxford, pp. 233–4.

34. WA Series 40/1, HQ NZMR Brigade War Diary, ANZ; D. Lange, quoted in Andrews, p. 181; Berrie, p. 150.

35. Some sources state that 150 horses died in a few days. The official British veterinary historian claimed that eating freshly threshed barley was the real cause of the losses, which amounted to only 15 deaths and 160 cases of serious illness across Chaytor's Force. Reakes, p. 157; Moore, pp. 163–4; Blenkinsop and Rainey, pp. 243–4; Sterling diary entry dated 2 Oct 1918.

36. A Jewish battalion which was supposed to join them did not arrive. According to one New Zealander, this inexperienced unit moved into the hills on two tracks. 'The heads of each column sighted each other on the high ground and each opened up. They got stuck into each other. Then both columns bolted and all met in a disorganised rabble back in the valley.' Andrews, p. 182; Preston, pp. 229–30, 241; WA Series 40/1, HQ NZMR Brigade War Diary, ANZ. The story of the railway raid is told in the Introduction.

37. Powles, p. 250.

38. Thalacker, p. 29.

39. Powles, p.250; Wilkie, p.228.

40. Gullett, p. 719; Nicol, pp. 227–8.

41. Preston, p. 241.

42. Moore, pp. 162–3.

43. Unlike the March raid, the ground was now hard enough to permit rapid off-road movement by horses. WA Series 40/1, HQ NZMR Brigade War Diary, ANZ; McMillan, p. 278; 'Narrative of Chaytor's Force', dated 6 Oct 1918, AWM4, 1/60/31, HQ Anzac Mounted Division War Diary, AWM; Powles, pp. 251–2.

44. A dressing station was opened at the ruined Roman amphitheatre to treat some of these men but the worst cases were evacuated to Jerusalem by ambulance. WA Series 40/1, HQ NZMR Brigade War Diary, ANZ; Downes, p. 722.

45. Powles, *Reveille*, p. 15; Judge and Sterling diary entries dated 25 Sep 1918.

46. WA Series 40/1, HQ NZMR Brigade War Diary, ANZ; Cameron diary entry dated 29 Sep 1918; McNeur letter dated 21 Oct 1918.

47. With the railway line at Dera cut by the Arabs, the Turks who did escape from Amman had nowhere to go. Allenby decided that they could be dealt with by the 4th Cavalry Division and the Arabs, and he ordered Chaytor not to pursue them to the north. Most of these Turks died of sickness or thirst, or were massacred by vengeful Arabs. With Amman in Chaytor's hands, the Turks of the 2nd Corps were caught in a trap. Their only other possible escape route, along the Pilgrim's Road to the east of Amman, was closed on 27 September when the 1st LH Brigade captured the water supply (and 300 prisoners) at Wadi el Hammam.

48. Falls, *Military Operations*, p. 556.

49. Gullett, p. 725; Richardson, p. 103.

50. Cameron, Lieutenant Colonel D.C., report, quoted in Wilson and Wetherell, p.148.

51. WA Series 40/1, HQ NZMR Brigade War Diary, ANZ.

52. Wilson and Wetherell, p. 147; Falls, *Military Operations*, pp. 557–8.

53. Bruce, A., 'Strange Events at Ziza; Aussies Protected Turks against Allies,' *Reveille*, Volume 31, 1 Apr 1958, pp. 23–4; Nicol, p. 234.

54. Gullett, pp. 726–7.

55. Powles, p. 255; Gullett, p. 727; Judge diary entry dated 30 Sep 1918; Sterling diary entry dated 30 Sep 1918; Doherty diary entry dated 1 Oct 1918; Moore, p. 165.

56. Ryrie took the worst Turkish casualties with him in the camel cacolets of his field ambulance. Many other soldiers from the local area slipped away to their homes. According to Ryrie, 'Chaytor nearly had a fit when these fine troops marched into Amman fully armed.' Falls, *Military Operations*, p. 558; Woodward, p. 202; Falls, *Armageddon 1918*, pp. 98–9.

57. Annabell, Major N., *Official History of the New Zealand Engineers During the Great War, 1914–1919*, Evans, Cobb & Sharpe, Wanganui, 1927, pp. 290–2.

58. AWM4, 1/16/32, HQ Anzac Mounted Division War Diary, AWM; WA Series 40/1, HQ NZMR Brigade War Diary, ANZ; Powles, pp. 256–7. Ziza is adjacent to Jordan's Queen Alia International Airport.

59. Powles, pp. 256–7.

60. AWM4, 1/16/32, HQ Anzac Mounted Division War Diary, AWM. Five New Zealanders are buried in the Damascus War Cemetery, and one lies in the Ramleh War Cemetery. The remaining five are buried (one) or commemorated (five) in the Jerusalem War Cemetery.

61. Sixty-one NZEF men died from malaria during the war. It is highly likely that nearly all of them were from the NZMR Brigade. Another record states that 50 NZEF men died from malaria in late 1918. The disease killed a total of 865 EEF men, out of a total of 35,222 reported cases. Quinine tablets were not always effective, and intravenous injections of quinine were administered only in the worst cases. The influenza was characterised by a rapid onset, severe symptoms and unusual lethality, even among fit young people. Some victims were dead within 24 hours of the first symptoms. Powles, p. 262; Blackwell and Douglas, p.125; Downes, pp. 748–9; Carbery, p. 539; WA Series 40/4, HQ NZMR Brigade Unregistered Files, ANZ; Barry, J.M., *The Great Influenza: the Epic Story of the Deadliest Plague in History*, Viking/Penguin, New York, 2004, pp. 1–7, 151.

62. Andrews, p. 183.

63. Moore, pp. 165–6; Sterling diary entry dated 4 Oct 1918.

64. Falls, *Military Operations*, p. 559.

65. Allenby had intended to bring the Anzac Mounted Division up to Damascus to rejoin the DMC, but this was not required. Chaytor appointed Colonel Mackesy as the Military Governor of Es Salt and Amman, but Mackesy was soon ordered to hand control to the Hejaz Arabs. He did so on 27 and 30 October in impressive ceremonies at Amman and Es Salt. A Guard of Honour of 65 Anzacs saluted as the Hejaz flag was hoisted over both towns. The last horsemen then withdrew from the region. Between 21 September and 5 October, the NZMR Brigade captured 3190 prisoners of war, 40 machine guns, fifteen artillery pieces and two wireless sets. Allenby telegram to Wilson dated 25 Sep 1918, in Hughes, *Allenby in Palestine*, p. 188; WA Series 40/1, HQ NZMR Brigade War Diary, ANZ; AWM4, 1/60/32, HQ Anzac Mounted Division War Diary, AWM; Gullett, p. 783.

66. Last Days with the Mounteds', in *Chronicles of the NZEF*, 22 Nov 1918, p. 205; Sterling diary entry dated 4 Oct 1918; McMillan, p. 281.

67. WA Series 40/1, HQ NZMR Brigade War Diary, ANZ; Andrews, p. 183; Sterling diary entry dated 4 Oct 1918.

68. Chaytor's Force was disbanded in Jericho on 3 Nov 1918. WA Series 40/1, HQ NZMR Brigade War Diary, ANZ; AWM4, 1/60/32, HQ Anzac Mounted Division War Diary, AWM.

69. Judge diary entries dated 6 and 7 Oct 1918.

70. Hull, G.B. letter dated 18 Oct 1918, 2001.1035, KMARL. For non-New Zealand readers, Rangitoto is an island in Auckland's Waitemata Harbour.

71. Liddell Hart, B.H., *History of the First World War*, Cassell edition, London, 1970, p. 561; Falls, *Military Operations*, p. 618.

72. Doherty diary entry dated 31 Oct 1918.

73. Judge diary entries dated 30, 31 Oct 1918.

74. Andrews, p. 185; Nicol, p. 237.

75. WA Series 40/4, HQ NZMR Brigade Unregistered Files, ANZ.

76. Ranstead letter dated 11–18 Nov 1918, in Harper, *Letters from the Battlefield: New Zealand Soldiers Write Home 1914–18*, p. 91.

Chapter 17: The horses stay behind

1. Priority was given to Gallipoli veterans if they were fit. The 7th ALH Regiment also went to Gallipoli. 81 horses went to Gallipoli with the CMR. WA Series 40/1, HQ NZMR Brigade War Diary, ANZ; Powles, *CMR*, pp. 243–5; McMillan, p. 290; Medical Report dated 2 Feb 1919 and CMR Report dated 4 Feb 1919, AWM4, 1/60/35, HQ Anzac Mounted Division War Diary, AWM.

2. Doherty letter dated 19 Dec 1918.

3. Powles, *CMR*, p. 246; Richardson, p.109; reports dated 18 Jan and 4 Feb 1919, AWM4, 1/60/35, HQ Anzac Mounted Division War Diary, AWM.

4. One hundred and twelve New Zealand men were hospitalised. The 7th ALH Regiment suffered one death from complications of influenza. These men are buried in the Chanak Consular Cemetery in Canakkale. Medical Report appended to CMR Report, AWM4, 1/60/35, HQ Anzac Mounted Division War Diary, AWM; Judge diary entries dated 7 Dec 1918 and 23/24 Jan 1919; Ranstead letter dated 24 Jan 1919.

5. Ranstead letter dated 20 Nov 1918, in Harper, *Letters from the Battlefield: New Zealand Soldiers Write Home 1914–18*, p. 91.

6. Wilkie, p. 235.

7. The Turks needed to be disarmed, fed and repatriated; freed Allied POWs and starving local people had to be taken care of; the malaria and influenza outbreaks had to be brought under control; military administrations had to be set up to govern the former Turkish province; and the already troublesome Hejaz Arab Army had to be dealt with. All of this required Allenby to maintain fighting troops in the field, ready for any eventuality. The men from the Ayun Kara graveyard were later reburied in the Ramleh War Cemetery. The Ayun Kara memorial has been destroyed.

8. Ranstead letter dated 29 Nov 1918. Along with Allsop, William Martin, Arthur Pearce and John McLennan survived the war; James Saunders, Christopher Bowen, Colin McLeod and David Quintal did not.

9. Leslie Lowry sailed from New Zealand in Feb 1918 with the 35th Mounted Rifles Reinforcements. After being posted to the 1st New Zealand Machine Gun Squadron in May, he spent the next two months in the field before being evacuated sick. By the time Lowry returned to the brigade in October 1918, the war was practically over. AABK 18805, W5544, Box 32, Record No. 0069645, Lowry, L.T., ANZ.

10. Corporal C.H. Carr heard the sounds of men running, followed by confused shouting and then a shot. 'This was followed by a cry of "help", then moaning.' Carr found Lowry lying face-down on the sand, about 40 metres from the tent lines, bleeding from a single wound to the chest. Lowry did not speak after his initial cry and Carr saw no-one else in the vicinity. The cause of death was determined to be blood loss. Statements by Cpl C.H. Carr, No.1 NZMGS, and Captain T.C. Fraser, NZMC, 'Proceedings of a Court of Inquiry Assembled at HQ No.1 NZMGS Richon, on the 10th December 1918, by order of Brigadier-General W. Meldrum, CMG, DSO, Commanding NZMR Brigade, for the purpose of inquiring into and reporting upon the circumstances under which No.65779 Trooper Lowry, L.T., of No.1 NZMGS met his death on the night of 9th/10th December 1918', WA Series 2/1, 90/60A, Box 3, Discipline, Surafend Raid, Jan–Feb 1919, ANZ; WA Series 1/3, XFE 1069, Courts of Inquiry, 65779 Tpr Lowry, L., 1st NZMG Sqn, ANZ. Leslie Lowry is buried in the Ramleh War Cemetery.

11. McMillan, pp. 294–5; Johnson, *Memoirs of a Soldier*, p. 83; Meldrum Court of Inquiry. The bullet that killed Lowry was fired from a Colt .45 revolver. This weapon was not on general issue to NZMR troops, but it was a common weapon in Turkish and Arab hands.

12. Hill, *Chauvel of the Light Horse*, p. 192; WA Series 1/3, XFE 1069: Courts of Inquiry, 65779 Tpr Lowry, L., 1st NZMG Sqn, ANZ.

13. Several witnesses stated that members of No.1 NZMGS organised the raid. Statement by Trooper H.S. Spaven, in HQ 2nd Light Horse Brigade report dated 11 Jan 1918 [*sic*], WA Series 2/1, 90/60A, Box 3, Discipline, Surafend Raid, Jan–Feb 1919, ANZ.

14. Andrews, p. 187.

15. Reuter, 'Anzac Episode in Palestine: Inquiry into 1914–18 War Allegation,' *The Times*, 19 May 1964; Anon, 'The Surafend Incident: Why Allenby Ignored the Anzacs, a Trooper's Story', *Quick March*, 10 Jan 1920, p. 64; Andrews, p. 187; Moore, p. 170; Birkbeck, G.T., diary entry dated 10 Dec 1918, quoted in Hughes, *Allenby in Palestine*, p. 309; King diary entry dated 10 Dec 1918. A few sources claim that some victims were castrated and/or thrown down a well, but the weight of evidence is against both assertions. D.J. Milnes points out that no veteran questioned by oral historian Nicholas Boyack about the castration allegation recalled this occurring. Owers interview; Adam-Smith, P., *The ANZACs*, Thomas Nelson, Melbourne, 1978, p. 239; Andrews, p. 187; Milnes, *Imperial Soldiers?*, p. 46.

16. Lieutenant Colonel McCarroll did not send any men from the AMR. He later claimed that he was not told of the cause of the fire, which was nearly out anyway. Memo by Brigadier General W. Meldrum and various witness statements, HQ NZMR Brigade BML/59 dated 31 Jan 1919, WA Series 2/1, 90/60A, Discipline, Surafend Raid, Jan–Feb 1919, ANZ.

17. Andrew, R.H., *Notes January 1918 to October 1919*, Allenby 6/9/7, Allenby Papers, LHCMA; WA Series 40/4, 29, Disturbance at Village of Surafend, 10 December 1918, ANZ.

18. Chaytor memo dated 4 Feb 1919, in HQ NZMR Brigade BML/59 dated 31 Jan 1919, WA Series 2/1, 90/60A, Discipline, Surafend Raid, Jan–Feb 1919, ANZ; HQ NZMR Brigade memo dated 16 Dec 1918, WA Series 40/4, 27 Discipline, Dress on Leave, Bounds, Punishments, etc from 7 Aug 1918–24 Jan 1919, ANZ; AD Series 10, Burning of Surafend Village, Palestine, ANZ.

19. Johnson, *Memoirs of a Soldier*, p. 84; Ranstead letter dated 25 Dec 1918; *War Memories of Robert Ellwood*, URL: http://www.jcu.edu.au/aff/history/net_resources/ellwood/016.html. Counting out involved a group of men counting from one to ten. If the target of the counting had not departed by the time the men reached 10, he would be hastened on his way by some form of physical violence.

20. The CMR and 7th ALH regiments were on Gallipoli, only one squadron of the 2nd ALH Regiment was present and the 5th ALH Regiment was at Semakh. According to Hill, the division was to be confined to camp at Rafah until ships became available for its repatriation. Allenby refused to approve awards to men of the division, for acts of gallantry and good work that took place before Surafend. Newell considers Allenby's public humiliation of the Anzac Mounted Division after Surafend to have been one of his 'most serious misjudgements in Palestine'. He attributes it to Allenby's 'uncontrollable temper'. Chauvel and others eventually persuaded Allenby to reverse his decision about awards. Porter interview; Hill, *Chauvel of the Light Horse*, p. 192; Newell, 'Learning the Hard Way: Allenby in Egypt and Palestine', pp. 382–3.

21. The EEF could not afford to have to deal with a rebellious population behind the front line, and it needed to keep the Hejaz Arabs on-side. Ted Andrews added the alleged looting of stores and murder of sentries to the list of grievances, and noted that 'the treacherous ambush of Ain [es] Sir was still fresh in the minds of the New Zealand troops'. There is no known case of New Zealanders abusing or killing Turkish or German prisoners during the Middle East campaign. They knew and obeyed the rules prohibiting such actions, yet the crimes that some of them committed at Surafend were more serious. It is clear that the Arab victims at Surafend were seen in a different light to enemy combatants, who were generally regarded with respect, if not sympathy, by the Anzacs. Andrews, p. 187. Gainfort interview; McKay, p. 167.

22. Powles, p. 268.

23. Andrews, p. 191.

24. Civics is the study of the rights and responsibilities of citizenship. There was little interest in Arabic, auditing, navigation, law, violin-playing, economics, ethics, chemistry, window dressing or butchering. Trooper John Robertson, who had been a school inspector in New Zealand before the war, suggested the scheme. Robertson was promoted to the rank of major and placed in charge of the project. WA Series 40/4, HQ NZMR Brigade Unregistered Files, ANZ; WA Series 40/4, 24, Box 5, Educational Facilities during Period of Armistice and Subsequent Period of Demobilisation, ANZ; Robertson, *With the Cameliers in Palestine*, pp. 232–4.

25. Ranstead letter dated 25 Dec 1918.

26. Men conducted training on machine gunnery, signalling and semaphore, bayonet fighting, saluting, bombing and guard duties. The cleaning and inspection of equipment was continual. HQ NZMR Brigade memo dated 6 Dec 1918, WA Series 40/4, HQ NZMR Brigade Unregistered Files, ANZ.

27. Routine Orders 3864 and 3919 dated 10 and 25 Dec 1918, WA Series 40/4, HQ NZMR Brigade Unregistered Files, ANZ.

28. In order to prevent the introduction of such equine diseases as glanders and anthrax, New Zealand's quarantine regulations 'absolutely prohibit the importation from Egypt of horses, cattle, dogs, or other animals under any circumstances whatever'. Memo from Lieutenant Colonel A.R. Young, for Director of Veterinary Services and Remounts, to HQ NZEF dated 16 Jun 1917, AD Series 1, 75/29, Box 1380, Demobilisation, Horses, Disposal Abroad, ANZ.

29. McKay, pp. 170–1.

30. War Office, *Statistics of the Military Effort of the British Empire during the Great War, 1914–1920*, 1922, p. 396; AD Series 1, 75/29, Box 1380, Demobilisation, Horses, Disposal of Abroad, ANZ. Some sources that list only three classes (A, B and C) probably combined classes A and B.

31. Nicol, p. 244.

32. This tallies closely with NZEF animal wastage records, which record a reduction of 418 horses between 31 October and 30 November 1918. New Zealand received £63 for each transferred horse. The fate of the 21 riding horses and 60 transport animals taken by the CMR to Gallipoli is unknown. AD Series 1, 75/29, Box 1380, Demobilisation, Horses, Disposal of Abroad, ANZ; Powles, *CMR*, p. 243; WA Series 1/3, XFE 1071, NZEF in Egypt, Wastage of Animals 1917–1918, ANZ; Judge diary entry dated 13 Nov 1918.

33. King diary entry dated 21 Nov 1918. As most of the horses transferred from the CMR would have been less

than 12 years old and sound, they should not have been destroyed. Some statements suggest that it was the old and sick horses in the Remount Depot that were killed first; according to George Ranstead 'a big clean up was made at the remount depot here the other day. All aged horses, unless they were particularly good, were destroyed – 500 were shot one day and 200 the next.' Sterling diary entries dated 20 and 21 Nov 1918; Andrews, pp. 185–6; Ranstead letter dated 29 Nov 1918.

34. Henderson, p. 25. The classes appear to be incorrect.

35. Bellis, p. 56.

36. Sterling diary entry dated 21 Feb 1919.

37. Undated statement in AD Series 1, 75/29, Box 1380, Demobilisation, Horses, Disposal of Abroad, ANZ. A further 200 horses are listed as 'transferred'. A total of 2350 NZMR horses were disposed of (389 CMR horses handed in at Ludd, 81 CMR horses taken to Gallipoli (fate unknown), 1680 to Moascar, 200 'transferred'). Other sources give slightly different numbers. When news of the disposal of the horses reached New Zealand in October 1919, a public campaign was launched to try and save them, but it was too late and nothing could be done. In 1930, Dorothy Brooke, the wife of the commander of the British Cavalry Brigade in Egypt, began a campaign that rescued over 5,000 ex-Army horses by 1934. It is possible that some old New Zealand horses were among this number.

38. Luckily for Bess, the fact that she had lived in the Middle East for over three years was overlooked or ignored by the authorities. The other horses belonged to Major General Russell, the late Lieutenant Colonel George King and the late Captain Richard Riddiford. The four horses were shipped from France to England in February 1919 to undergo the mandatory year-long quarantine. They were used at Sling Camp until September, boarded out for the remaining six months, then shipped home. Attempts to recover the cost (£683) from their owners met with no success. All except King's horse were Main Body animals. There is a memorial cairn for Bess near Flock House, Bulls. WA Series 22/6, 40, Horses returned for Sentimental Reasons, ANZ; Chaytor memo dated 1 Jul 1920, AD Series 1, 75/29, Box 1380, Demobilisation, Horses, Disposal of Abroad, ANZ.

39. Judge diary entry dated 26 Apr 1919. In Jan 1919, the War Office asked New Zealand to consider calling for volunteers for a composite mounted rifles regiment, to form part of an Anzac brigade which would be used for occupation duties in Egypt. The request was refused. In February, a scheme to allow some of the men to take leave in England was put in place. Three hundred and fifty mounted riflemen applied but the scheme was cancelled when the uprising began in Egypt. AD Series 1, 75/39, Box 1381, Demobilization, Leave to Visit England, extension of to Troops Serving in Palestine and Egypt, ANZ.

40. Chaytor believed that the disturbances resulted from a lack of control in Ismailia, and incitement by men from Kantara. He replaced Lieutenant Colonel Charles Dick, the Commanding Officer of the New Zealand Training Unit and Depot, who Chaytor thought lacked experience and firmness. New Zealand's share of the compensation paid to the shopkeepers was 2,477 Egyptian pounds. A number of New Zealanders were court-martialled for looting, receiving terms of imprisonment with hard labour. WA Series 1, Item 3, Box 6, File XFE 1024: Courts of Inquiry: Disturbances at Ismailia 7th/11th December 1918, 14th/15th July 1919, ANZ; WA Series 1 Item 3 Box 6 File XFE 1024: Courts of Inquiry: Disturbances at Ismailia 7th/11th December 1918, 14th/15th July 1919, ANZ; Pugsley, C., *On the Fringe of Hell: New Zealanders and Military Discipline in the First World War*, Hodder & Stoughton, Auckland, 1991, p. 288.

41. Studholme, pp. 18, 378–80; Ranstead letter dated 27 Feb 1919.

42. Mitchell interview.

43. Sterling diary entry dated 29 Dec 1918.

44. According to Andrews, the Chaytors joined a party of Europeans and Indians in Assiut, where they were besieged. An aircraft reportedly dropped them a machine gun with enough ammunition to hold off the attackers until a relief force arrived. In April, three British soldiers were ambushed and killed in another village. Fromkin, D., *A Peace to End All Peace: the Fall of the Ottoman Empire and the Creation of the Modern Middle East*, Henry Holt, New York, 2001, p. 419; Jones, I., *Who Are the Blokes in the Black Hats? Australian Light Horse and the Egyptian Rebellion of 1919*, Proceedings of the Australian War Memorial History Conference, July 1989; Andrews, p. 195; Allenby telegrams to Curzon dated 19 Apr and 4 May 1919, in Hughes, *Allenby in Palestine*, pp. 240–1, 250.

45. Allenby was at the Versailles Peace Conference, arriving back in Cairo on 25 March. Jones, *Who Are the Blokes in the Black Hats?*; Allenby letter to Chetwode dated 29 Mar 1919, in Hughes, *Allenby in Palestine*, p. 232; Olden, p. 305.

46. Mousa, S., 'Unrest in Egypt', *Purnell's History of the First World War*, pp.3326–7.

47. According to Harry Judge, some men 'think it is only a gag to get us away from the "Aussies" who seem very inclined to make trouble over the delay in demobilisation.' One hundred horses were taken from Rafah. Judge diary entry dated 17 Mar 1919; WA Series 40/4, HQ NZMR Brigade Unregistered Files, ANZ.
48. Moore, p. 173.
49. Sterling diary entry dated 20 Mar 1919; Berrie, p. 163.
50. Moore, p. 173. More than half of the 2207 New Zealanders remaining in Egypt after the departure of the *Kaikoura* were deployed to various places in the Nile Delta, including Damanhur, Kafr Sheikh and Mansoura (see Map 1, p.23).
51. The composite regiment, consisting of the WMR squadron, light horsemen and mounted artillerymen, was under the command of Major William Foley of the WMR. Wilkie, p. 239; Andrews, p. 195.
52. In May 1919 the NZMR Brigade was in bivouac over the periods 11–19, 23–4 May and 26–30 May. WA Series 40/1, HQ NZMR Brigade War Diary, ANZ.
53. *New Zealand Herald*, 12 Sep 1919.
54. Sterling diary entry dated 14 Apr 1919; Powles, p. 270; Doherty letter dated 31 Mar 1919.
55. Andrews, p. 196.
56. Allenby telegram to War Office dated 16 May 1919, Allenby letter to Wilson dated 5 Jun 1919, Allenby telegrams to Curzon dated 4 May and 4 Jun 1919, in Hughes, *Allenby in Palestine*, pp. 255–6,159, 251, 273; Jones, *Who Are the Blokes in the Black Hats?*
57. Powles, p. 272.
58. Andrews, p. 198.
59. Twelve hundred horses were handed in at Bilbeis. The men moved from Tanta to Ismailia by rail, arriving between 21 and 23 June. WA Series 40/4, HQ NZMR Brigade Unregistered Files, ANZ.
60. Special Order by Major General Sir EWC Chaytor, KCMG, CB, ADC, Commanding Anzac Mounted Division, dated 27 Jun 1919, AWM4, 1/60/40, HQ Anzac Mounted Division War Diary, AWM.
61. Quoted in Bostock, p. 231.
62. Chaytor wanted men with businesses in New Zealand to go first, followed by men with guaranteed employment, then men with trades for which there was a shortage in New Zealand, and lastly, all the others. AD Series 1, 75/34, Box 1381, Demobilization, Leave to Visit England, extension of to Troops Serving in Palestine and Egypt, ANZ; Sterling diary entry dated 3 Jul 1919.
63. Sixteen nurses also returned to New Zealand on these ships. This total is 540 more than the official strength of the NZEF in Egypt on 31 Oct 1918, which was 3707. The difference is probably accounted for by men already struck off the NZEF strength, but not yet embarked for New Zealand. Studholme, pp.18, 378–80.
64. Andrews, p. 198; Murray, *A Collection of Memories*, p. 144.
65. Andrews, p. 198.
66. Quoted in Nicol, p. 240.
67. *New Zealand Herald*, 12 Sep 1919.

Conclusion

1. McNeur letter dated 18 Dec 1918.
2. Three times as many New Zealanders lost their lives in six weeks on the Somme in 1916 as died in the entire three-year Middle East campaign. No two sources for NZEF casualty figures agree completely. I chose to use the CWGC database for fatalities, and the *NZEF Alphabetical List of Casualties* for the numbers of wounded men. The missing men probably can all be added to the list of deaths. The post-Gallipoli fatalities include 57 men who died after being discharged from the NZEF. Particularly bad periods for the mounteds were 8–9 Aug 1915 (137 deaths on Chunuk Bair), 27–8 Aug 1915 (132 deaths at Hill 60), 14 Nov 1917 (49 deaths at Ayun Kara) and 23 Mar–1 Apr 1918 (38 deaths at or near Amman). A total of 16,366 EEF men (including 1,374 AIF men) died and 38,090 (including 3341 AIF men) were wounded during the Middle East war. *New Zealand Expeditionary Force, Alphabetical List of Casualties, Books 1–14*, Government Printer, Wellington, 1916–1919; *Statistics*, pp. 739, 769.
3. WA Series 40/4, HQ NZMR Brigade Unregistered Files, ANZ; various regimental records. The worst months for equine battle casualties were April 1917 (41 horses killed), November 1917 (108), March 1918 (63) and April 1918 (57).
4. Casualties attributed to artillery fire and shell-shock seldom appear in the NZMR Brigade's Record of

Casualties. Instances of injury from bayonets and poison gas are rare and non-existent respectively. There were a few cases of self-inflicted wounding, and suicide was not unheard-of (including one case during the trip home after the war). Several men drowned when their ships were sunk by mines or torpedoes, or accidentally while swimming. According to one contemporary study, one-quarter of wounds from high velocity bullets were fatal; serious wounds (which often resulted in death) comprised another 15%, with minor (probably survivable) wounds making up the remaining 60%. WA Series 40/5, NZ Mounted Rifles Brigade Record of Casualties, ANZ; Delorme, E., *War Surgery*, H.K. Lewis, London, 1915, The World War One Document Archive, University of Kansas, URL: http://www.ku.edu/carrie/specoll/medical/delorme/delorme.htm

5. Algar, B., *In the Shadow of War*, p. 123.

6. Gas gangrene and tetanus killed many wounded men on the Western Front, but this was less common in the Middle East because of the absence of manure-rich soil to contaminate wounds. Gabriel, R.A. and K.S. Metz, *A History of Military Medicine, Volume 2, From the Renaissance through Modern Times*, Greenwood Press, New York, 1992, pp. 240, 243; Bosanquet, N., 'Health Systems in Khaki: the British and American Medical Experience', in Cecil and Liddle, *Facing Armageddon: the First World War Experience*, pp. 451–65.

7. Three at Gallipoli and thirteen in the Middle East (including eight at Romani). Trooper Ronald Gowland is buried in the Haidar Pasha Cemetery in Istanbul. The graves of the other five POWs who died are lost. Nearly 17,000 British and Empire troops were taken prisoner by the Turks during the war (13,000 from Kut el Amara, in Mesopotamia). Between 3300 and 5500 of them died in captivity. WA Series 235/2, *Report on the Treatment of British Prisoners of War in Turkey*, HMSO, November 1918, ANZ.

8. A figure of 17,723 is quoted in Powles for the number of men who left New Zealand to serve in the ranks of the NZMR Brigade during the war, but I cannot account for that many men in the reinforcement records. Powles, p. 6.

9. Over the entire war, the percentage of men killed and wounded in the EEF was just over 6% (one casualty for every sixteen men sent out). Compare this to France, where the casualty rate was over 50%, and Gallipoli, where the rate was nearly 25%. *Statistics*, p. 248.

10. Pugsley, *The Anzac Experience: New Zealand, Australia and Empire in the First World War*, p. 147.

11. Wood, *Tackling the Turk*, pp. 118–19.

12. Report of the General Officer Commanding for the Period from 1st July 1918 to 30th June 1919, 'New Zealand Horses on Active Service', *Appendix of the Journal of the House of Representatives of New Zealand*, Wellington, 1919.

13. The Battle of Romani took place three and a half months after the New Zealanders crossed the Suez Canal and entered Sinai, and there was a similar interval between Romani and the next battle at Magdhaba.

14. Falls, *Military Operations*, p. 644.

15. Field punishment and imprisonment with hard labour were typical punishments for serious crimes, while lesser offences attracted fines, loss of pay, extra duties and reprimands. Some interesting offences include receiving stolen goods, disorderly behaviour in a brothel, using another man's leave pass, resisting arrest and losing a horse and bridle by neglect. WA Series 9/5, 9, Box 2, Egyptian Court Martial Register, ANZ; *Field Service Pocket Book*, p. 216, Pugsley, *On the Fringe of Hell*, p. 56.

16. Finkel, p. 530. Mustafa Kemal rejected the harsh terms of the 1920 peace treaty, seized power and took Turkey to war again. In 1922, he drove the Allied occupying armies from Anatolia and advanced on the Dardanelles. For a brief period, a large-scale war was in the offing and New Zealand offered an infantry brigade and a mounted rifles brigade (7000 men). In the end, the Allies gave in, returning eastern Thrace to the Turks and withdrawing from Istanbul. Mustafa Kemal became Kemal Ataturk, the first President of the Republic of Turkey.

17. Liddell Hart, *History of the First World War*, p. 399.

18. Mitchell interview. It should not be forgotten that Turkey was responsible for the systematic killing of at least one million Christian Armenians in 1915. These civilians were murdered by Turkish soldiers and policemen, or callously deported from Anatolia to starve or die from disease in the deserts of Mesopotamia and Syria.

19. See www.gov-gen.govt.nz/utilities/printspeech.asp?ID=235, accessed 6 Mar 2007.

20. Under the terms of the secret Sykes–Picot Agreement of 1916, Syria, Mesopotamia and Palestine were to be divided into French and British areas of influence once the Turks were defeated. The Balfour Declaration of 1917 promised the Jews a national homeland in Palestine after the war, but not at the expense of the indigenous Arab inhabitants. These two documents frustrated Arab dreams of independence after the war.

21. Meldrum, Brigadier General W., *Notes on Campaigns of NZMR*, KMARL.
22. The first Commanding Officer of the 'Div Cav', Lieutenant Colonel C.J. Pierce, served throughout the First World War with the WMR.

Index